...e lady to my right is ...unko Minagawa, who ...ays Ryoma in the ...nime.

I get really busy toward the end of the year, but it's the time of year when I get the opportunity to meet the readers, so I really enjoy it. I got a lot of inspiration from everybody last year. I hope to continue putting out pieces that will surprise all of you.

Takeshi Konomi

About Takeshi Konomi

Takeshi Konomi exploded onto the manga scene with the incredible **THE PRINCE OF TENNIS**. His refined art style and sleek character designs proved popular with **Weekly Shonen Jump** readers, and **THE PRINCE OF TENNIS** became the No. 1 sports manga in Japan almost overnight. Its cast of fascinating male tennis players attracted legions of female readers even though it was originally intended to be a boys' comic. The manga continues to be a success in Japan. A hit anime series was created, as well as several video games and mountains of merchandise.

THE PRINCE OF TENNIS
VOL. 12
The SHONEN JUMP Manga

**STORY AND ART BY
TAKESHI KONOMI**

English Adaptation/Michelle Pangilinan
Translation/Joe Yamazaki
Touch-up Art & Lettering/Andy Ristaino
Graphics and Cover Design/Janet Piercy
Editor/Michelle Pangilinan

Managing Editor/Elizabeth Kawasaki
Director of Production/Noboru Watanabe
Vice President of Publishing/Alvin Lu
Vice President & Editor in Chief/ Yumi Hoashi
Sr. Director of Acquisitions/Rika Inouye
Vice President of Sales & Marketing/Liza Coppola
Publisher/Hyoe Narita

Printed in the U.S.A.

Published by VIZ Media, LLC
P.O. Box 77010
San Francisco, CA 94107

SHONEN JUMP Manga Edition
10 9 8 7 6 5 4 3 2 1
First printing, March 2006

www.viz.com

PARENTAL ADVISORY
THE PRINCE OF TENNIS
is rated A and is suitable
for readers of all ages.

THE WORLD'S
MOST POPULAR MANGA

SHONEN JUMP

GRAPHIC NOVEL

www.shonenjump.com

Shonen Jump Graphic Novel

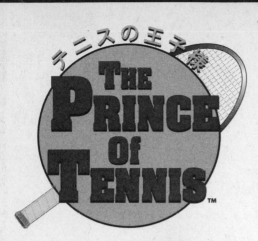

テニスの王子様

THE PRINCE OF TENNIS™

VOL. 12
Invincible Man

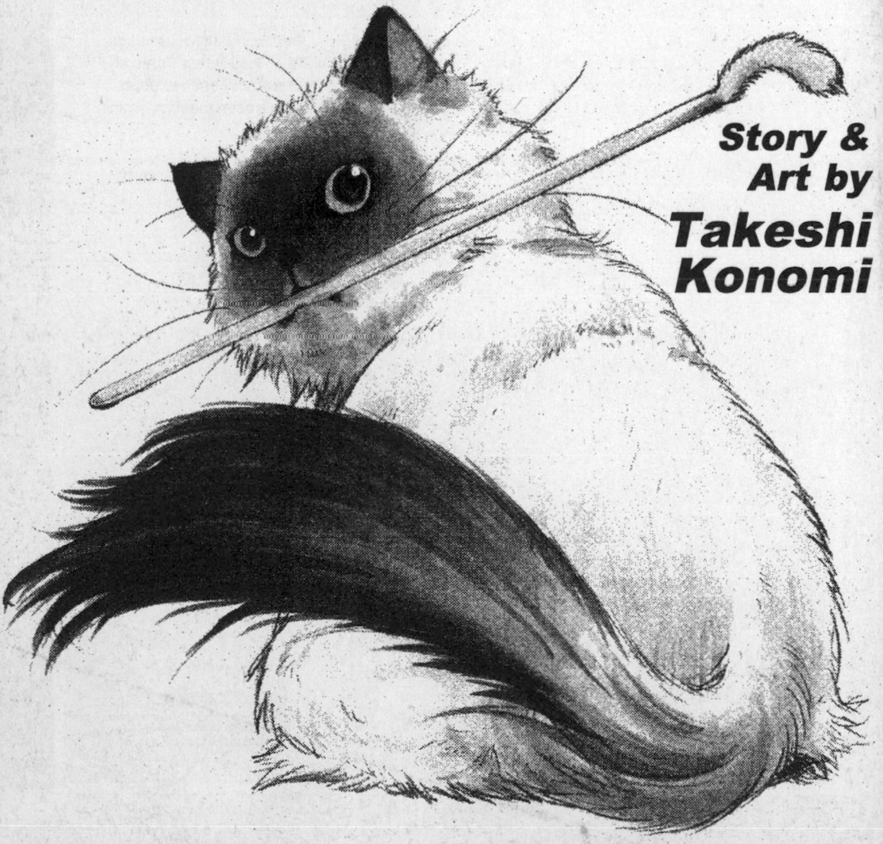

Story & Art by
Takeshi Konomi

Shusuke Fuji

Seishun Academy
Tennis Team (9th Grade)

Shuichiro Oishi

Seishun Academy Tennis Team
Alternate Captain (9th Grade)

Kunimitsu Tezuka

Seishun Academy Tennis Team
Captain (9th Grade)

STORY
&
CHARACTERS

VOLUME 1 ▶ 12

Ryoma Echizen

Seishun Academy Tennis Team (7th Grade)

THE PRINCE OF TENNIS

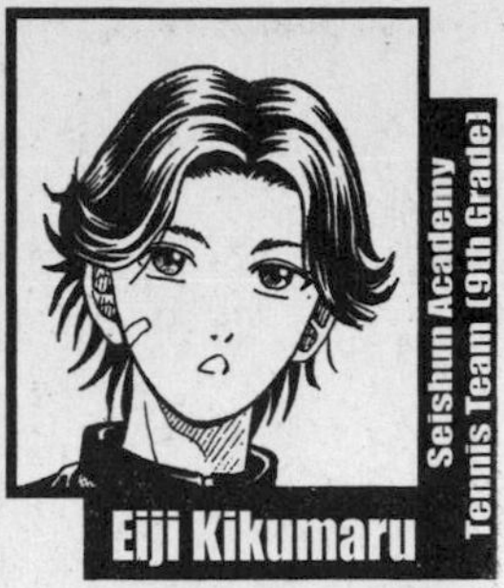
Seishun Academy Tennis Team (9th Grade)
Eiji Kikumaru
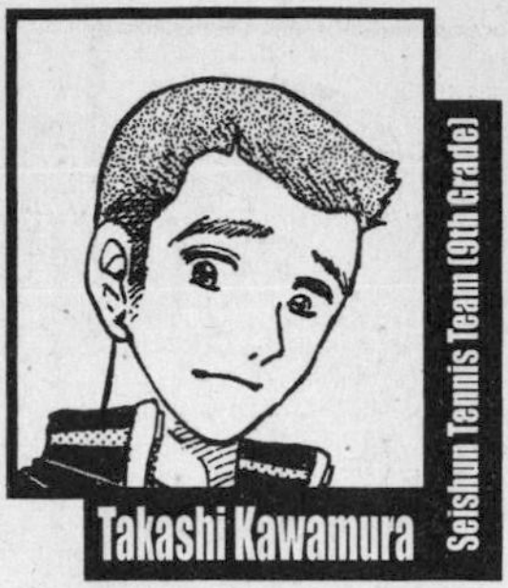
Seishun Tennis Team (9th Grade)
Takashi Kawamura
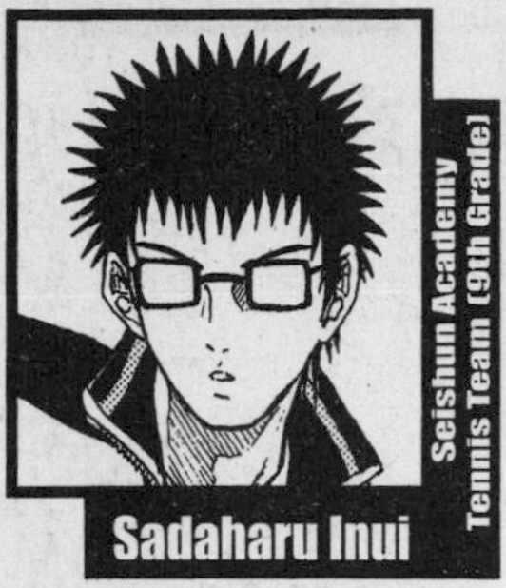
Seishun Academy Tennis Team (9th Grade)
Sadaharu Inui
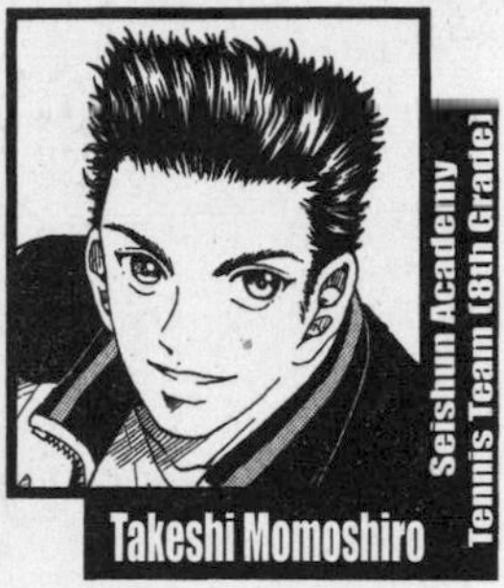
Seishun Academy Tennis Team (8th Grade)
Takeshi Momoshiro
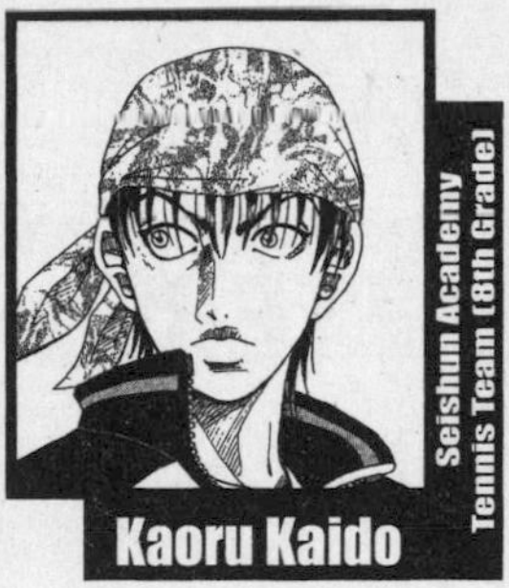
Seishun Academy Tennis Team (8th Grade)
Kaoru Kaido
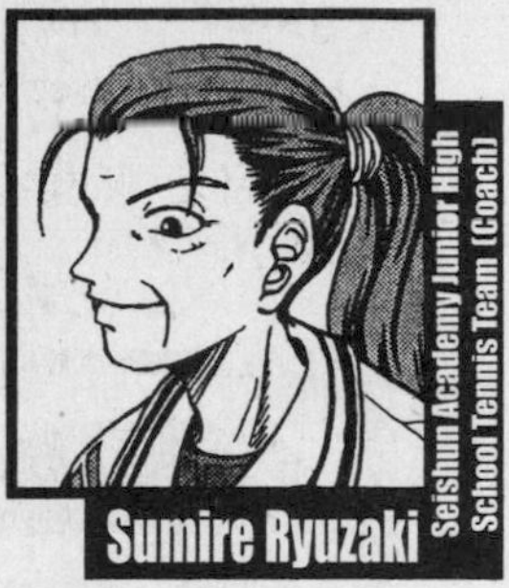
Seishun Academy Junior High School Tennis Team (Coach)
Sumire Ryuzaki

Ryoma Echizen, who has enrolled at Seishun Academy, is a tennis prodigy who won four consecutive U.S. Junior tournaments. The first ever 7th grade starter, he has led his team to the District Preliminaries! Despite a few mishaps, Seishun has advanced to the finals of the City Tournament. They will play the powerhouse team of Yamabuki Junior High School—home of the national level doubles pair. But Seishun has emerged from doubles play with one win and one loss. There are high expectations for the singles matches, and Momo's opponent is a formidable ex all-star player!

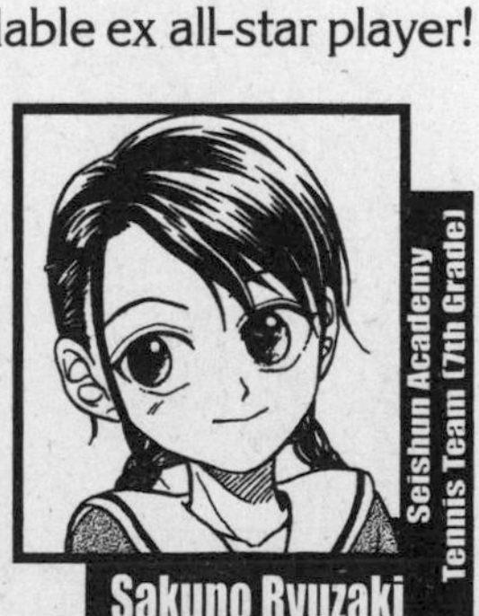
Seishun Academy Tennis Team (7th Grade)
Sakuno Ryuzaki
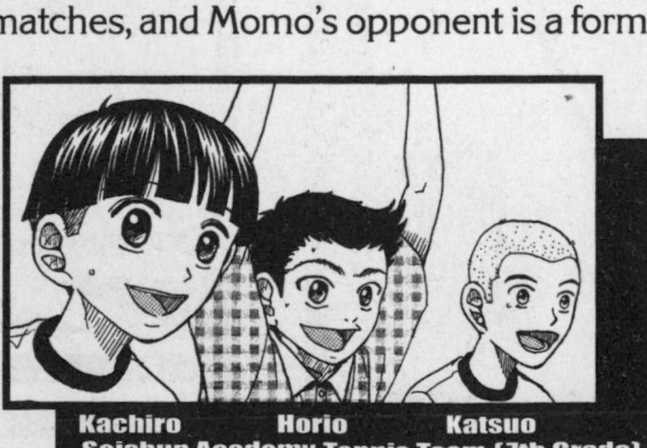
Kachiro
Horio
Katsuo
Seishun Academy Tennis Team (7th Grade)

CONTENTS

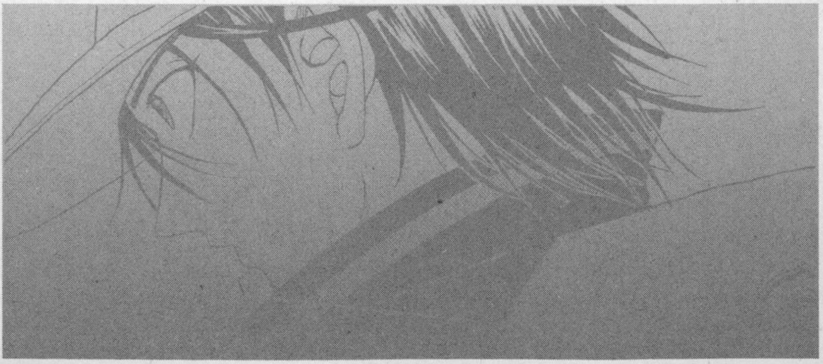

GENIUS 97: TRICKSTER

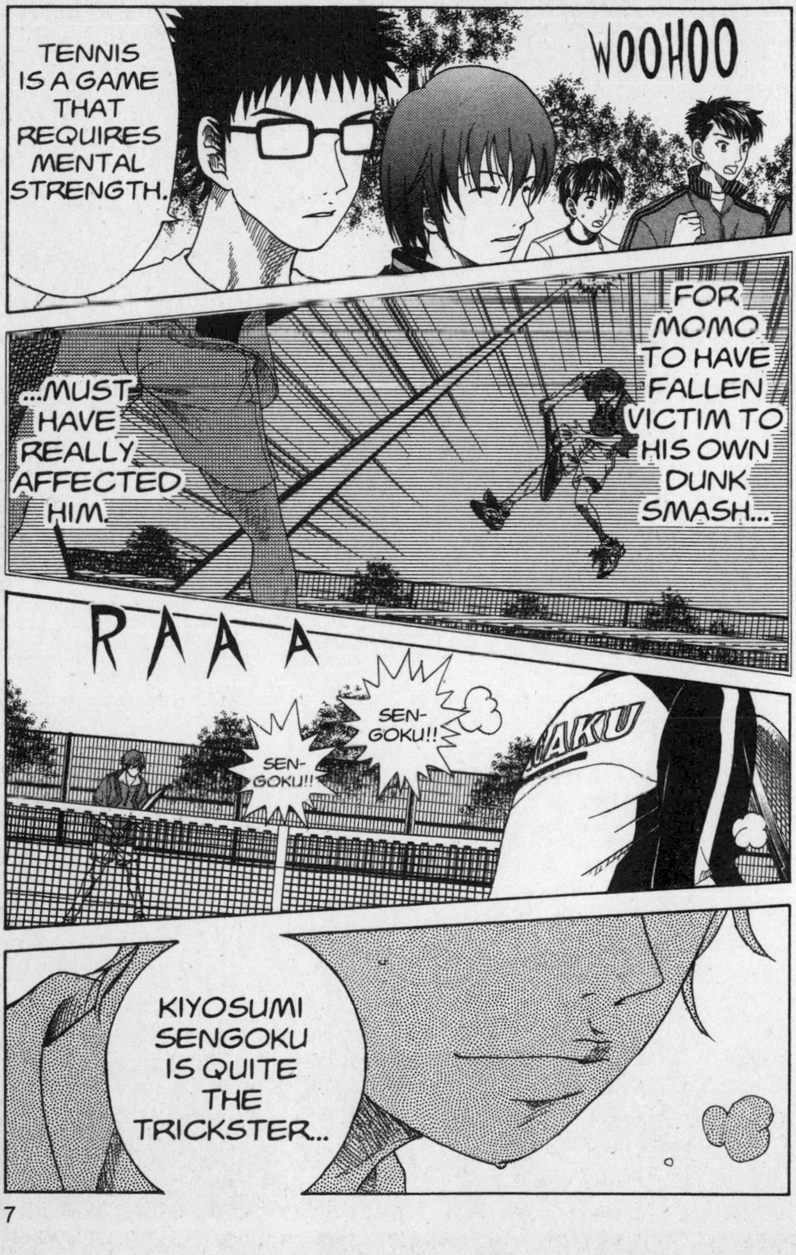
WOOHOO
TENNIS IS A GAME THAT REQUIRES MENTAL STRENGTH.
FOR MOMO TO HAVE FALLEN VICTIM TO HIS OWN DUNK SMASH...
...MUST HAVE REALLY AFFECTED HIM.
RAAA
SEN-GOKU!!
SEN-GOKU!!
KIYOSUMI SENGOKU IS QUITE THE TRICKSTER...

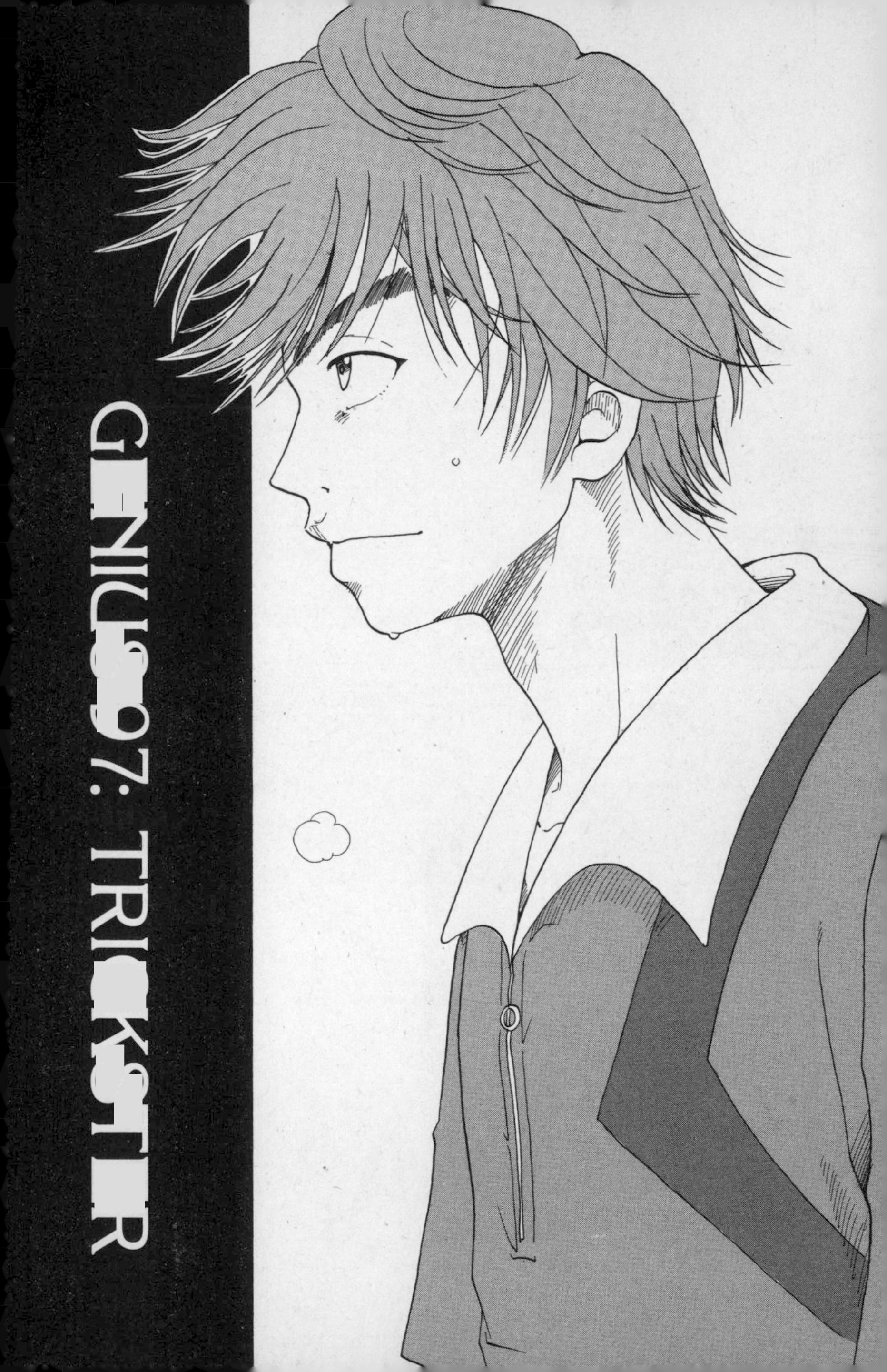
G[redacted]NIU[redacted] 97: TRI[redacted]K[redacted]T[redacted]R

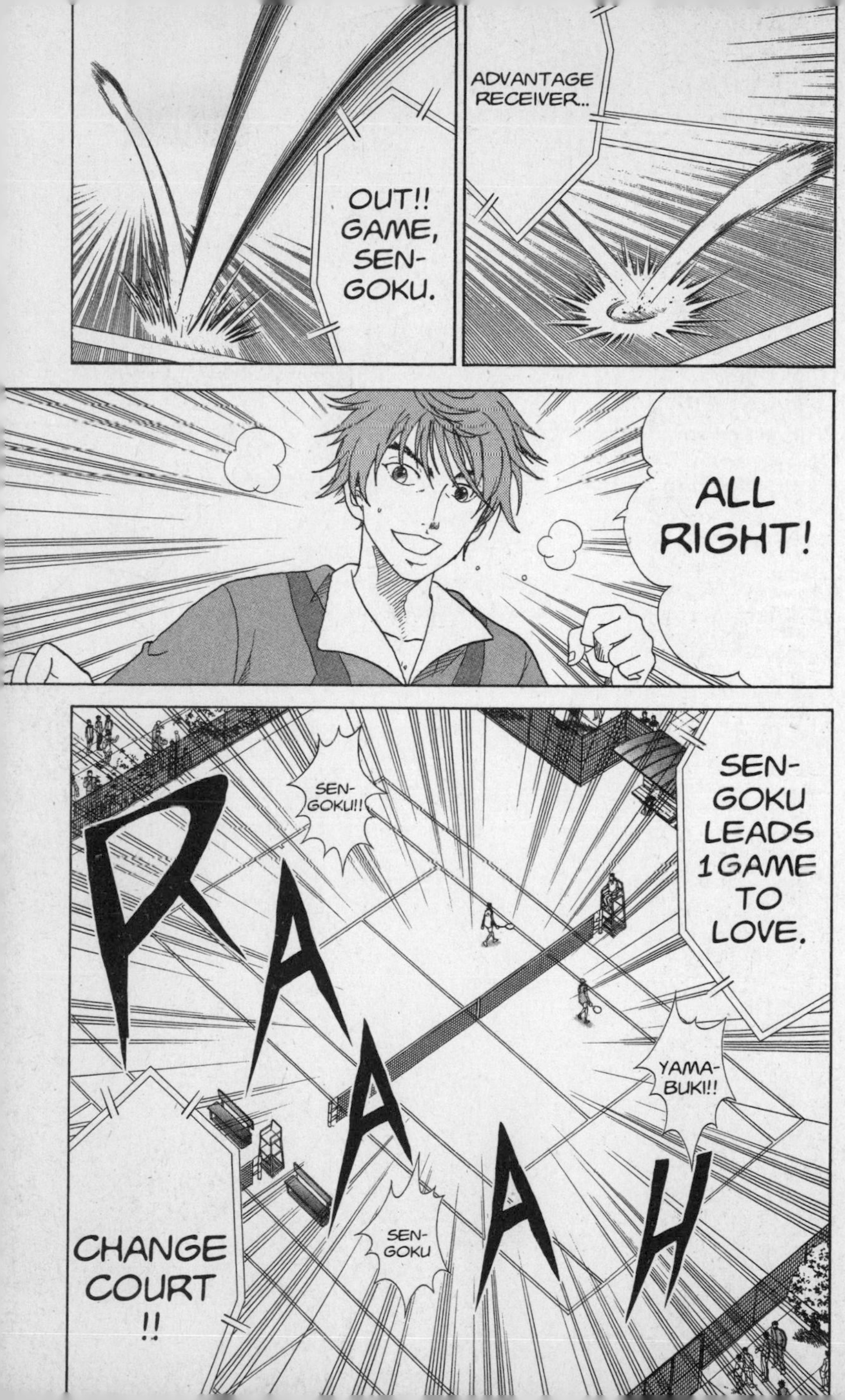
ADVANTAGE RECEIVER...
OUT!! GAME, SEN-GOKU.
ALL RIGHT!
SEN-GOKU LEADS 1 GAME TO LOVE.
SEN-GOKU!!
RAAAH
YAMA-BUKI!!
SEN-GOKU
CHANGE COURT !!

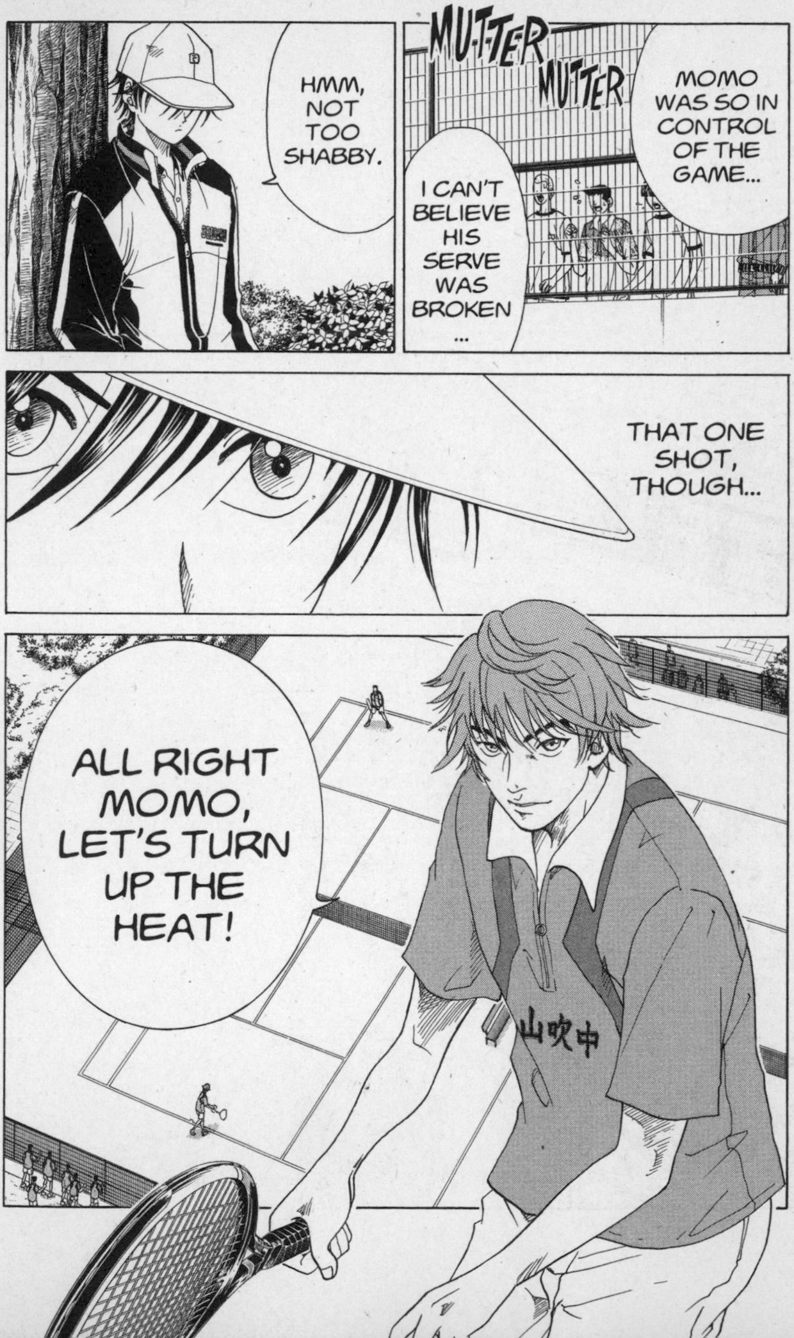
MUTTER MUTTER
MOMO WAS SO IN CONTROL OF THE GAME...
I CAN'T BELIEVE HIS SERVE WAS BROKEN ...
HMM, NOT TOO SHABBY.
THAT ONE SHOT, THOUGH...
ALL RIGHT MOMO, LET'S TURN UP THE HEAT!
山吹中

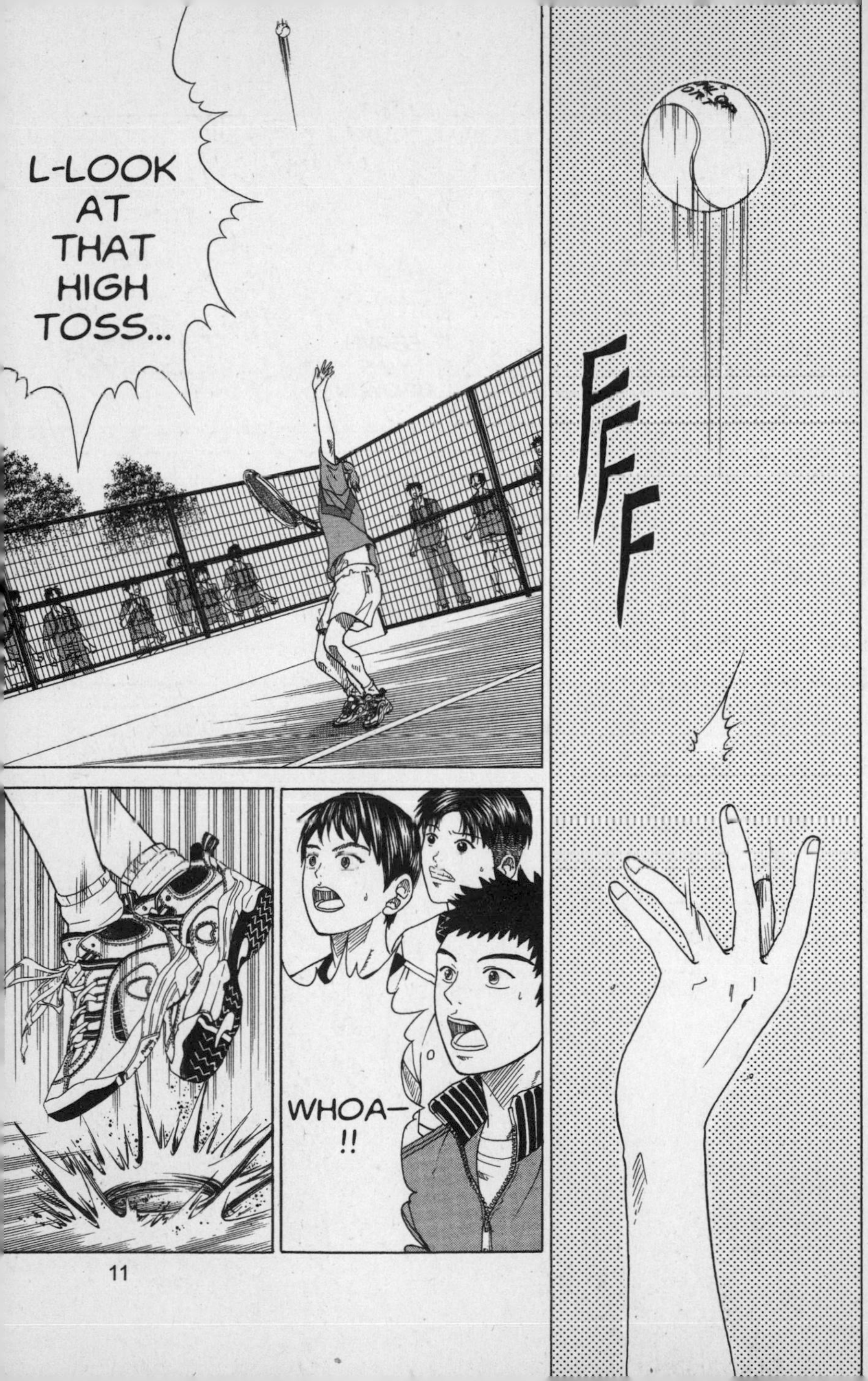
FFF
L-LOOK AT THAT HIGH TOSS...
WHOA-!!

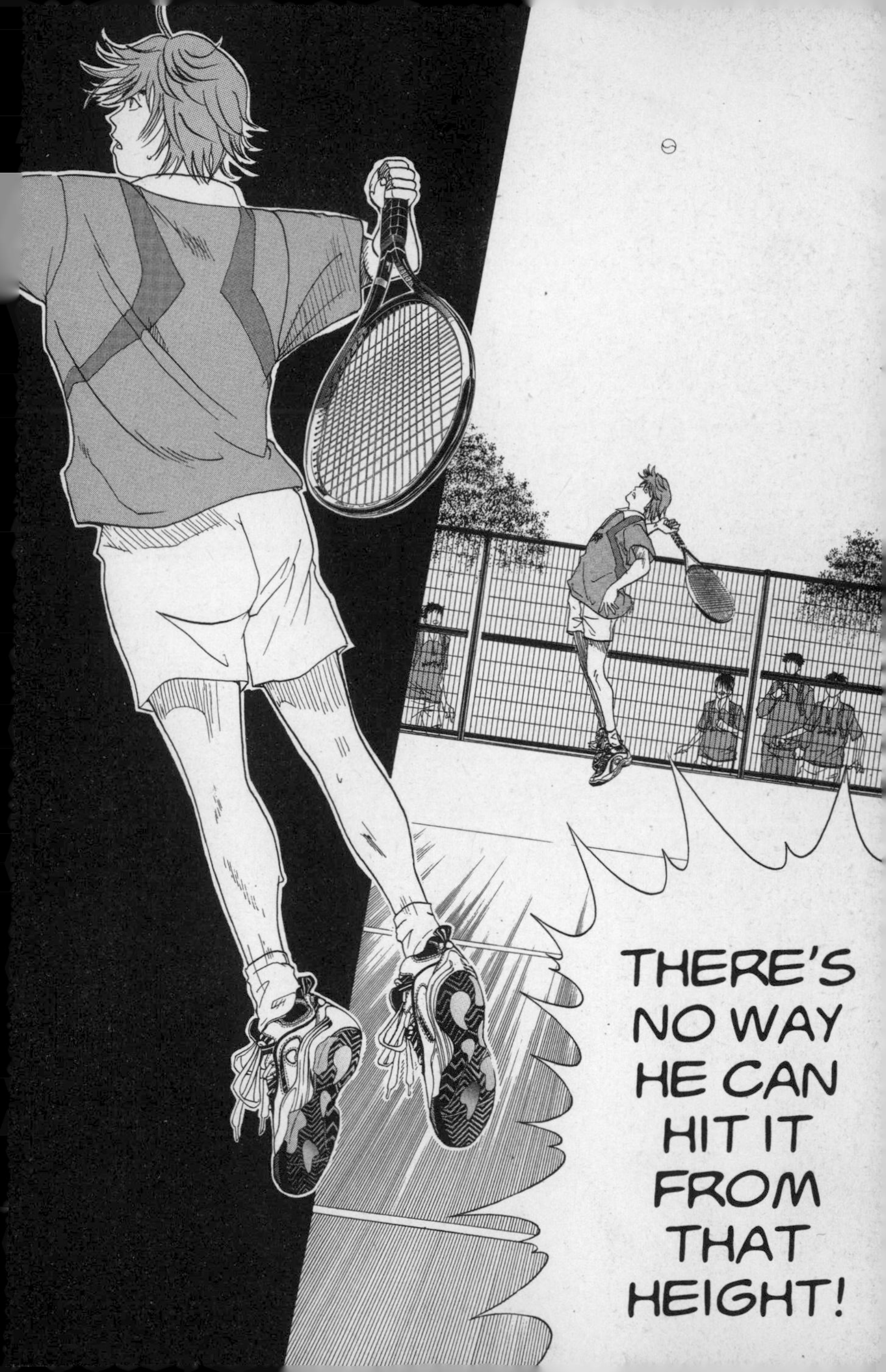
THERE'S NO WAY HE CAN HIT IT FROM THAT HEIGHT!

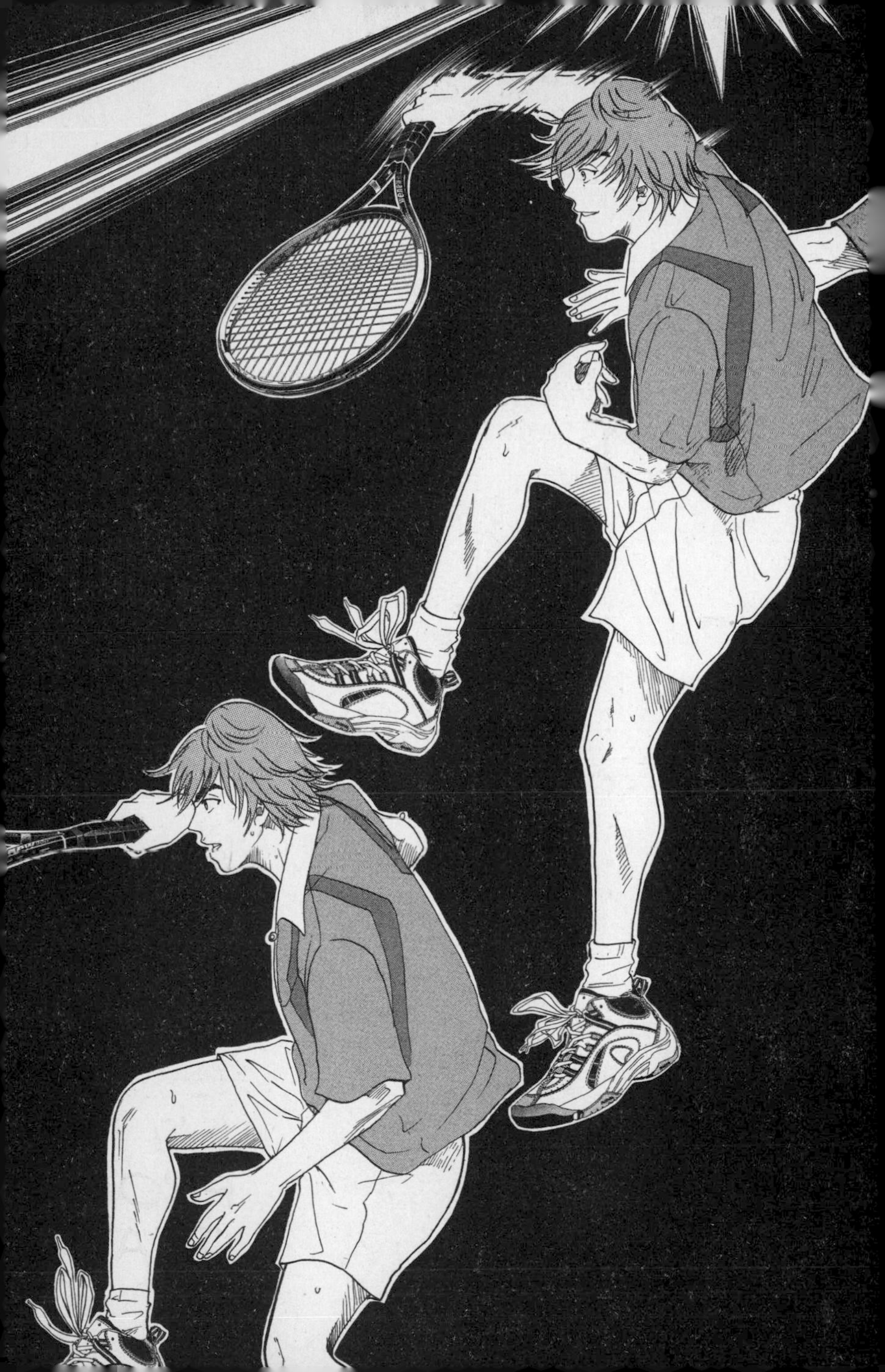

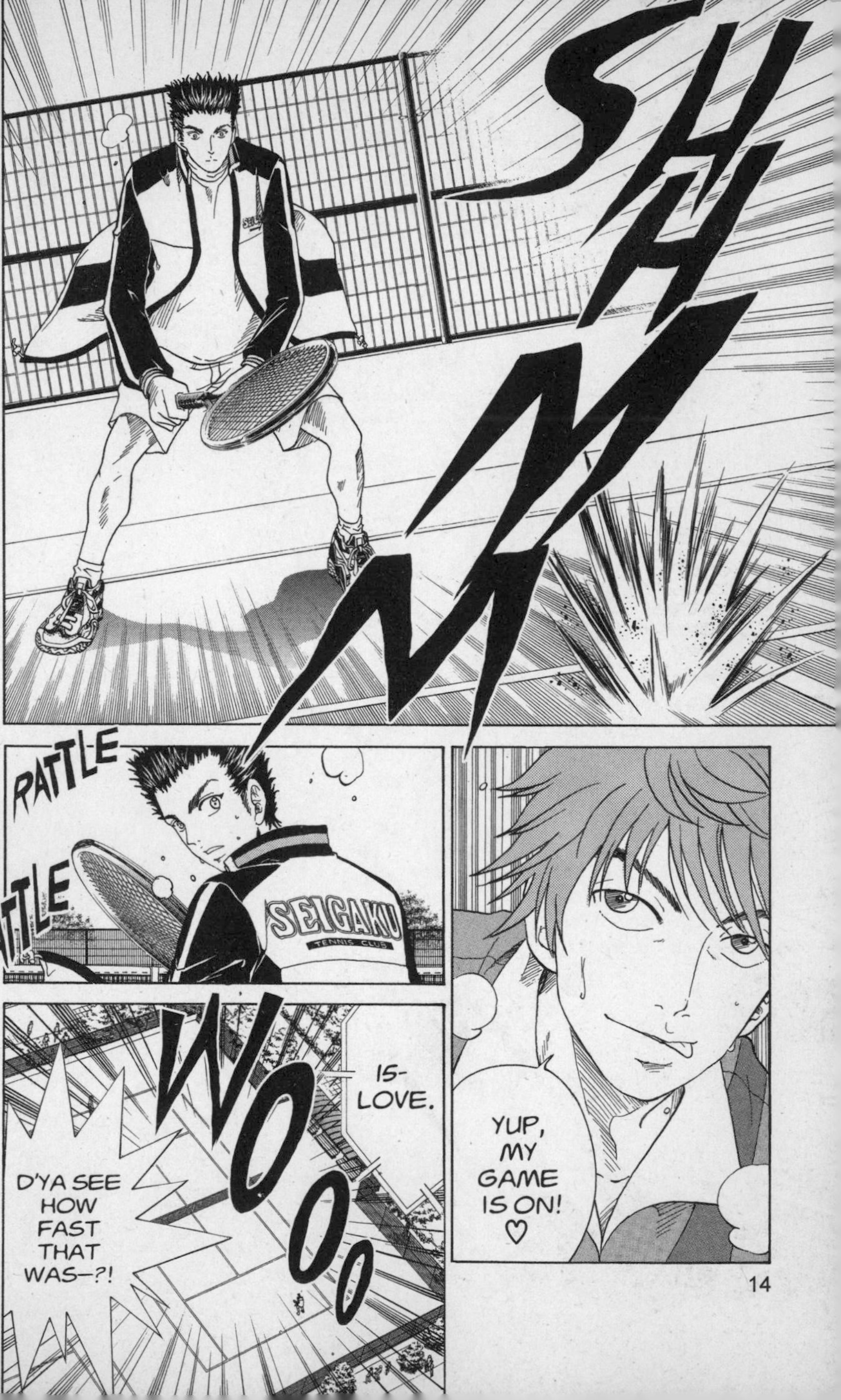
SHHMM
YUP, MY GAME IS ON! ♡
RATTLE
RATTLE
WOOOO
IS- LOVE.
D'YA SEE HOW FAST THAT WAS—?!

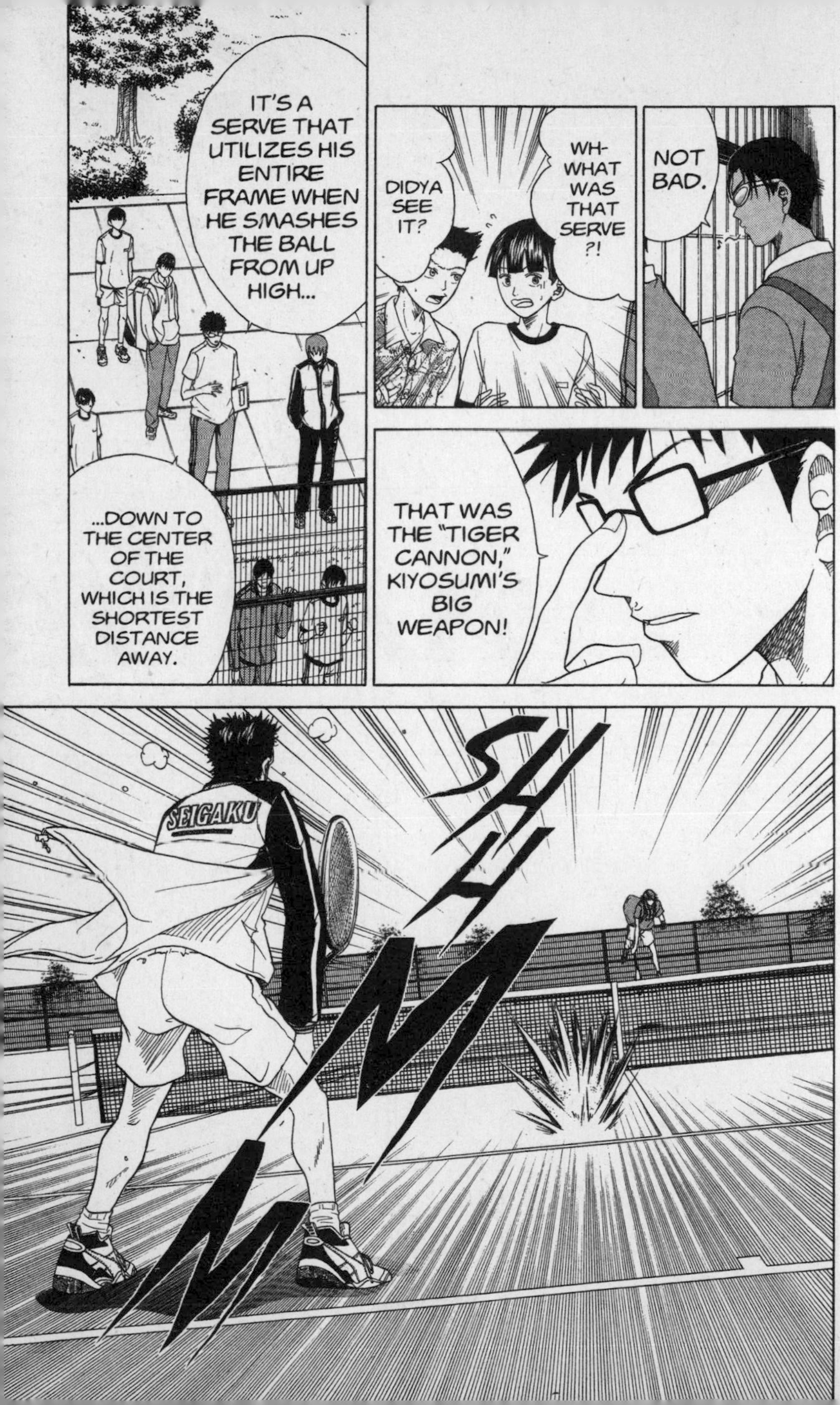
NOT BAD.
WH- WHAT WAS THAT SERVE ?!
DIDYA SEE IT?
THAT WAS THE "TIGER CANNON," KIYOSUMI'S BIG WEAPON!
IT'S A SERVE THAT UTILIZES HIS ENTIRE FRAME WHEN HE SMASHES THE BALL FROM UP HIGH...
...DOWN TO THE CENTER OF THE COURT, WHICH IS THE SHORTEST DISTANCE AWAY.
SEIGAKU
SHHMM

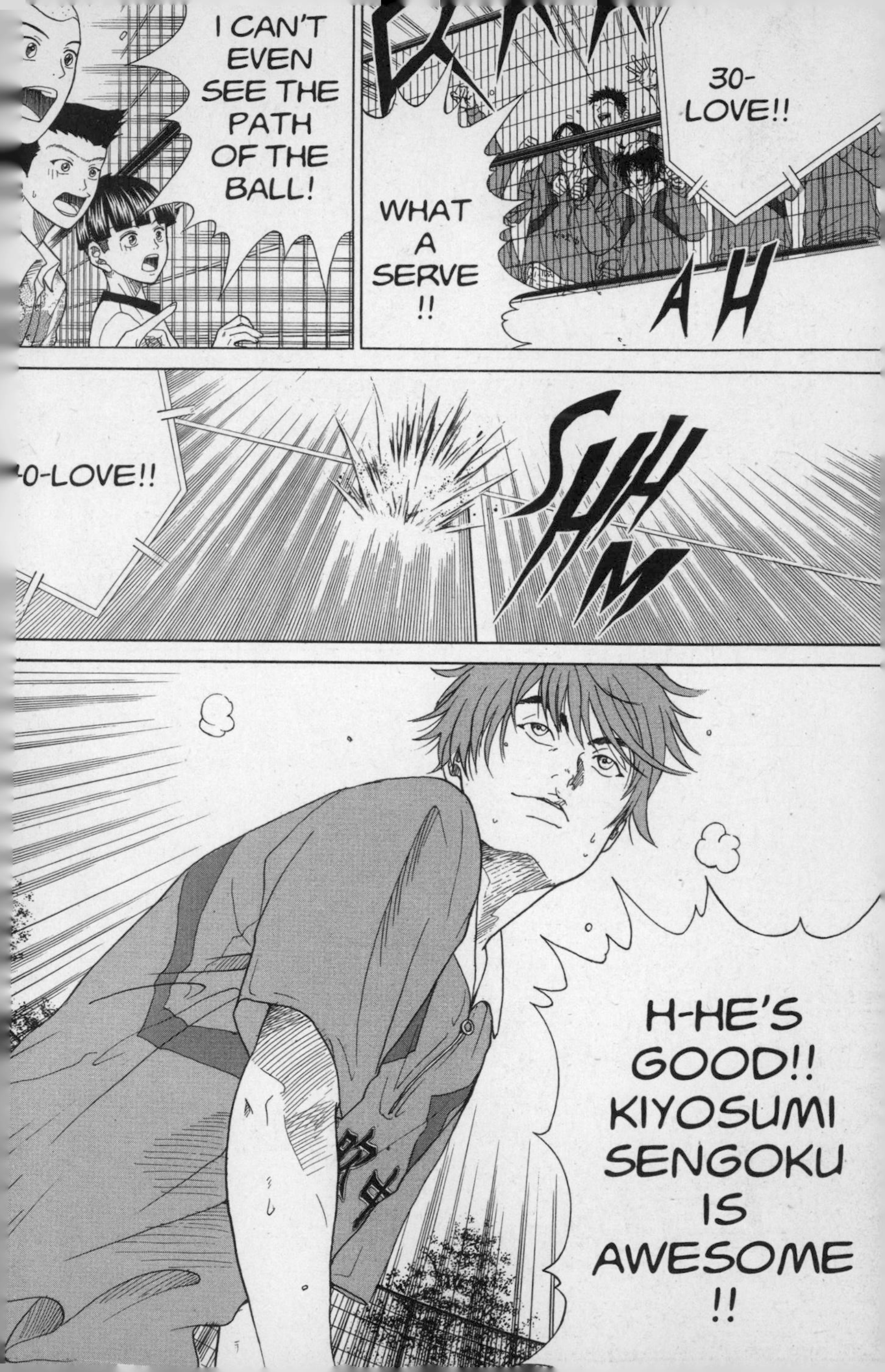
30-LOVE!!
AH
WHAT A SERVE !!
I CAN'T EVEN SEE THE PATH OF THE BALL!
SHHM
0-LOVE!!
H-HE'S GOOD!! KIYOSUMI SENGOKU IS AWESOME !!

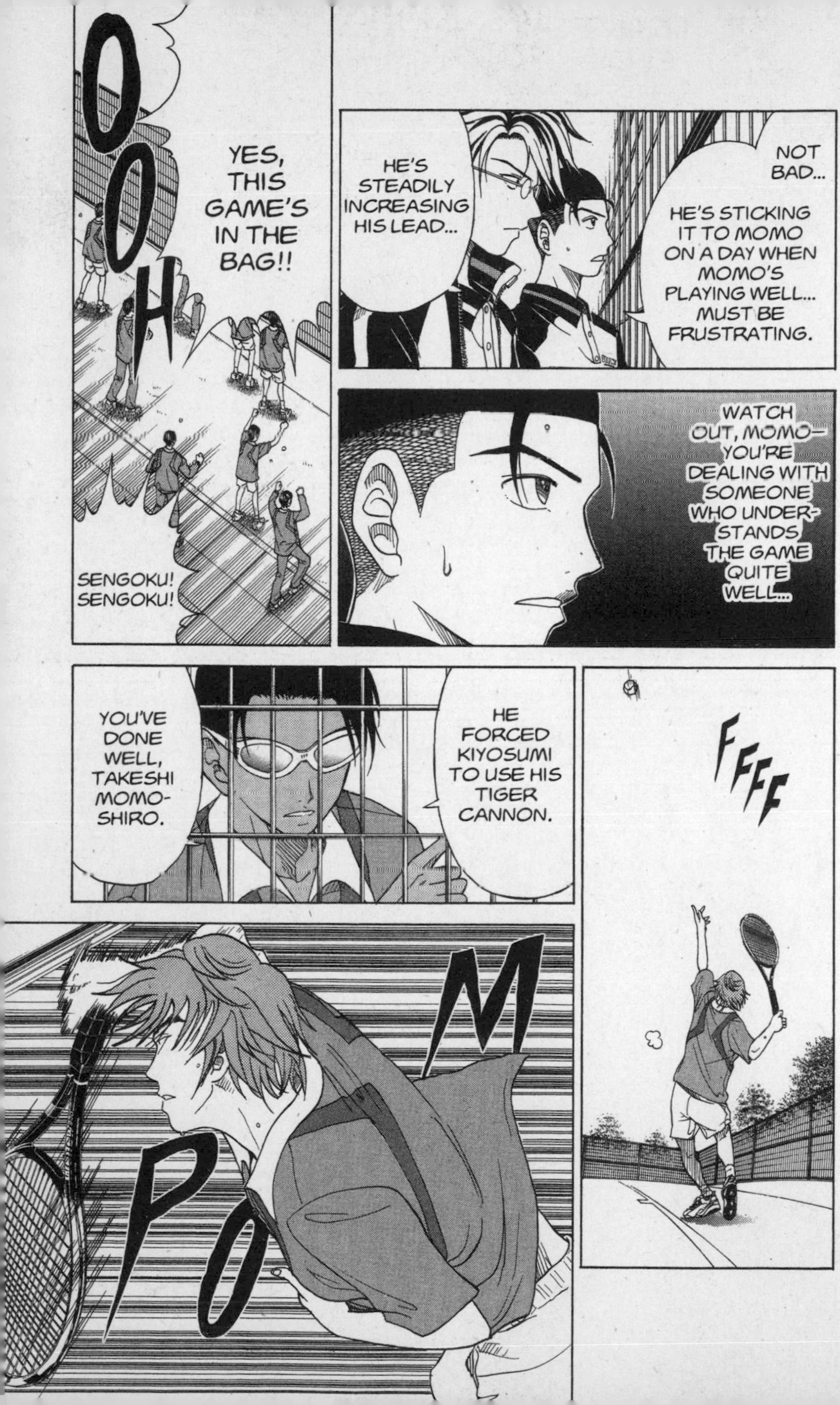
NOT BAD...
HE'S STICKING IT TO MOMO ON A DAY WHEN MOMO'S PLAYING WELL... MUST BE FRUSTRATING.
HE'S STEADILY INCREASING HIS LEAD...
WATCH OUT, MOMO— YOU'RE DEALING WITH SOMEONE WHO UNDER-STANDS THE GAME QUITE WELL...
OOOH
YES, THIS GAME'S IN THE BAG!!
SENGOKU! SENGOKU!
FFFF
HE FORCED KIYOSUMI TO USE HIS TIGER CANNON.
YOU'VE DONE WELL, TAKESHI MOMO-SHIRO.
POM

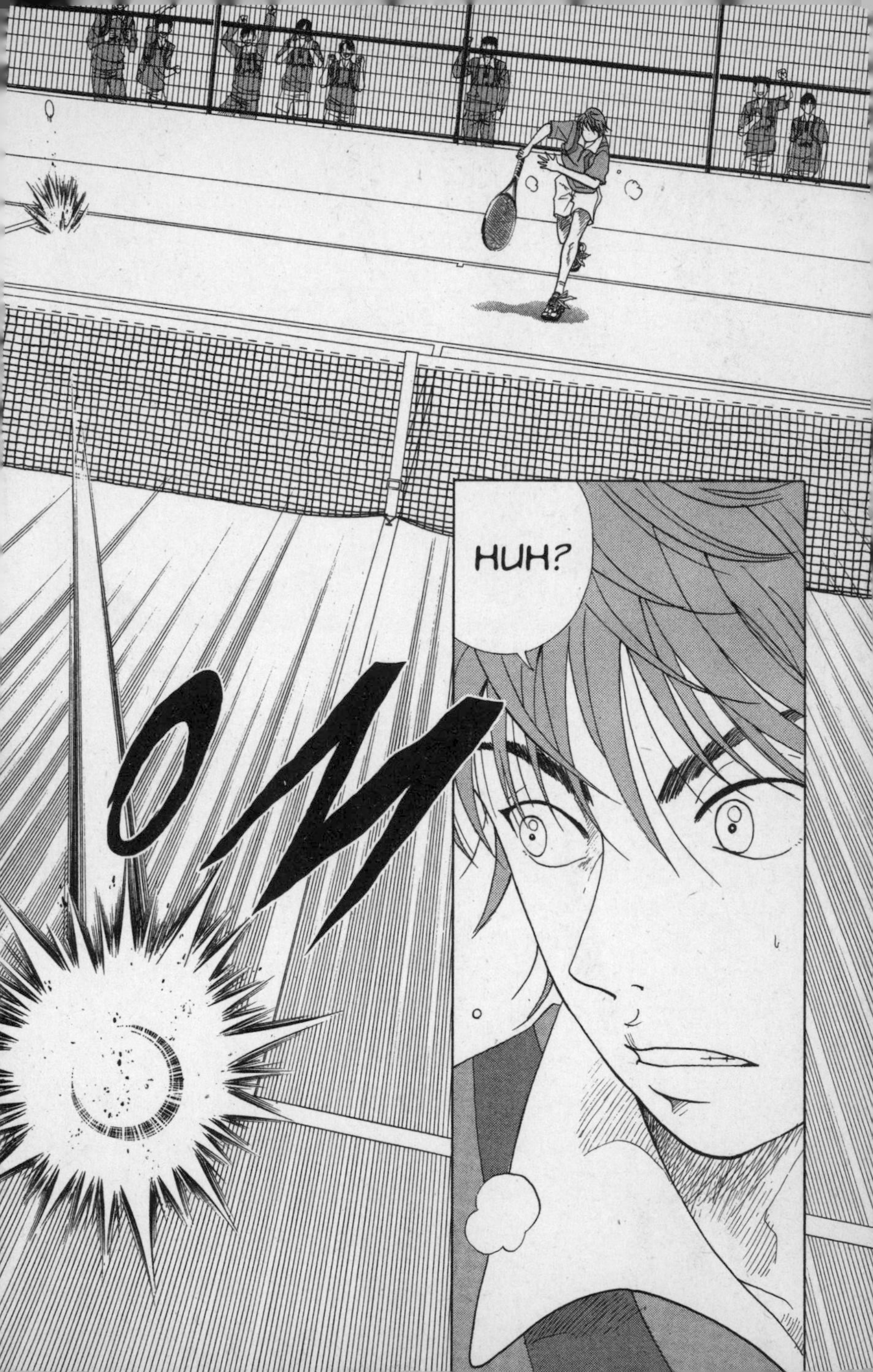
HUH?

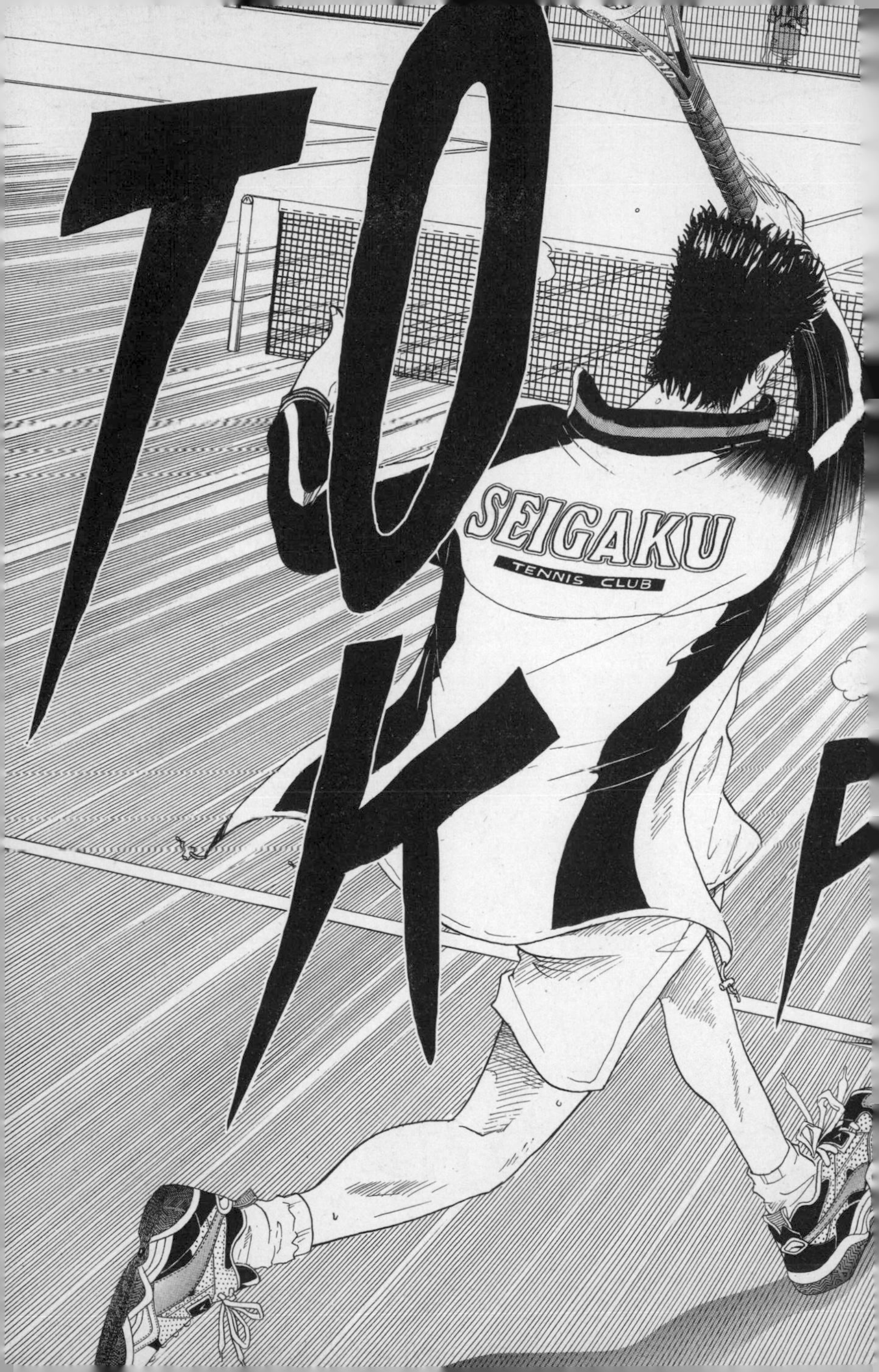
SEIGAKU
TENNIS CLUB

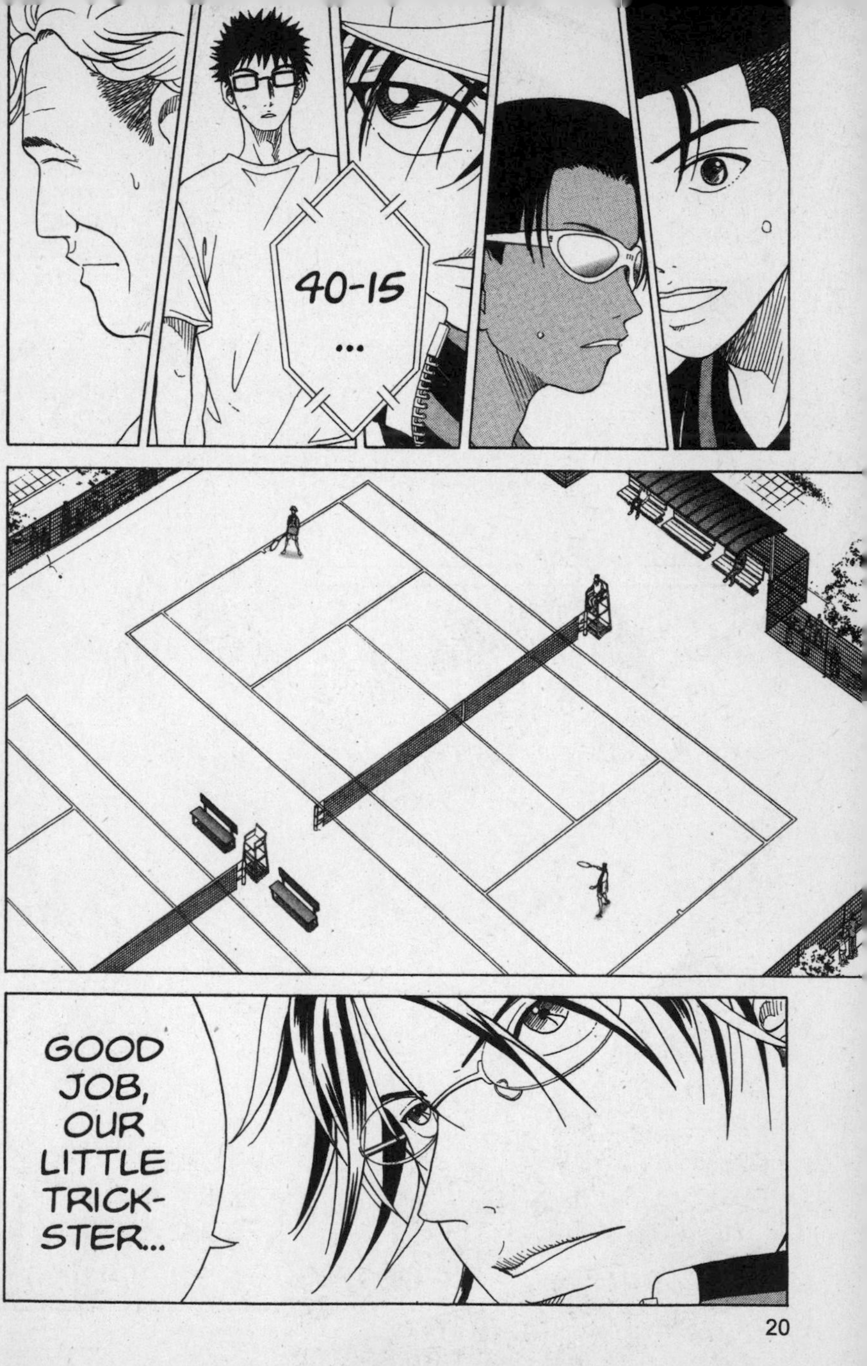
40-15
...
GOOD JOB, OUR LITTLE TRICK-STER...

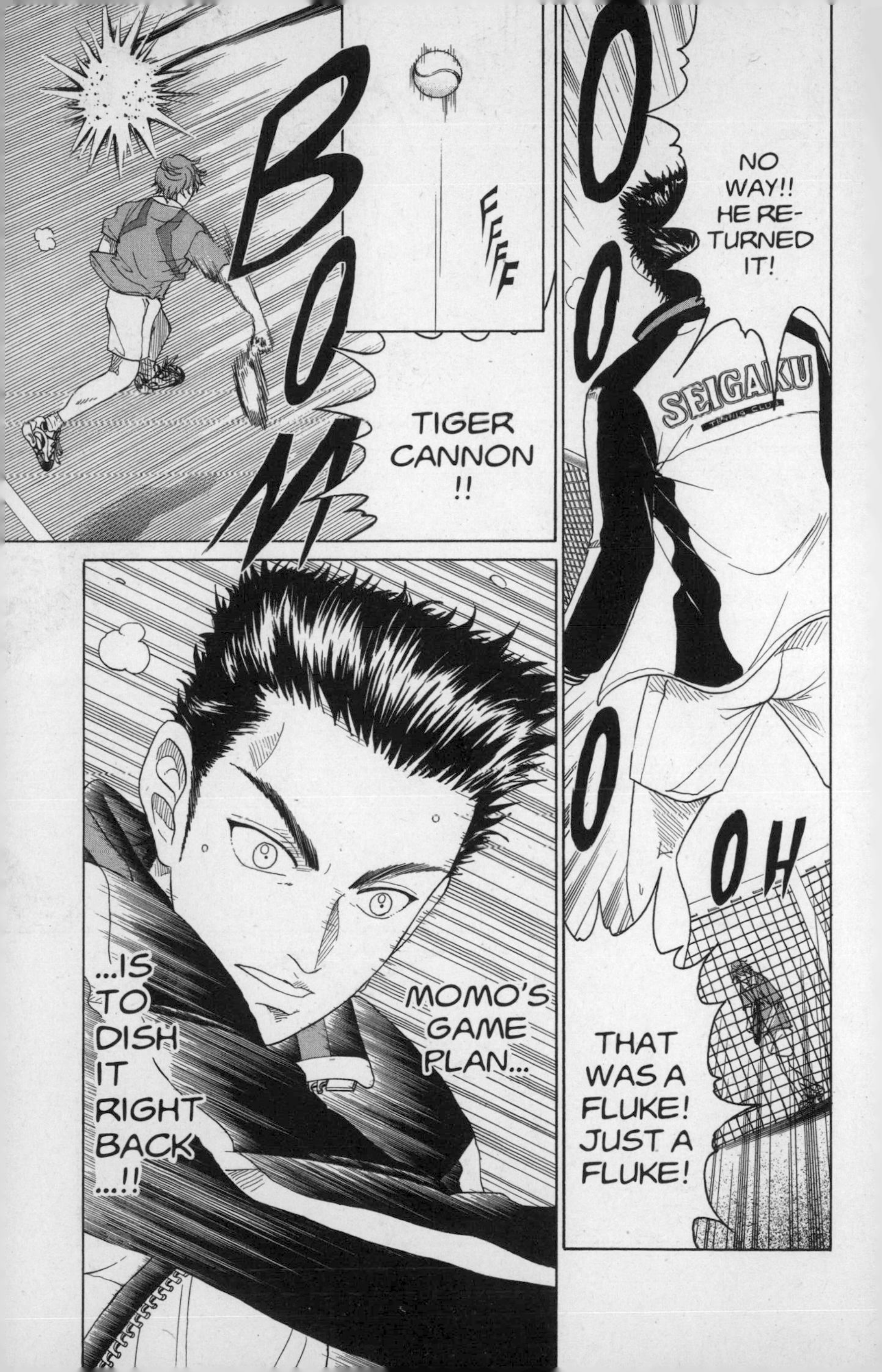
OOOO
OH
NO WAY!! HE RE-TURNED IT!
SEIGAKU
THAT WAS A FLUKE! JUST A FLUKE!
FFFF
TIGER CANNON !!
BOOM
MOMO'S GAME PLAN...
...IS TO DISH IT RIGHT BACK ...!!

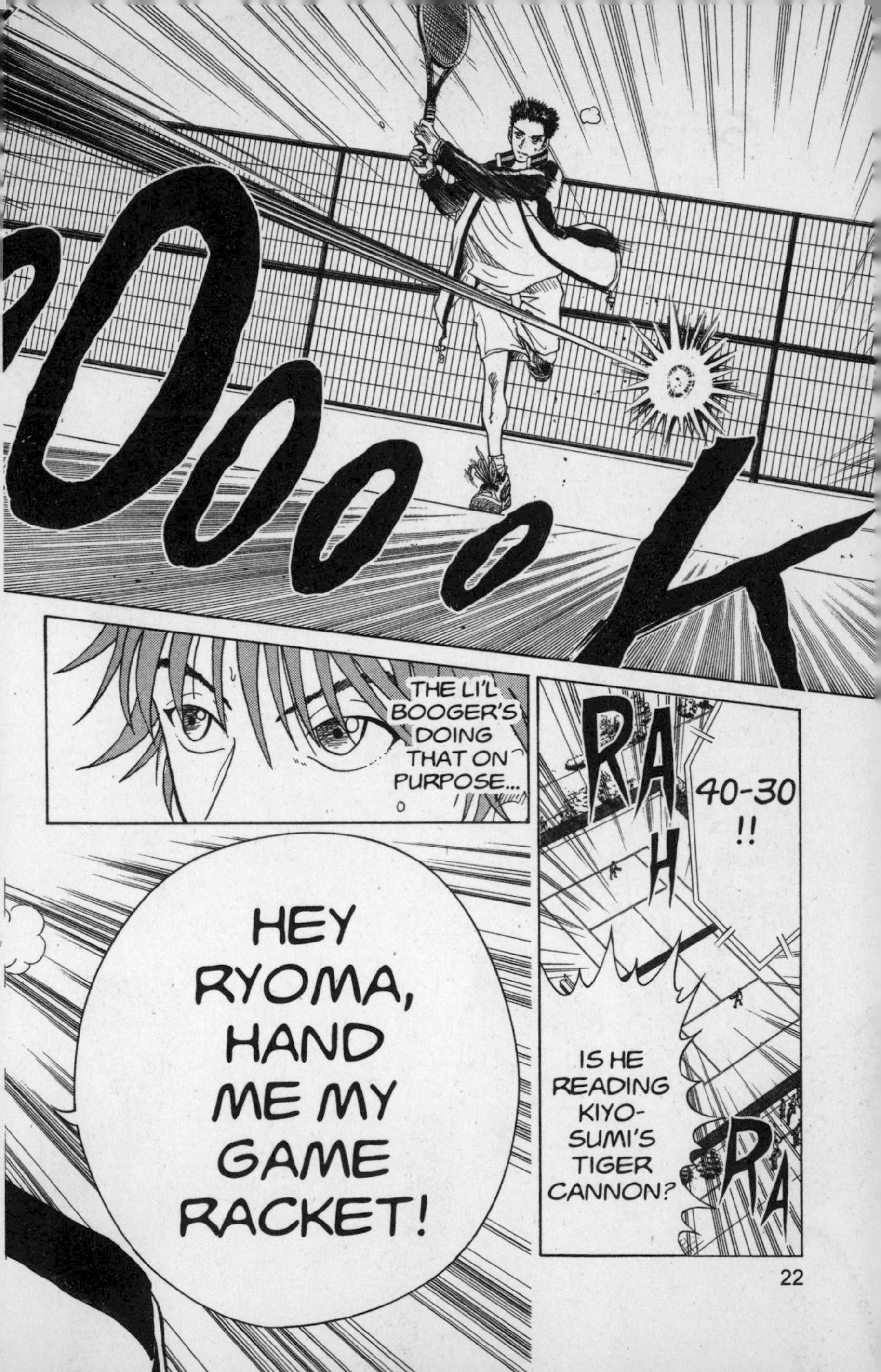
RAH
40-30 !!
IS HE READING KIYO-SUMI'S TIGER CANNON?
RA
THE LI'L BOOGER'S DOING THAT ON PURPOSE...
HEY RYOMA, HAND ME MY GAME RACKET!

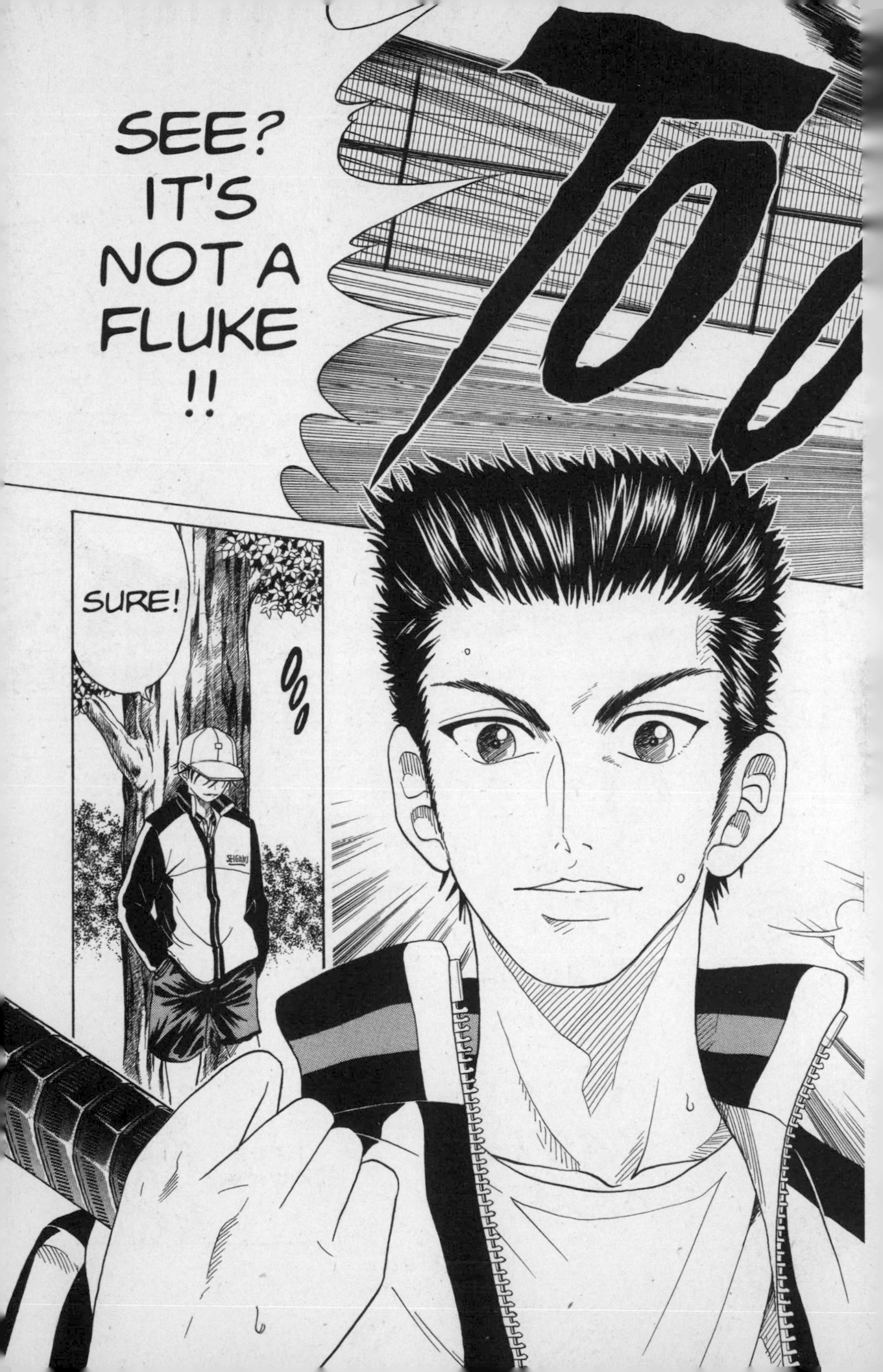
SEE? IT'S NOT A FLUKE !!
SURE!

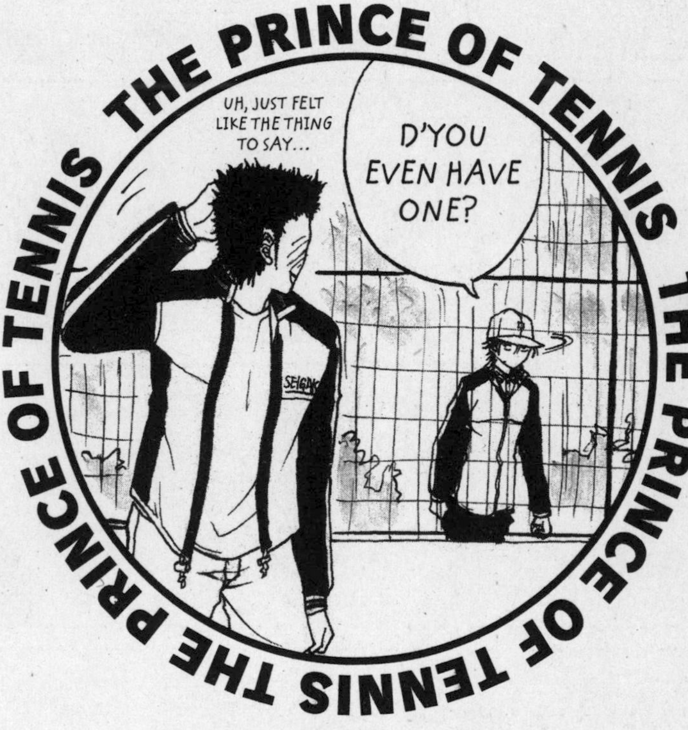
THE PRINCE OF TENNIS THE PRINCE OF TENNIS THE PRINCE OF TENNIS
D'YOU EVEN HAVE ONE?
UH, JUST FELT LIKE THE THING TO SAY...

GENIUS 98: DETERMINATION

SHF
PWIK
FWT
FWT
FWT
FWT
PW IK
PW IK
2-YEAR ANNIVERSARY
BNG
BNG

THIS WAS THE FIRST EPISODE OF THE PRINCE OF TENNIS' SECOND YEAR IN SERIALIZATION IN WEEKLY SHONEN JUMP IN JAPAN.

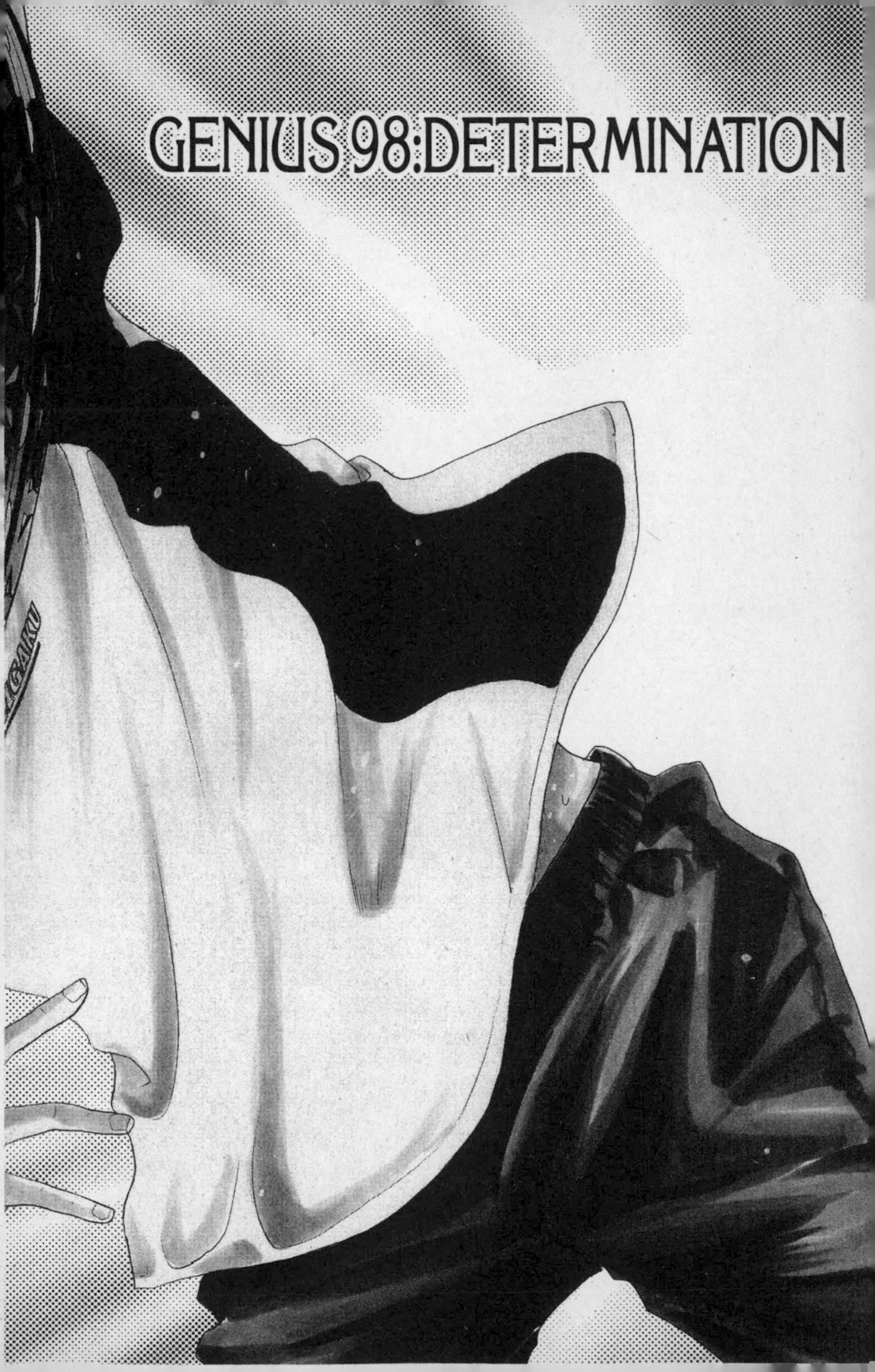
GENIUS 98: DETERMINATION

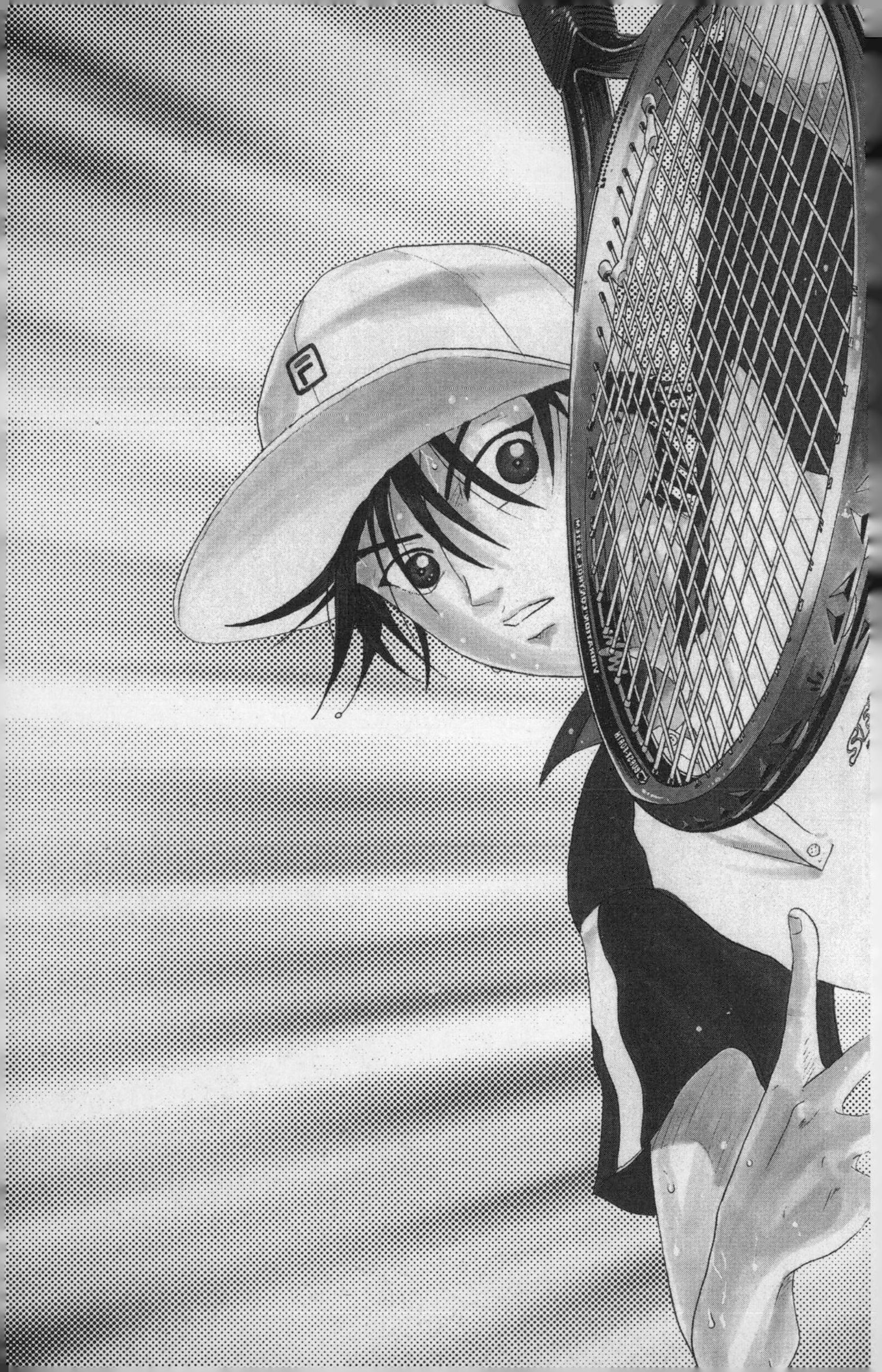

KALPIN
  AGE: TWO YEARS OLD
  BIRTHDAY: MARCH
  LIKES: CAT TOYS
  FAVORITE FOOD: CAT SNACKS
  BEST MOVE: HIND LEG CAT KICK
  FAVORITE LINE: "HOARA"
  (SUPPOSED TO BE A MEOW)

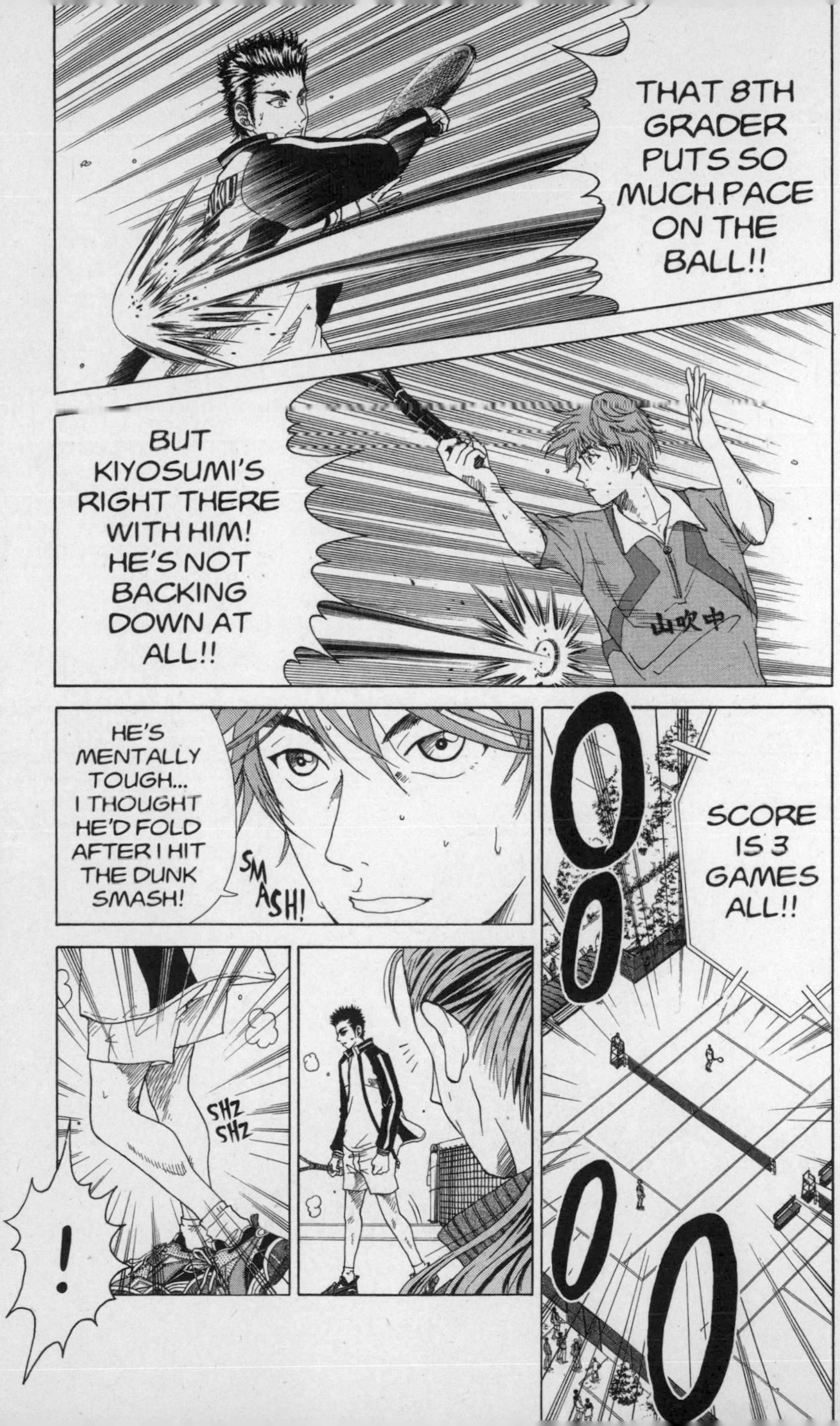
THAT 8TH GRADER PUTS SO MUCH PACE ON THE BALL!!
BUT KIYOSUMI'S RIGHT THERE WITH HIM! HE'S NOT BACKING DOWN AT ALL!!
山吹中
SCORE IS 3 GAMES ALL!!
HE'S MENTALLY TOUGH... I THOUGHT HE'D FOLD AFTER I HIT THE DUNK SMASH!
SMASH!
SHZ SHZ
!

HMPH! HIS LEFT LEG IS CRAMPING UP!!

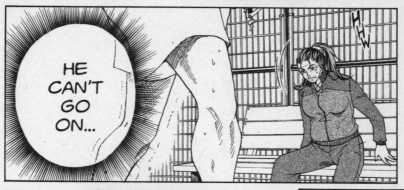

HE CAN'T GO ON...

!

SEIGAKU

READ THIS WAY

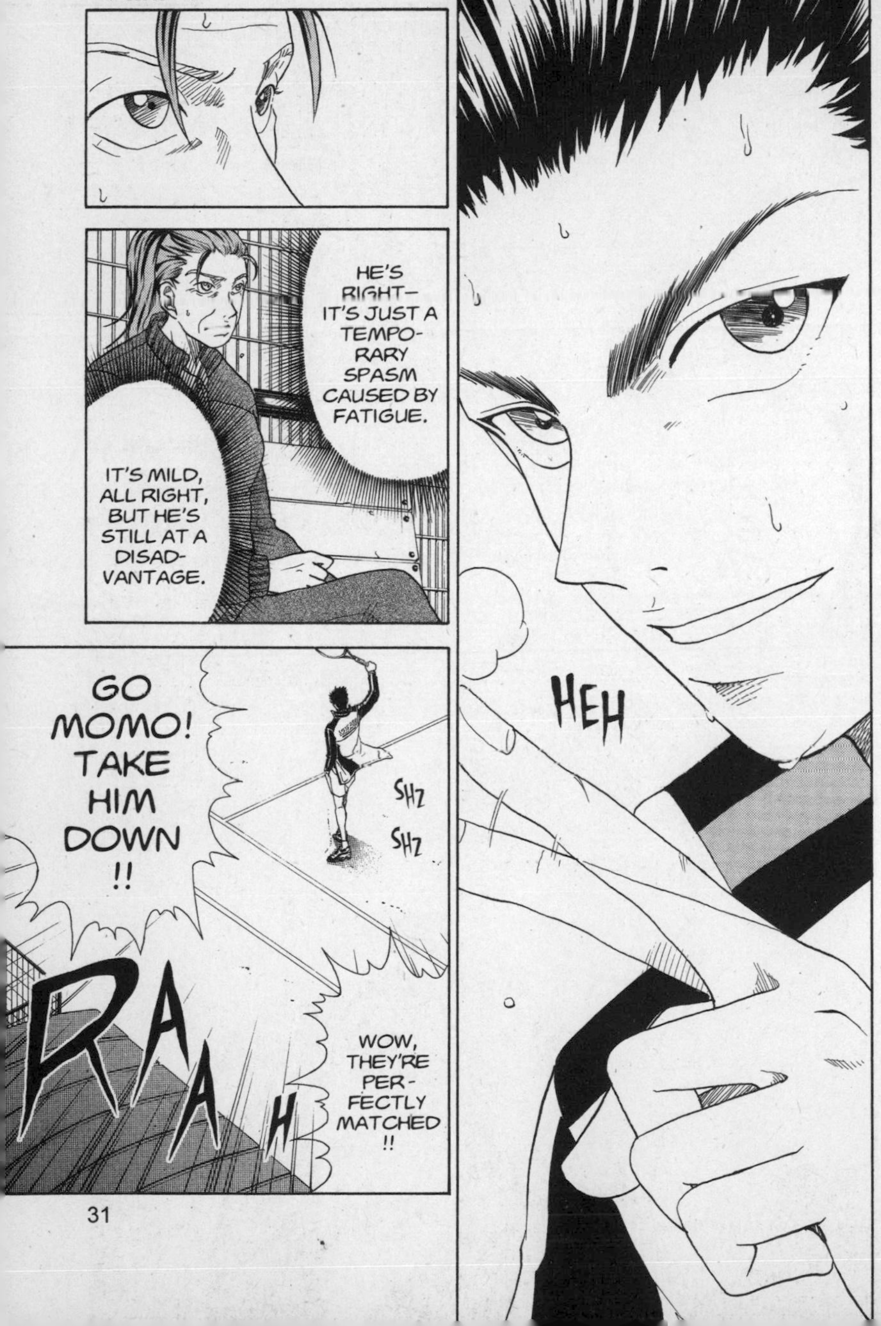
HEH
HE'S RIGHT— IT'S JUST A TEMPORARY SPASM CAUSED BY FATIGUE.
IT'S MILD, ALL RIGHT, BUT HE'S STILL AT A DISADVANTAGE.
SHZ SHZ
GO MOMO! TAKE HIM DOWN!!
WOW, THEY'RE PERFECTLY MATCHED!!
RAAH

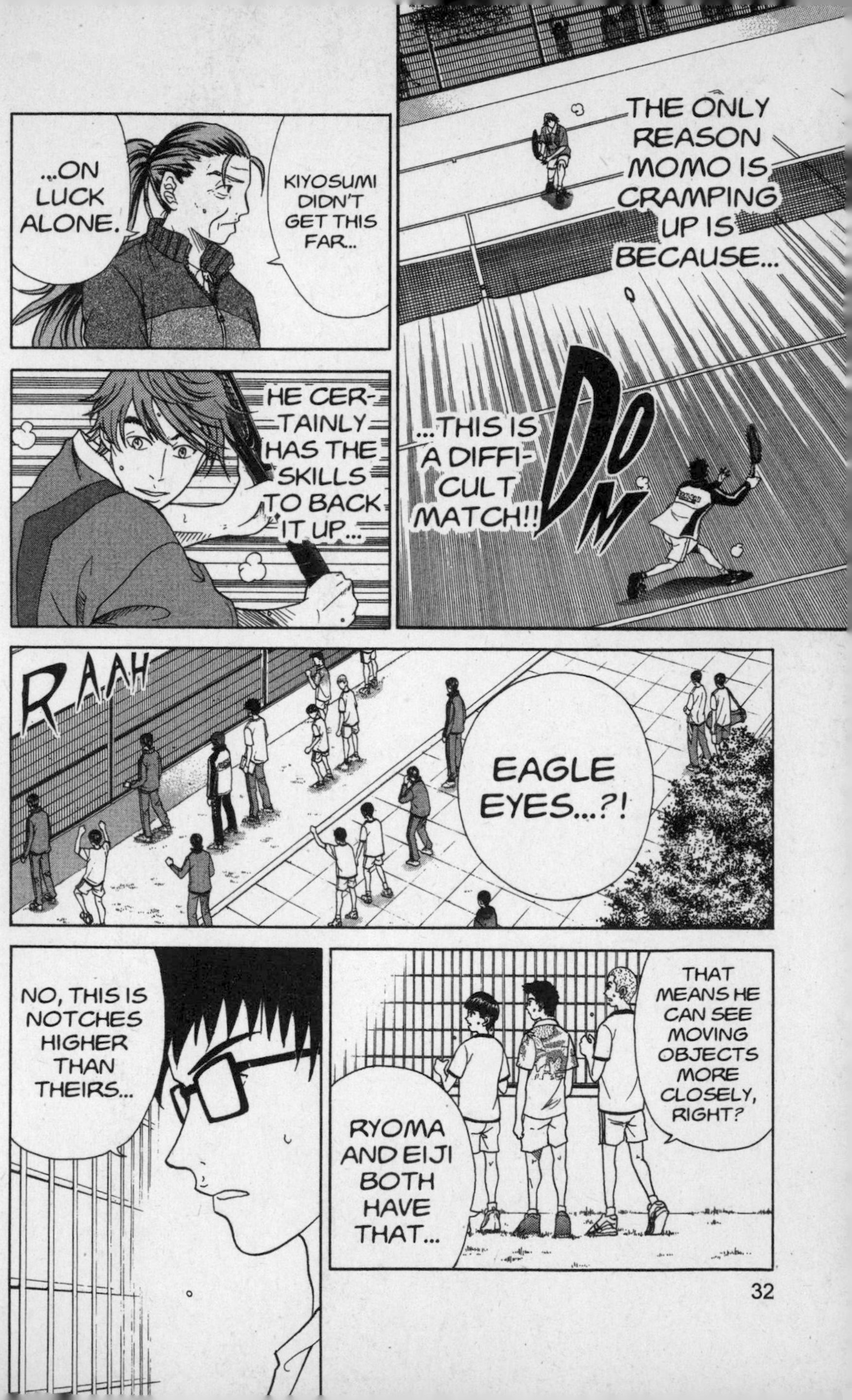
THE ONLY REASON MOMO IS CRAMPING UP IS BECAUSE...
...THIS IS A DIFFICULT MATCH!!
DOM
KIYOSUMI DIDN'T GET THIS FAR...
...ON LUCK ALONE.
HE CERTAINLY HAS THE SKILLS TO BACK IT UP...
RAAH
EAGLE EYES...?!
THAT MEANS HE CAN SEE MOVING OBJECTS MORE CLOSELY, RIGHT?
RYOMA AND EIJI BOTH HAVE THAT...
NO, THIS IS NOTCHES HIGHER THAN THEIRS...

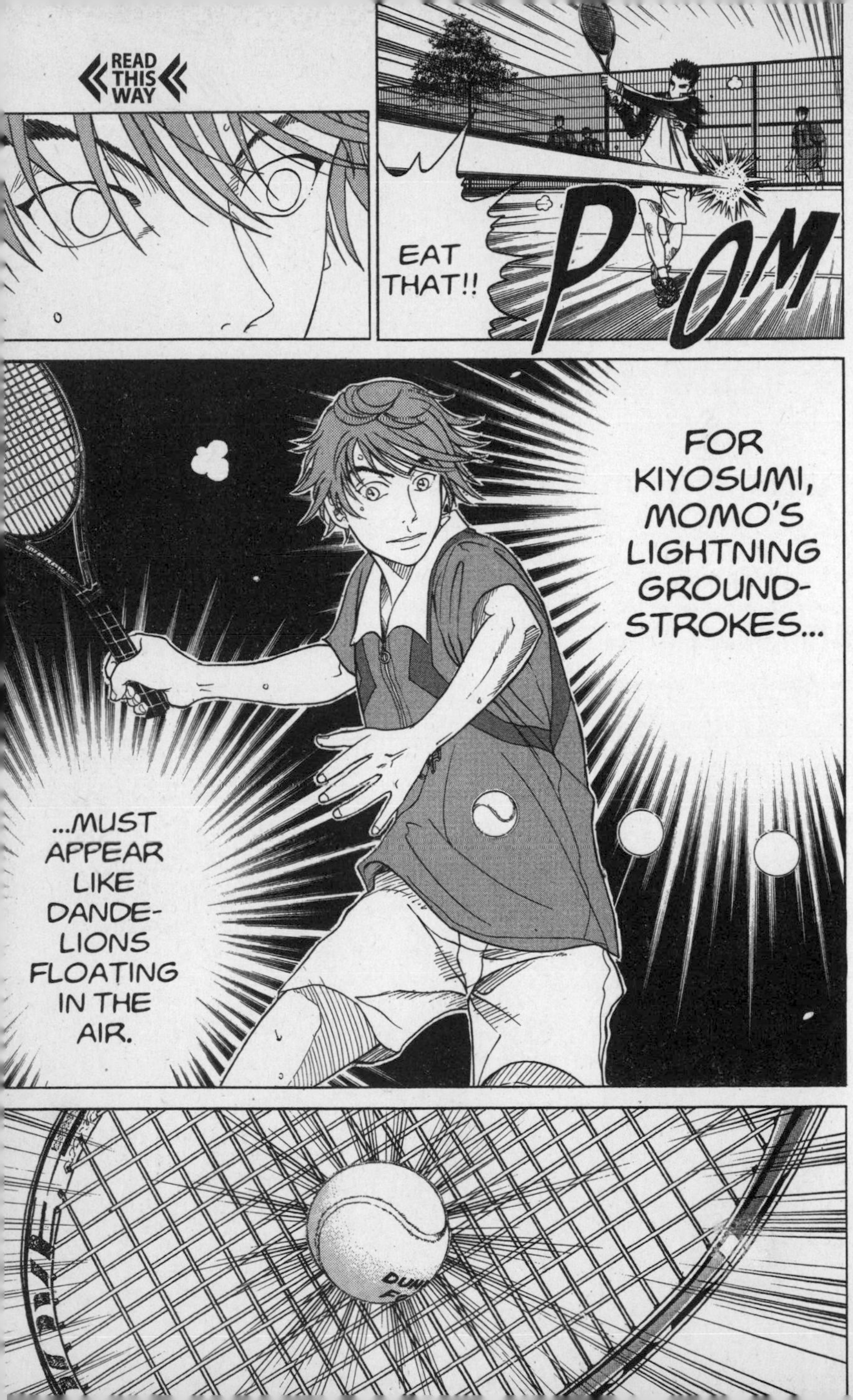
READ THIS WAY
EAT THAT!!
POM
FOR KIYOSUMI, MOMO'S LIGHTNING GROUND-STROKES...
...MUST APPEAR LIKE DANDE-LIONS FLOATING IN THE AIR.

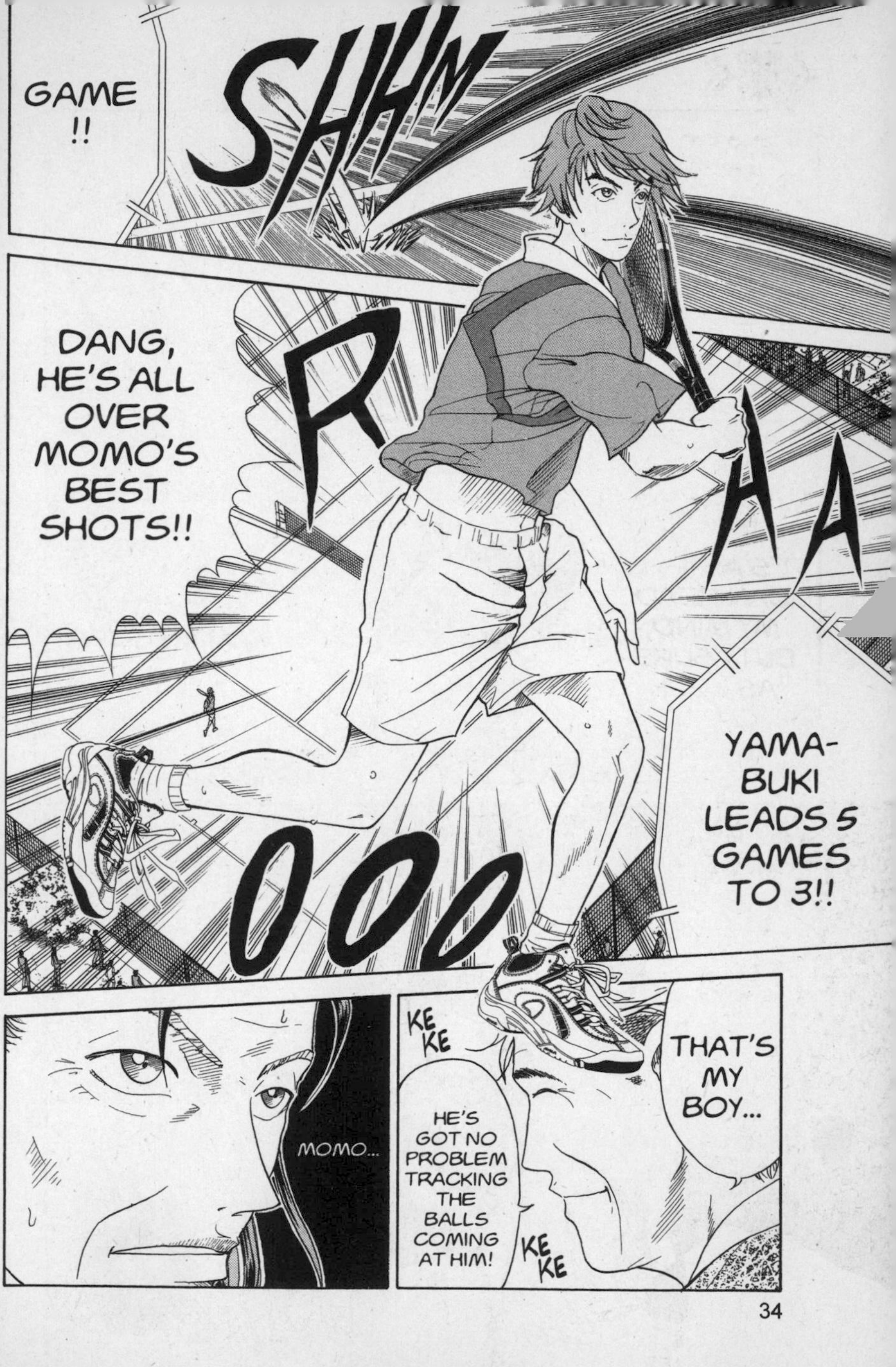
GAME !!
SHHM
YAMA-BUKI LEADS 5 GAMES TO 3!!
RAAOOO
DANG, HE'S ALL OVER MOMO'S BEST SHOTS!!
KE KE
THAT'S MY BOY...
HE'S GOT NO PROBLEM TRACKING THE BALLS COMING AT HIM!
KE KE
MOMO...

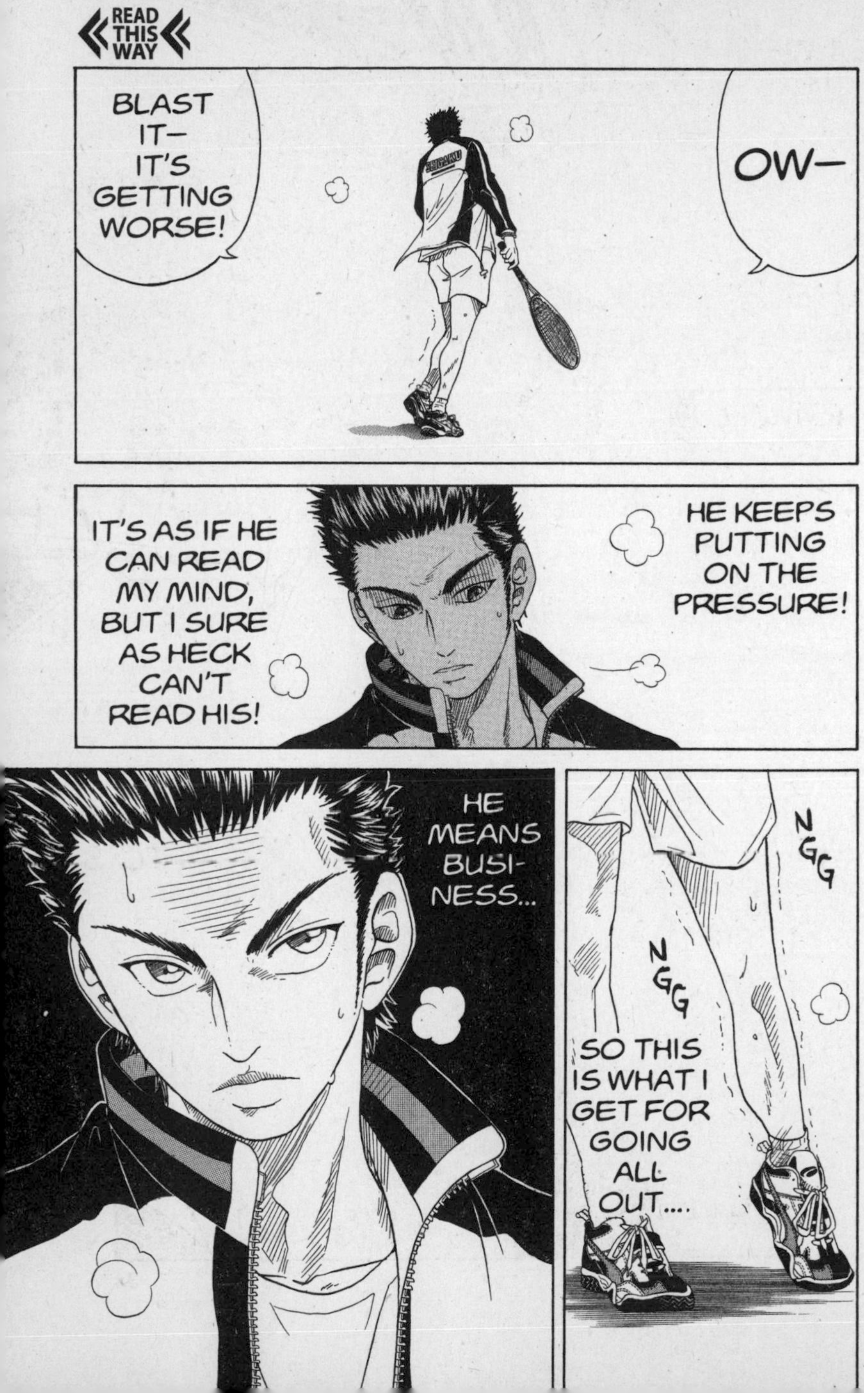
READ THIS WAY
OW—
BLAST IT— IT'S GETTING WORSE!
HE KEEPS PUTTING ON THE PRESSURE!
IT'S AS IF HE CAN READ MY MIND, BUT I SURE AS HECK CAN'T READ HIS!
NGG
NGG
SO THIS IS WHAT I GET FOR GOING ALL OUT....
HE MEANS BUSI-NESS...

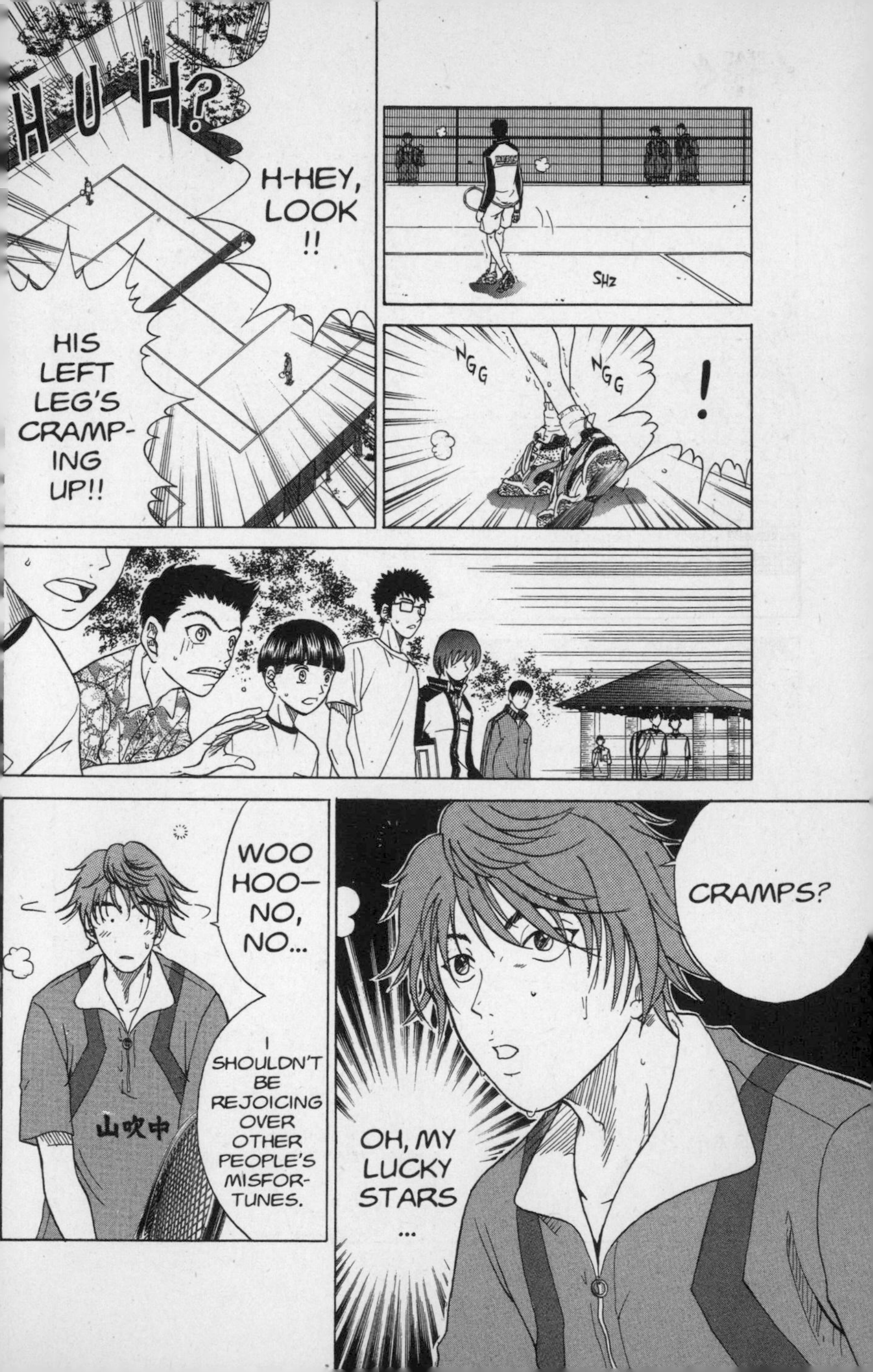
SHZ
NGG
NGG
!
HUH?
H-HEY, LOOK!!
HIS LEFT LEG'S CRAMPING UP!!
CRAMPS?
OH, MY LUCKY STARS...
WOO HOO— NO, NO...
I SHOULDN'T BE REJOICING OVER OTHER PEOPLE'S MISFORTUNES.
山吹中

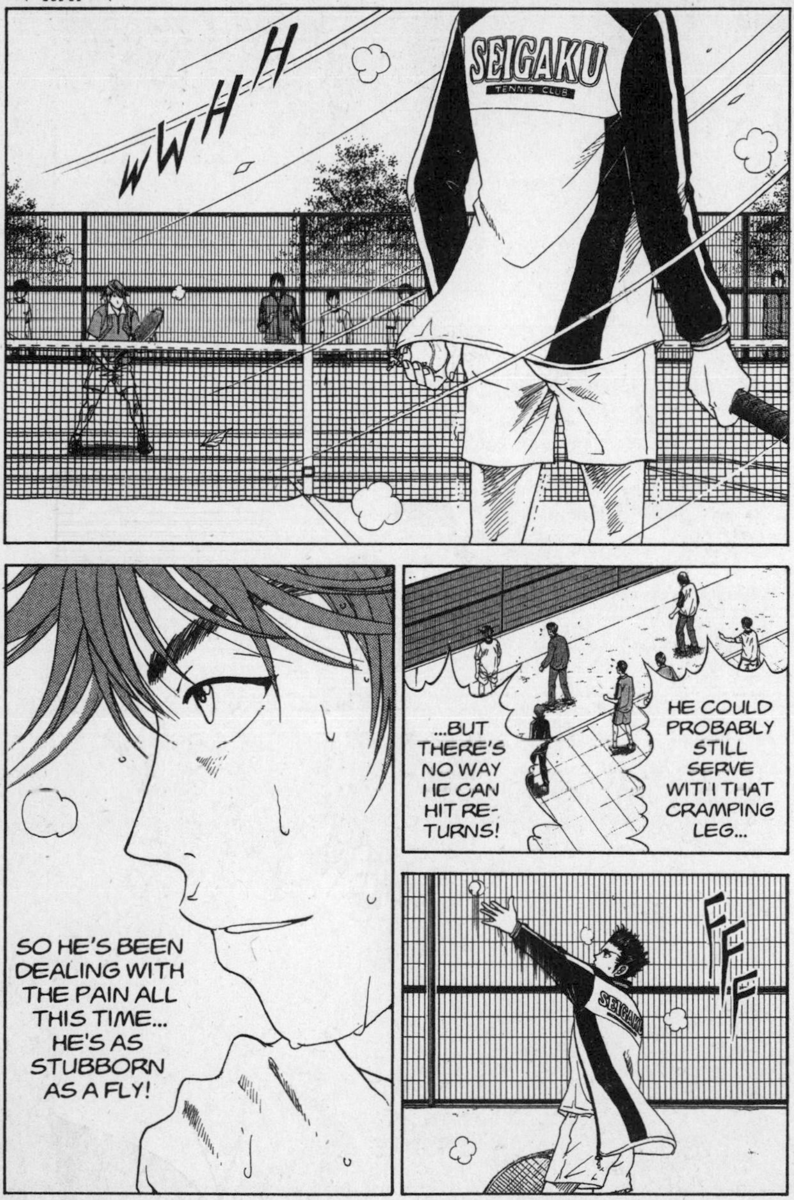
WWHH
HE COULD PROBABLY STILL SERVE WITH THAT CRAMPING LEG...
...BUT THERE'S NO WAY HE CAN HIT RE-TURNS!
FFF
SO HE'S BEEN DEALING WITH THE PAIN ALL THIS TIME... HE'S AS STUBBORN AS A FLY!

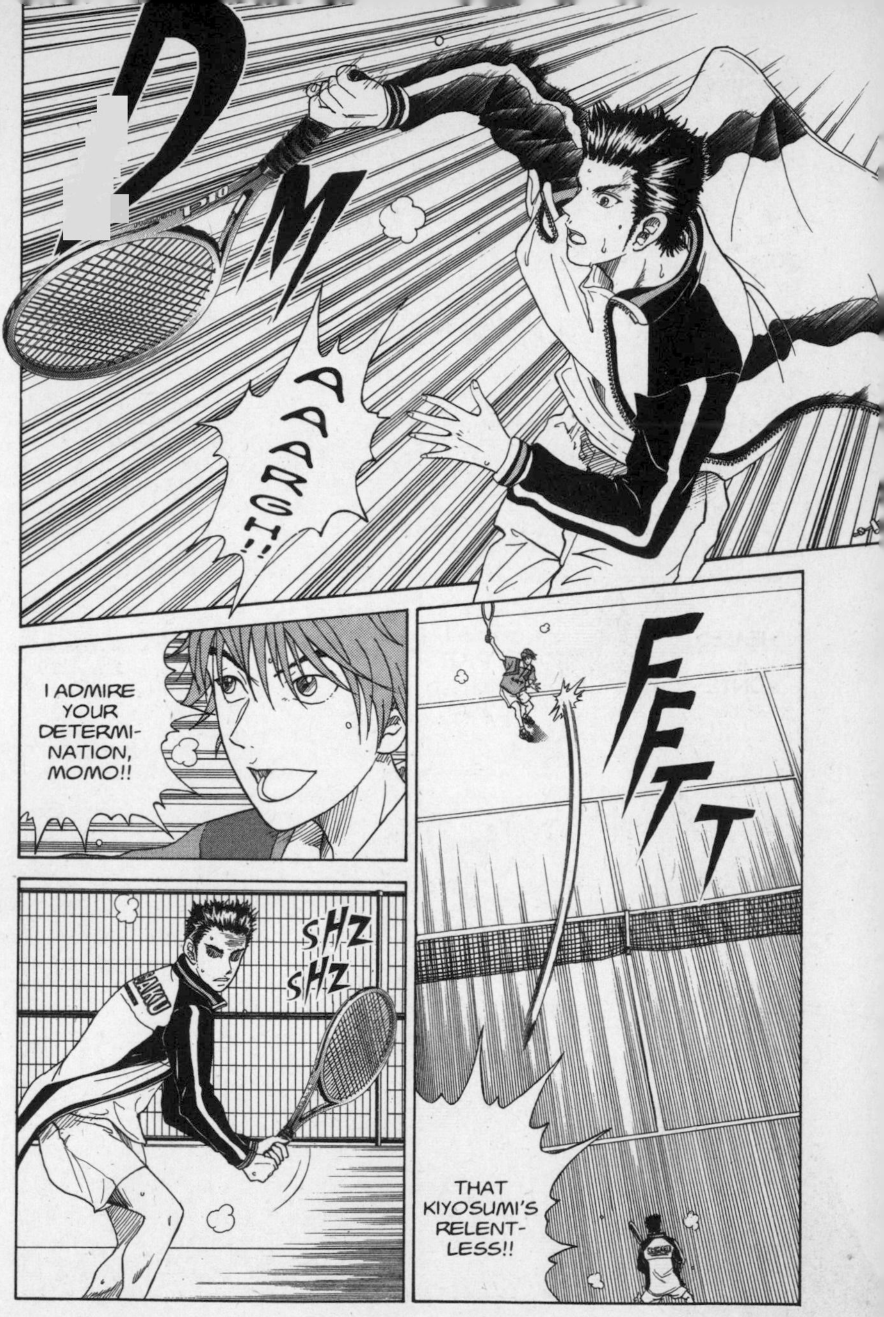
DM
AAARGH!!
FFTT
THAT KIYOSUMI'S RELENT-LESS!!
I ADMIRE YOUR DETERMI-NATION, MOMO!!
SHZ SHZ

READ THIS WAY

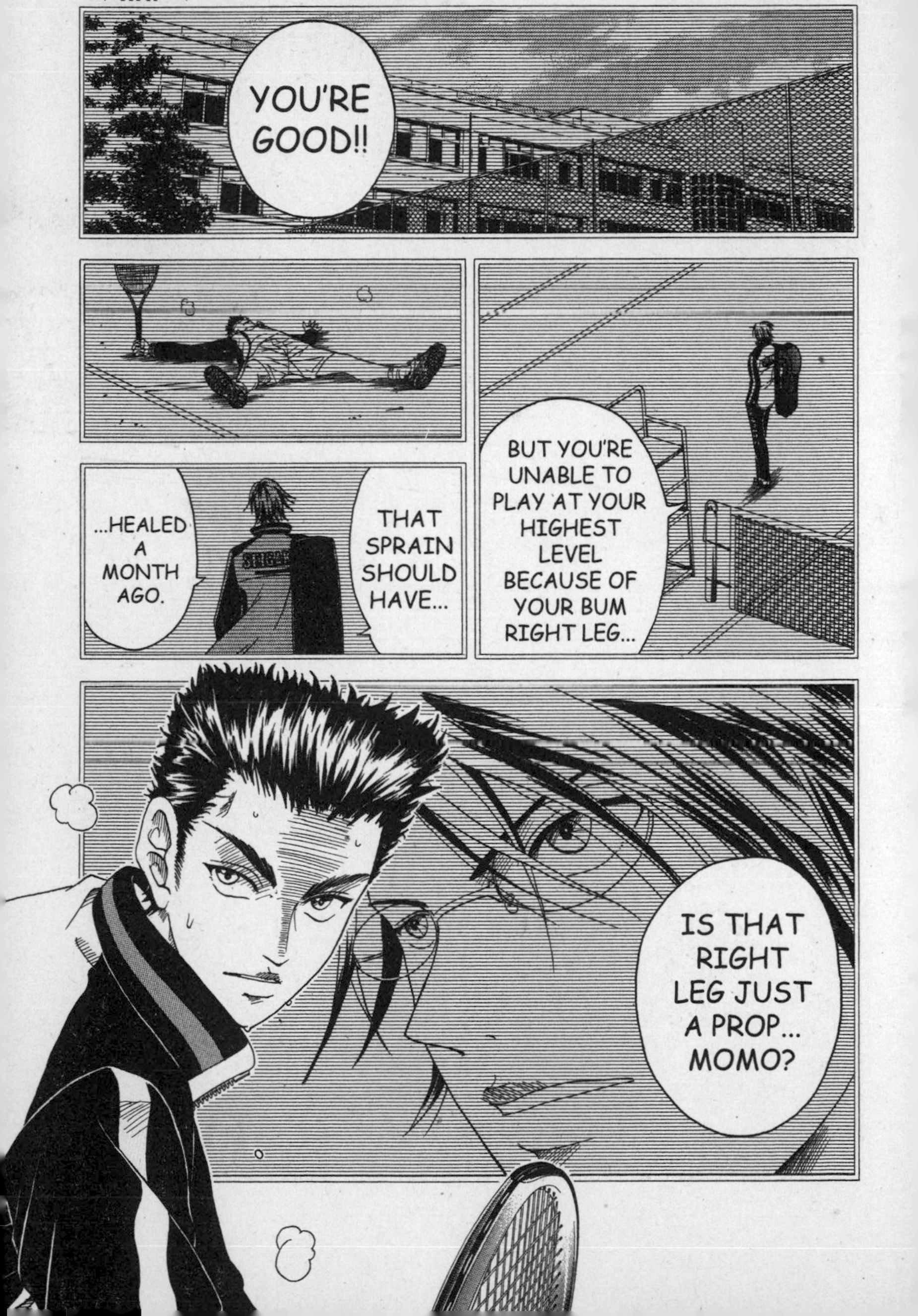
YOU'RE GOOD!!
BUT YOU'RE UNABLE TO PLAY AT YOUR HIGHEST LEVEL BECAUSE OF YOUR BUM RIGHT LEG...
THAT SPRAIN SHOULD HAVE...
...HEALED A MONTH AGO.
IS THAT RIGHT LEG JUST A PROP... MOMO?

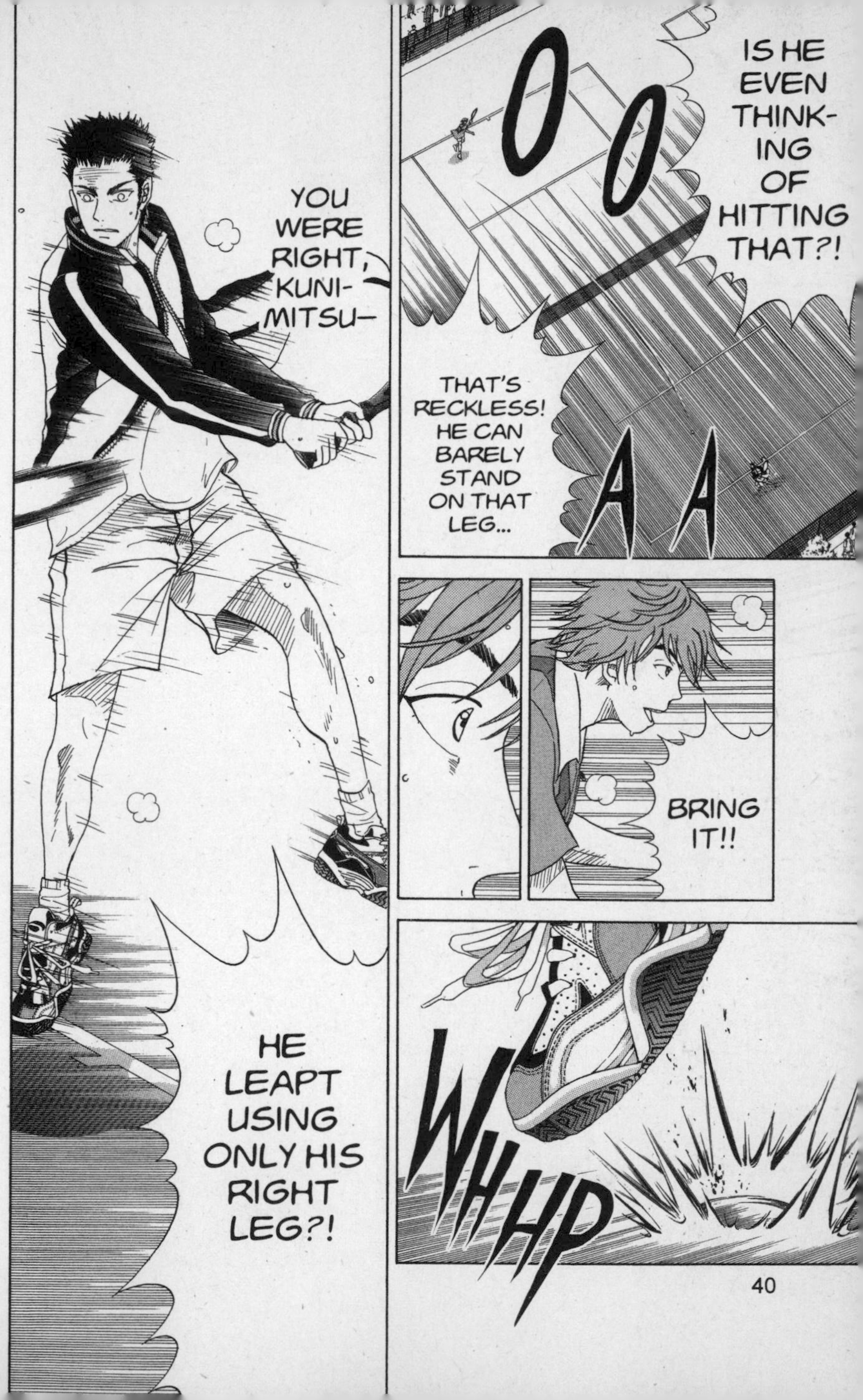
IS HE EVEN THINKING OF HITTING THAT?!
OO
THAT'S RECKLESS! HE CAN BARELY STAND ON THAT LEG...
AA
BRING IT!!
WHHP
YOU WERE RIGHT, KUNIMITSU—
HE LEAPT USING ONLY HIS RIGHT LEG?!

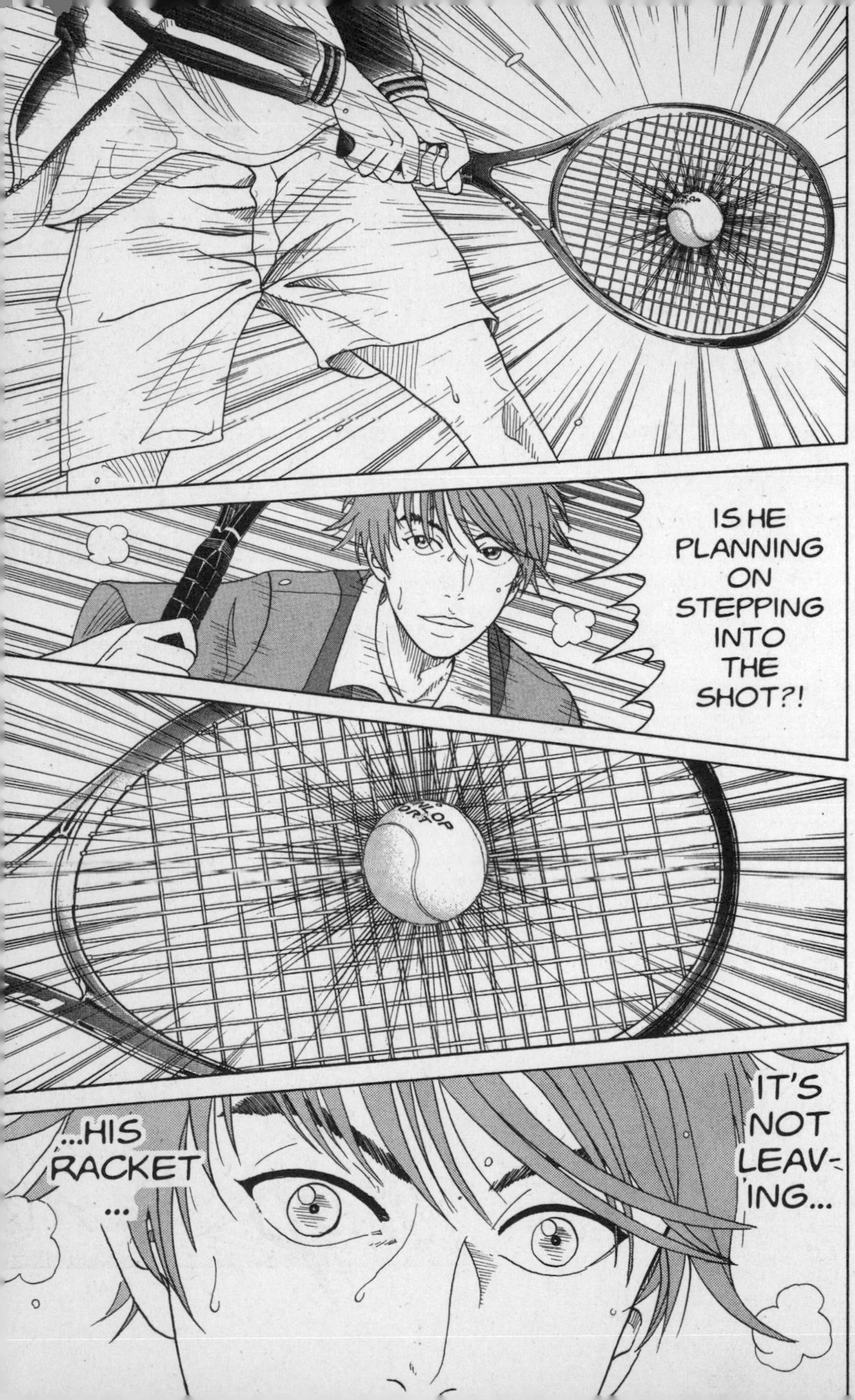
IS HE PLANNING ON STEPPING INTO THE SHOT?!
IT'S NOT LEAV-ING...
...HIS RACKET ...

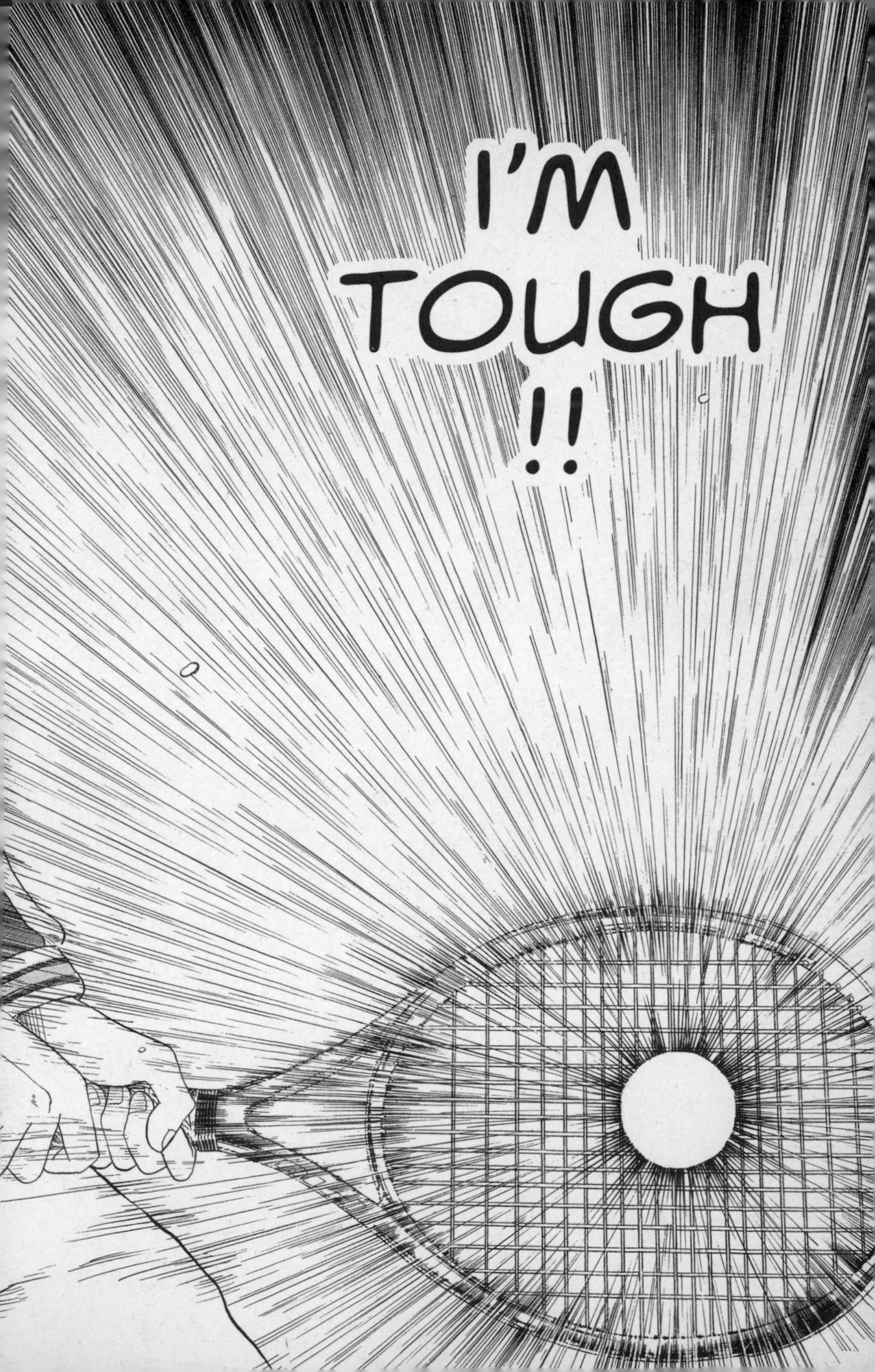
I'M TOUGH !!

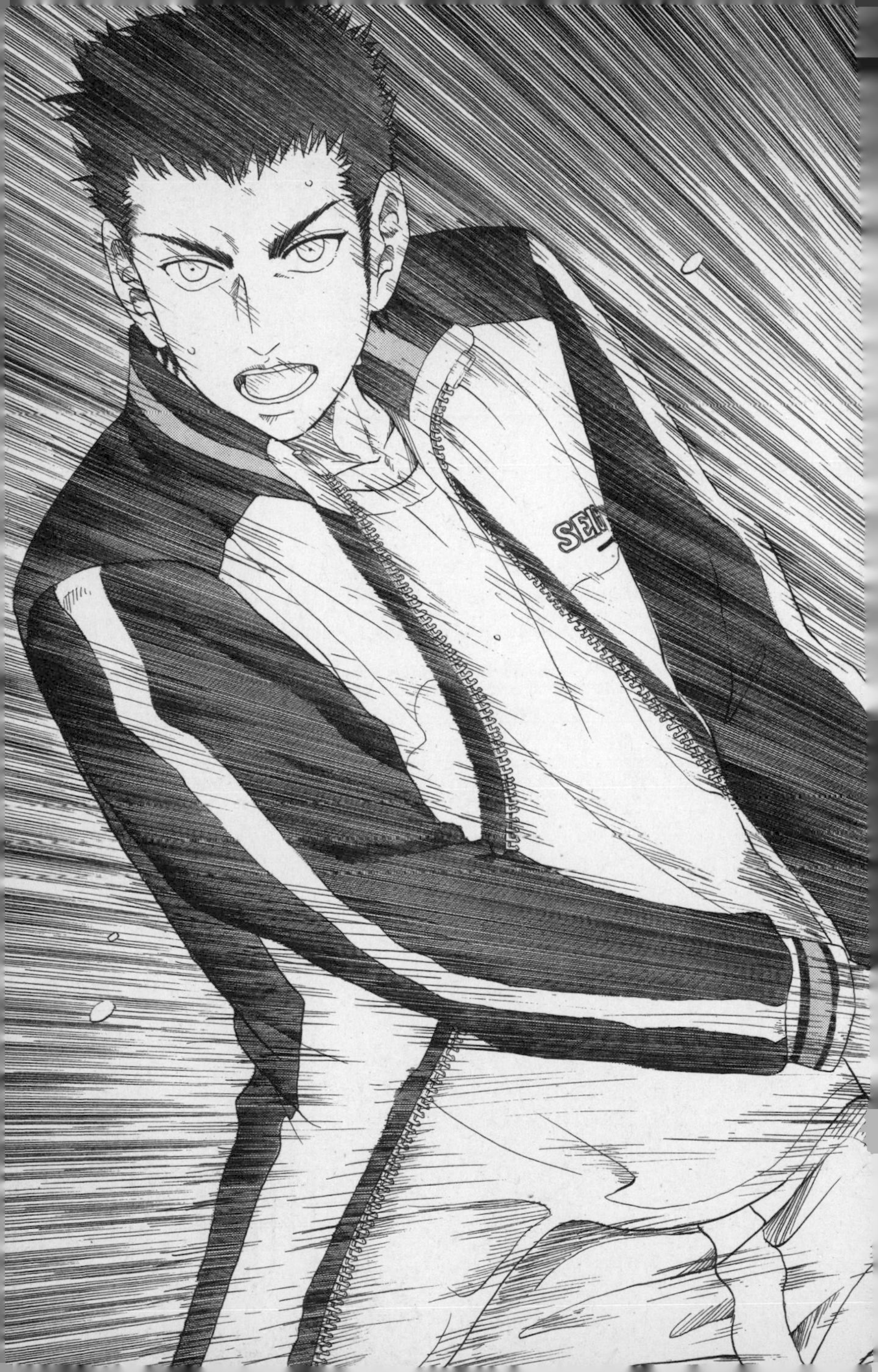

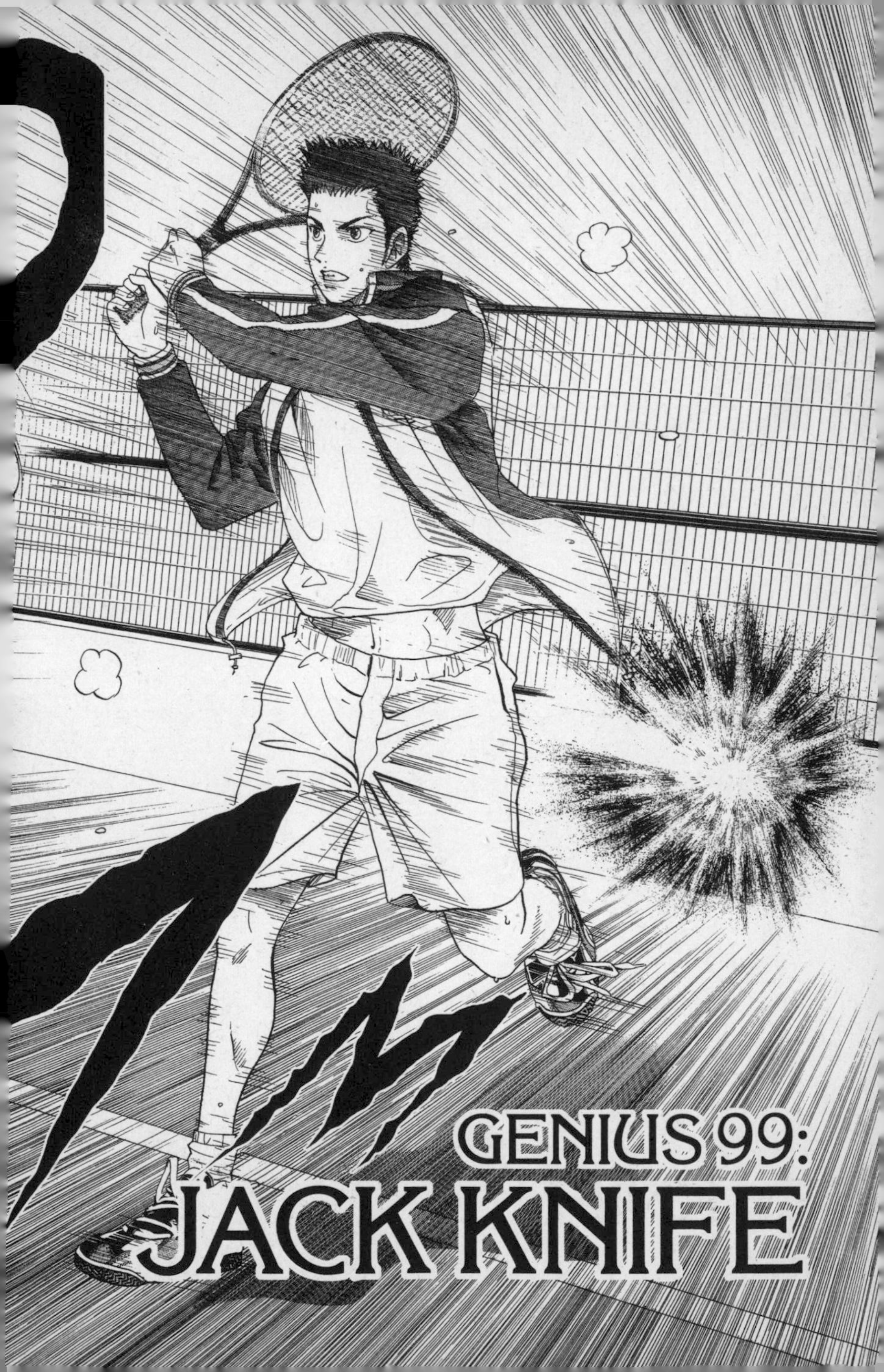
GENIUS 99:
JACK KNIFE

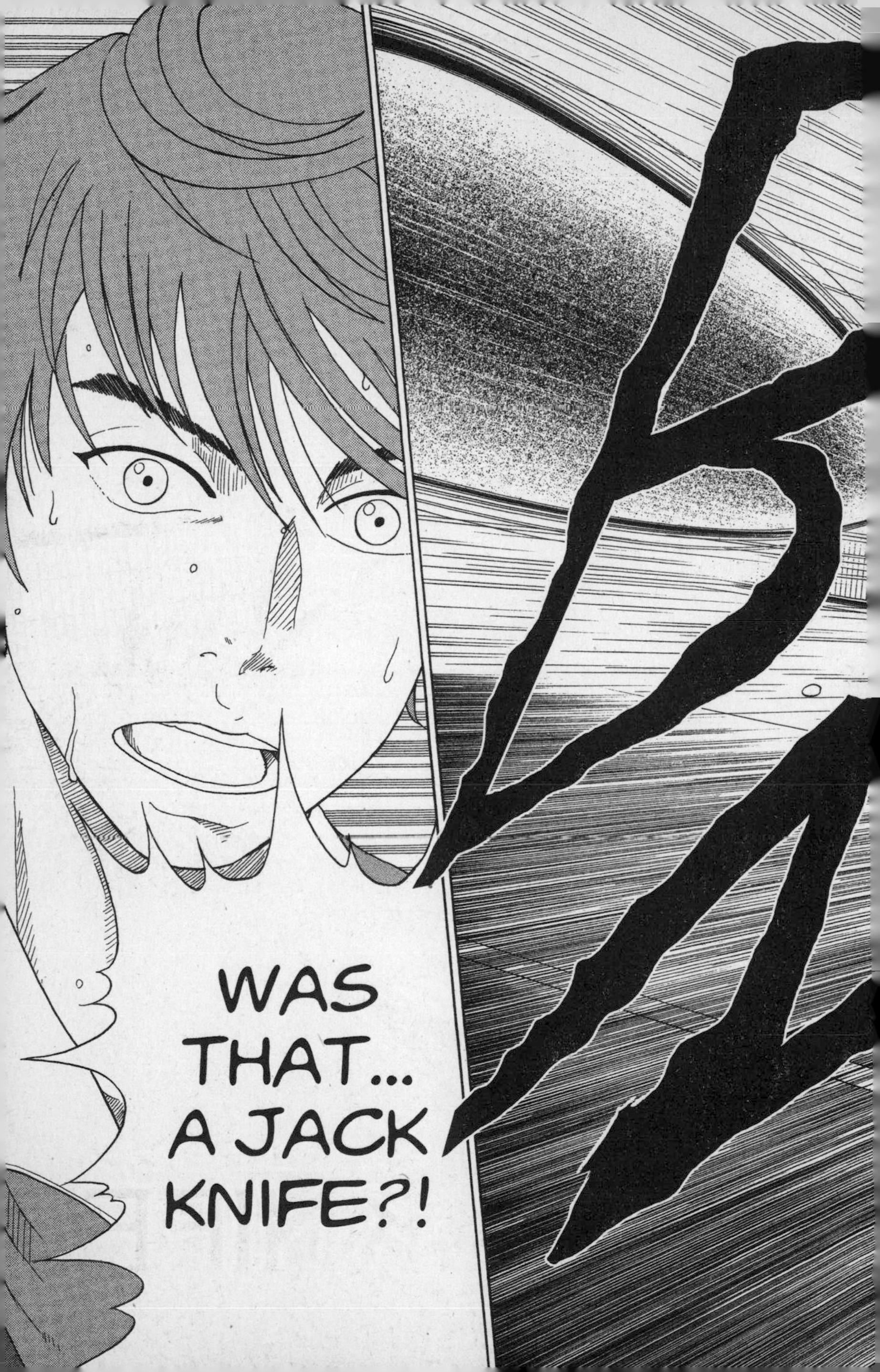
WAS THAT... A JACK KNIFE?!

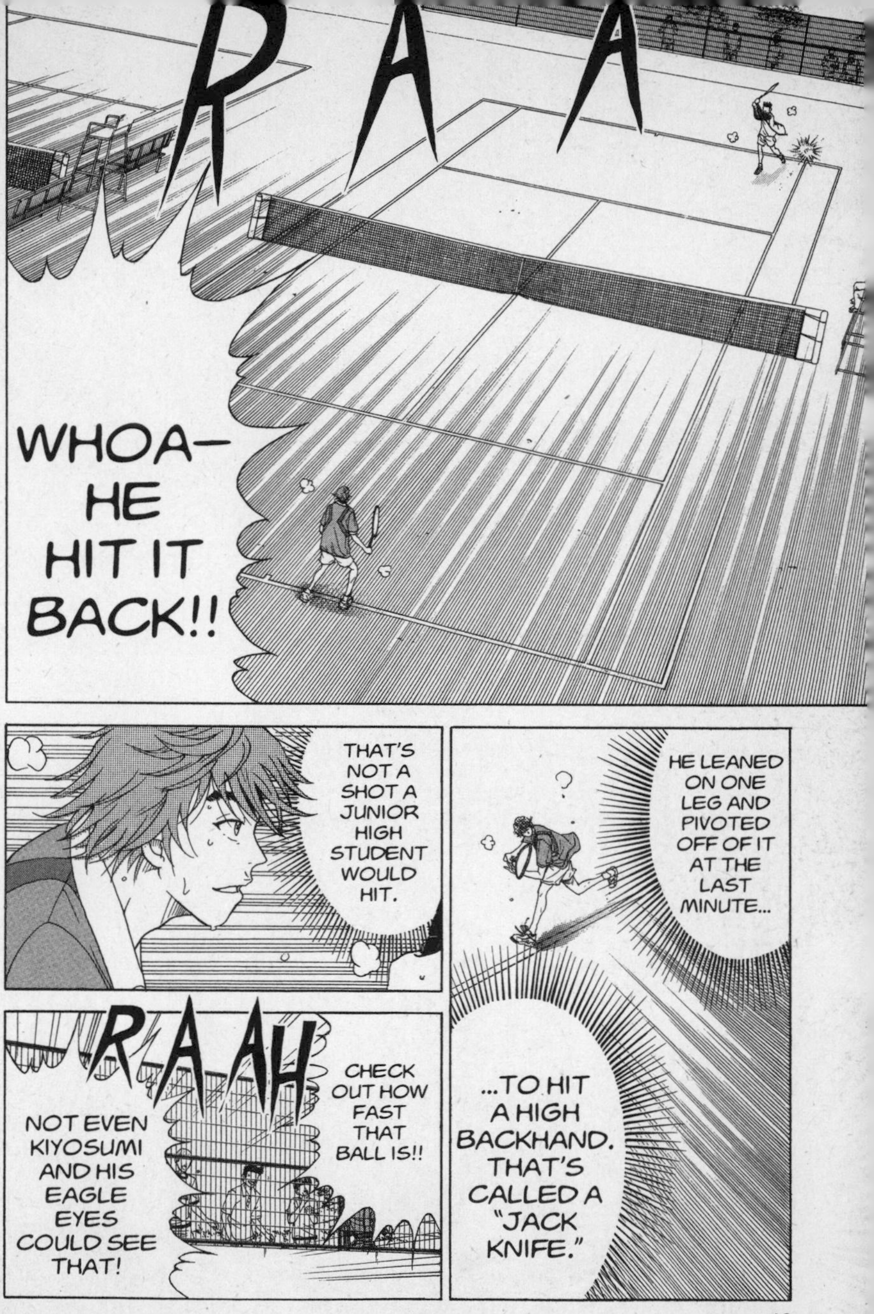
RAA
WHOA—HE HIT IT BACK!!
HE LEANED ON ONE LEG AND PIVOTED OFF OF IT AT THE LAST MINUTE...
...TO HIT A HIGH BACKHAND. THAT'S CALLED A "JACK KNIFE."
THAT'S NOT A SHOT A JUNIOR HIGH STUDENT WOULD HIT.
RAAH
CHECK OUT HOW FAST THAT BALL IS!!
NOT EVEN KIYOSUMI AND HIS EAGLE EYES COULD SEE THAT!

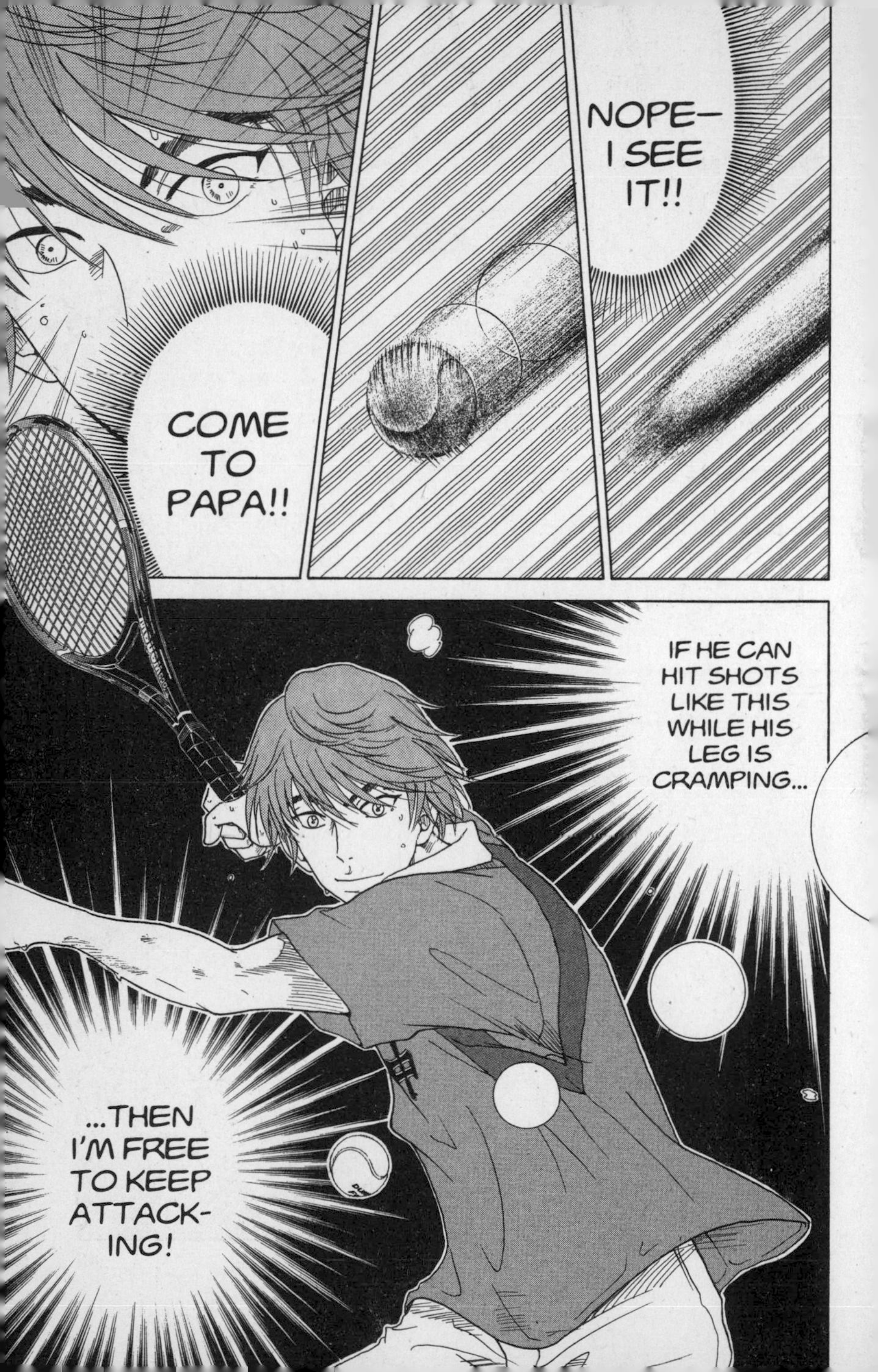
NOPE— I SEE IT!!
COME TO PAPA!!
IF HE CAN HIT SHOTS LIKE THIS WHILE HIS LEG IS CRAMPING...
...THEN I'M FREE TO KEEP ATTACK-ING!

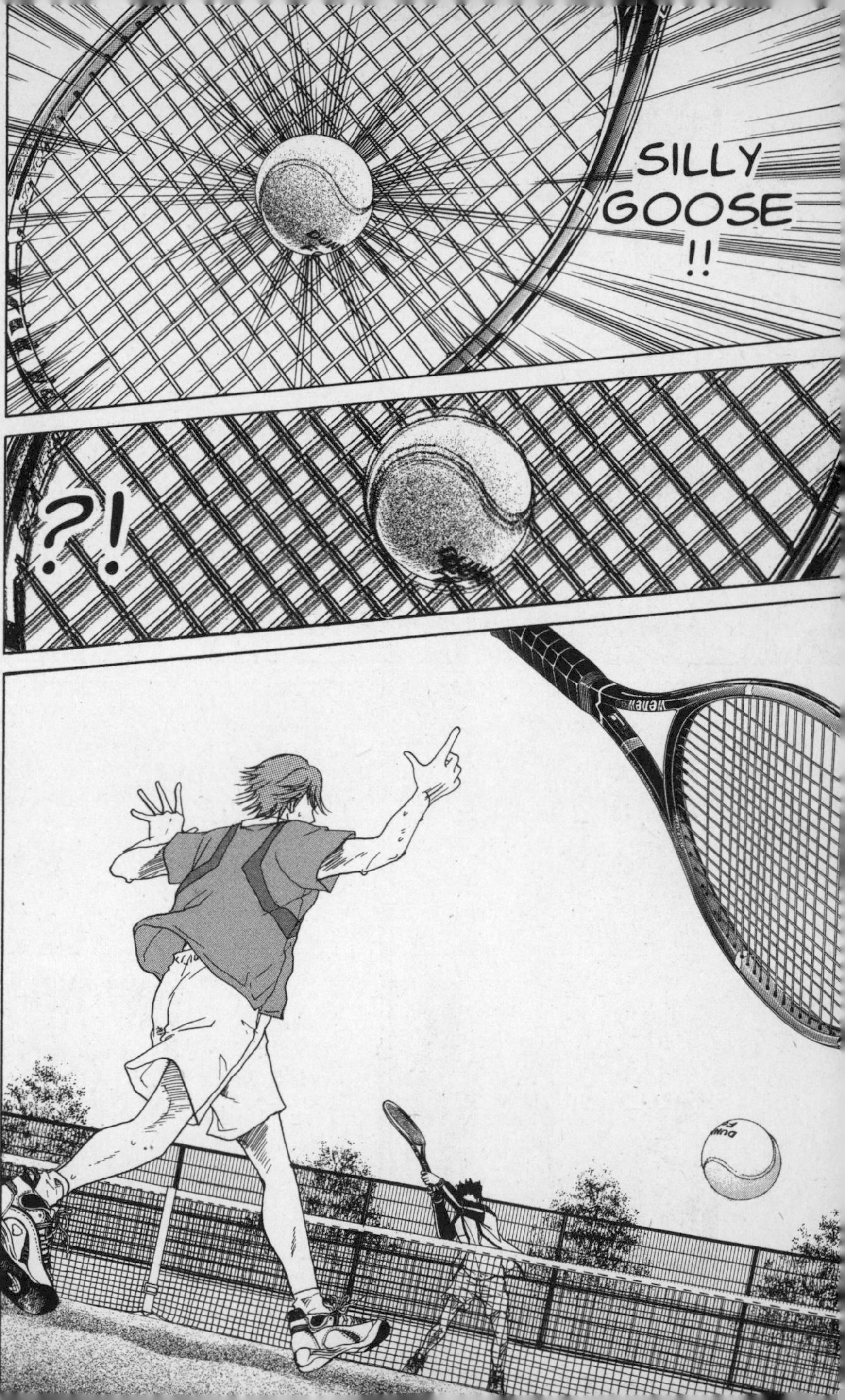
SILLY GOOSE !!
?!

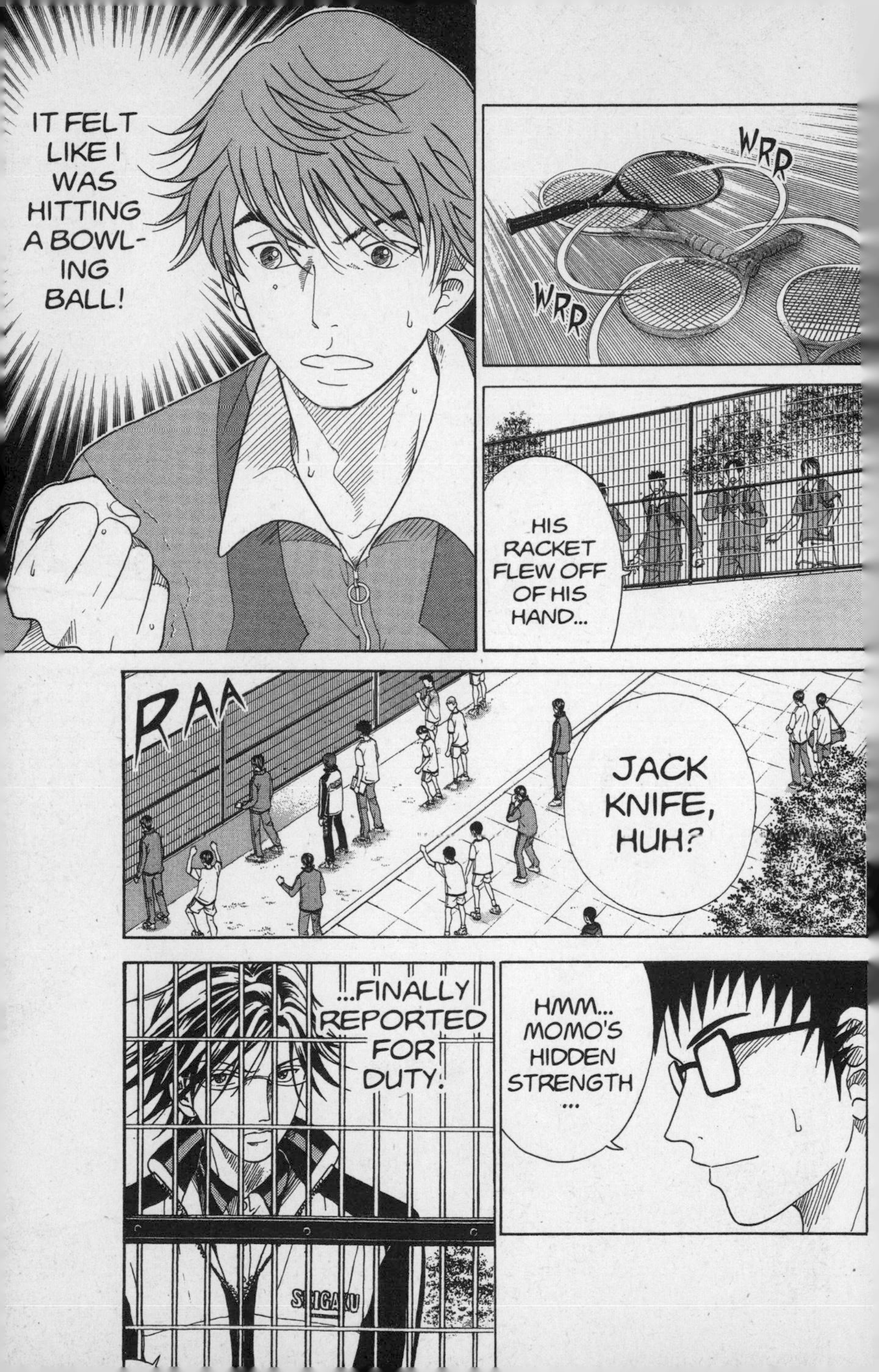
WRR
WRR
HIS RACKET FLEW OFF OF HIS HAND...
IT FELT LIKE I WAS HITTING A BOWL-ING BALL!
RAA
JACK KNIFE, HUH?
HMM... MOMO'S HIDDEN STRENGTH ...
...FINALLY REPORTED FOR DUTY.
SEIGAKU

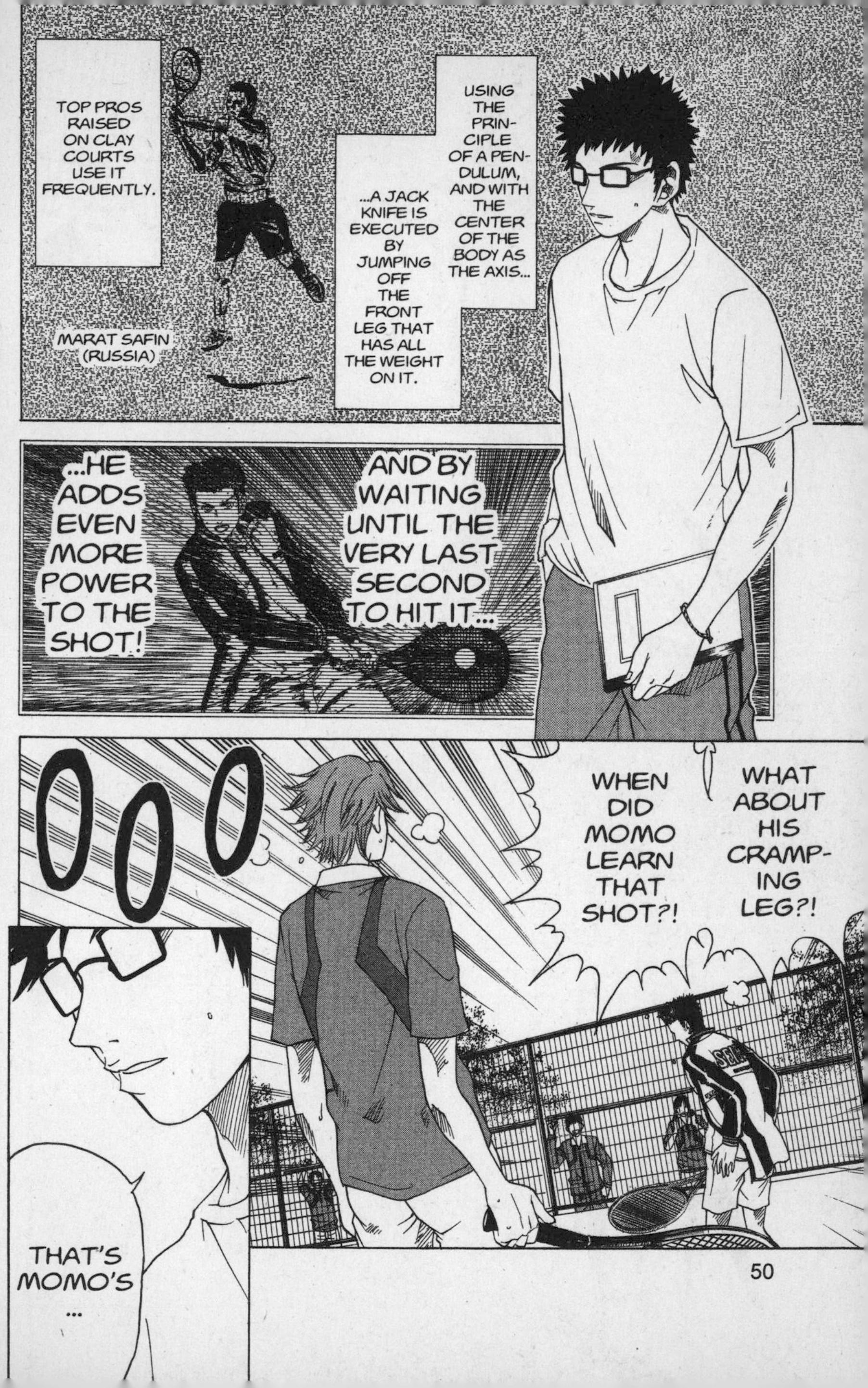
USING THE PRINCIPLE OF A PENDULUM, AND WITH THE CENTER OF THE BODY AS THE AXIS...
...A JACK KNIFE IS EXECUTED BY JUMPING OFF THE FRONT LEG THAT HAS ALL THE WEIGHT ON IT.
TOP PROS RAISED ON CLAY COURTS USE IT FREQUENTLY.
MARAT SAFIN (RUSSIA)
AND BY WAITING UNTIL THE VERY LAST SECOND TO HIT IT...
...HE ADDS EVEN MORE POWER TO THE SHOT!
WHAT ABOUT HIS CRAMPING LEG?!
WHEN DID MOMO LEARN THAT SHOT?!
OOO
THAT'S MOMO'S ...

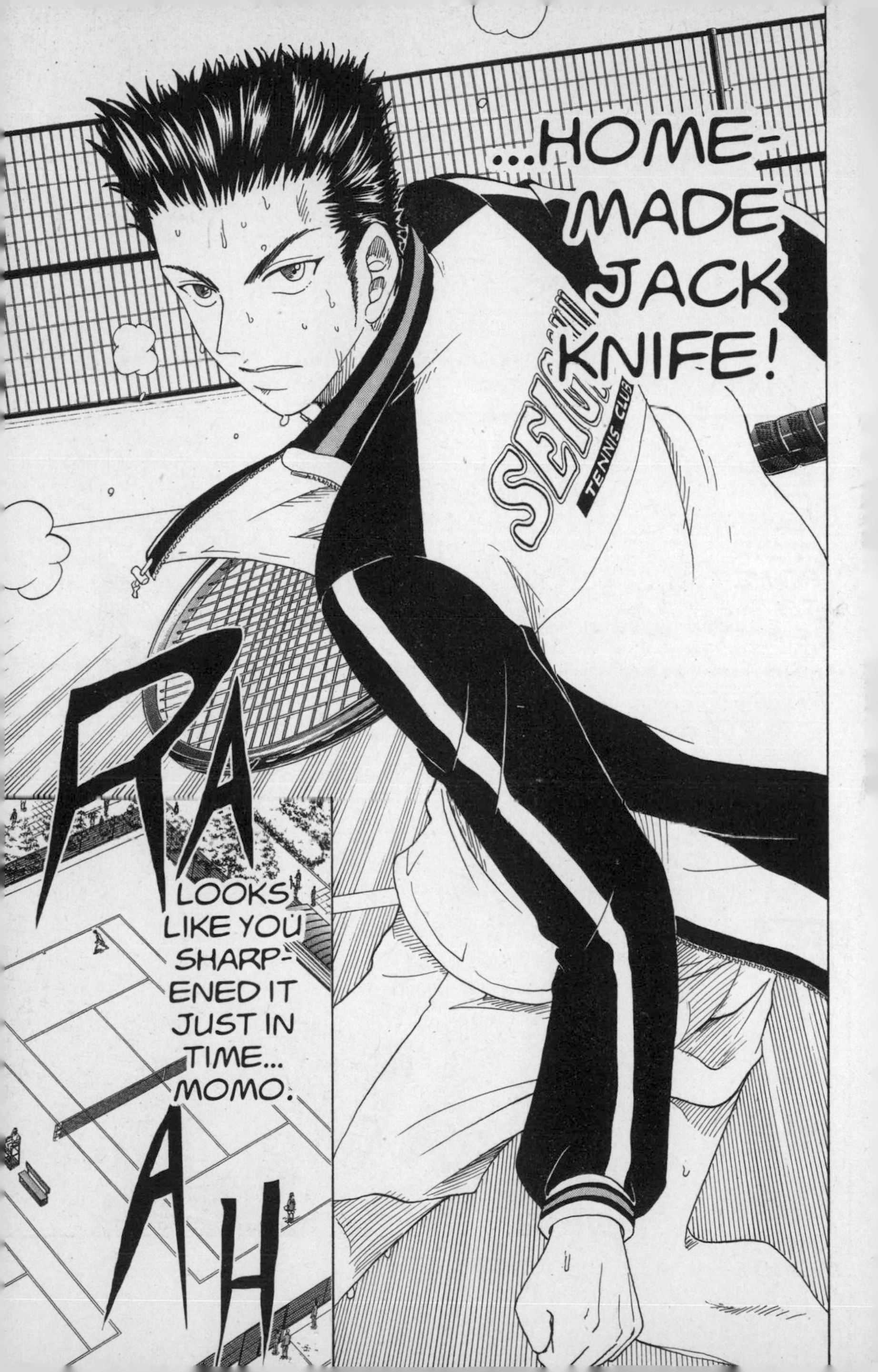
...HOME-MADE JACK KNIFE!
SEIGAKU
TENNIS CLUB
FRAAH
LOOKS LIKE YOU SHARP-ENED IT JUST IN TIME... MOMO.

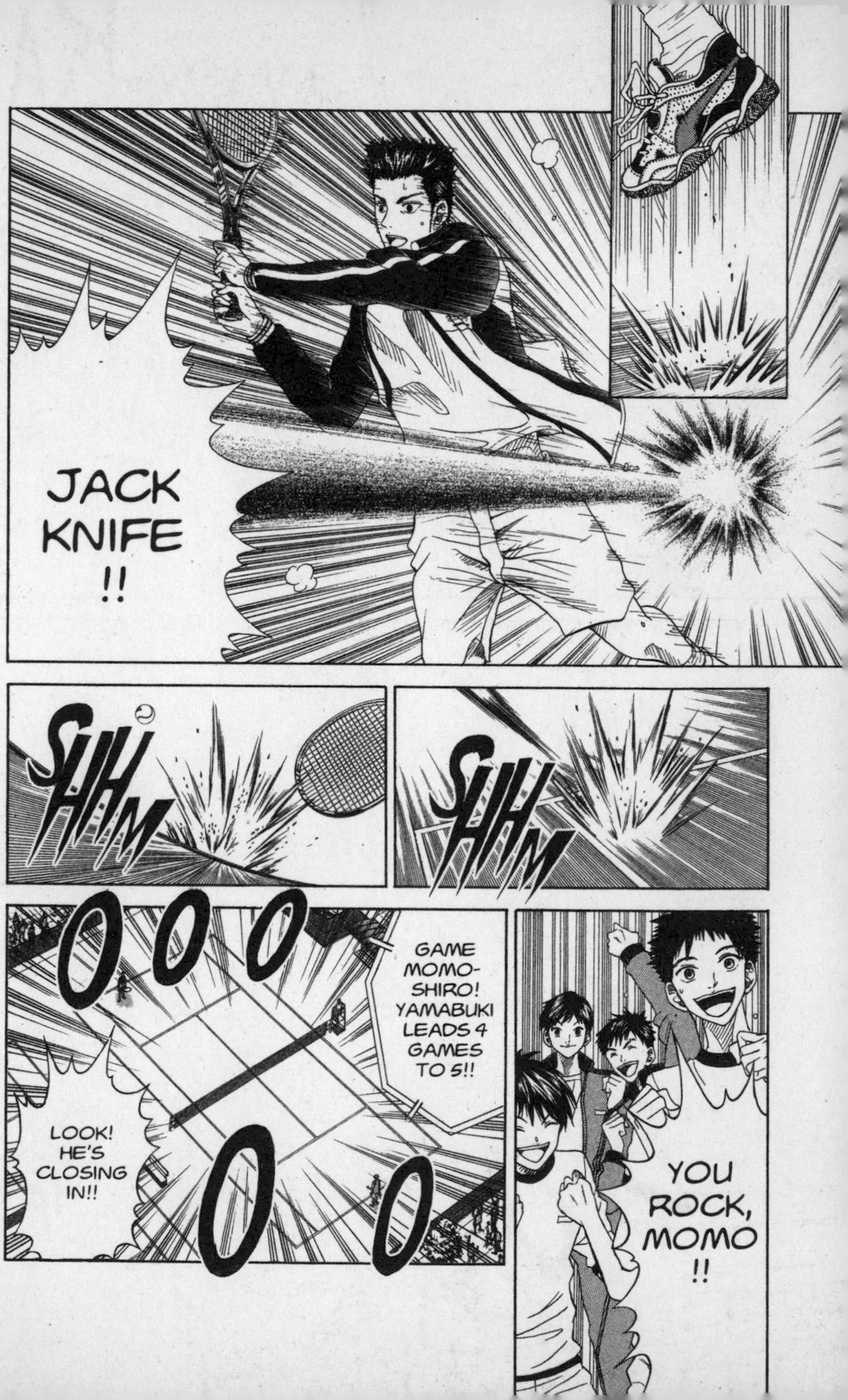
JACK KNIFE !!
SHHM
SHHM
YOU ROCK, MOMO !!
GAME MOMO-SHIRO! YAMABUKI LEADS 4 GAMES TO 5!!
OOOOO
LOOK! HE'S CLOSING IN!!

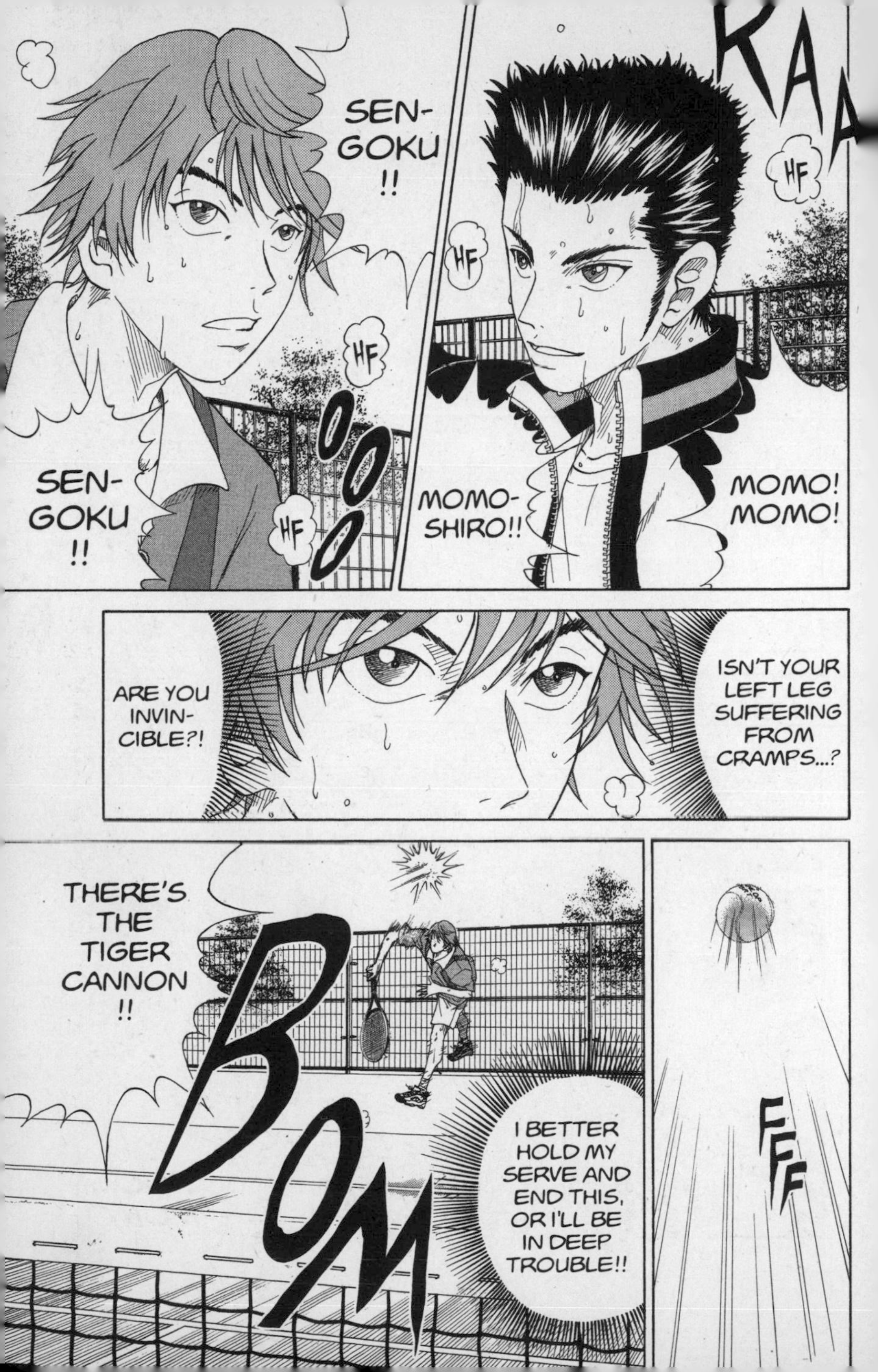
KAA
HF
HF
MOMO! MOMO!
MOMO-SHIRO!!
SEN-GOKU!!
HF
OOO
HF
SEN-GOKU!!
ISN'T YOUR LEFT LEG SUFFERING FROM CRAMPS...?
ARE YOU INVINCIBLE?!
FFF
THERE'S THE TIGER CANNON!!
BOM
I BETTER HOLD MY SERVE AND END THIS, OR I'LL BE IN DEEP TROUBLE!!

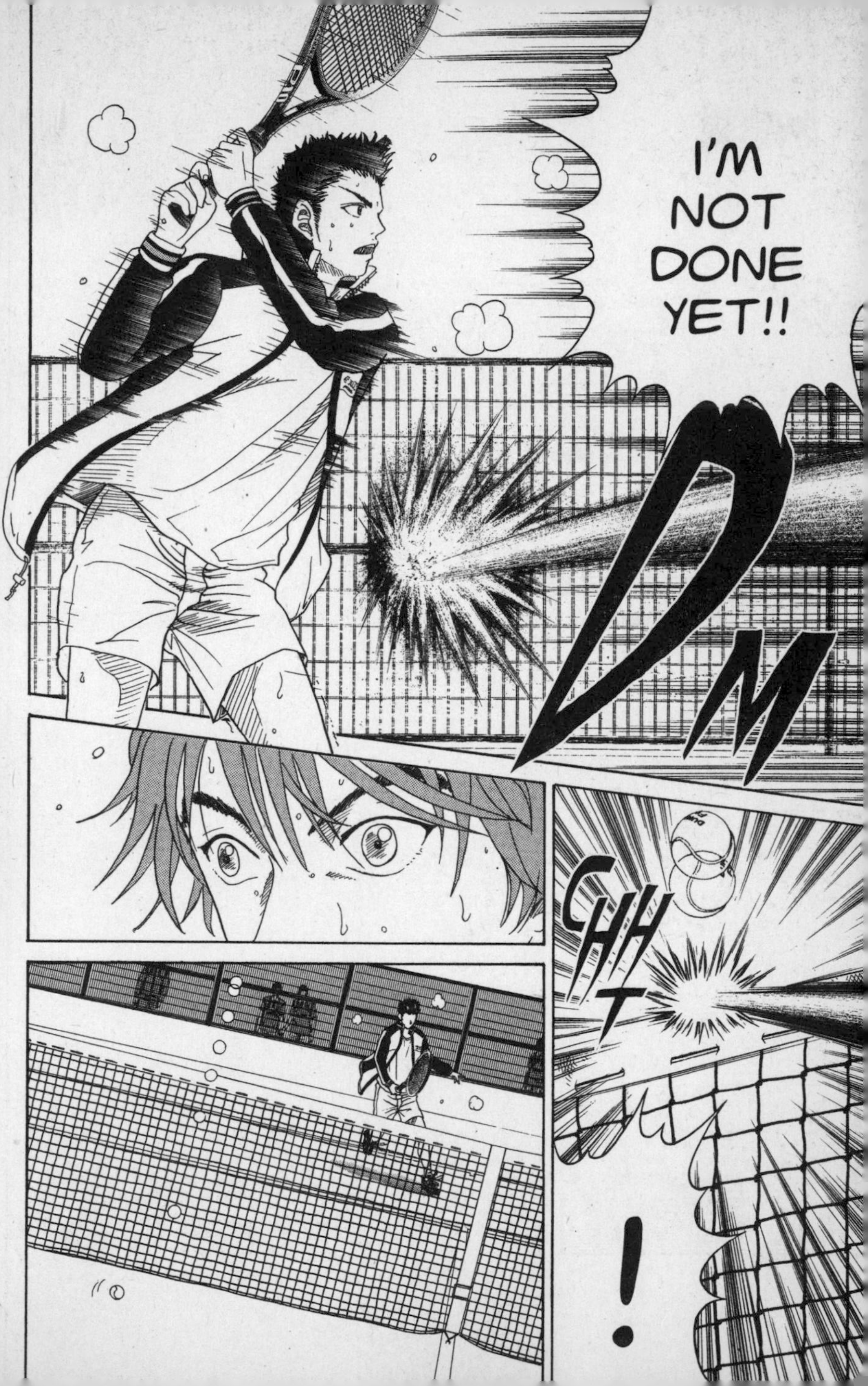
I'M NOT DONE YET!!
DM
CHHT
!

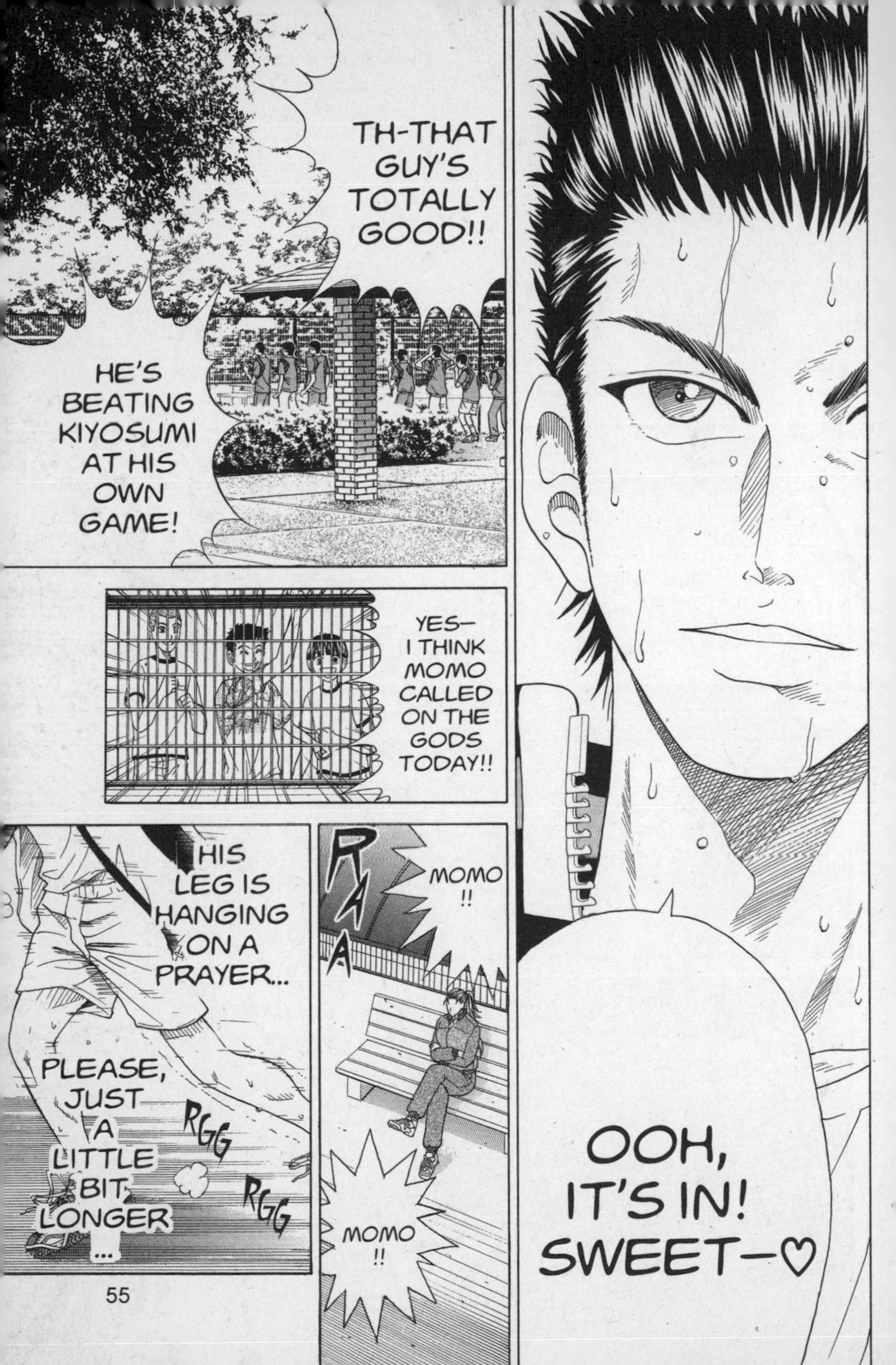
OOH, IT'S IN! SWEET—♡
TH-THAT GUY'S TOTALLY GOOD!!
HE'S BEATING KIYOSUMI AT HIS OWN GAME!
YES— I THINK MOMO CALLED ON THE GODS TODAY!!
RAA
MOMO!!
MOMO!!
HIS LEG IS HANGING ON A PRAYER...
PLEASE, JUST A LITTLE BIT LONGER ...
RGG
RGG

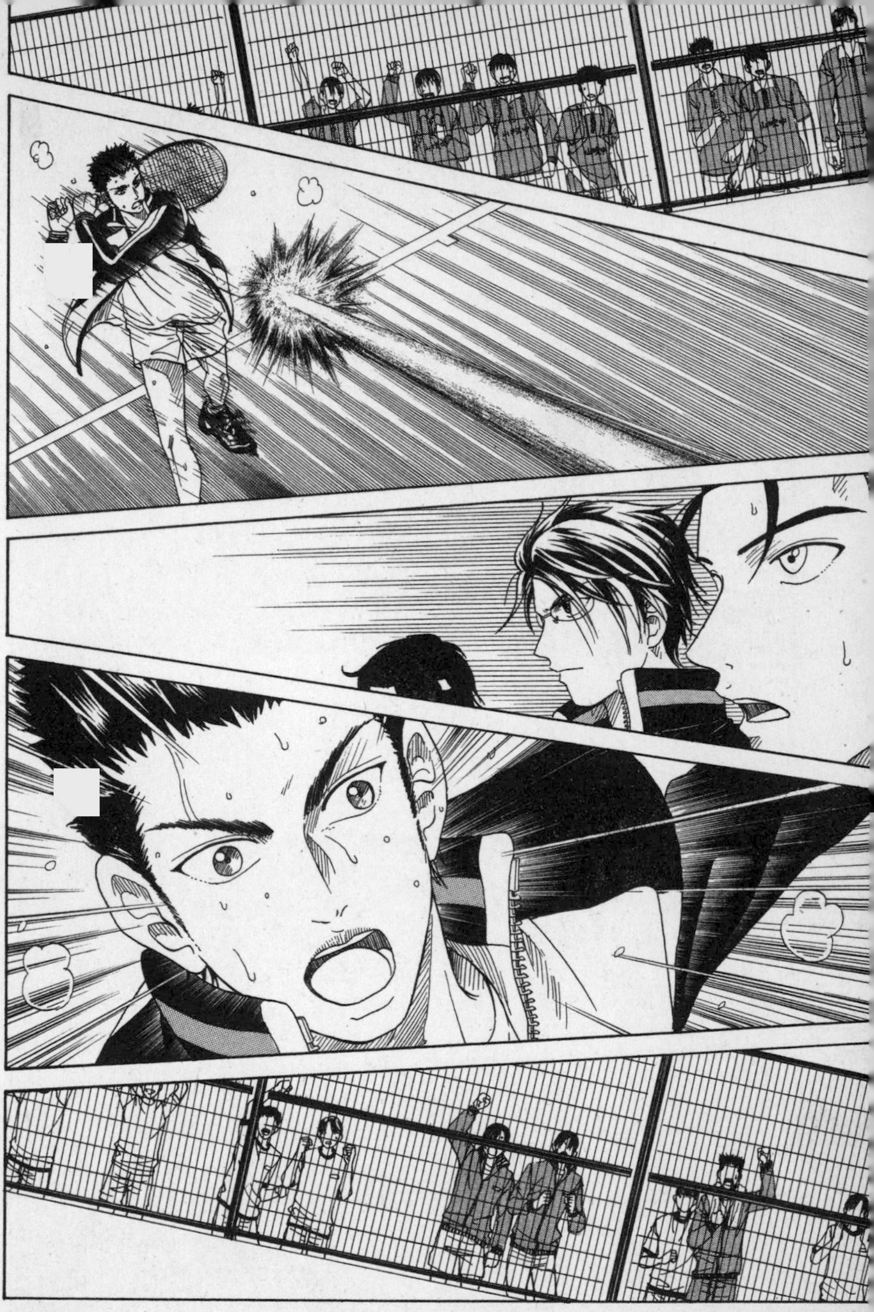

READ THIS WAY

RGG
RGG

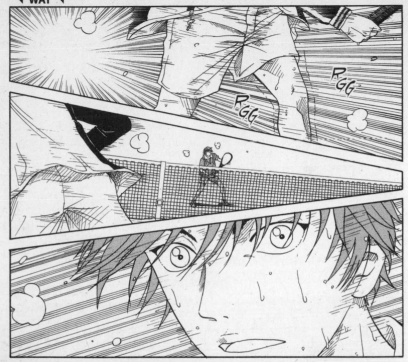

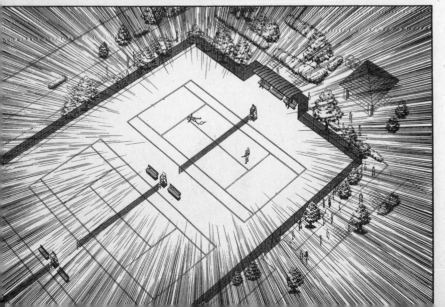

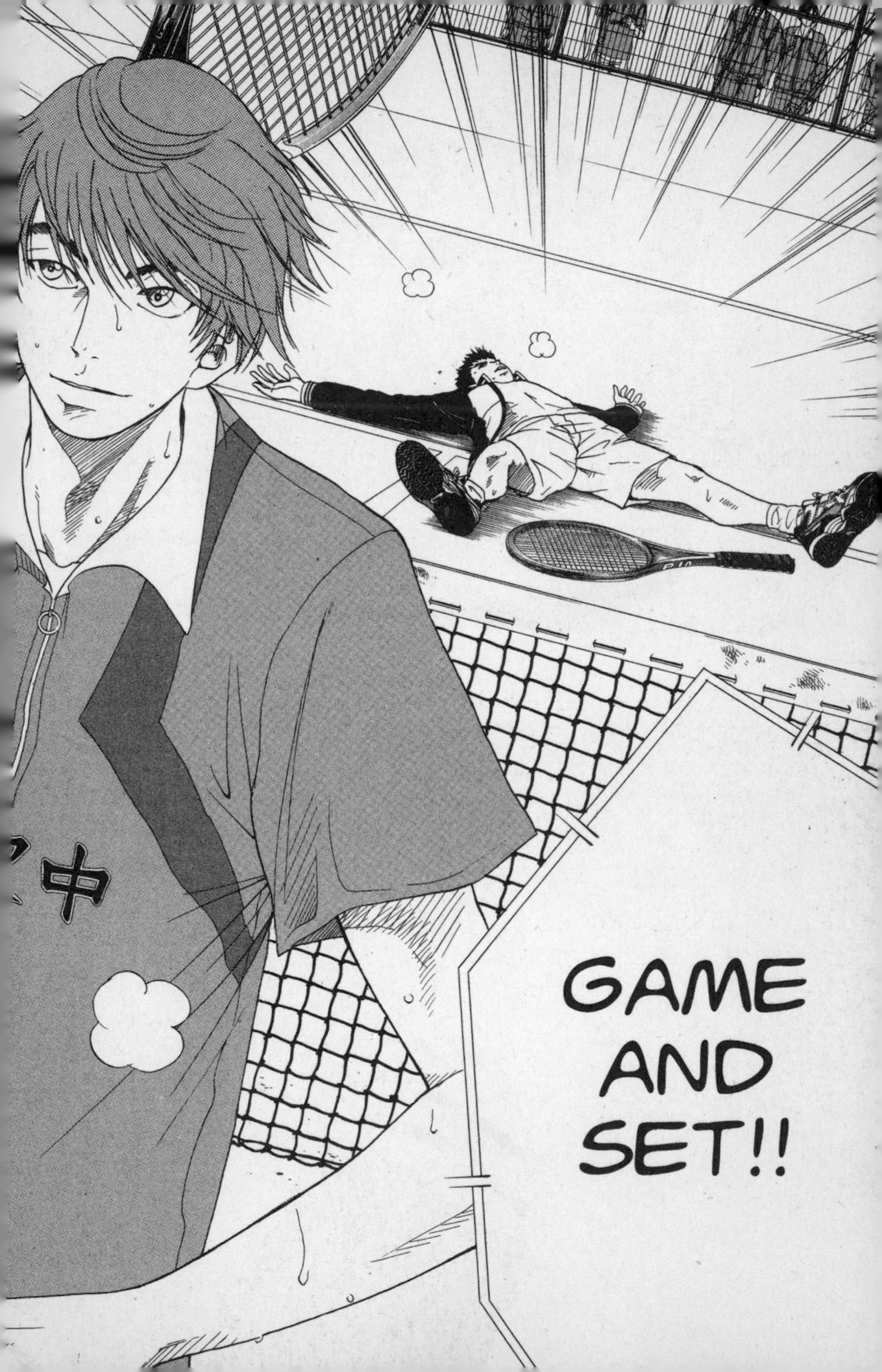
GAME AND SET!!

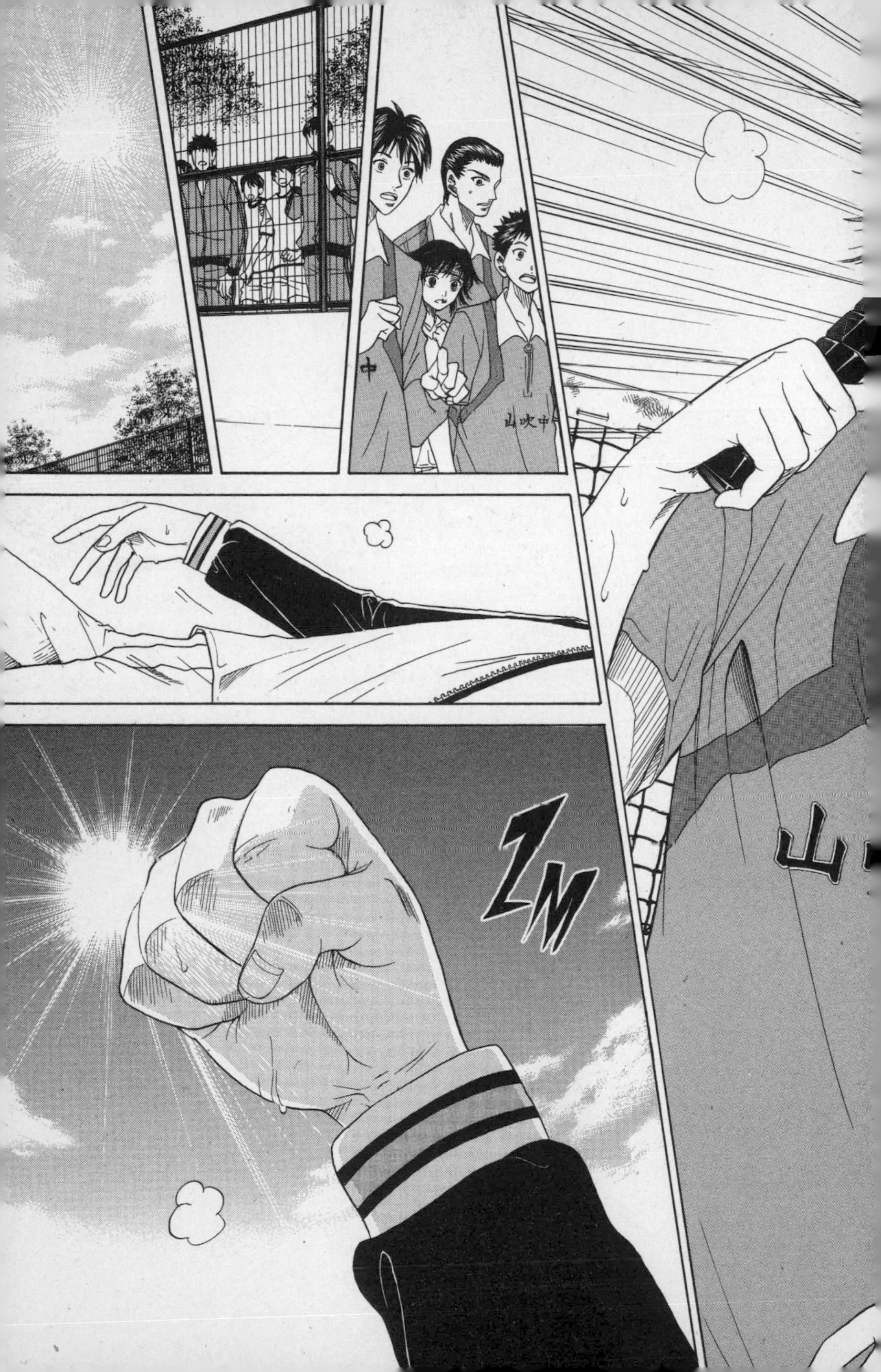
山吹中
ZM

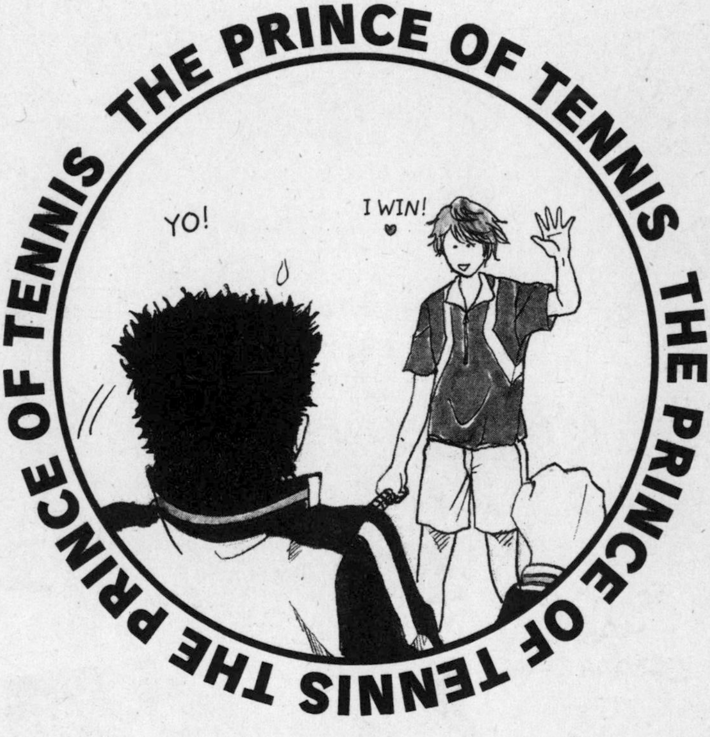
THE PRINCE OF TENNIS THE PRINCE OF TENNIS THE PRINCE OF TENNIS
I WIN!
YO!

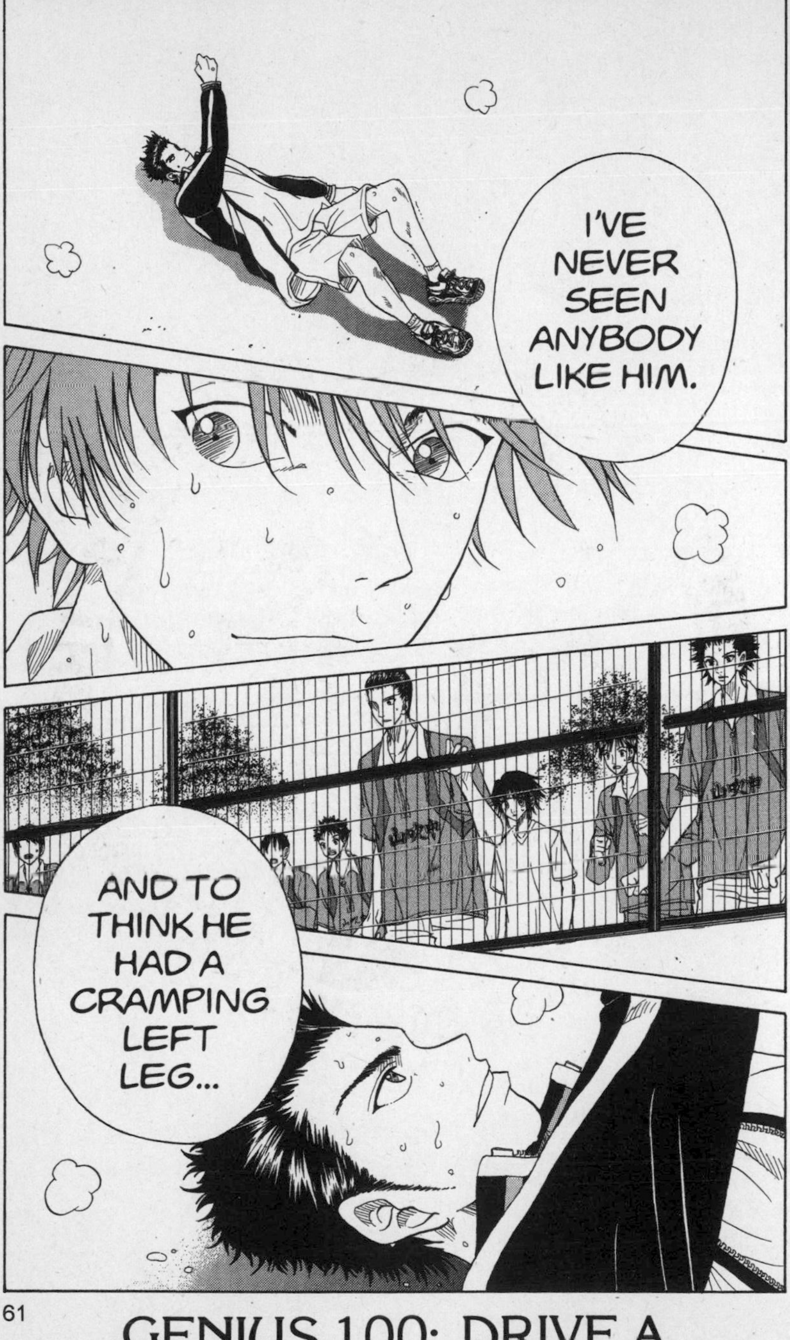
I'VE NEVER SEEN ANYBODY LIKE HIM.
AND TO THINK HE HAD A CRAMPING LEFT LEG...

GENIUS 100: DRIVE A

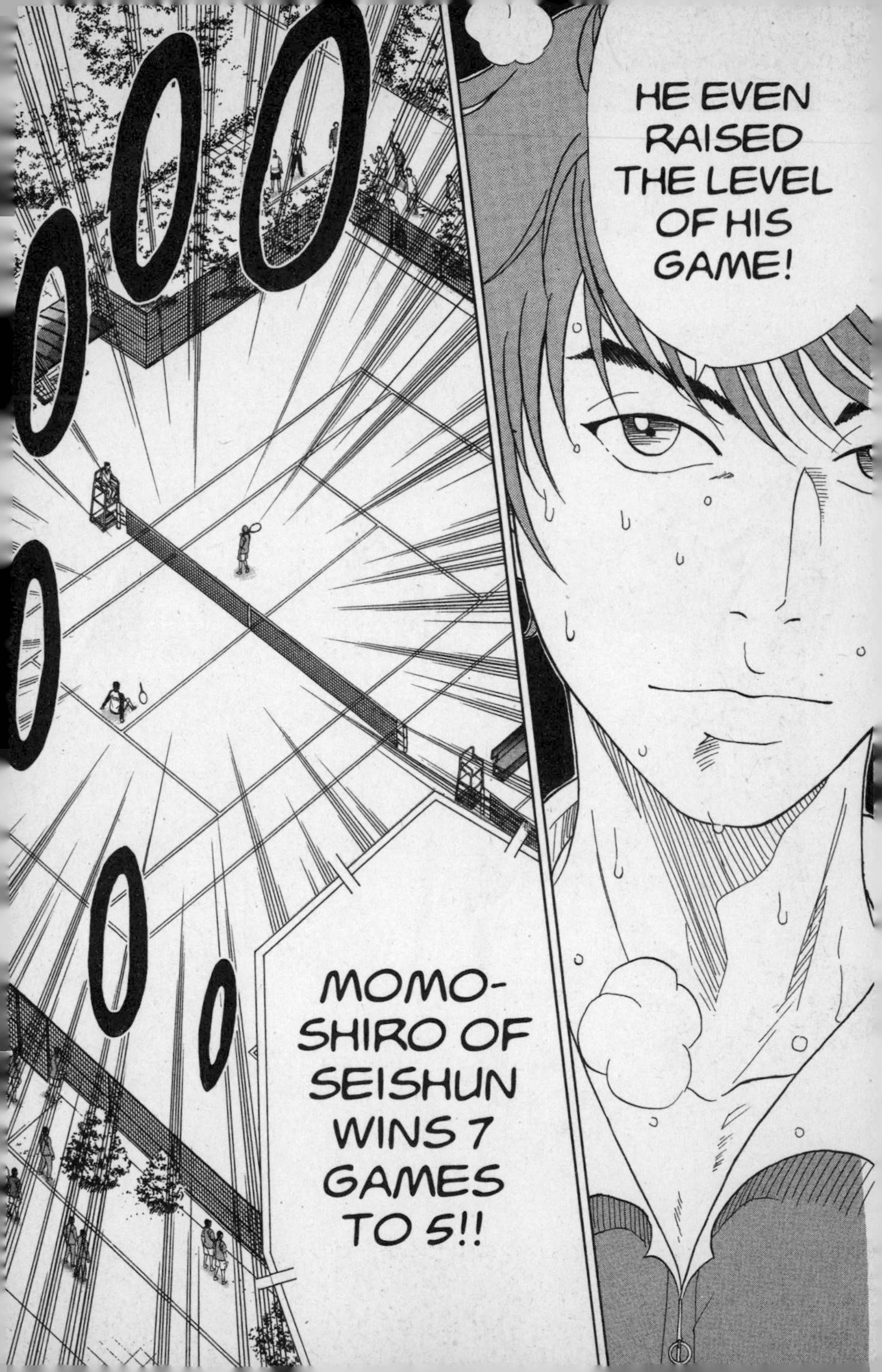
HE EVEN RAISED THE LEVEL OF HIS GAME!
MOMO-SHIRO OF SEISHUN WINS 7 GAMES TO 5!!

GENIUS 100: DRIVE A

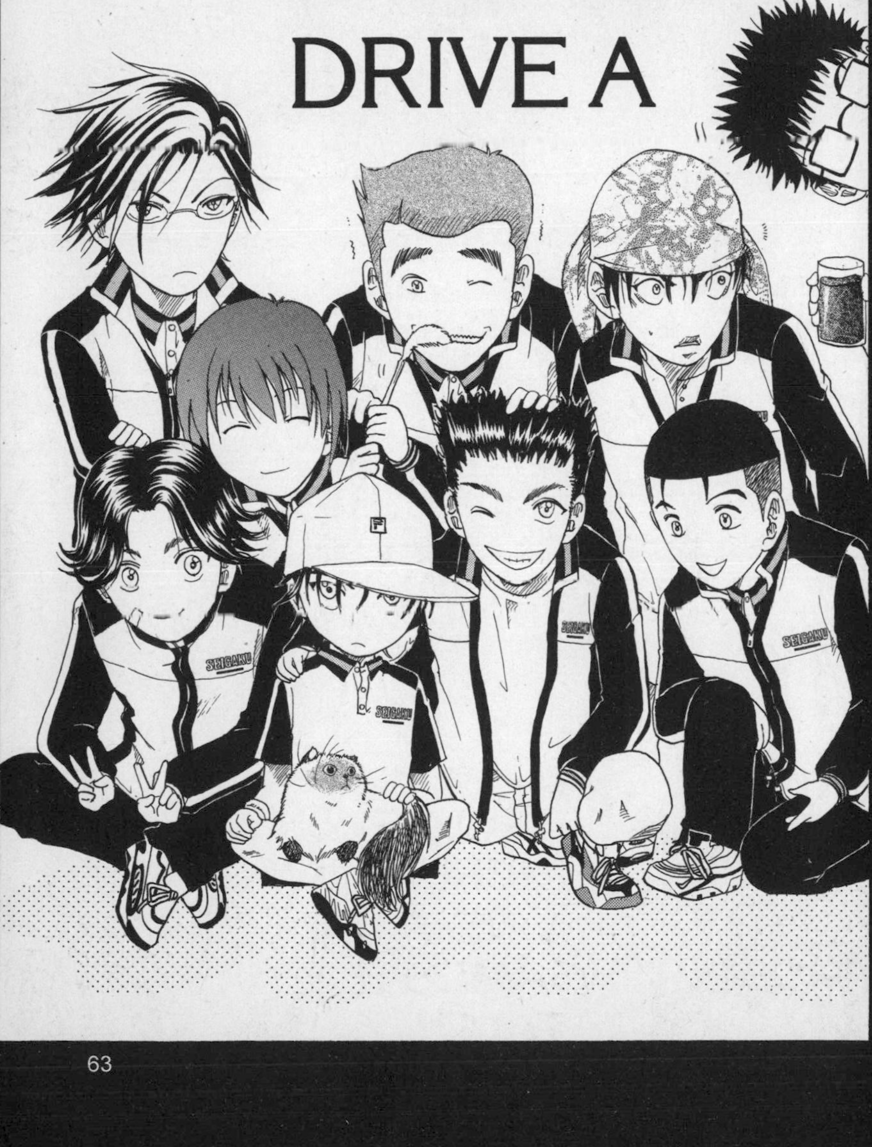
SEIGAKU
SEIGAKU
SEIGAKU
SEIGAKU

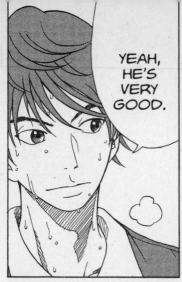

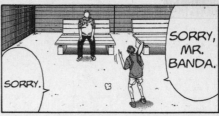

SORRY, MR. BANDA.
SORRY.
YOU WERE FORTUNATE TO PLAY HIM BEFORE THE KANTO TOURNAMENT.
YEAH, HE'S VERY GOOD.
YOU PLAYED A GOOD MATCH.
YOU REALLY ARE OUR STAR PLAYER.. COUGH-COUGH...
HIS LEG WAS CRAMPING, HUH...?
...
I SAID I WAS SORRY, MR. BANDA...
WOO HOO

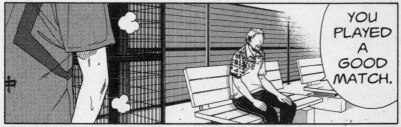

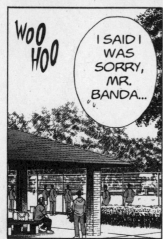

READ THIS WAY

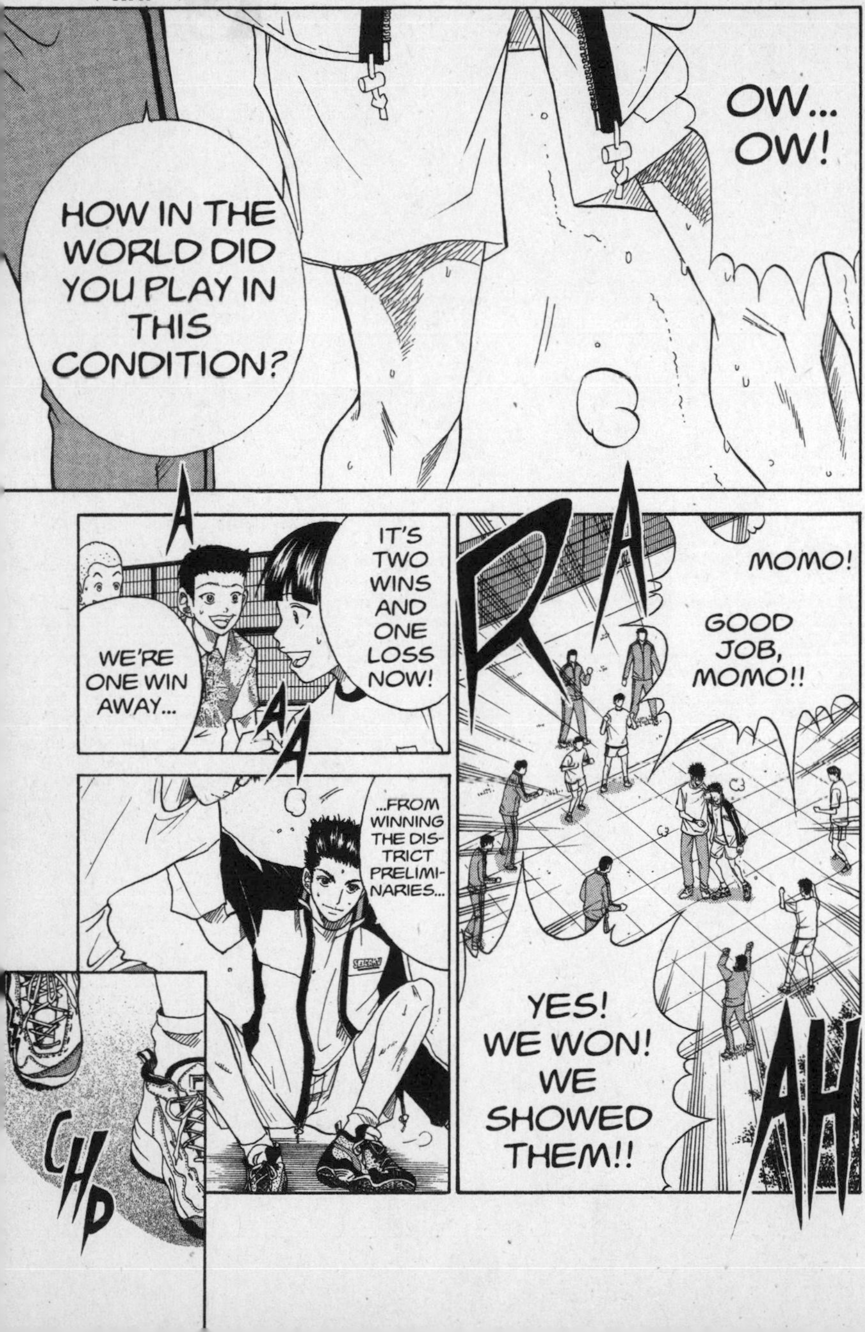
OW... OW!
HOW IN THE WORLD DID YOU PLAY IN THIS CONDITION?
MOMO!
GOOD JOB, MOMO!!
YES! WE WON! WE SHOWED THEM!!
RA
A
AH
A
A
A
IT'S TWO WINS AND ONE LOSS NOW!
WE'RE ONE WIN AWAY...
...FROM WINNING THE DISTRICT PRELIMINARIES...
CHP

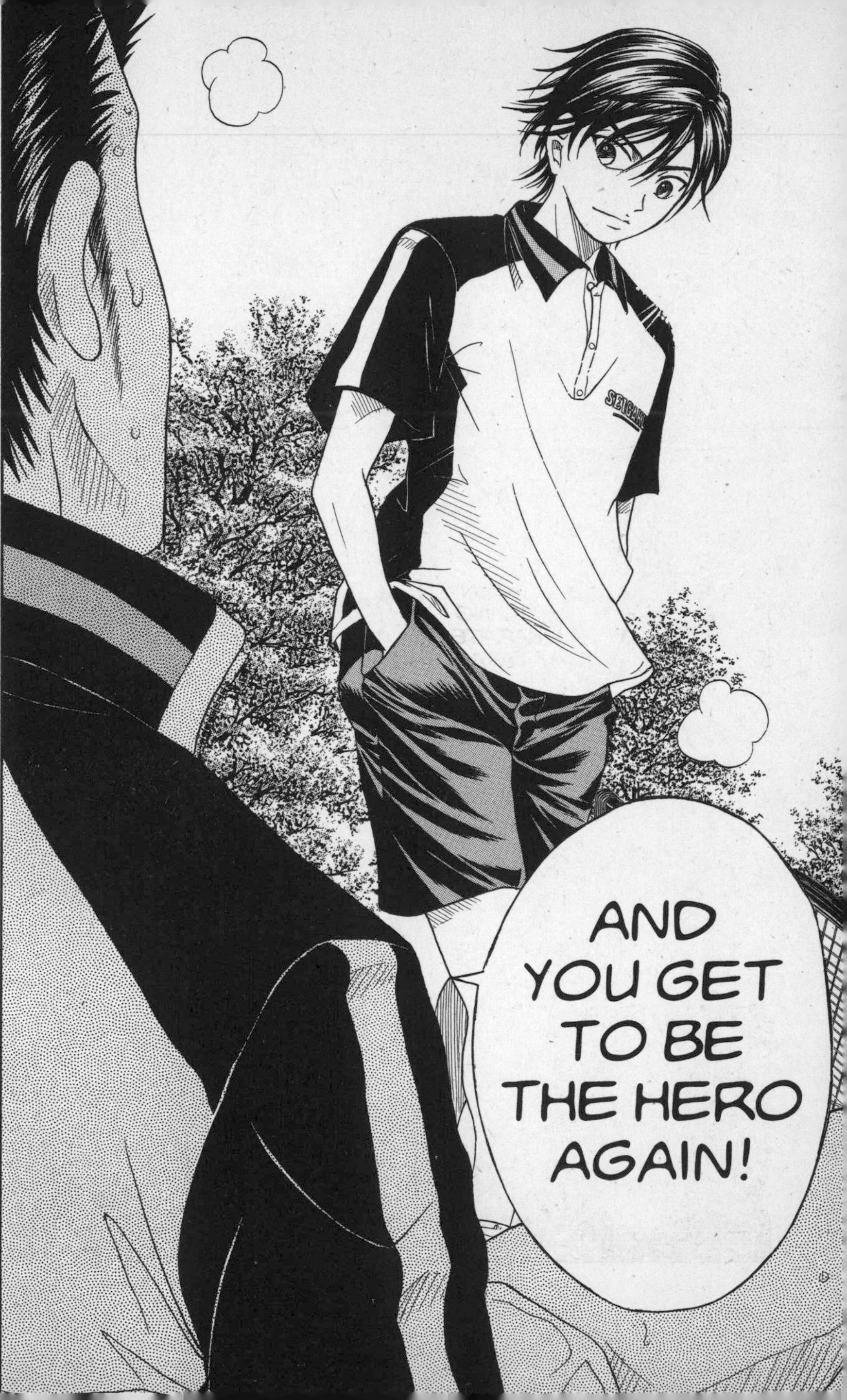
AND YOU GET TO BE THE HERO AGAIN!

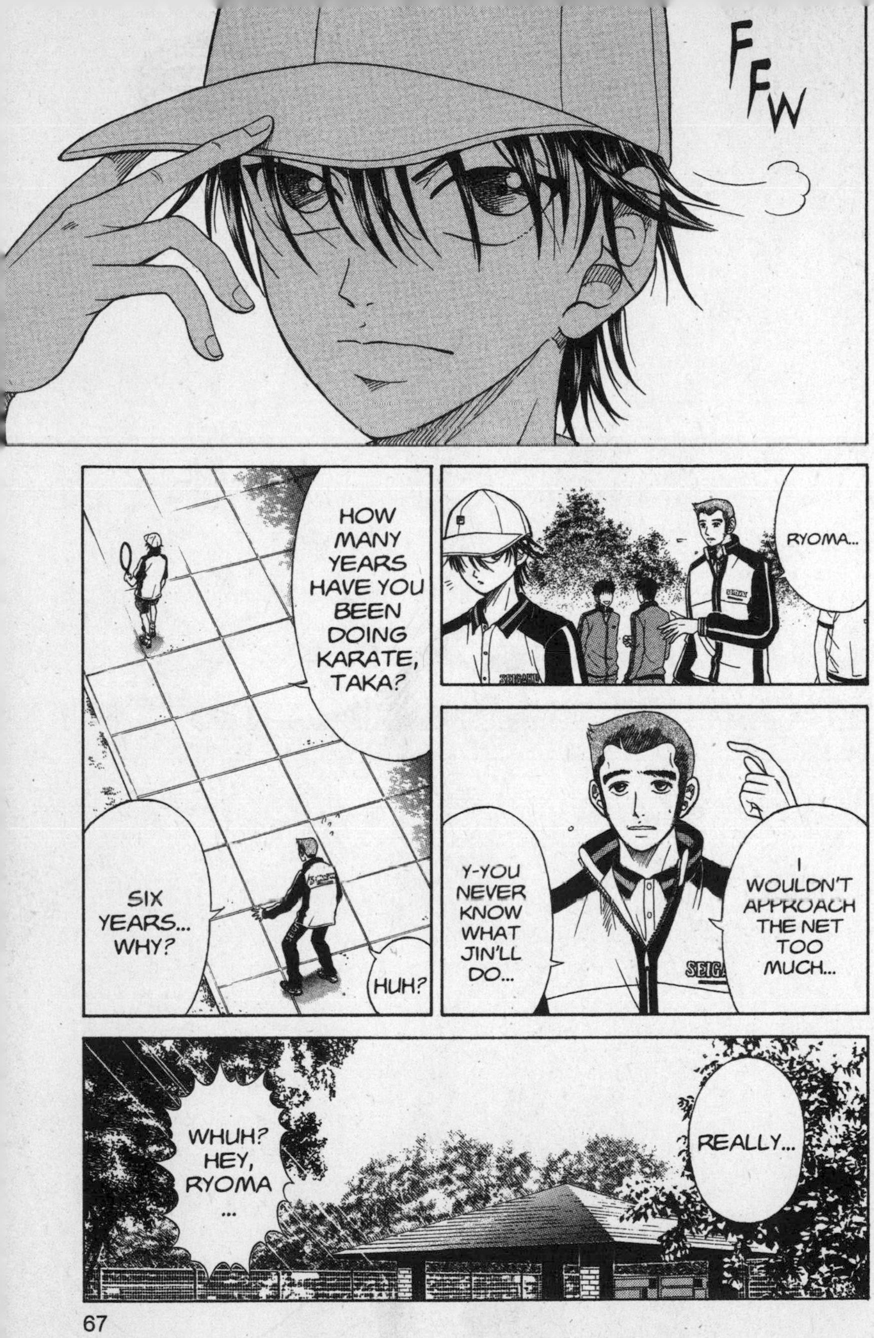
FFW
RYOMA...
I WOULDN'T APPROACH THE NET TOO MUCH...
Y-YOU NEVER KNOW WHAT JIN'LL DO...
HOW MANY YEARS HAVE YOU BEEN DOING KARATE, TAKA?
HUH?
SIX YEARS... WHY?
REALLY...
WHUH? HEY, RYOMA ...

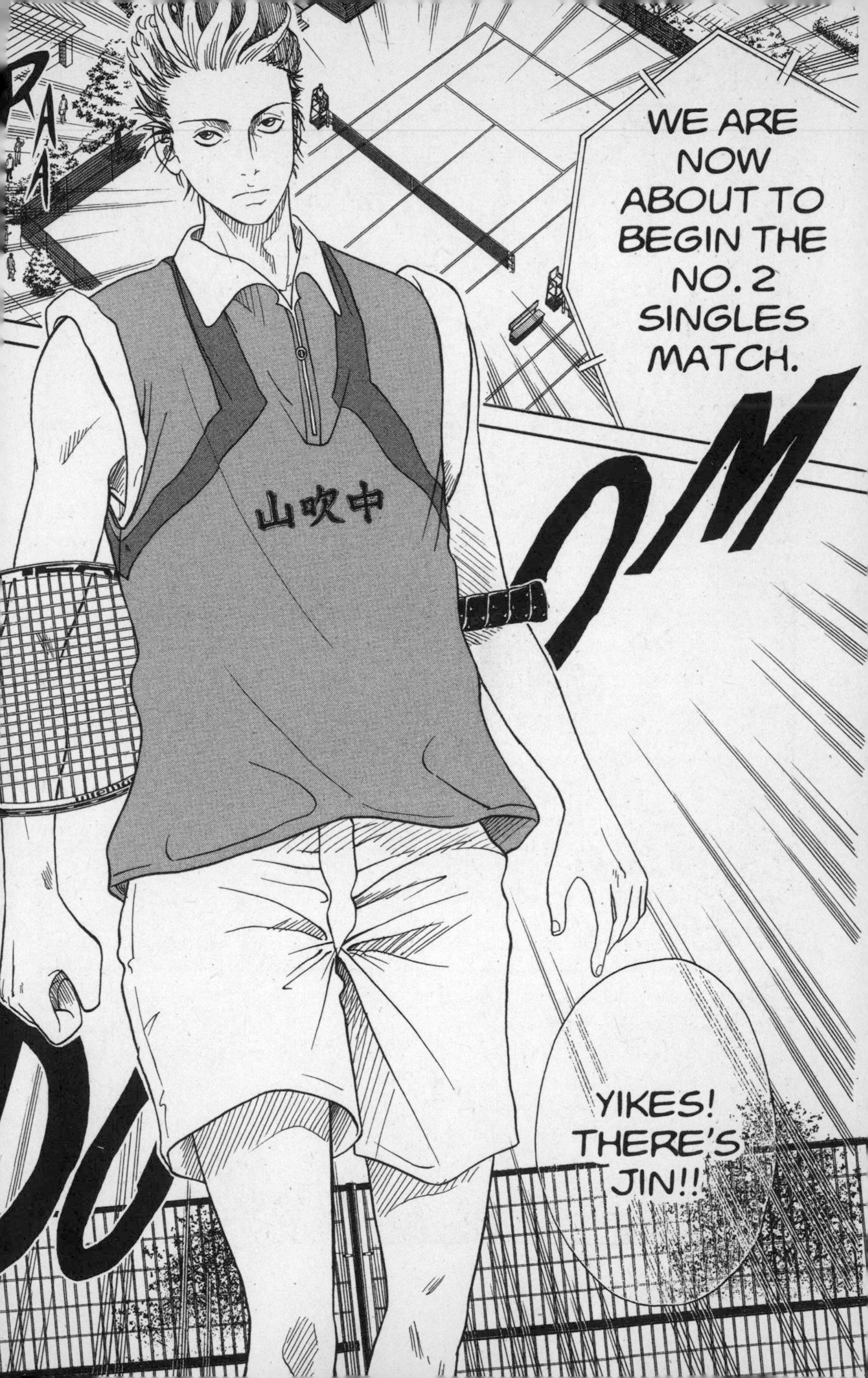
WE ARE NOW ABOUT TO BEGIN THE NO. 2 SINGLES MATCH.
YIKES! THERE'S JIN!!

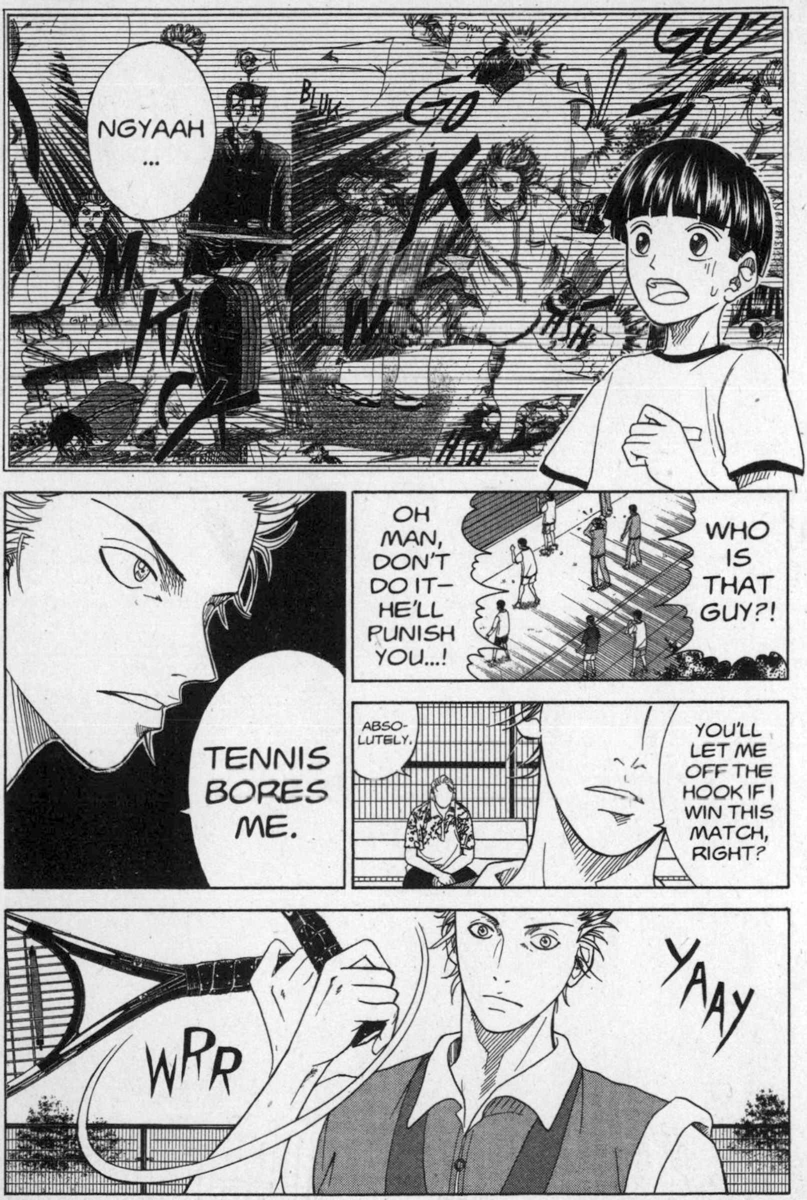
NGYAAH ...
WHO IS THAT GUY?!
OH MAN, DON'T DO IT—HE'LL PUNISH YOU...!
YOU'LL LET ME OFF THE HOOK IF I WIN THIS MATCH, RIGHT?
ABSO-LUTELY.
TENNIS BORES ME.
YAAY
WRR

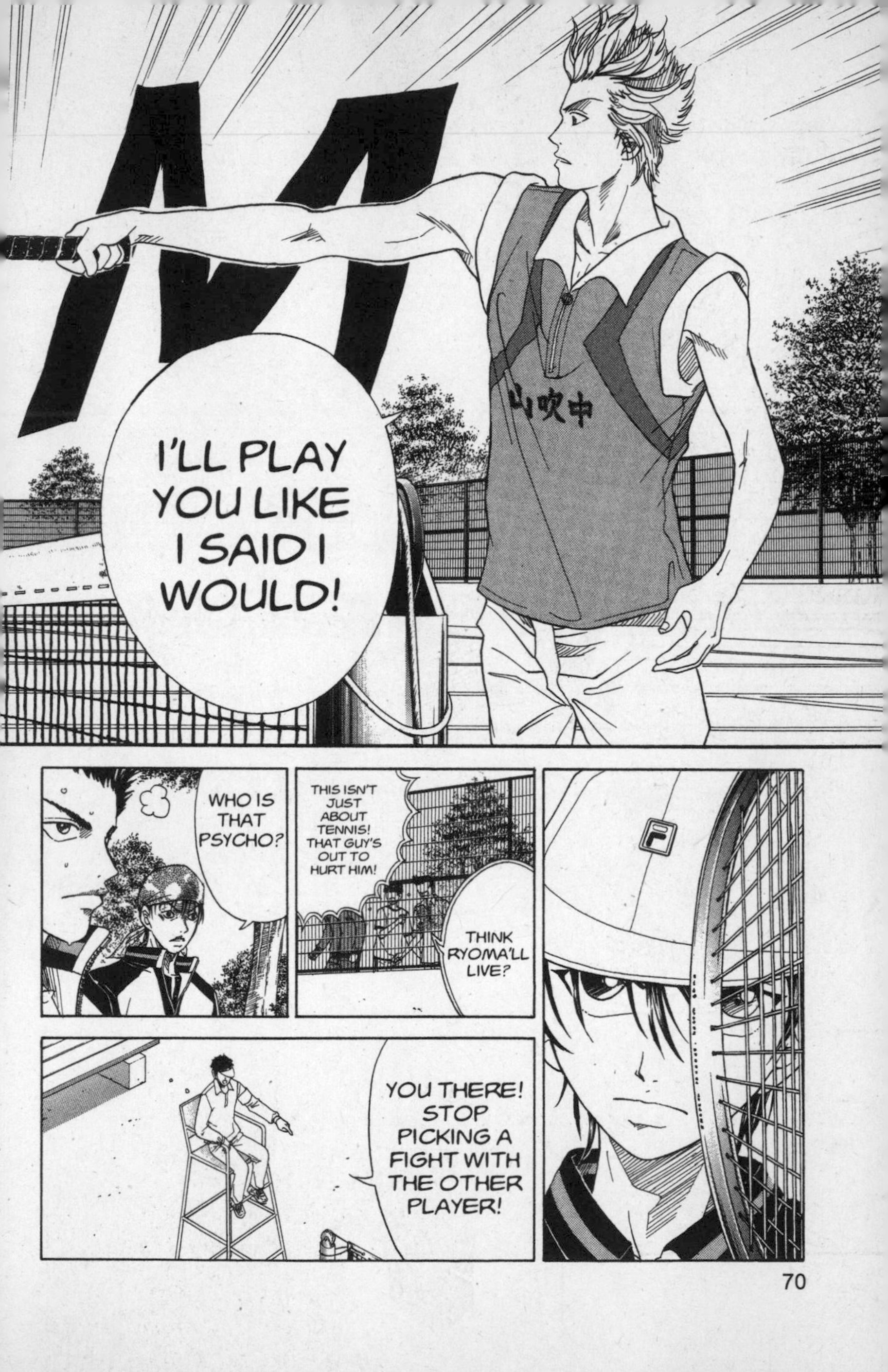
山吹中
I'LL PLAY YOU LIKE I SAID I WOULD!
THIS ISN'T JUST ABOUT TENNIS! THAT GUY'S OUT TO HURT HIM!
THINK RYOMA'LL LIVE?
WHO IS THAT PSYCHO?
YOU THERE! STOP PICKING A FIGHT WITH THE OTHER PLAYER!

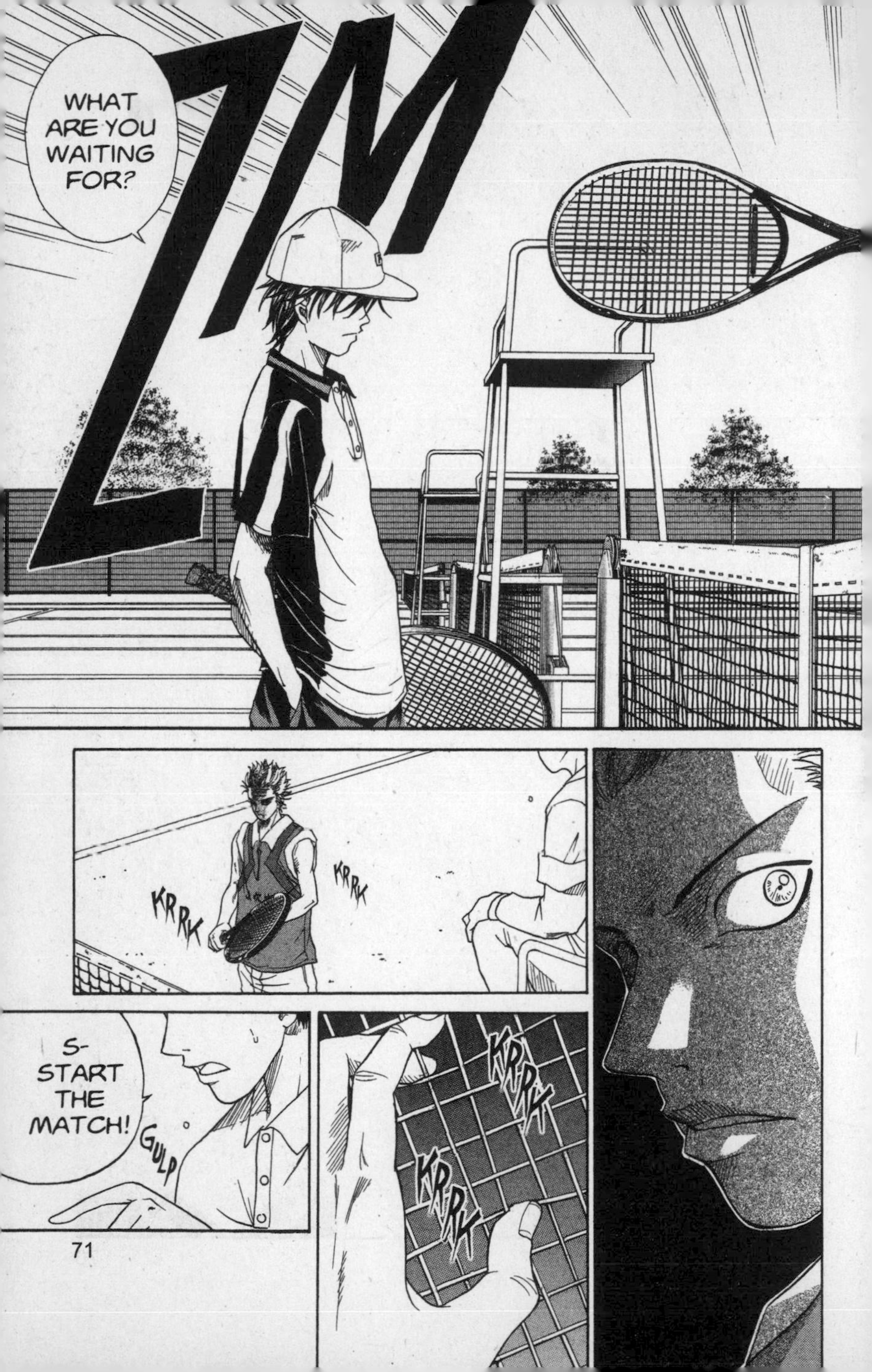
ZM
WHAT ARE YOU WAITING FOR?
KRRK
KRRK
KRRK
KRRK
S- START THE MATCH!
GULP

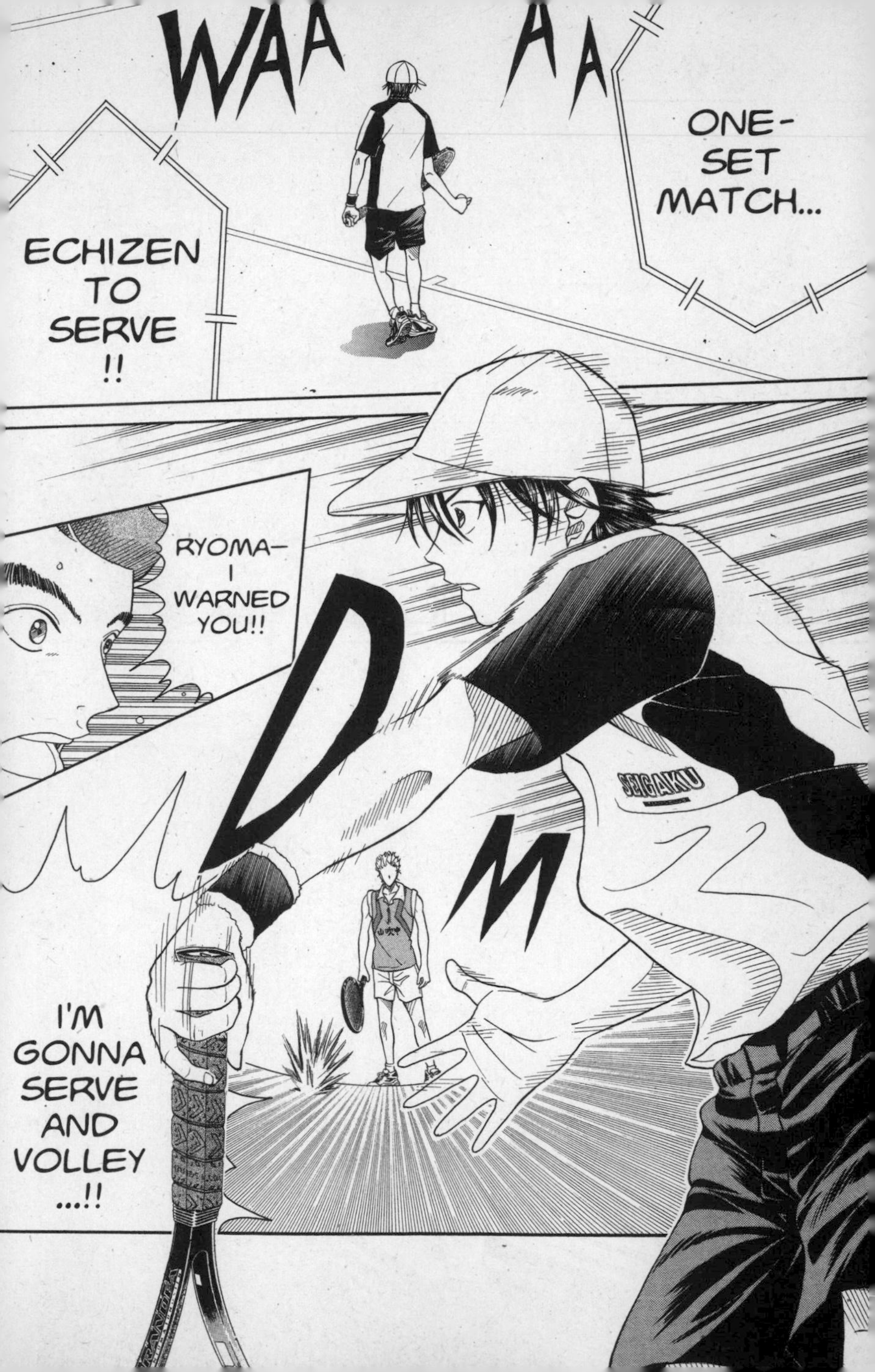
WAA AA
ONE-SET MATCH...
ECHIZEN TO SERVE !!
RYOMA-I WARNED YOU!!
DM
I'M GONNA SERVE AND VOLLEY ...!!

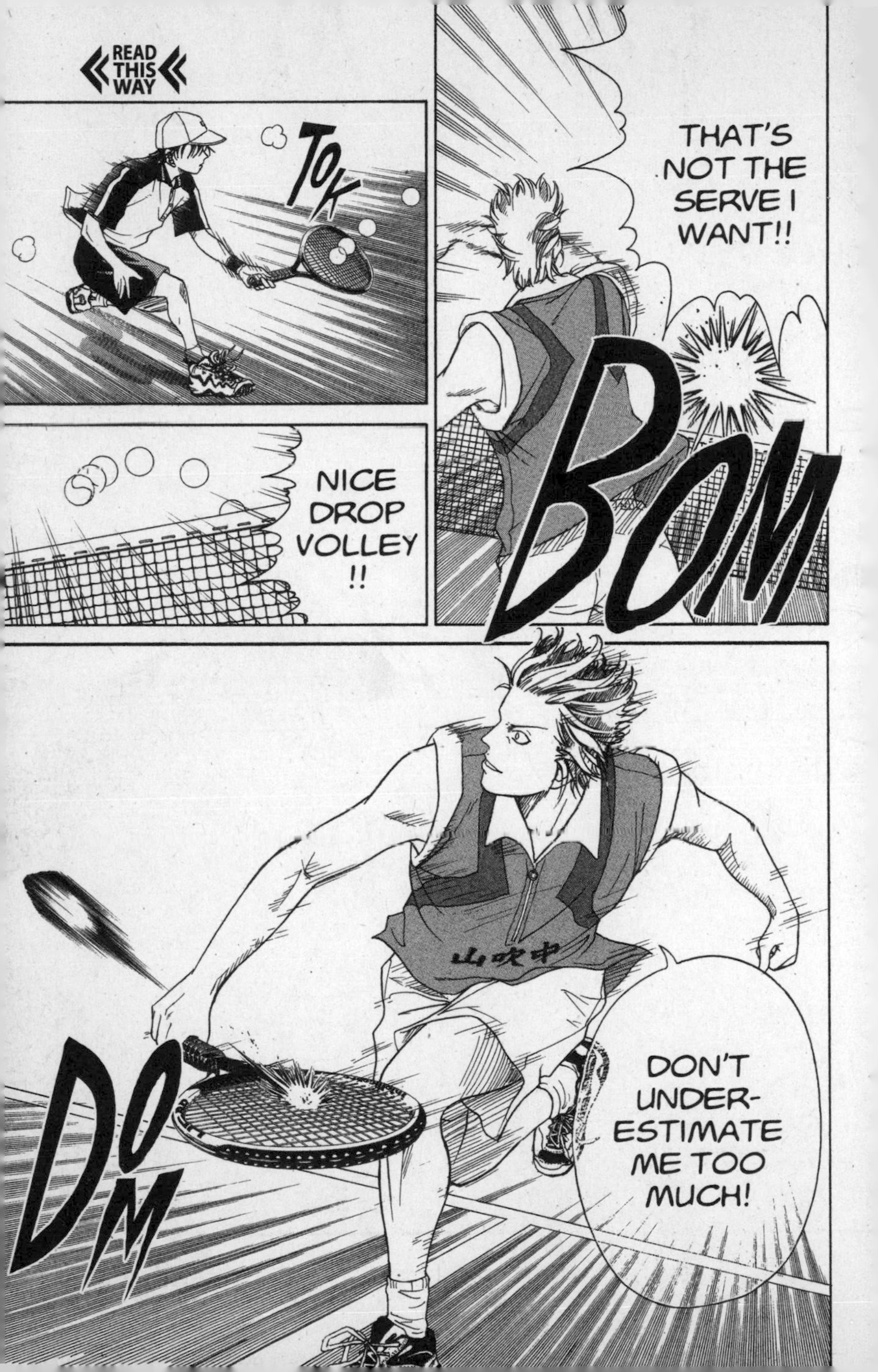
READ THIS WAY
THAT'S NOT THE SERVE I WANT!!
BOM
TOK
NICE DROP VOLLEY !!
山吹中
DOM
DON'T UNDER-ESTIMATE ME TOO MUCH!

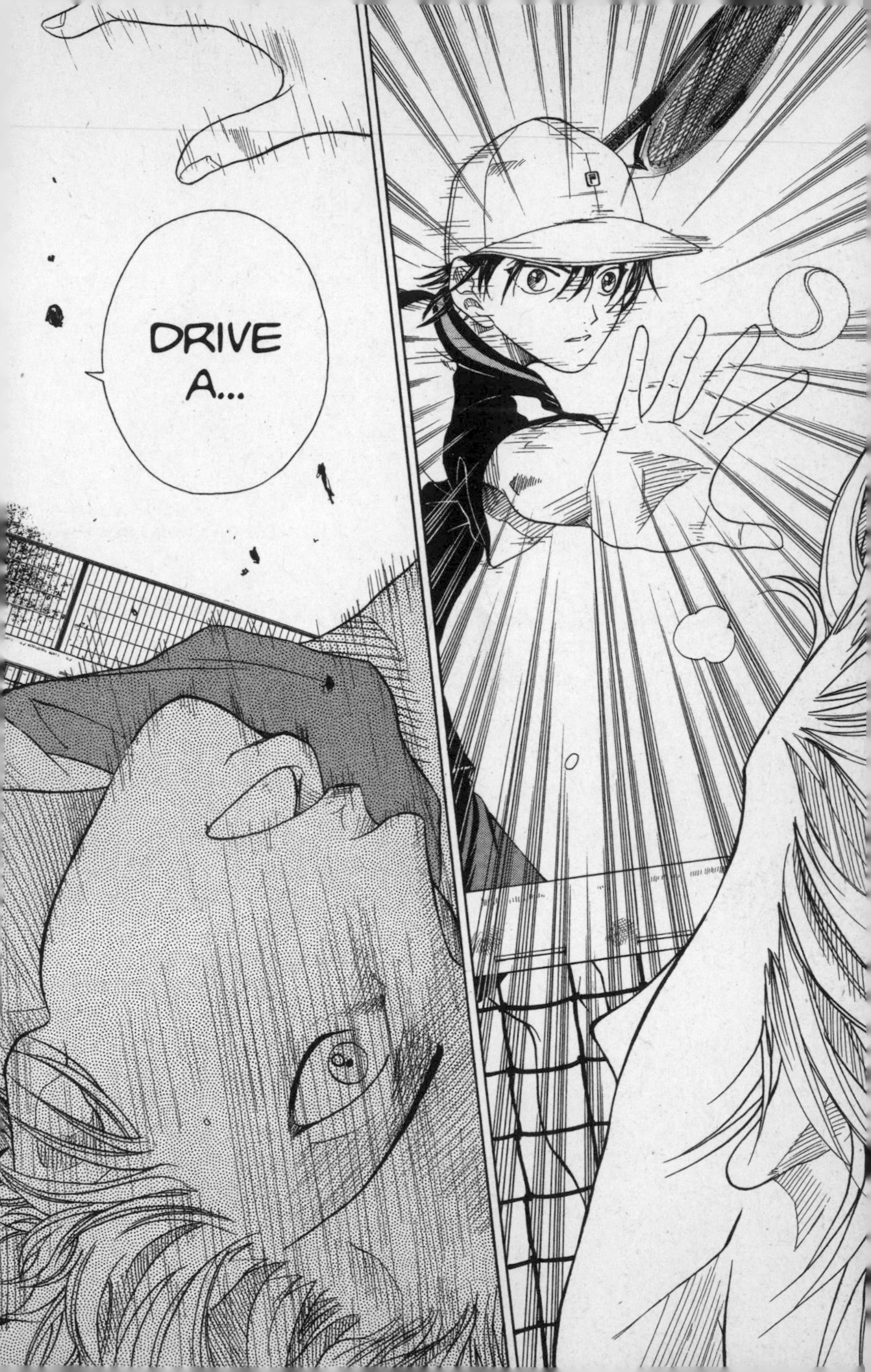
DRIVE A...

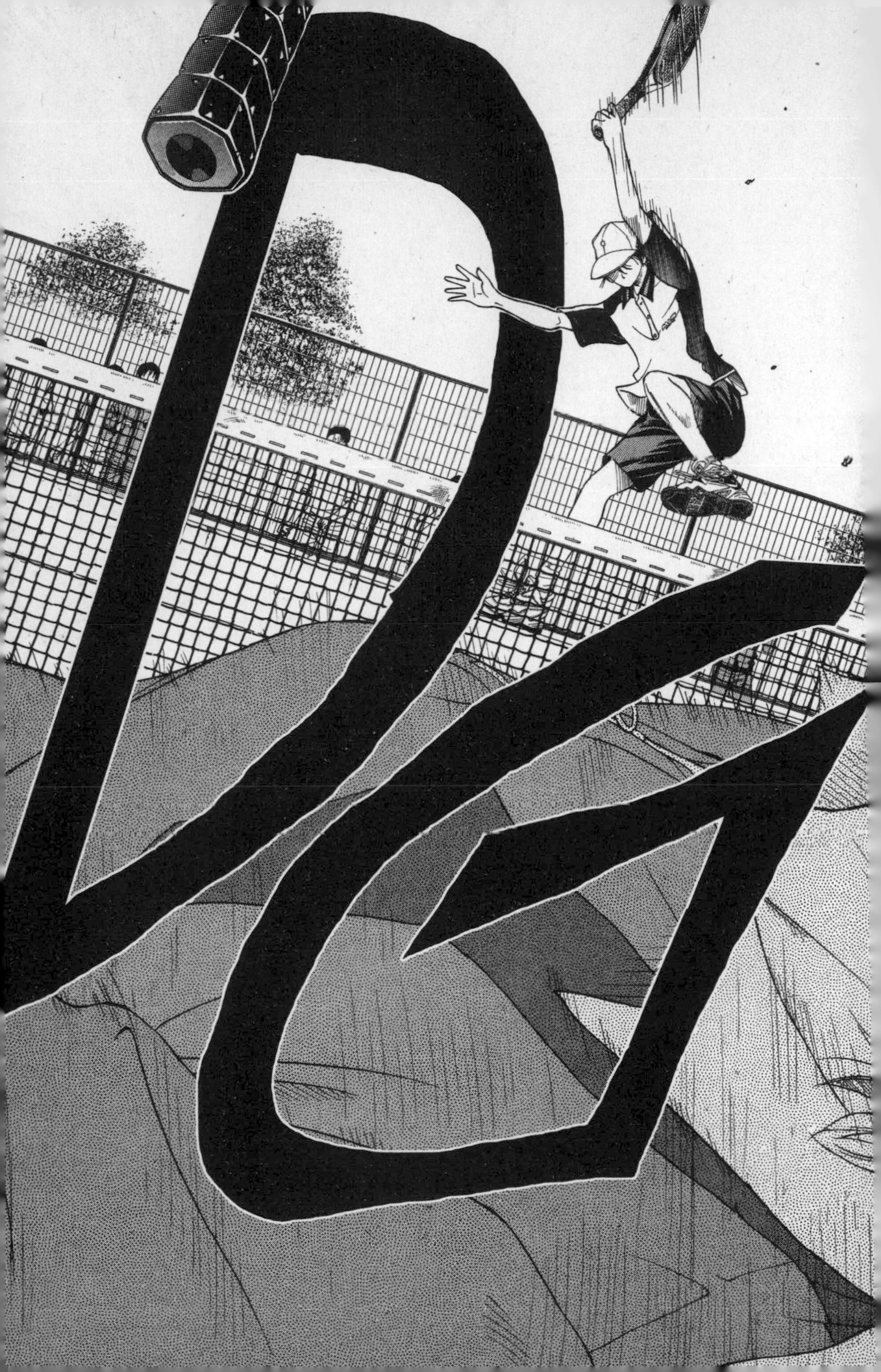

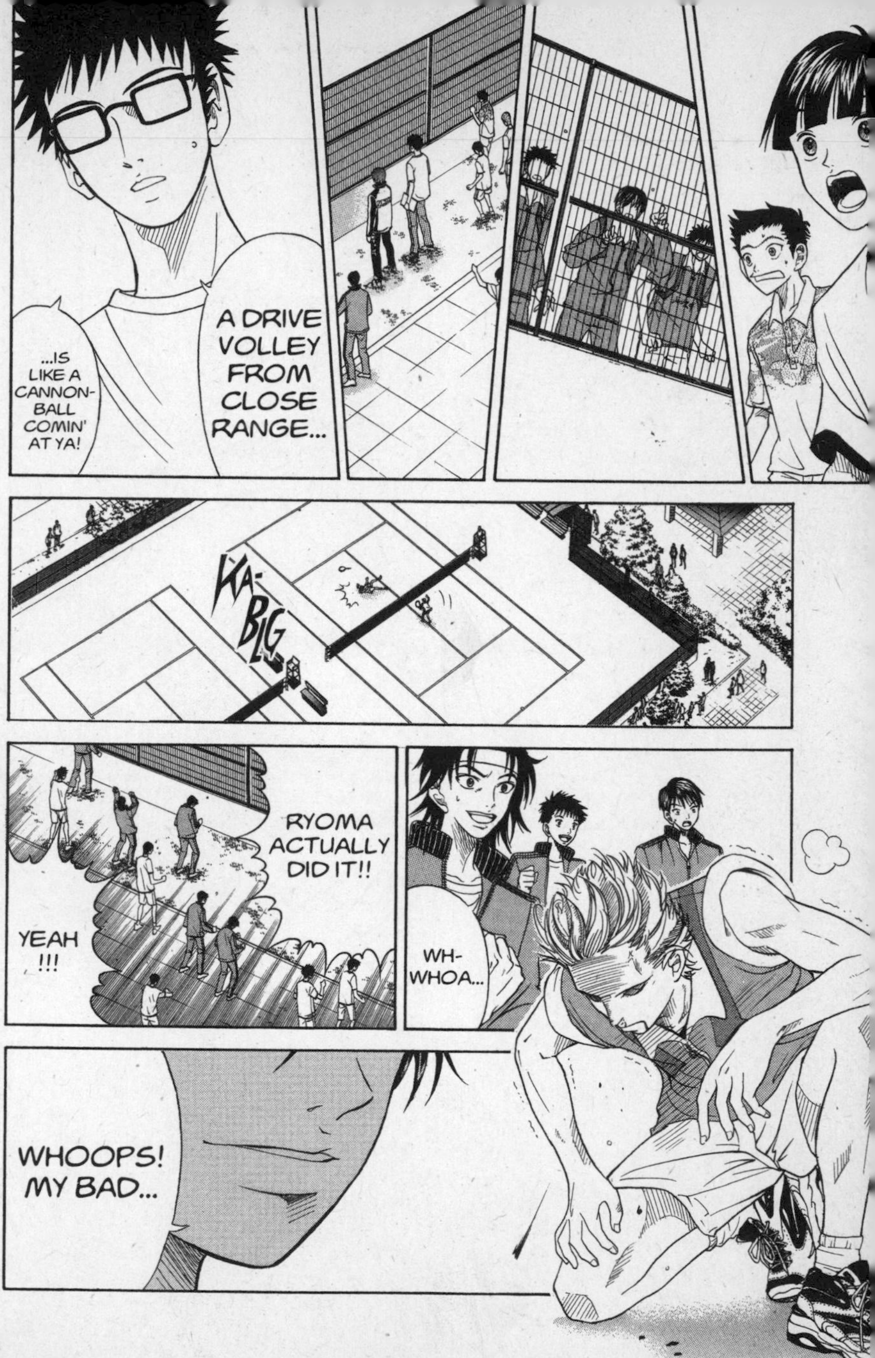
A DRIVE VOLLEY FROM CLOSE RANGE...
...IS LIKE A CANNON-BALL COMIN' AT YA!
KA-BLIG
WH-WHOA...
RYOMA ACTUALLY DID IT!!
YEAH !!!
WHOOPS! MY BAD...

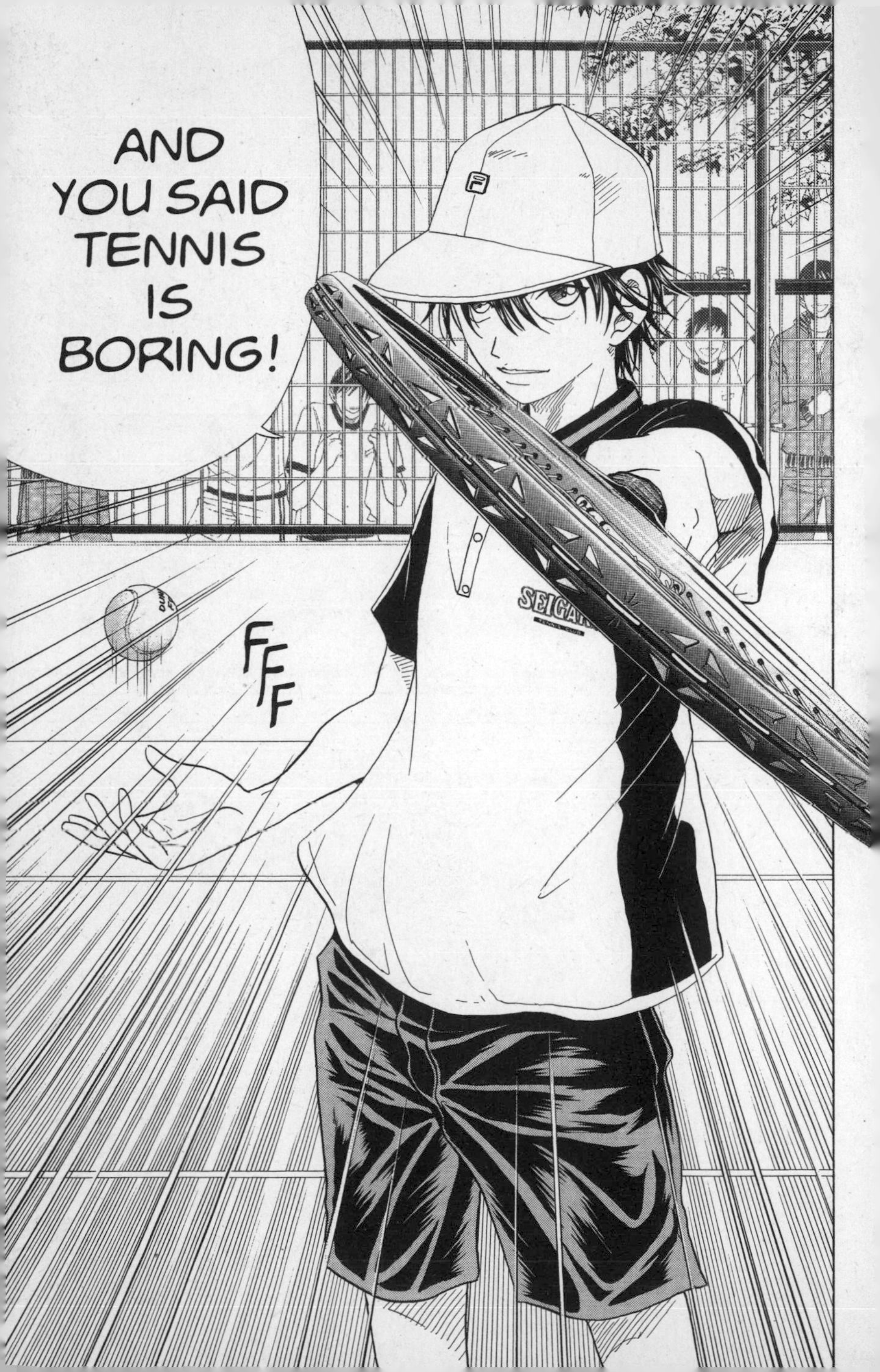
AND YOU SAID TENNIS IS BORING!
FFF

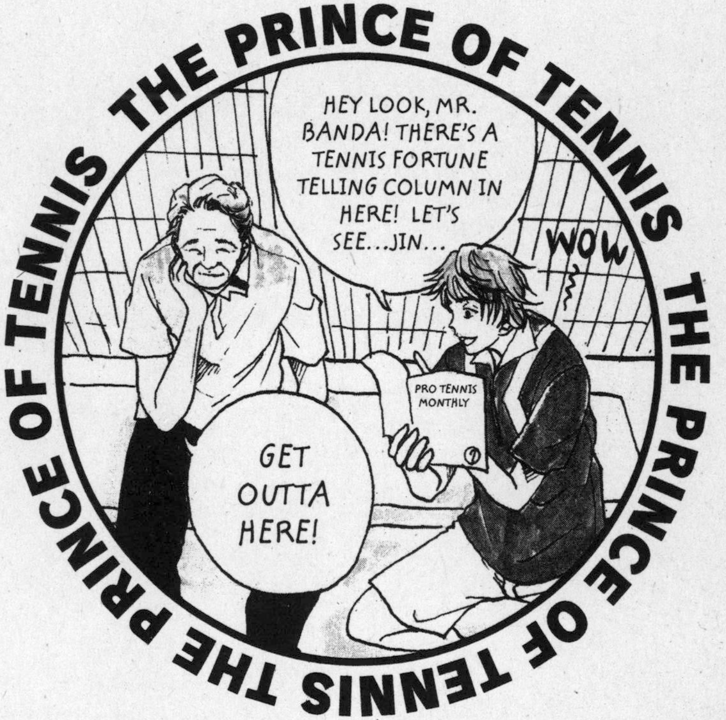
THE PRINCE OF TENNIS THE PRINCE OF TENNIS THE PRINCE OF TENNIS
HEY LOOK, MR. BANDA! THERE'S A TENNIS FORTUNE TELLING COLUMN IN HERE! LET'S SEE...JIN...
WOW
PRO TENNIS MONTHLY
GET OUTTA HERE!

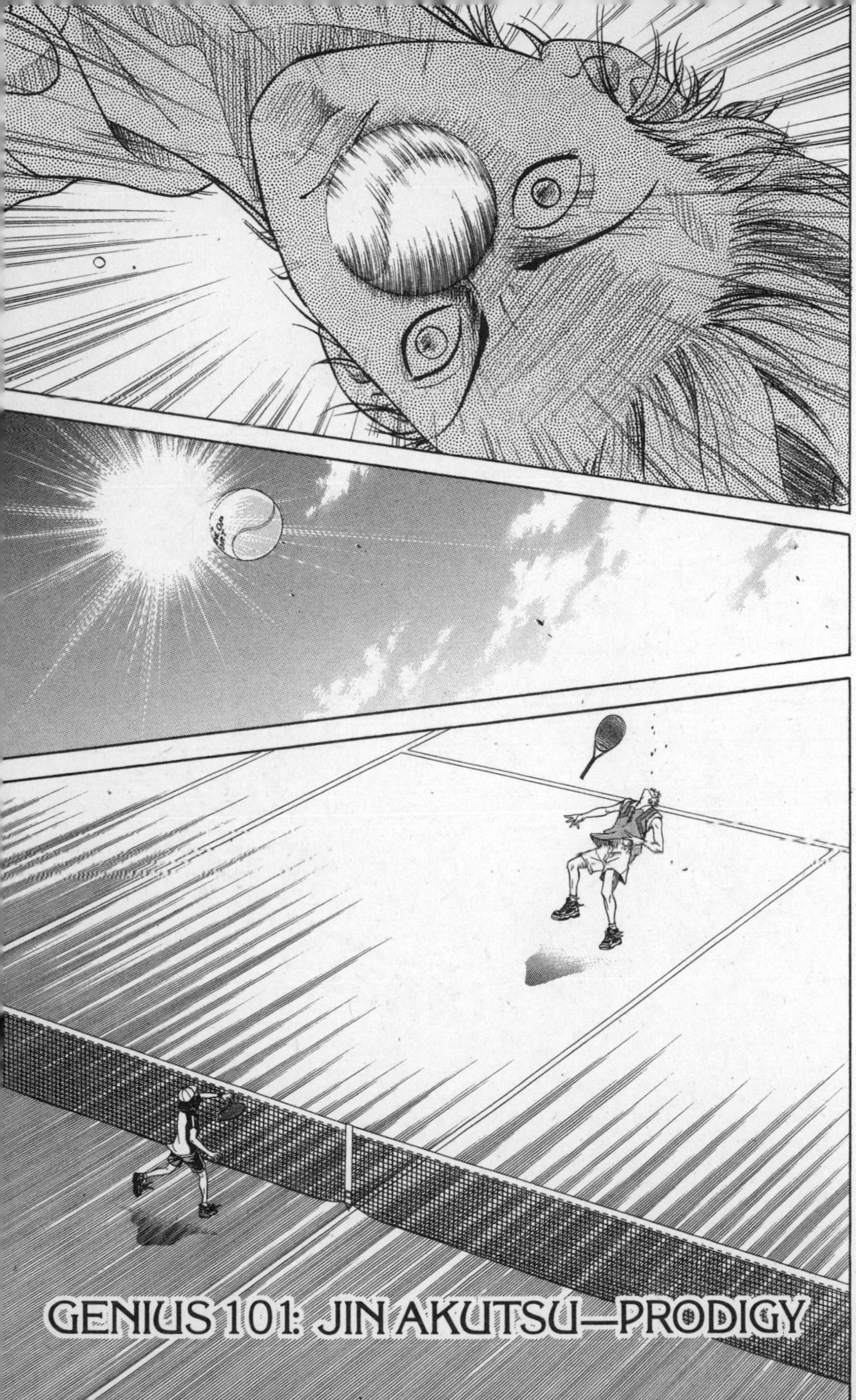
GENIUS 101: JIN AKUTSU—PRODIGY

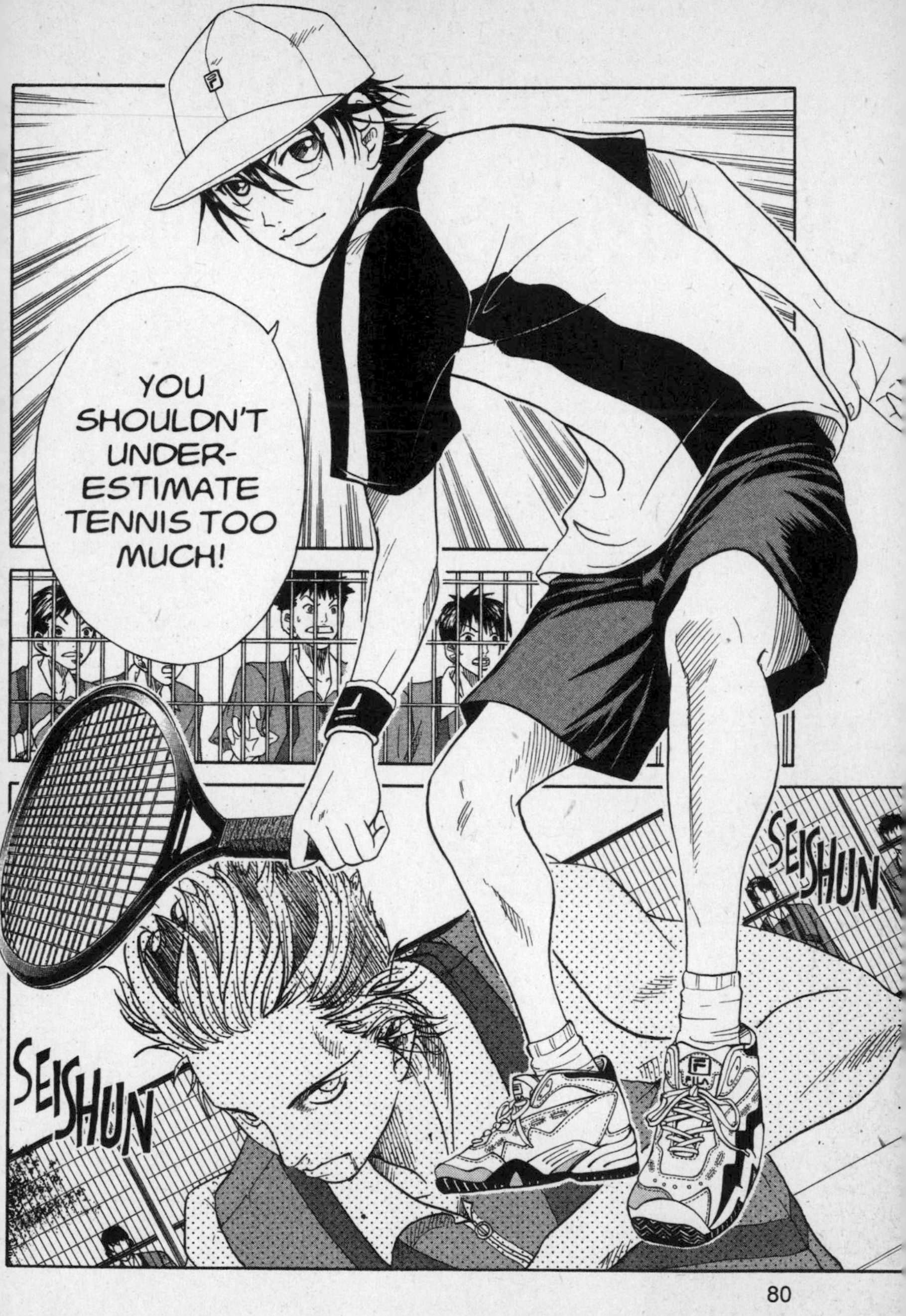
YOU SHOULDN'T UNDER-ESTIMATE TENNIS TOO MUCH!
SEISHUN
SEISHUN

GENIUS 101: JIN AKUTSU—PRODIG

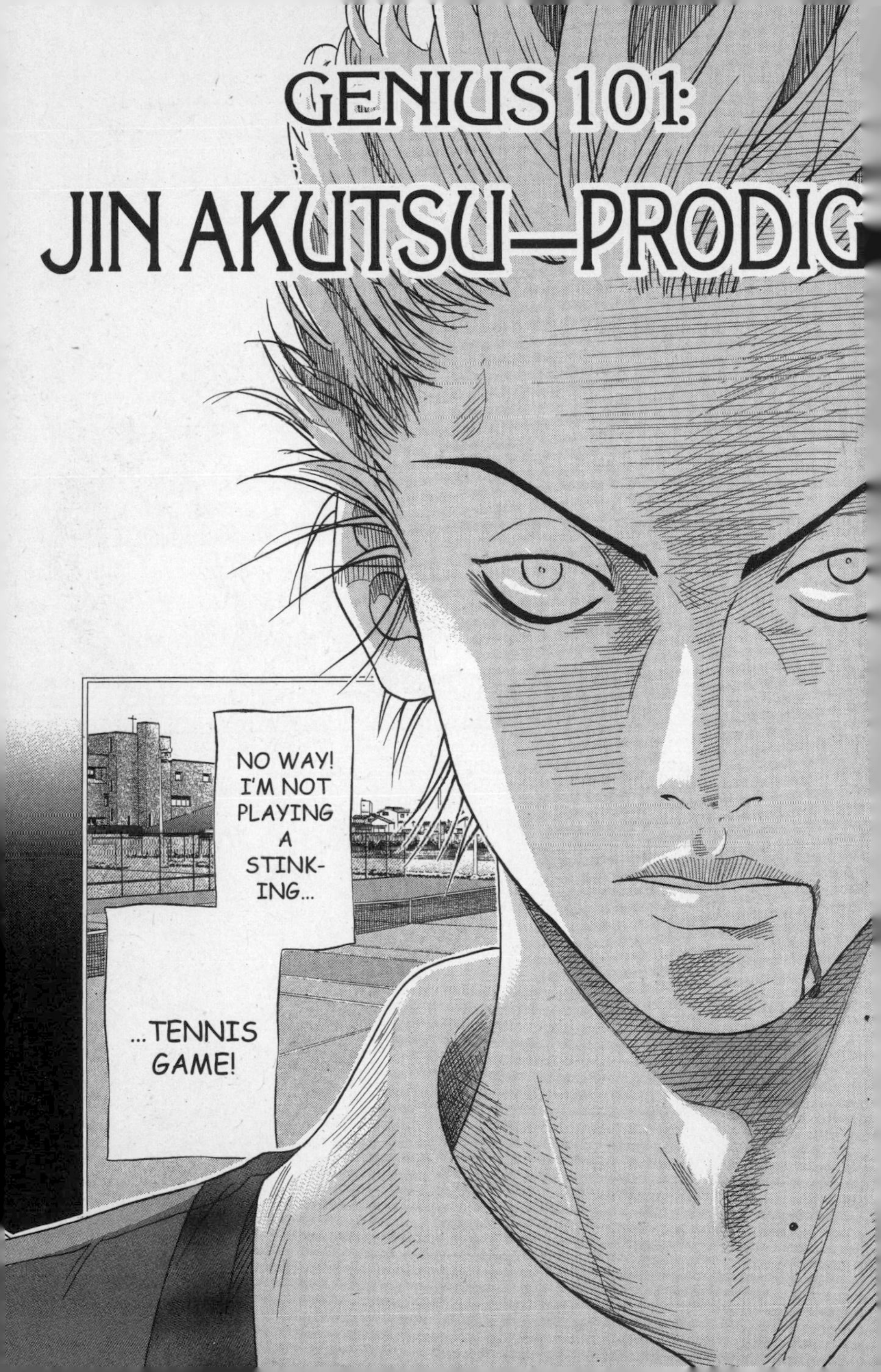
NO WAY! I'M NOT PLAYING A STINKING...
...TENNIS GAME!

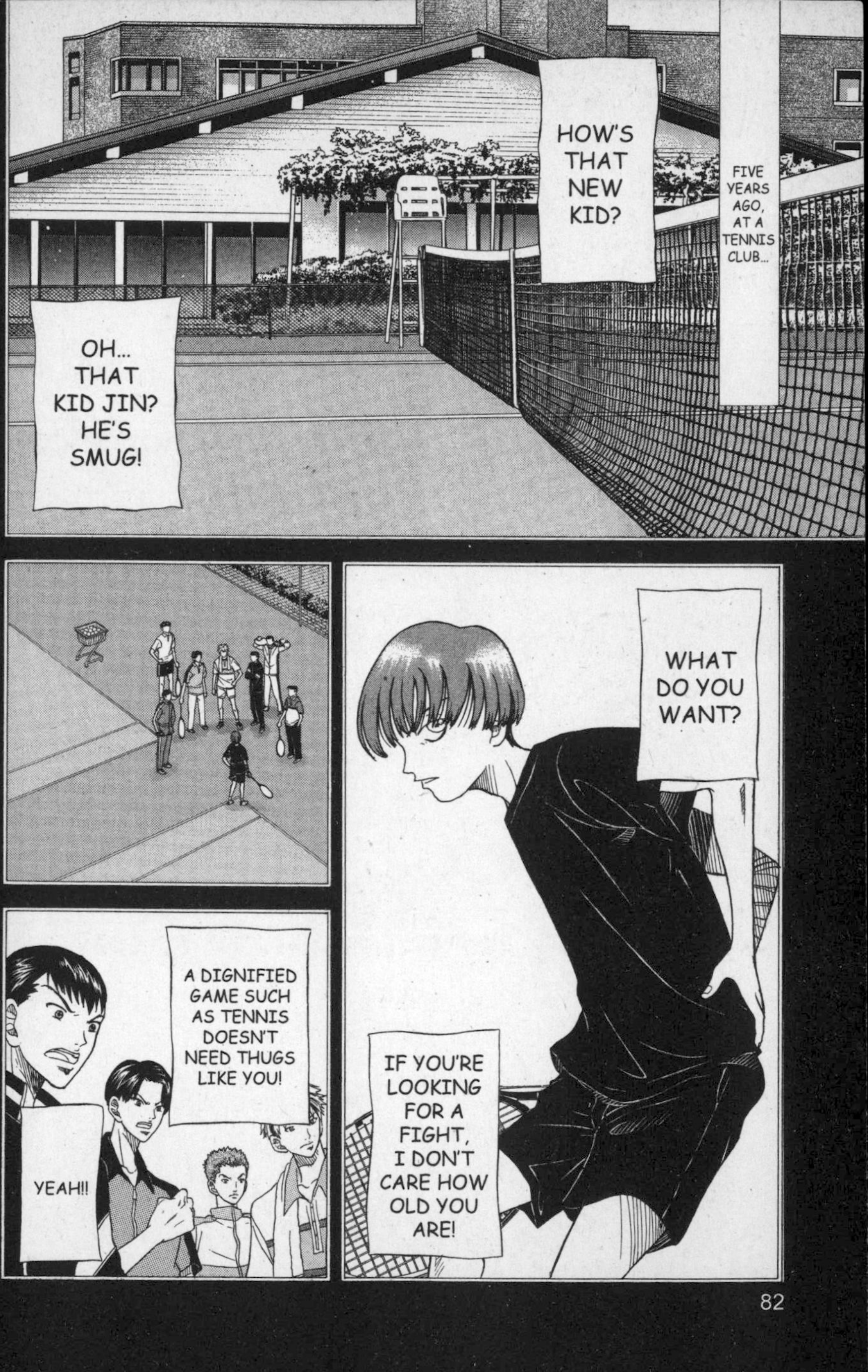
FIVE YEARS AGO, AT A TENNIS CLUB...
HOW'S THAT NEW KID?
OH... THAT KID JIN? HE'S SMUG!
WHAT DO YOU WANT?
IF YOU'RE LOOKING FOR A FIGHT, I DON'T CARE HOW OLD YOU ARE!
A DIGNIFIED GAME SUCH AS TENNIS DOESN'T NEED THUGS LIKE YOU!
YEAH!!

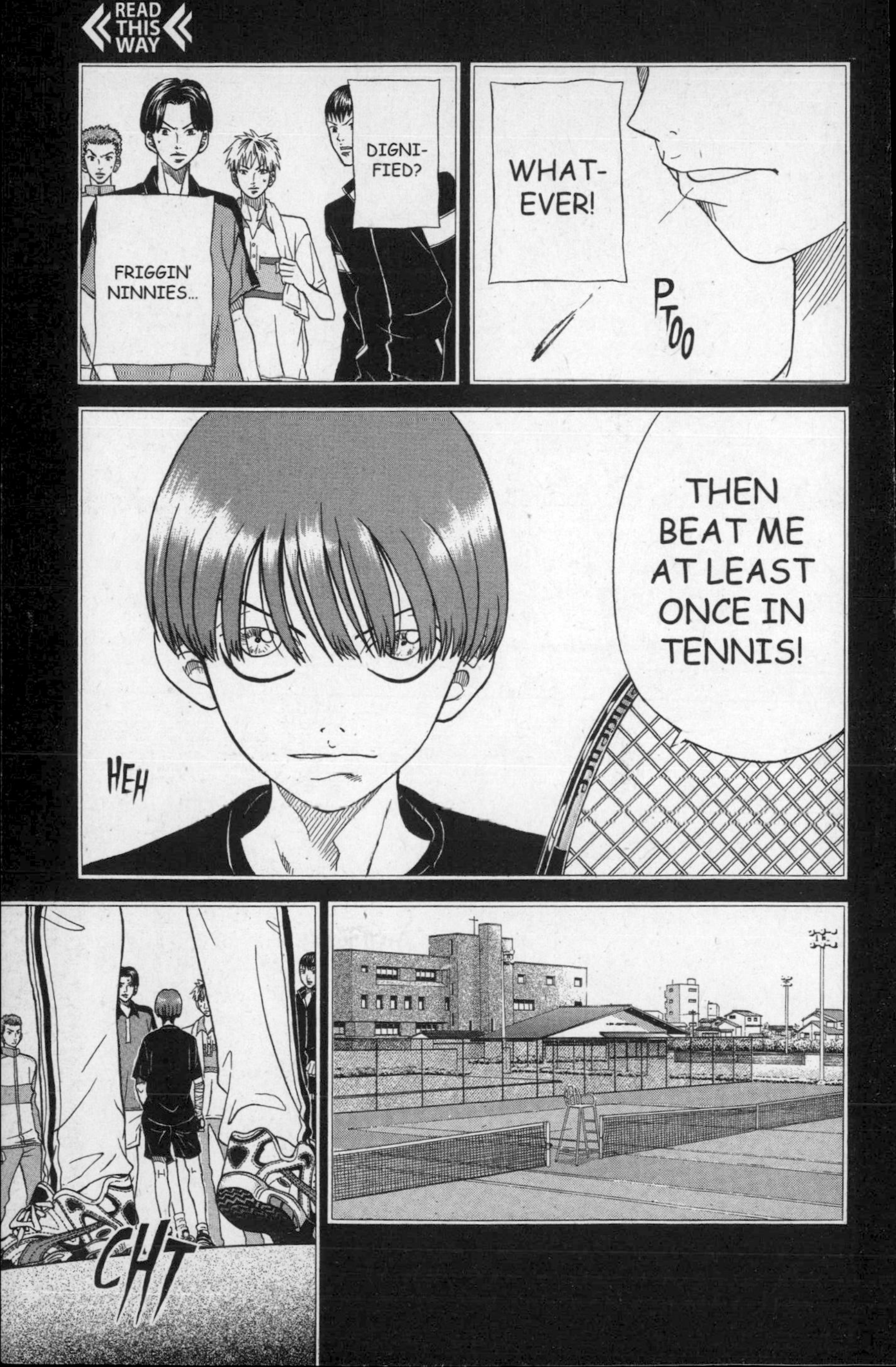
READ THIS WAY
WHAT-EVER!
PTOO
DIGNI-FIED?
FRIGGIN' NINNIES...
THEN BEAT ME AT LEAST ONCE IN TENNIS!
HEH
CHT

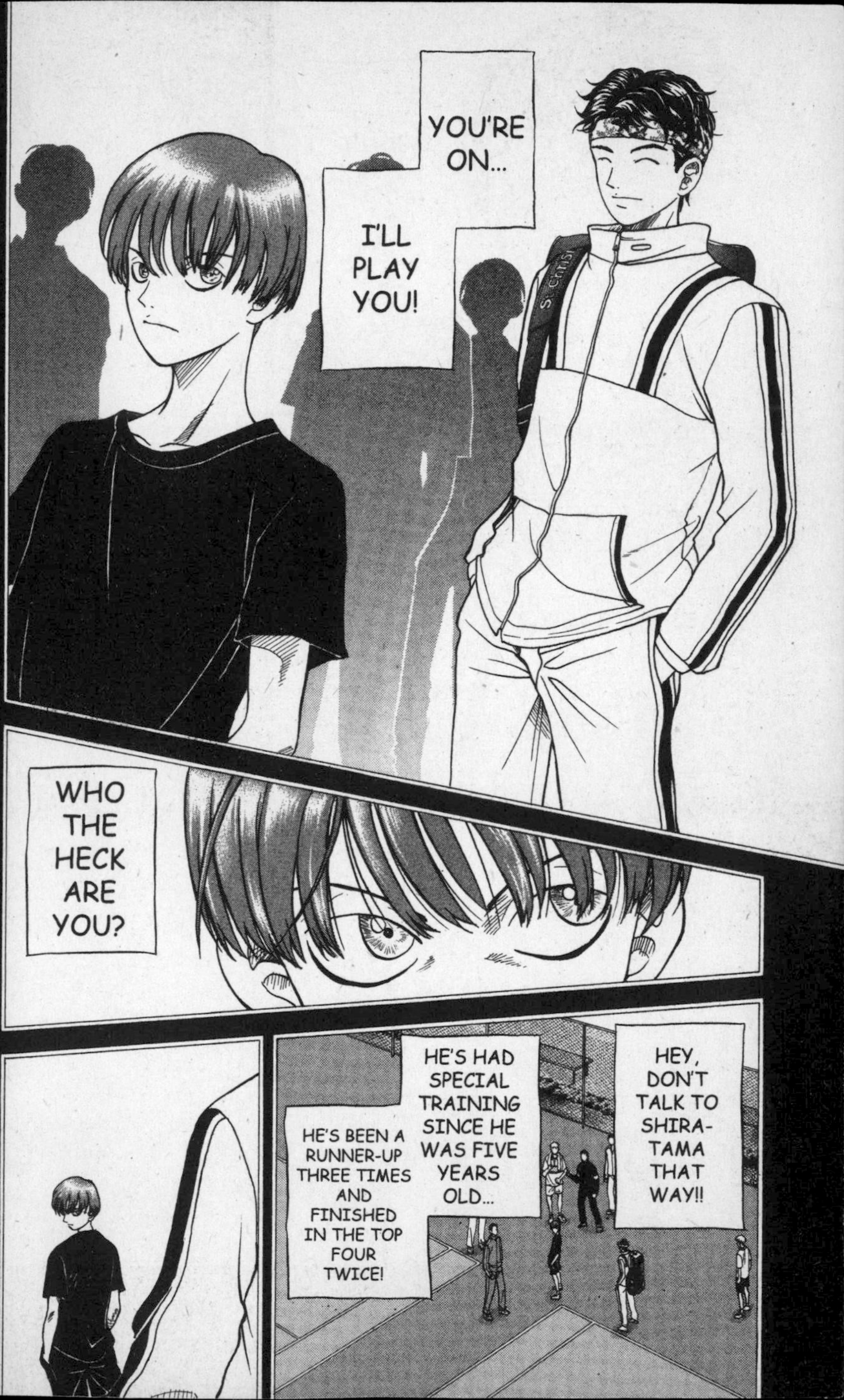
YOU'RE ON...
I'LL PLAY YOU!
WHO THE HECK ARE YOU?
HEY, DON'T TALK TO SHIRA-TAMA THAT WAY!!
HE'S HAD SPECIAL TRAINING SINCE HE WAS FIVE YEARS OLD...
HE'S BEEN A RUNNER-UP THREE TIMES AND FINISHED IN THE TOP FOUR TWICE!

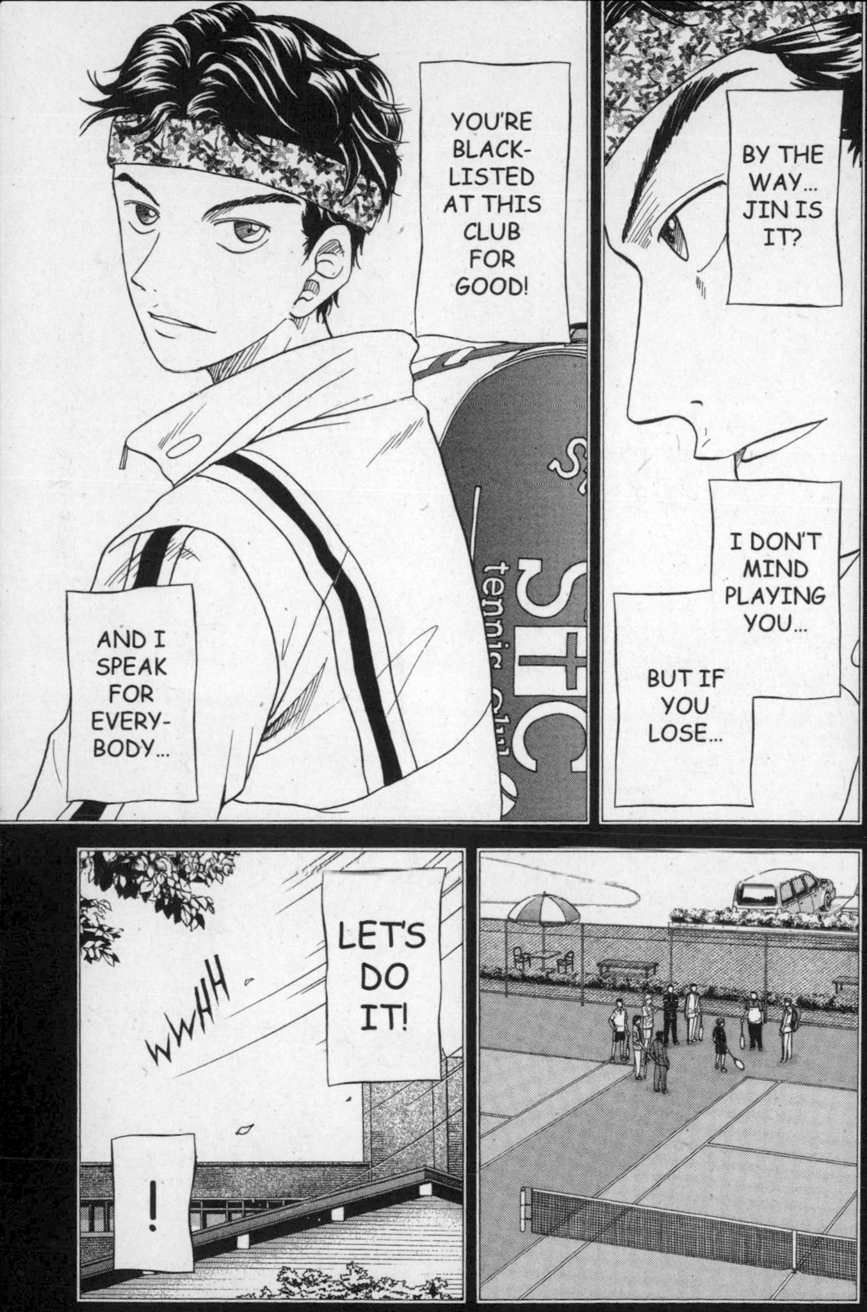
BY THE WAY... JIN IS IT?
I DON'T MIND PLAYING YOU...
BUT IF YOU LOSE...
YOU'RE BLACK-LISTED AT THIS CLUB FOR GOOD!
AND I SPEAK FOR EVERY-BODY...
STC tennis club
LET'S DO IT!
WWHH
!

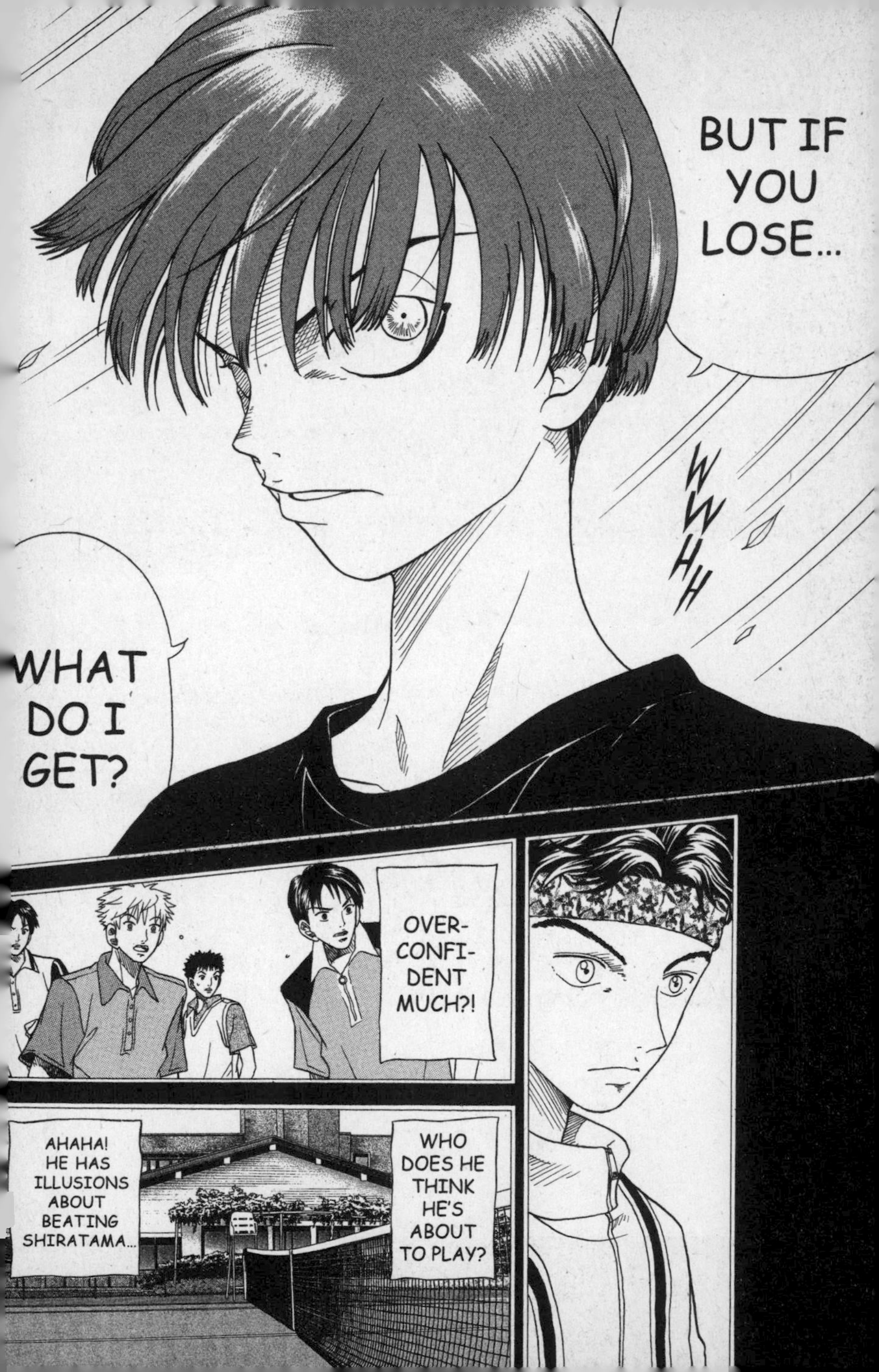
BUT IF YOU LOSE...
WHAT DO I GET?
WWHH
OVER-CONFIDENT MUCH?!
WHO DOES HE THINK HE'S ABOUT TO PLAY?
AHAHA! HE HAS ILLUSIONS ABOUT BEATING SHIRATAMA...

READ THIS WAY

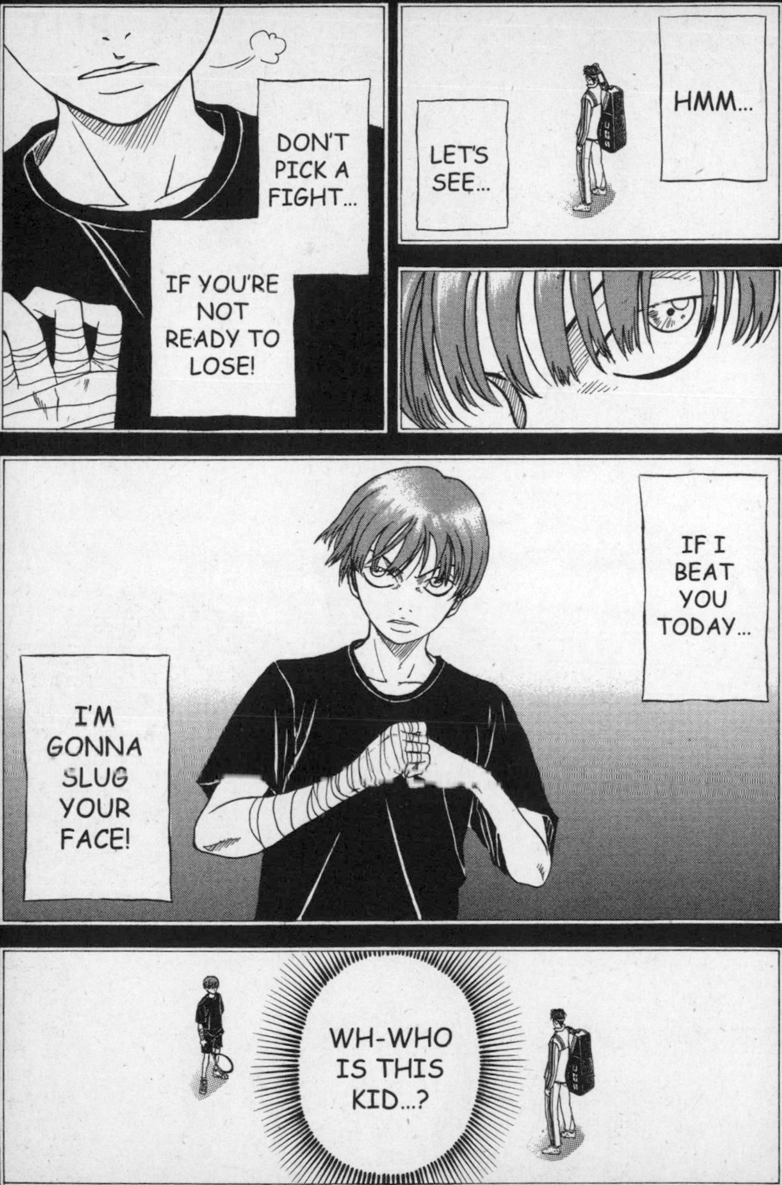
HMM...
LET'S SEE...
DON'T PICK A FIGHT...
IF YOU'RE NOT READY TO LOSE!
IF I BEAT YOU TODAY...
I'M GONNA SLUG YOUR FACE!
WH-WHO IS THIS KID...?

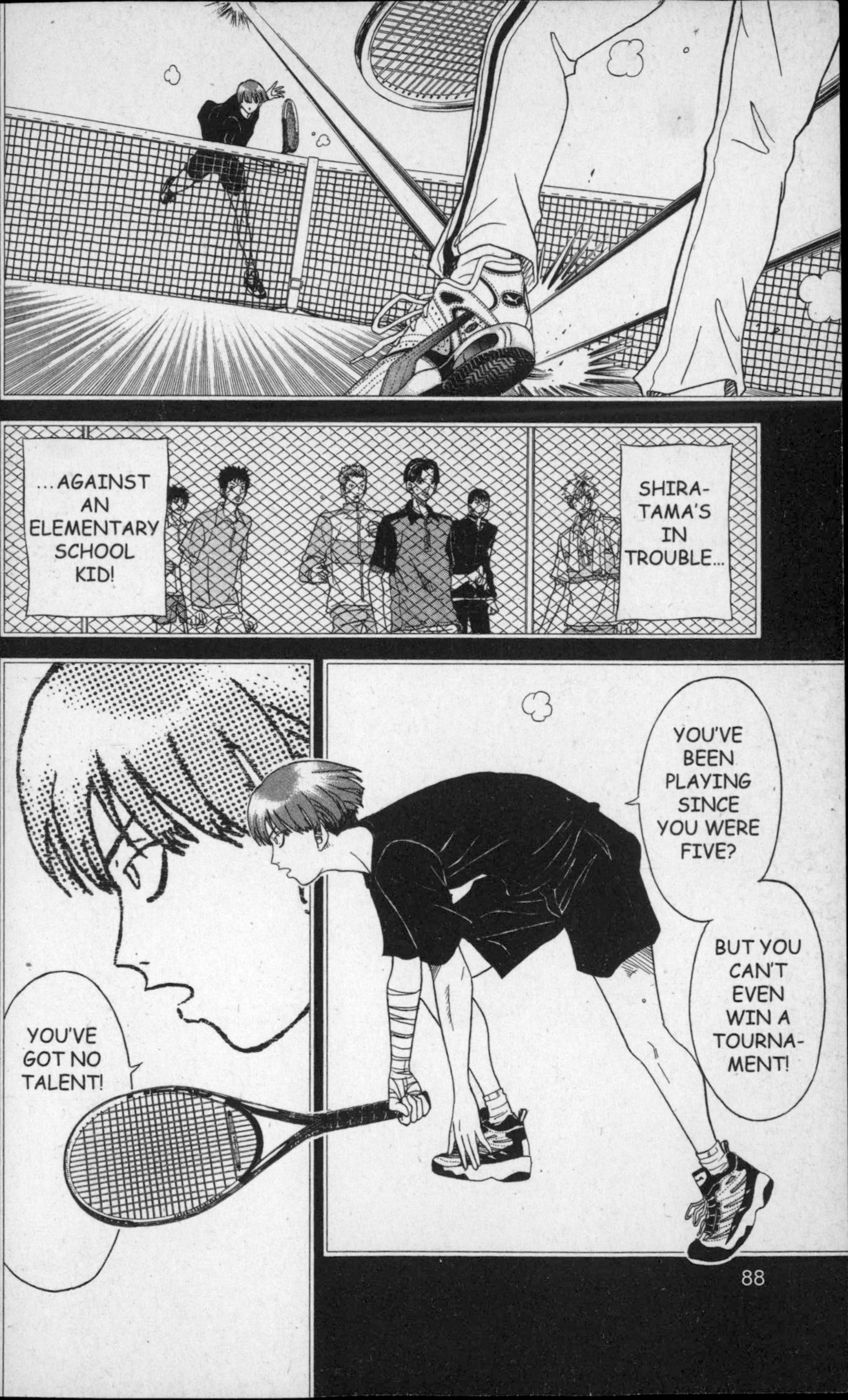
SHIRA-TAMA'S IN TROUBLE...
...AGAINST AN ELEMENTARY SCHOOL KID!
YOU'VE BEEN PLAYING SINCE YOU WERE FIVE?
BUT YOU CAN'T EVEN WIN A TOURNA-MENT!
YOU'VE GOT NO TALENT!

READ THIS WAY

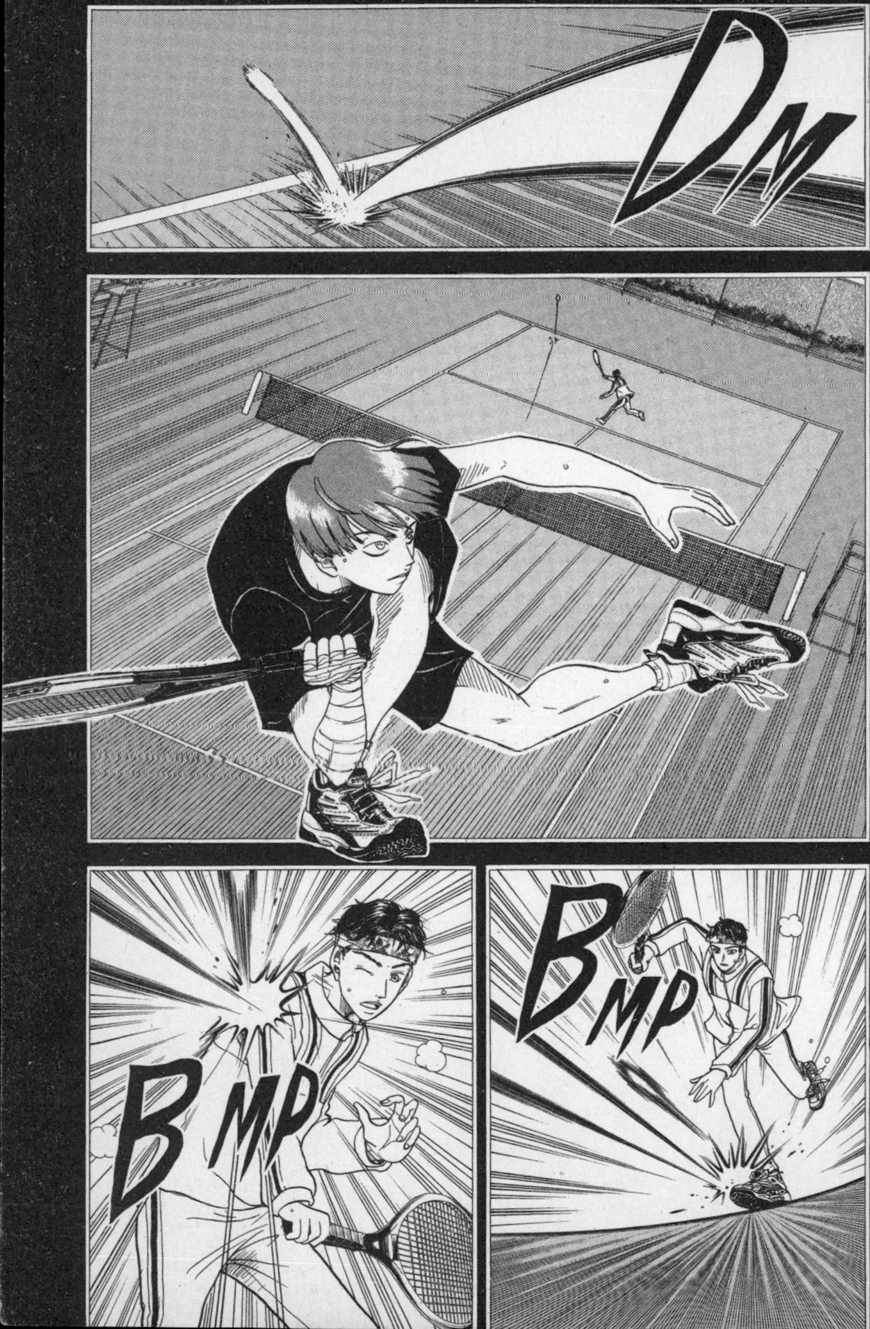
DM
BMP
BMP

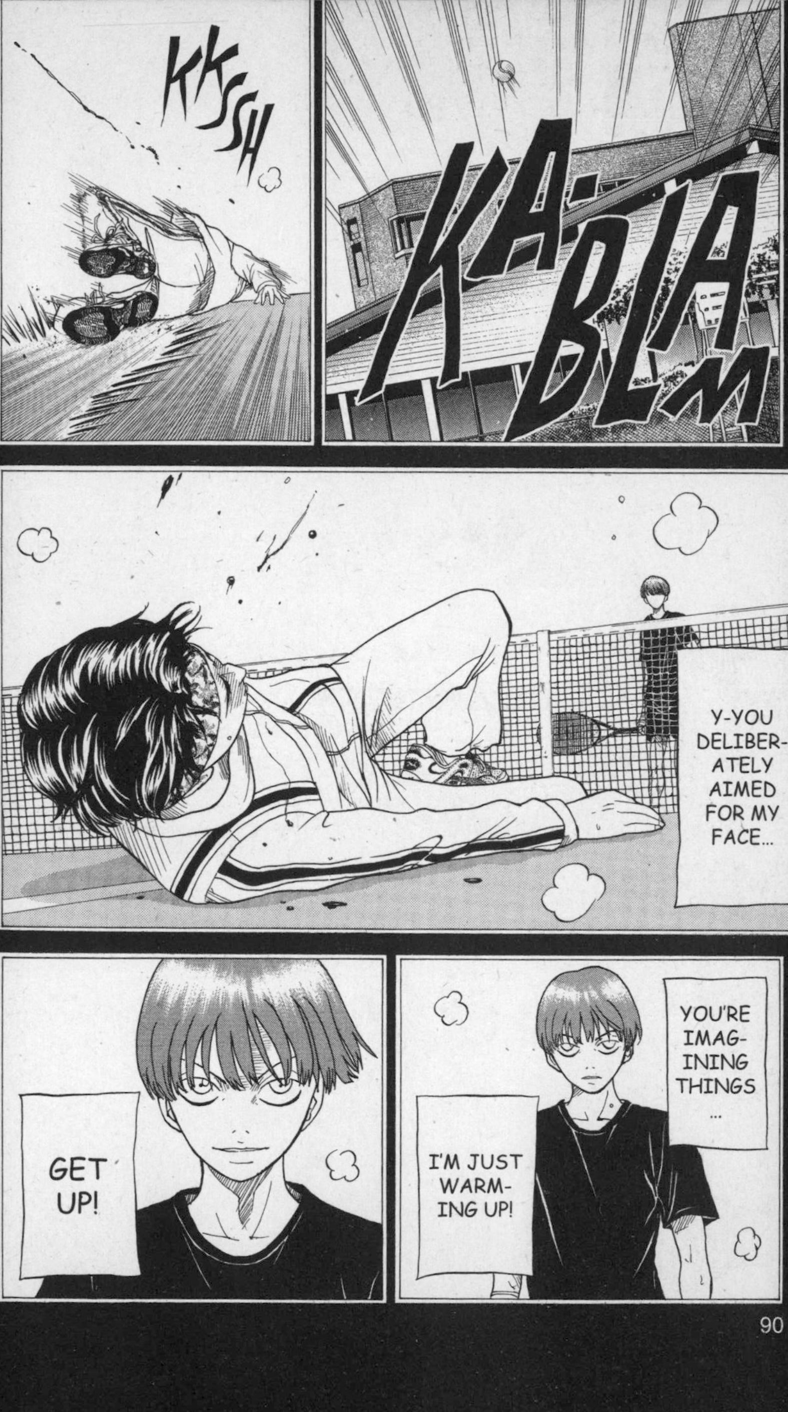
KA-BLAM
KKSSH
Y-YOU DELIBER-ATELY AIMED FOR MY FACE...
YOU'RE IMAG-INING THINGS ...
I'M JUST WARM-ING UP!
GET UP!

READ THIS WAY

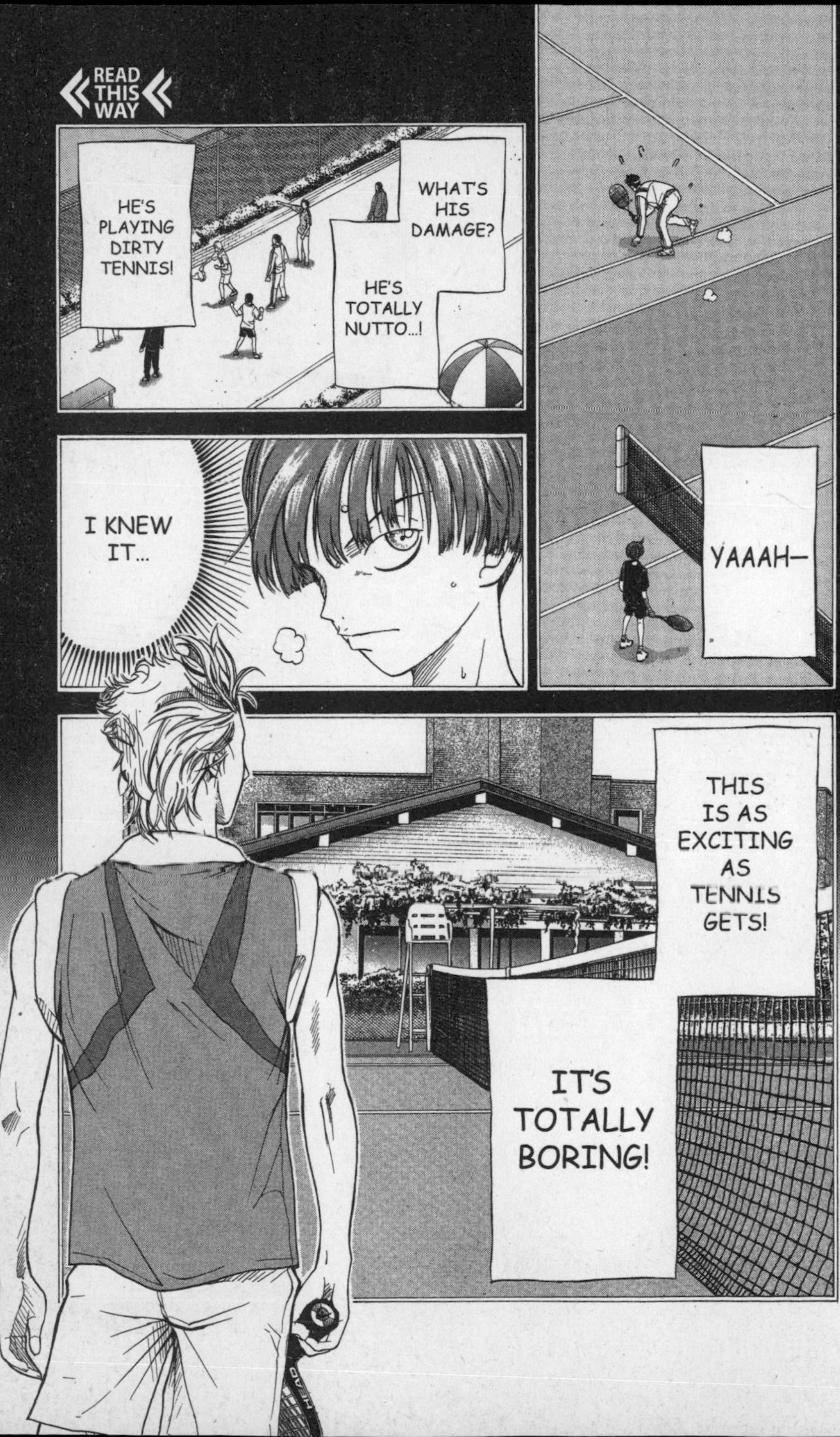
YAAAH—
WHAT'S HIS DAMAGE?
HE'S TOTALLY NUTTO...!
HE'S PLAYING DIRTY TENNIS!
I KNEW IT...
THIS IS AS EXCITING AS TENNIS GETS!
IT'S TOTALLY BORING!

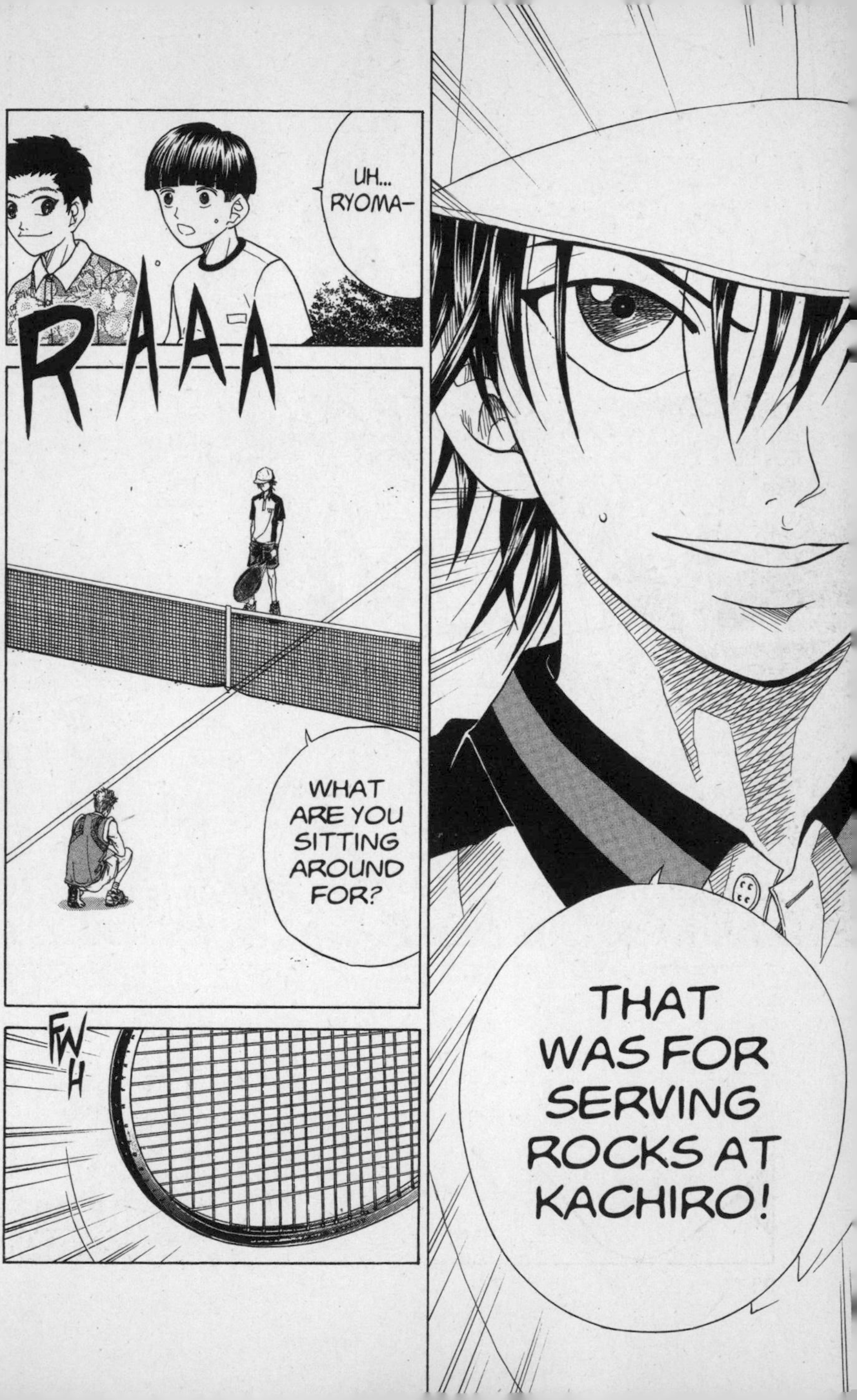
THAT WAS FOR SERVING ROCKS AT KACHIRO!
UH... RYOMA-
RAAA
WHAT ARE YOU SITTING AROUND FOR?
FWH

YOU STILL OWE ME FOR TAKA...

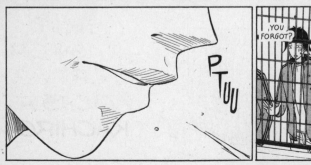

PTUU

YOU FORGOT?

OH, AND I ALMOST FORGOT ARAI...

93

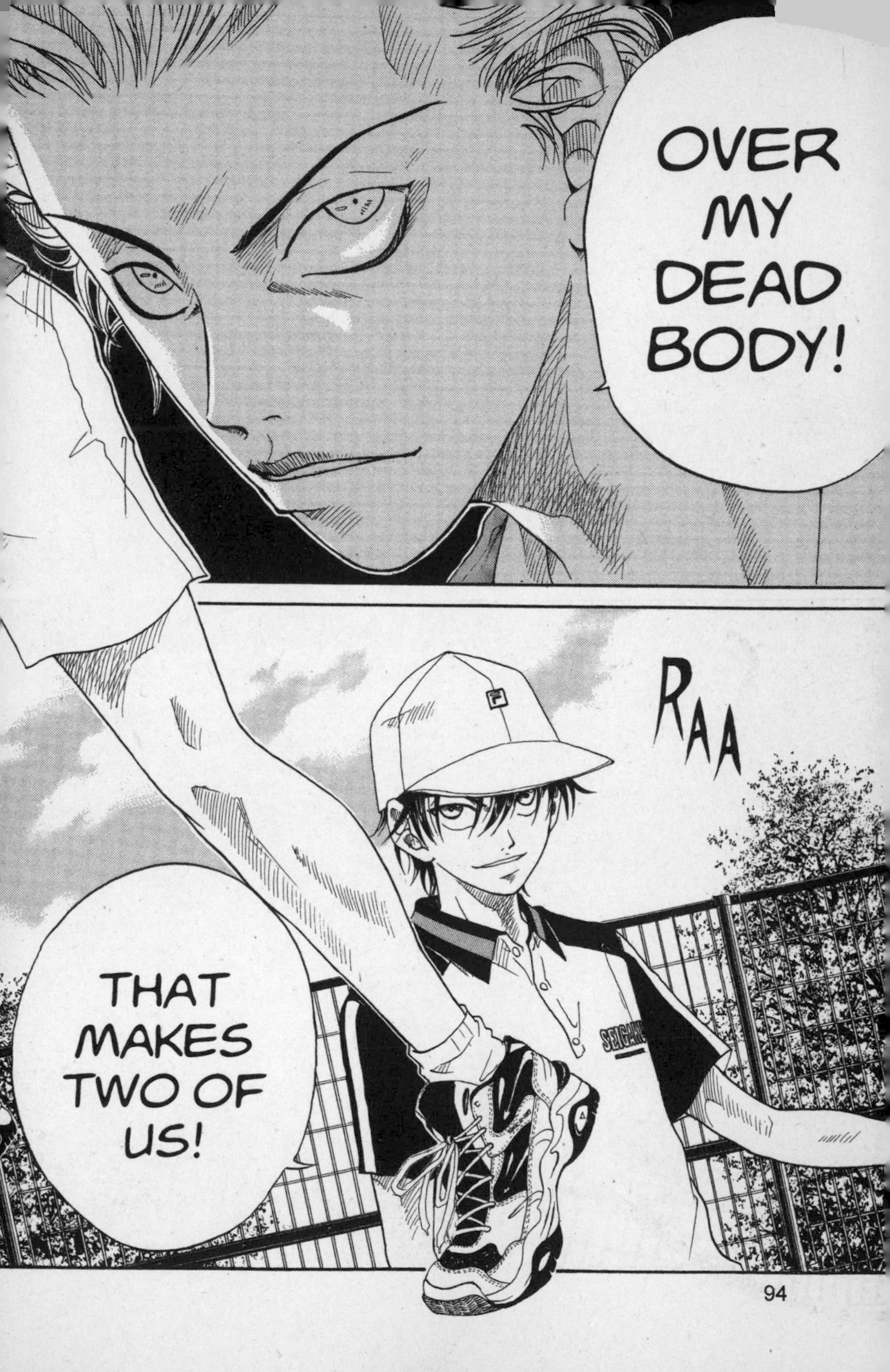
OVER MY DEAD BODY!
RAA
THAT MAKES TWO OF US!

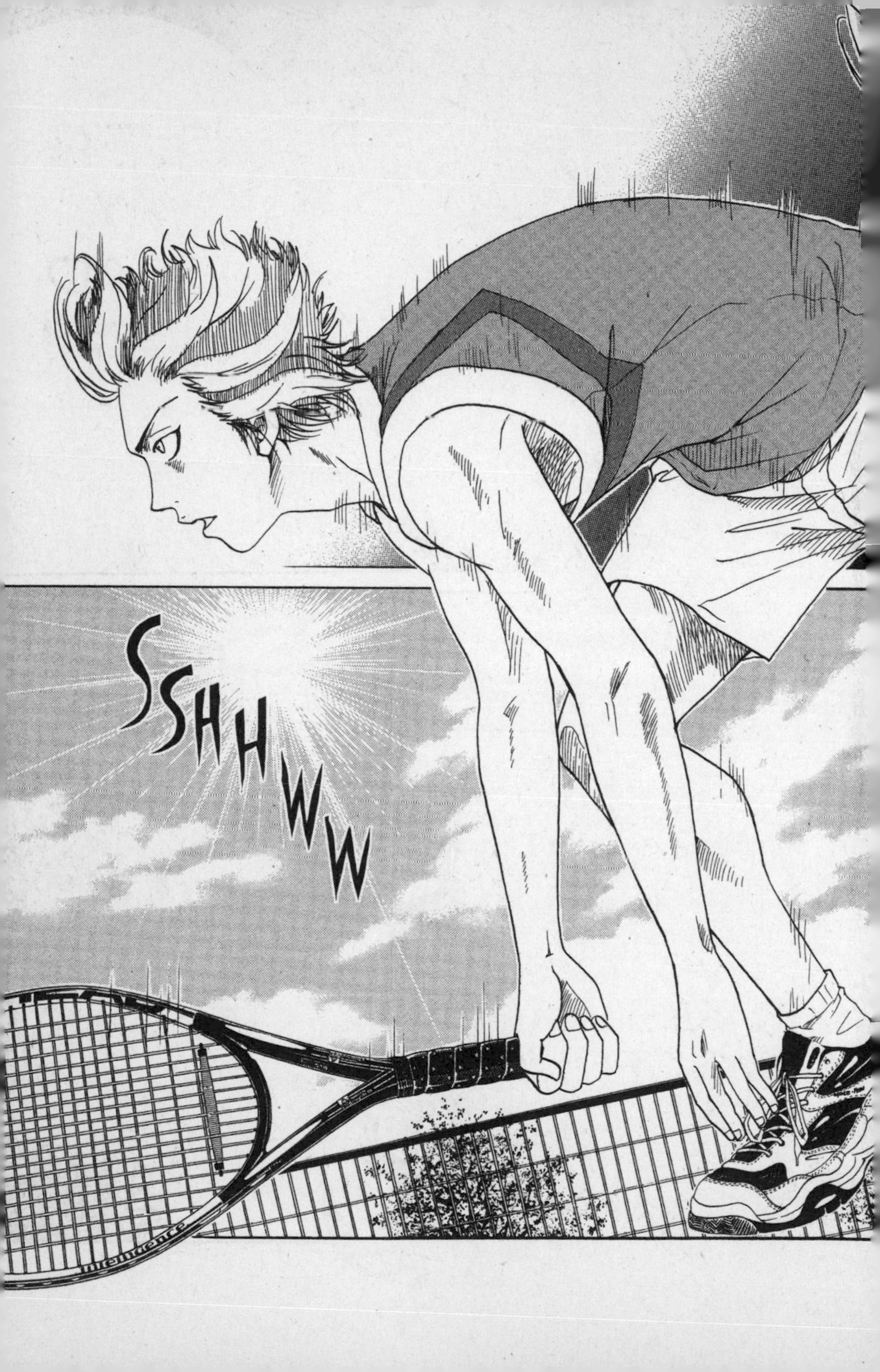
SSHHWWW

Thank you for reading Prince of Tennis Volume 12!

I know it's sudden, but in a previous volume I wrote, "I'm planning on attending the Jump Festa Tokyo Tournament in December of 2001, so I hope to wander around there too. For those of you who are going, come say hello if you see me around." Unfortunately, I was called aside and told that "...for safety reasons, authors may not wander around...especially the author of The Prince of Tennis." (Come to think of it, they have a point. Sorry.) To the fans that wrote and told me they'd look for me, I apologize. In any case, to those who attended the Jump Festa Tokyo Tournament, thank you for your support! To those of you who wrote, "I can't be there, but I'm cheering for you," thank you so much! And to the voice actors who made the stage exciting and dynamic, thank you! I had a wonderful time. I hope everybody who attended had fun too.

I've been receiving a ton of letters from fans of the anime. Many of them were family letters, sent in by a mother and child who sat down to write one together. I couldn't be happier. Thank you!

Of course, I'm still receiving letters from fans who have been following The Prince of Tennis since it first came out. I'm really grateful!

I wrestled with time during the second half of 2001. There were many close calls, but I was able to overcome them with your support. I'm hoping to do my best in 2002 as well!

I included a special project at the end of this volume! First timers, those trying again, those busy with the fan book, and especially those who love that "cool" guy—please participate!!

Well then...keep supporting The Prince of Tennis and Ryoma! See you in the next volume!!

T. Konomi
2002. 1. 12

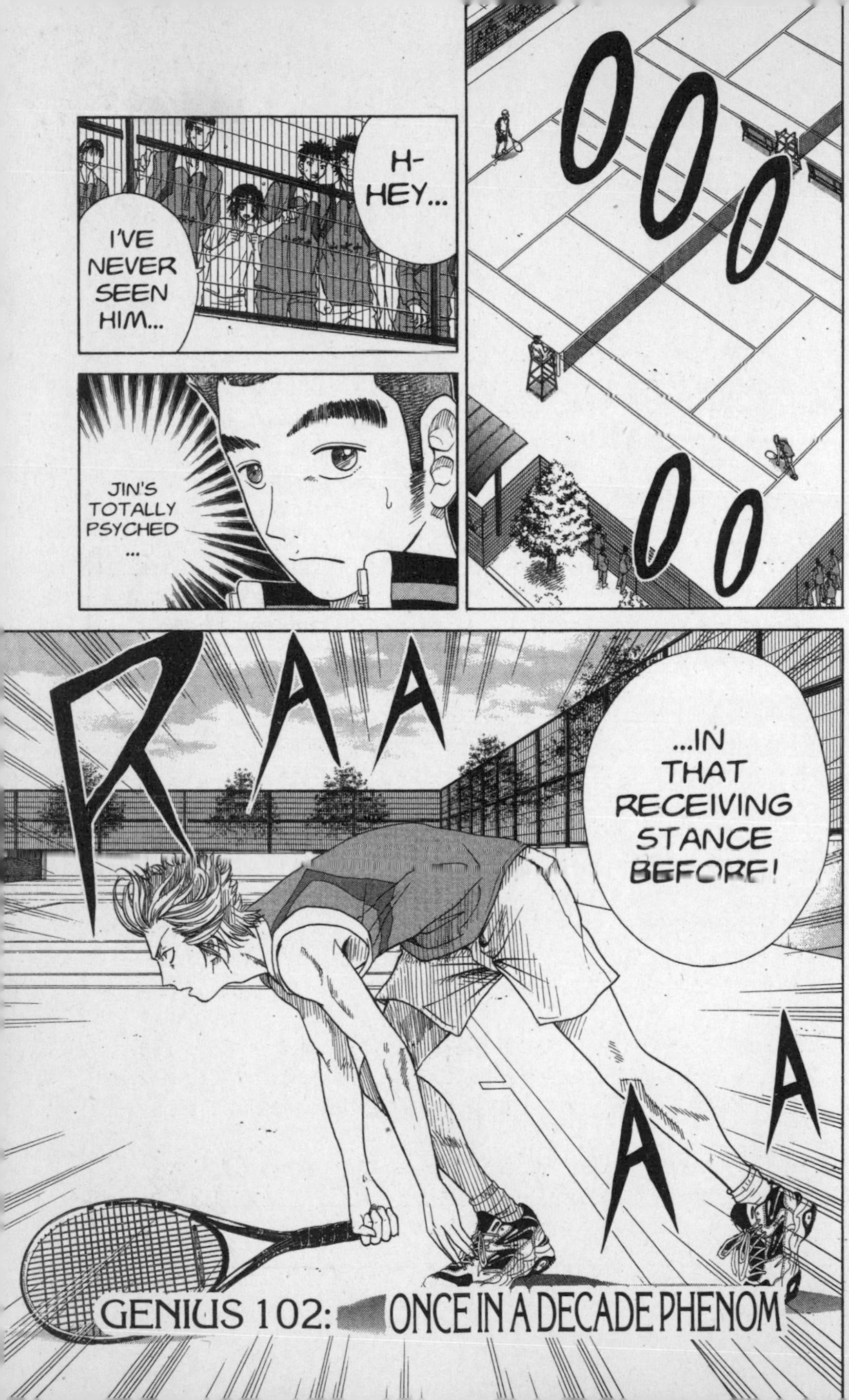
OOOOOO
H-HEY...
I'VE NEVER SEEN HIM...
JIN'S TOTALLY PSYCHED...
RAAAA
...IN THAT RECEIVING STANCE BEFORE!
GENIUS 102: ONCE IN A DECADE PHENOM

GENIUS 102: ONCE IN A DECADE PHENOM

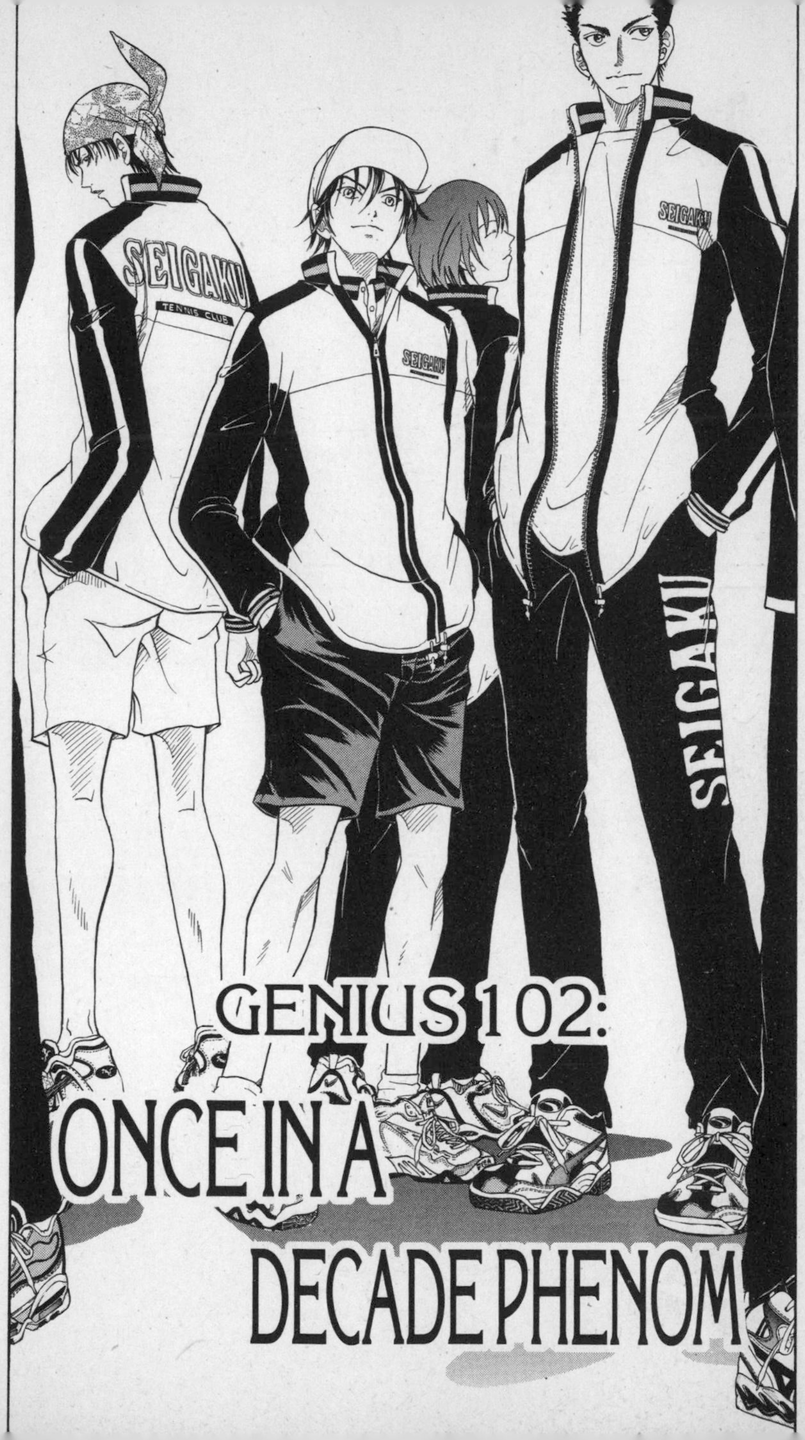
SEIGAKU
TENNIS CLUB
SEIGAKU
SEIGAKU
SEIGAKU

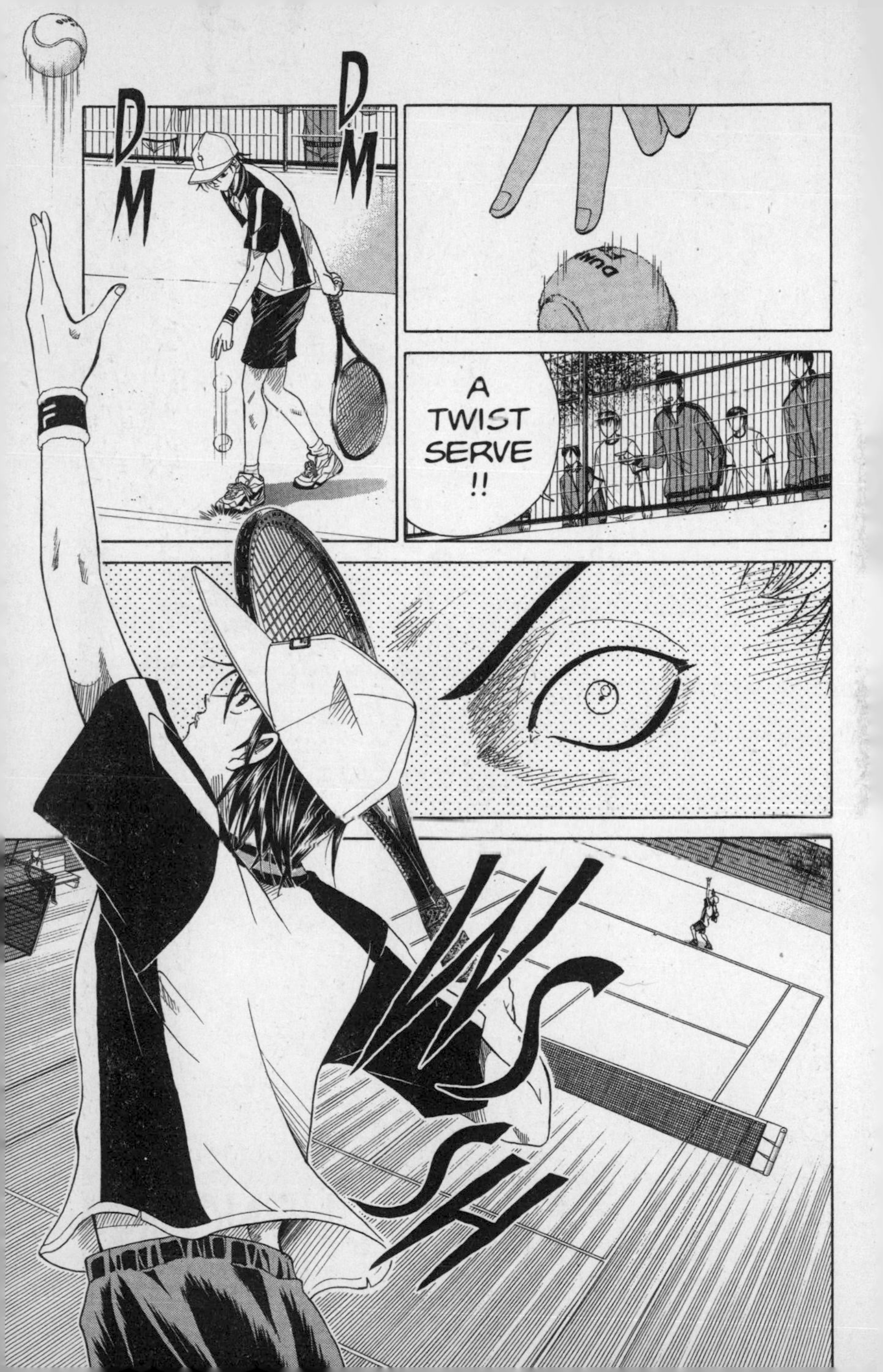
D
M
D
M
A TWIST SERVE !!
WHSH

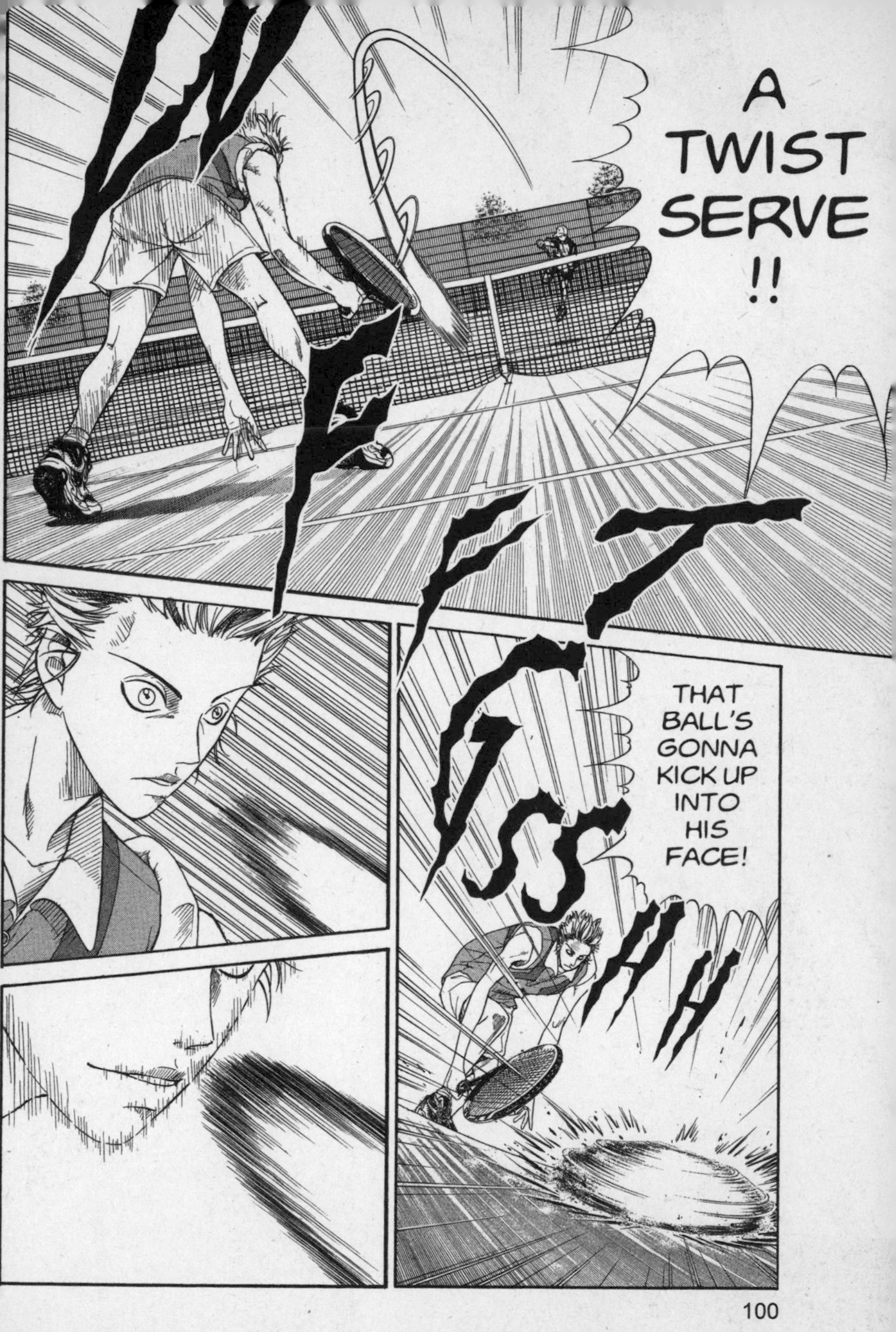
A TWIST SERVE!!
THAT BALL'S GONNA KICK UP INTO HIS FACE!

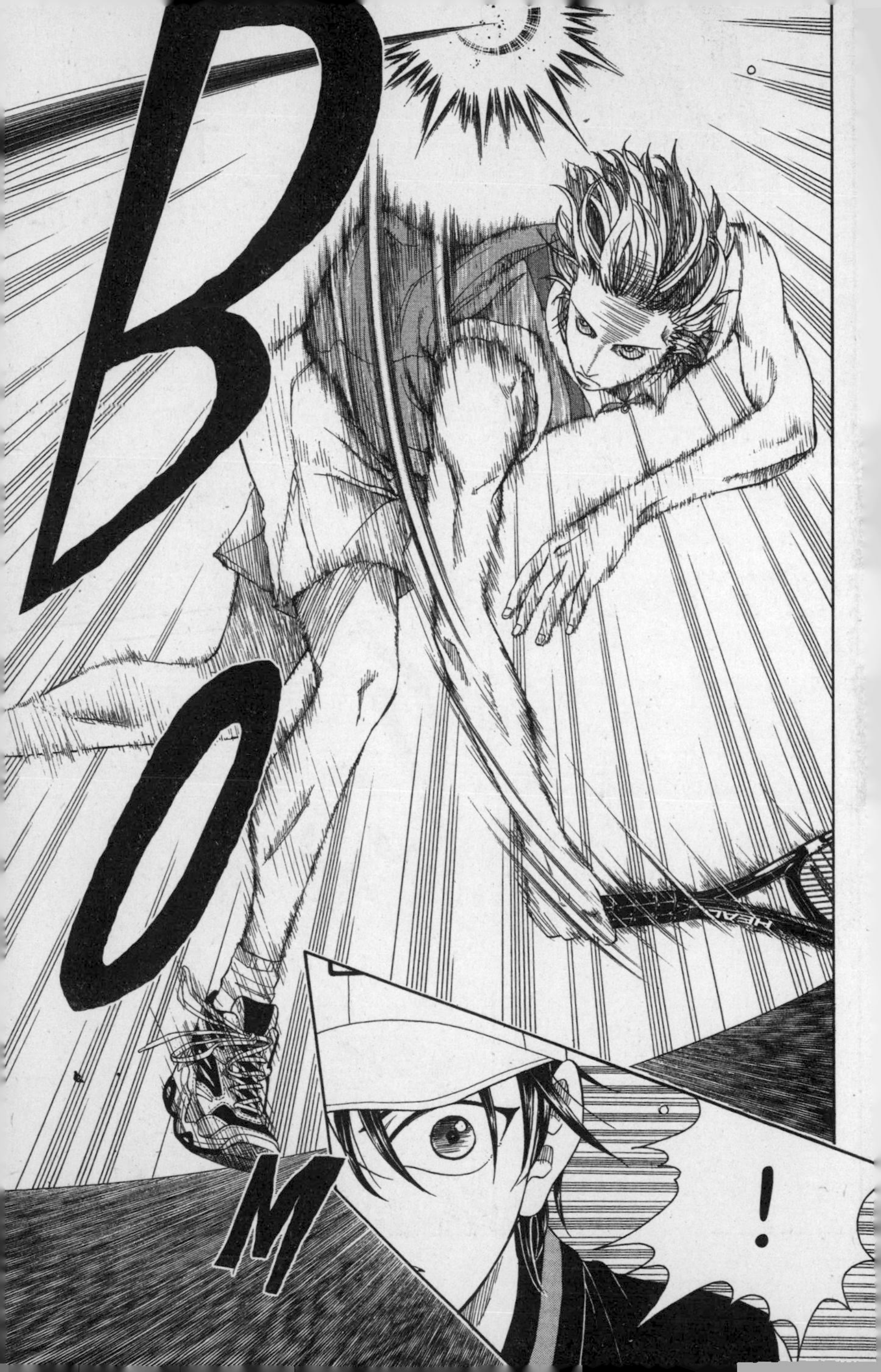
BOOM
!

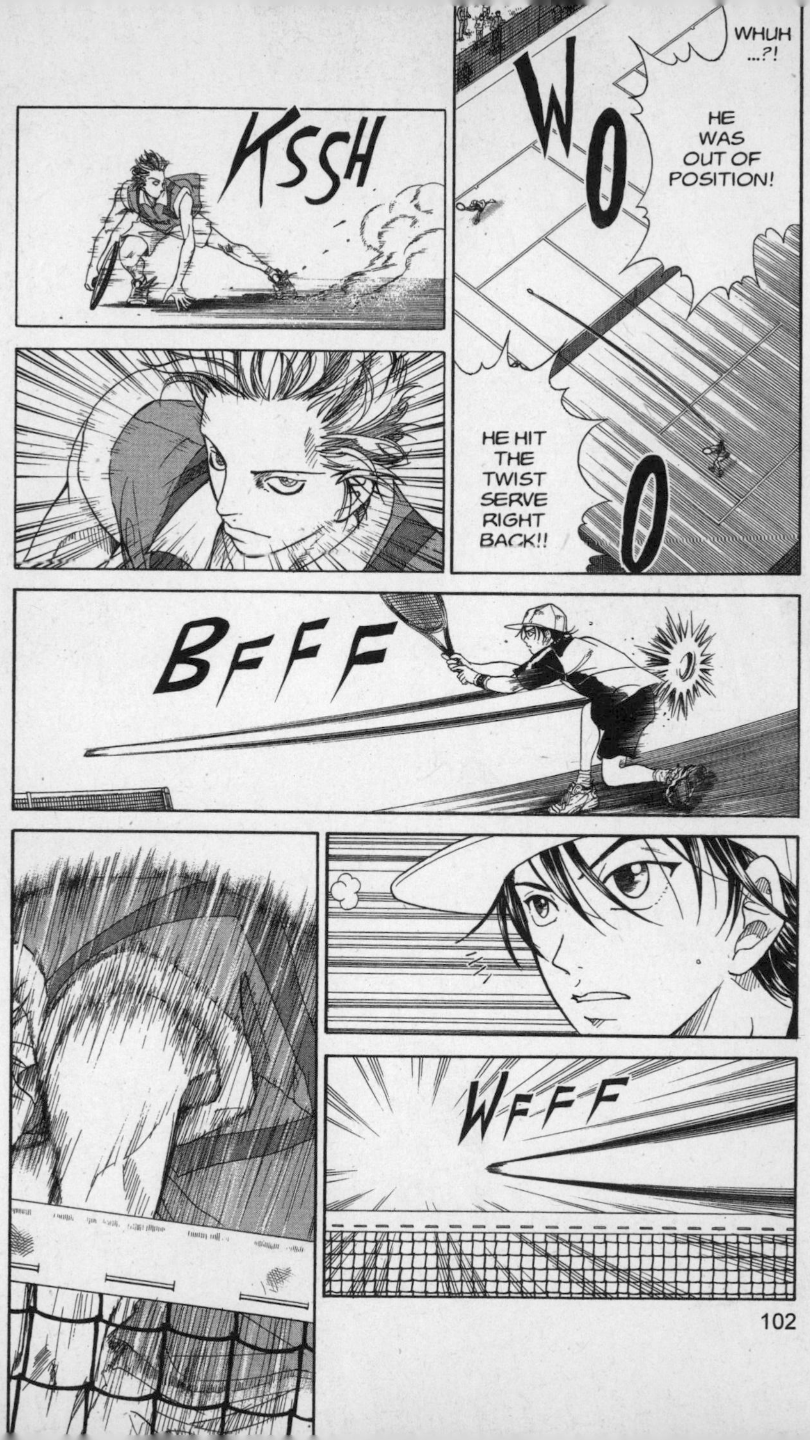
WHUH ...?!
WO
HE WAS OUT OF POSITION!
O
HE HIT THE TWIST SERVE RIGHT BACK!!
KSSH
BFFF
WFFF

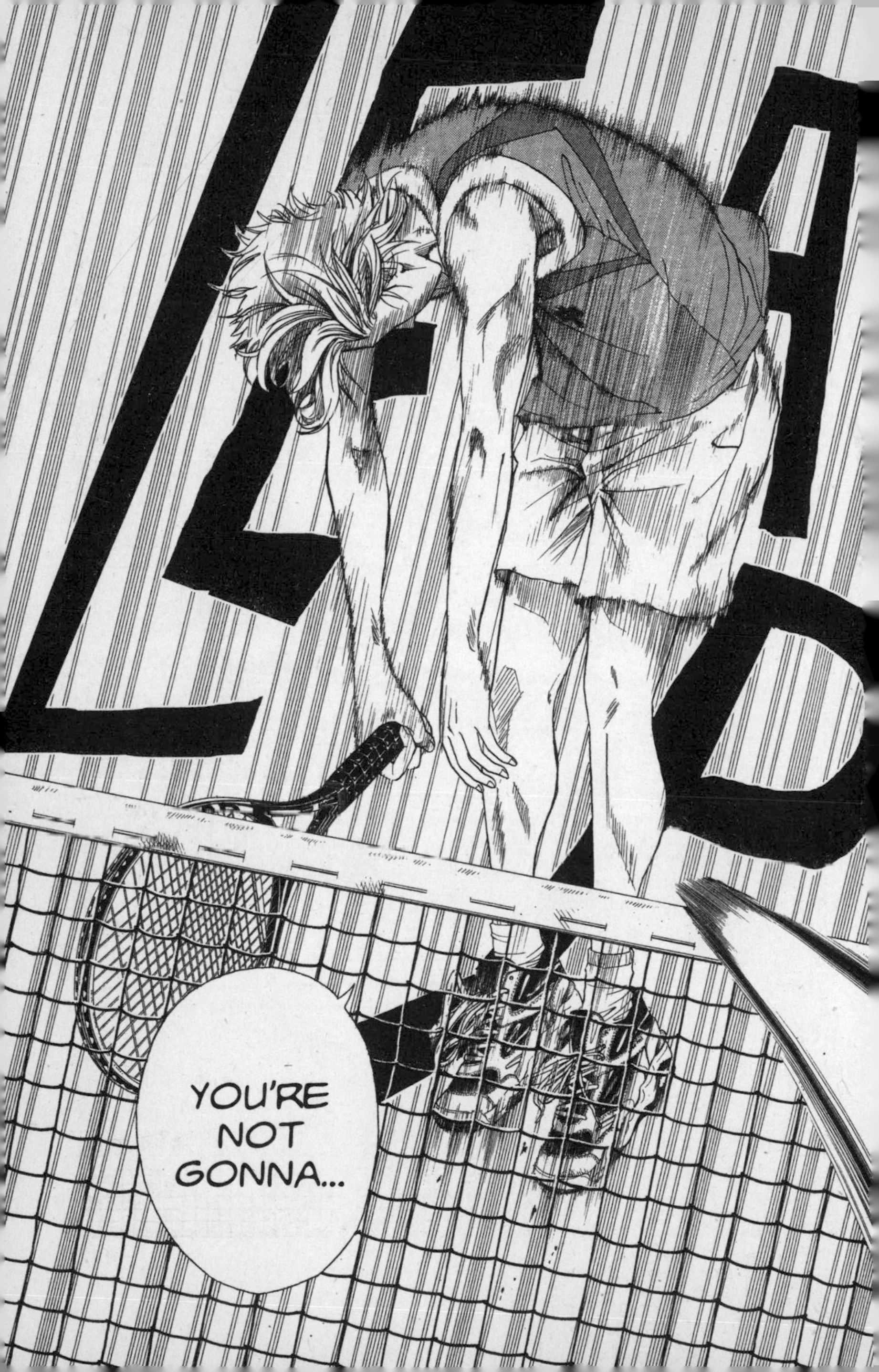
YOU'RE NOT GONNA...

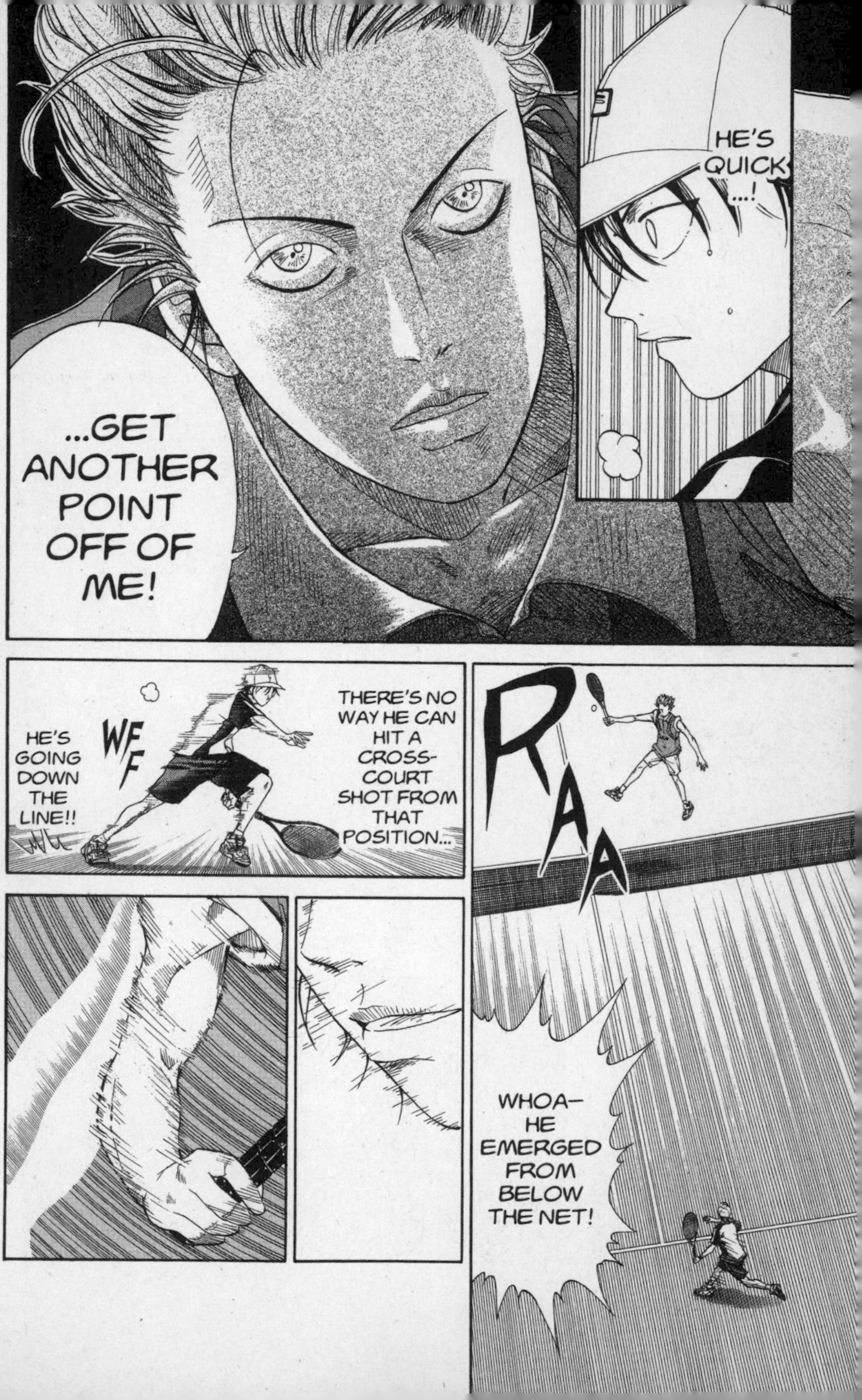
HE'S QUICK ...!
...GET ANOTHER POINT OFF OF ME!
THERE'S NO WAY HE CAN HIT A CROSS-COURT SHOT FROM THAT POSITION...
HE'S GOING DOWN THE LINE!!
WFF
RAA
WHOA— HE EMERGED FROM BELOW THE NET!

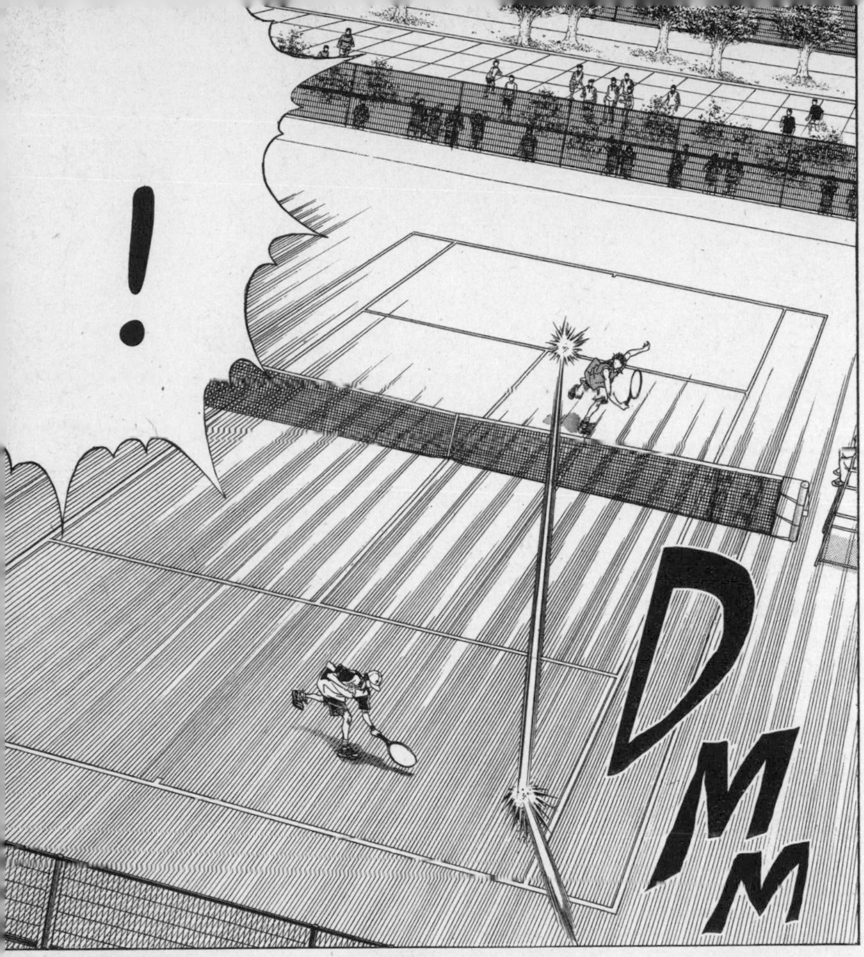
!
DMM
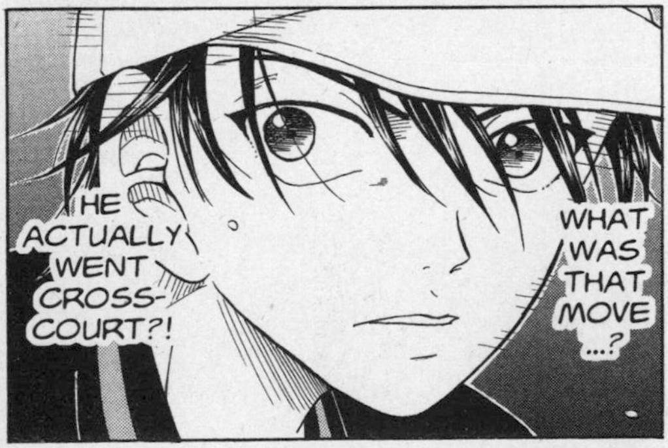
WHAT WAS THAT MOVE ...?
HE ACTUALLY WENT CROSS-COURT?!
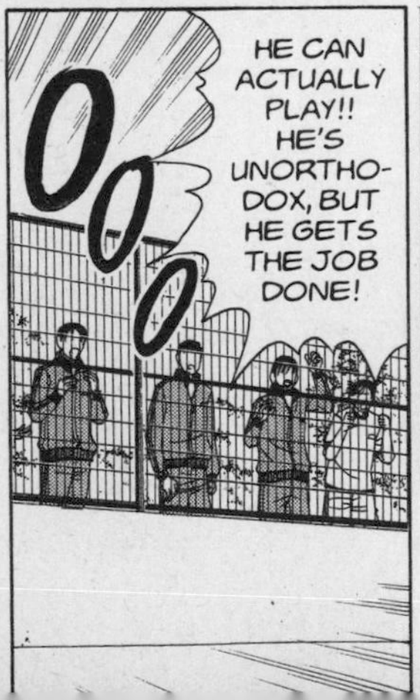
HE CAN ACTUALLY PLAY!! HE'S UNORTHODOX, BUT HE GETS THE JOB DONE!
OOO

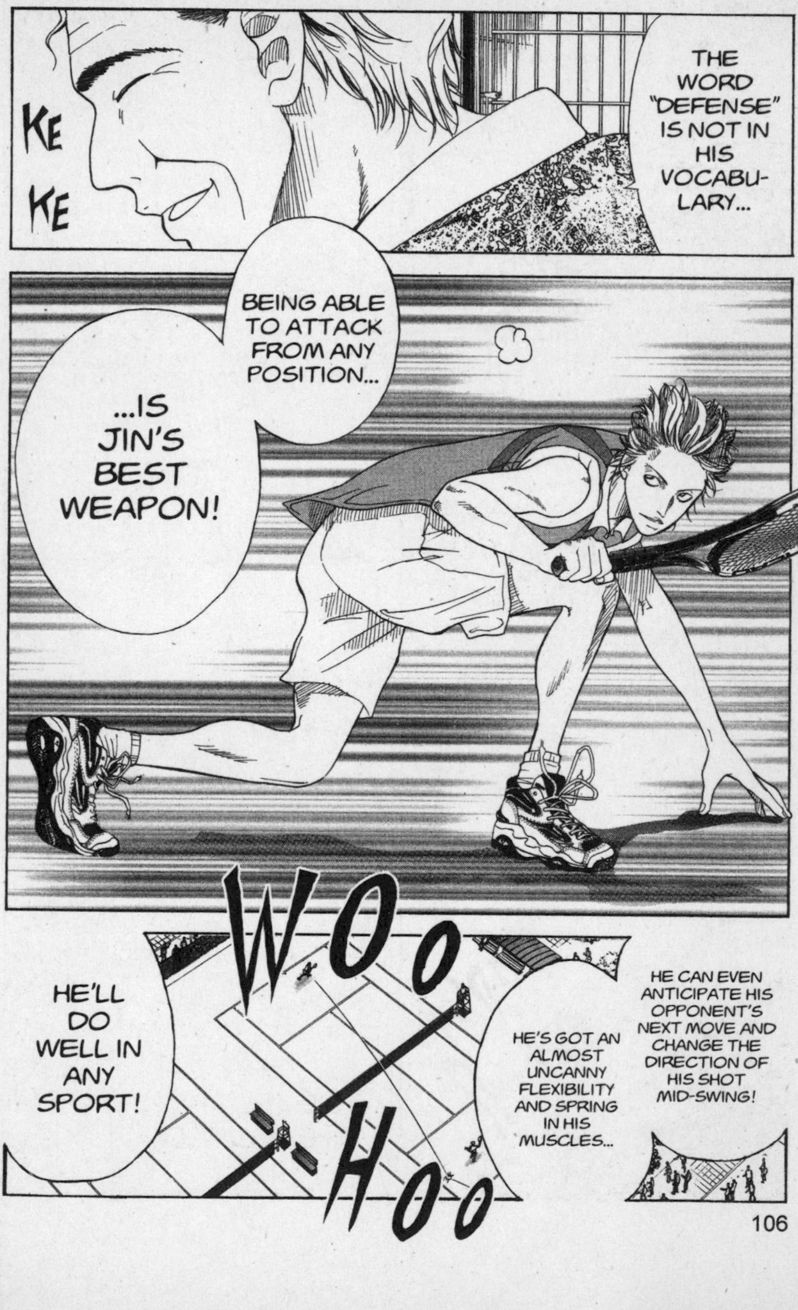
THE WORD "DEFENSE" IS NOT IN HIS VOCABULARY...
KE KE
BEING ABLE TO ATTACK FROM ANY POSITION...
...IS JIN'S BEST WEAPON!
HE'S GOT AN ALMOST UNCANNY FLEXIBILITY AND SPRING IN HIS MUSCLES...
HE CAN EVEN ANTICIPATE HIS OPPONENT'S NEXT MOVE AND CHANGE THE DIRECTION OF HIS SHOT MID-SWING!
WOO HOO
HE'LL DO WELL IN ANY SPORT!

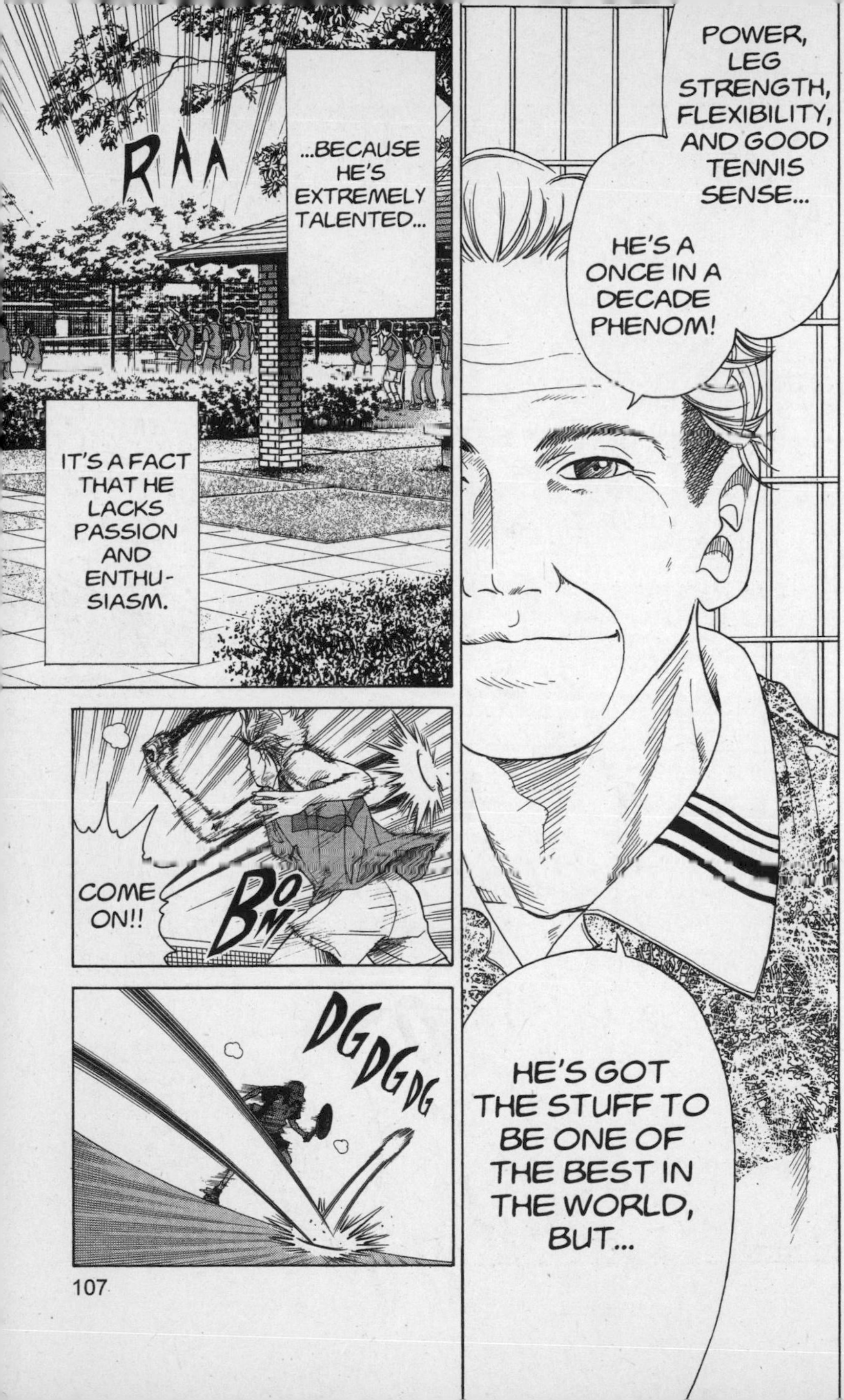
POWER, LEG STRENGTH, FLEXIBILITY, AND GOOD TENNIS SENSE...
HE'S A ONCE IN A DECADE PHENOM!
HE'S GOT THE STUFF TO BE ONE OF THE BEST IN THE WORLD, BUT...
...BECAUSE HE'S EXTREMELY TALENTED...
RAA
IT'S A FACT THAT HE LACKS PASSION AND ENTHUSIASM.
BOM
COME ON!!
DG DG DG

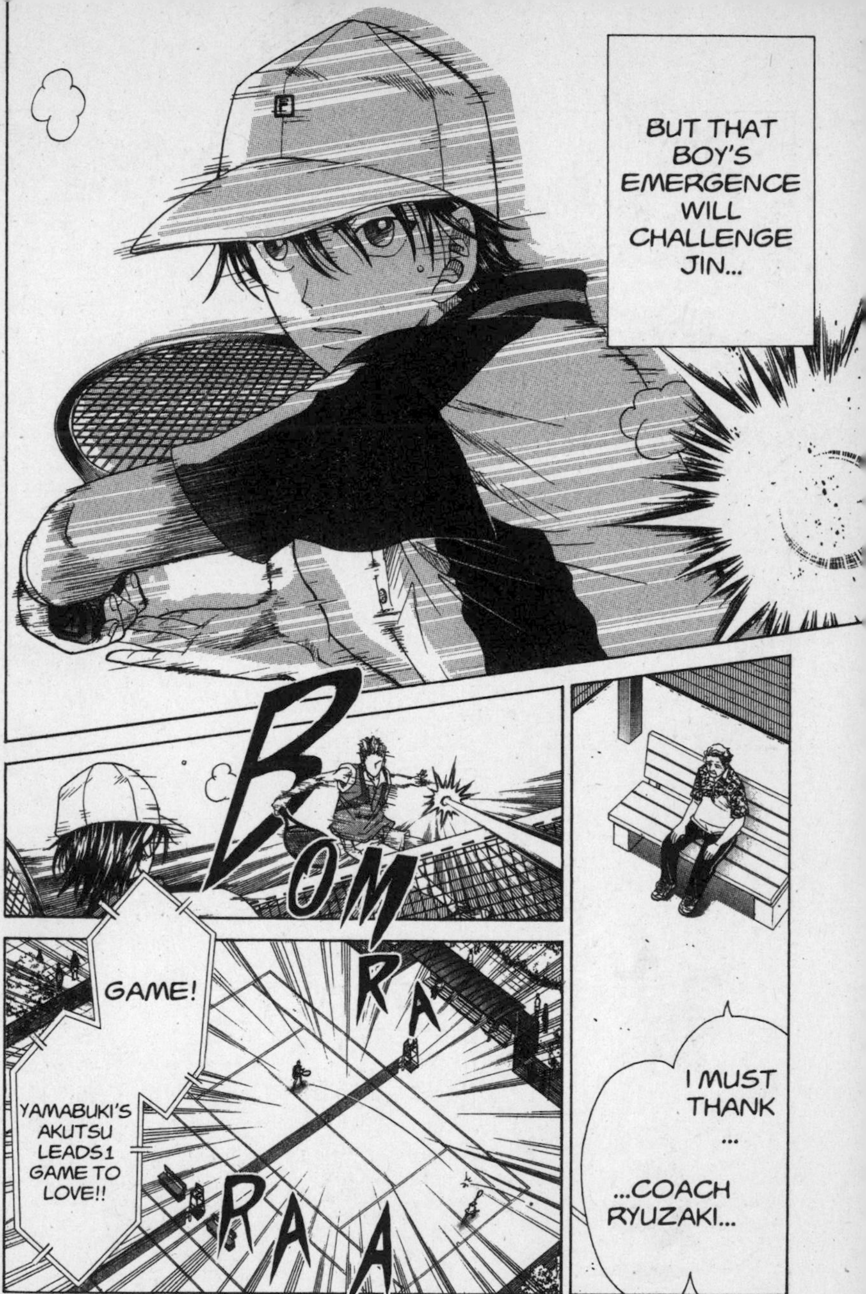

BUT THAT BOY'S EMERGENCE WILL CHALLENGE JIN...
I MUST THANK ... ...COACH RYUZAKI...
BOMRA
RAA
GAME!
YAMABUKI'S AKUTSU LEADS 1 GAME TO LOVE!!

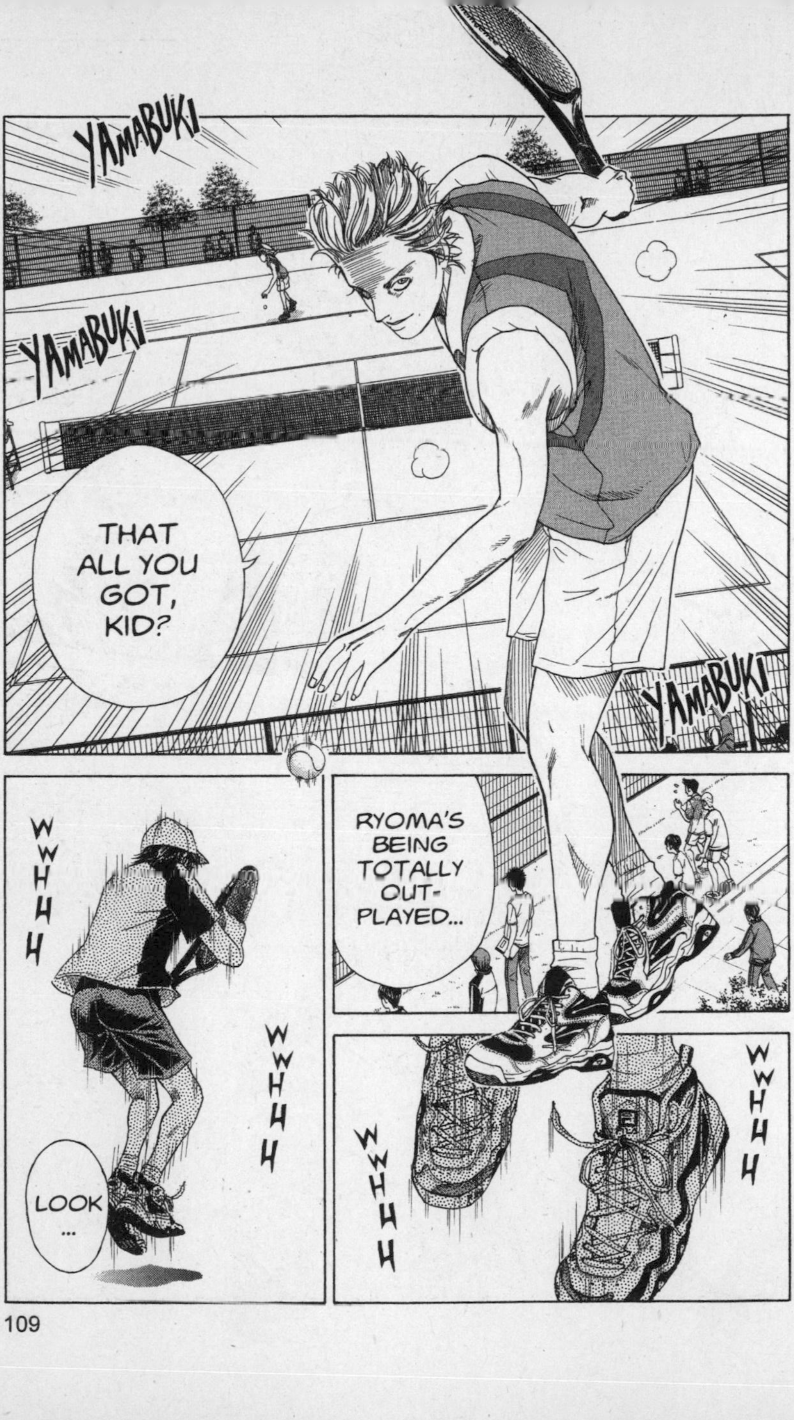
YAMABUKI
YAMABUKI
YAMABUKI
THAT ALL YOU GOT, KID?
RYOMA'S BEING TOTALLY OUT-PLAYED...
WWHHHH
WWHHHH
WWHHHH
WWHHHH
LOOK ...

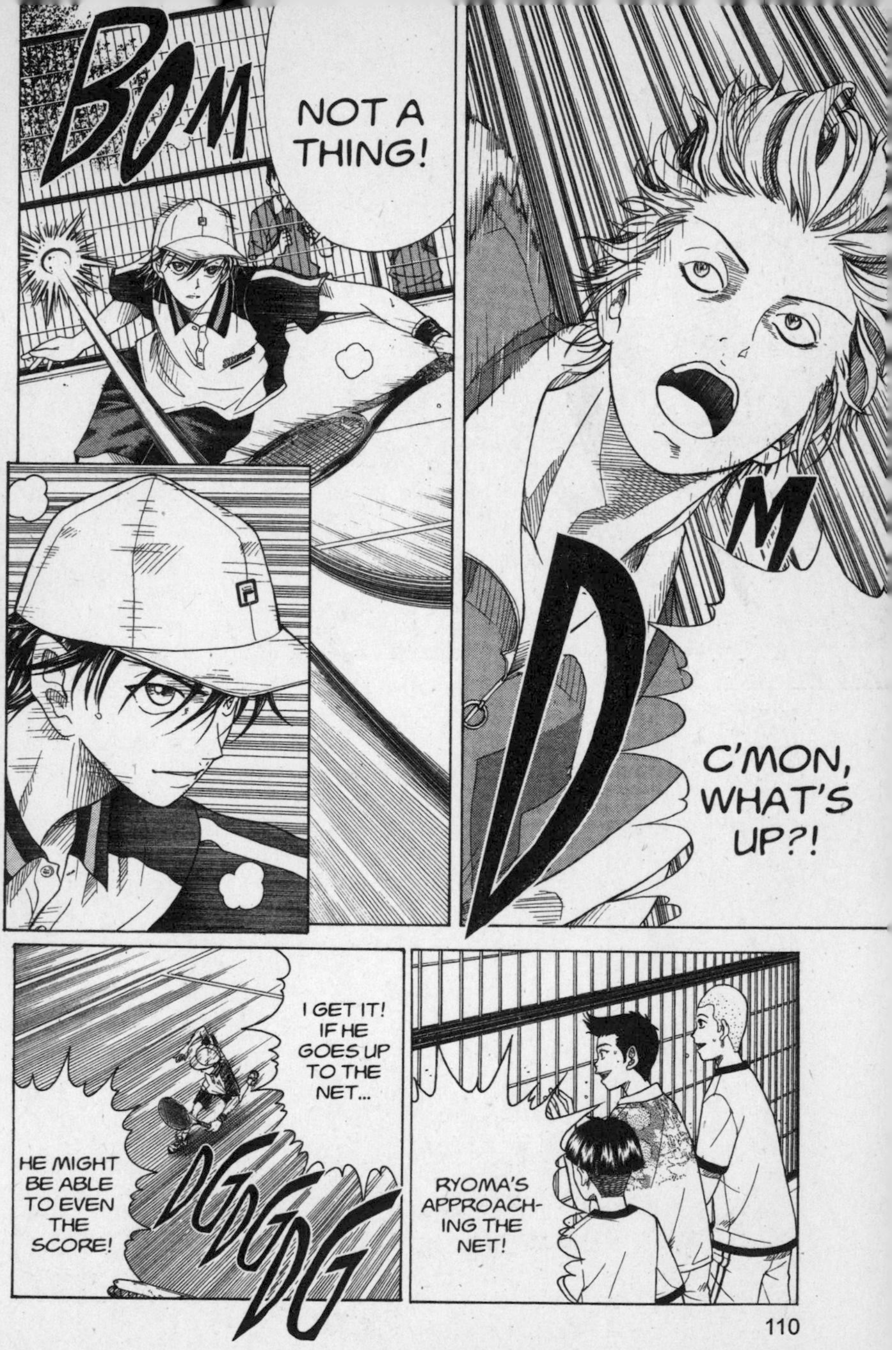
DM
C'MON, WHAT'S UP?!
BOM
NOT A THING!
RYOMA'S APPROACH-ING THE NET!
I GET IT! IF HE GOES UP TO THE NET...
HE MIGHT BE ABLE TO EVEN THE SCORE!
DGDGDG

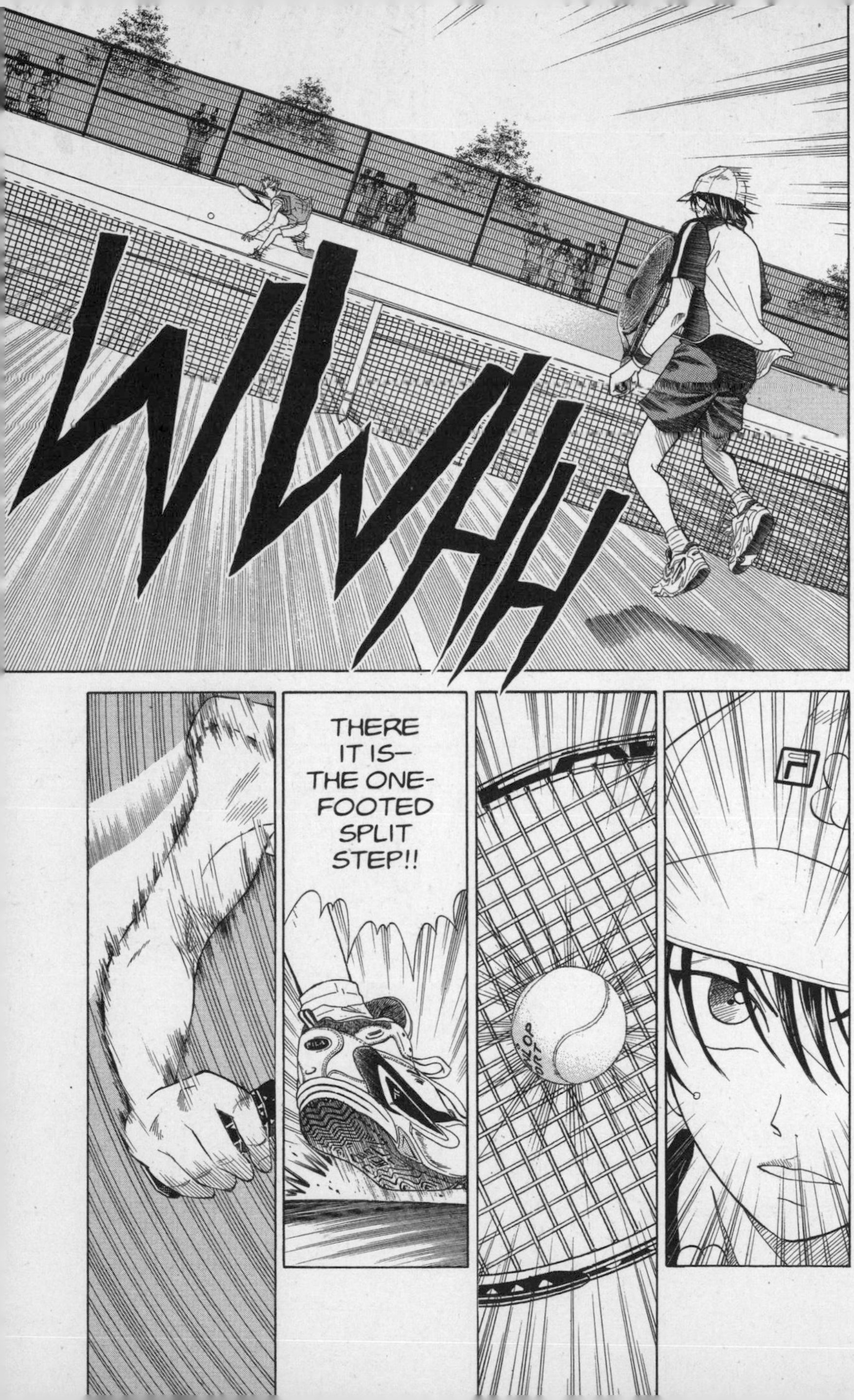
WWAHH
THERE IT IS— THE ONE-FOOTED SPLIT STEP!!

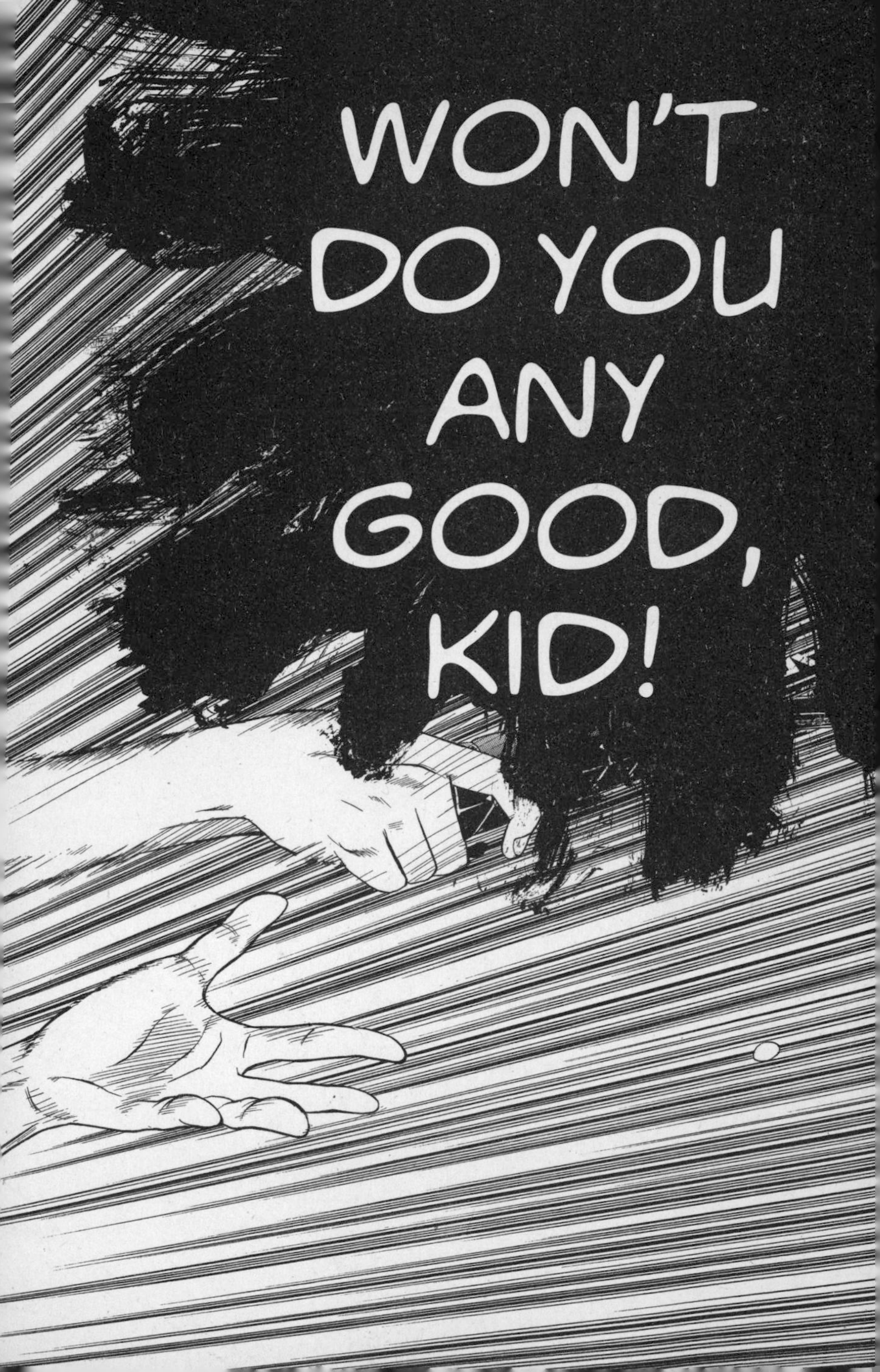
WON'T DO YOU ANY GOOD, KID!

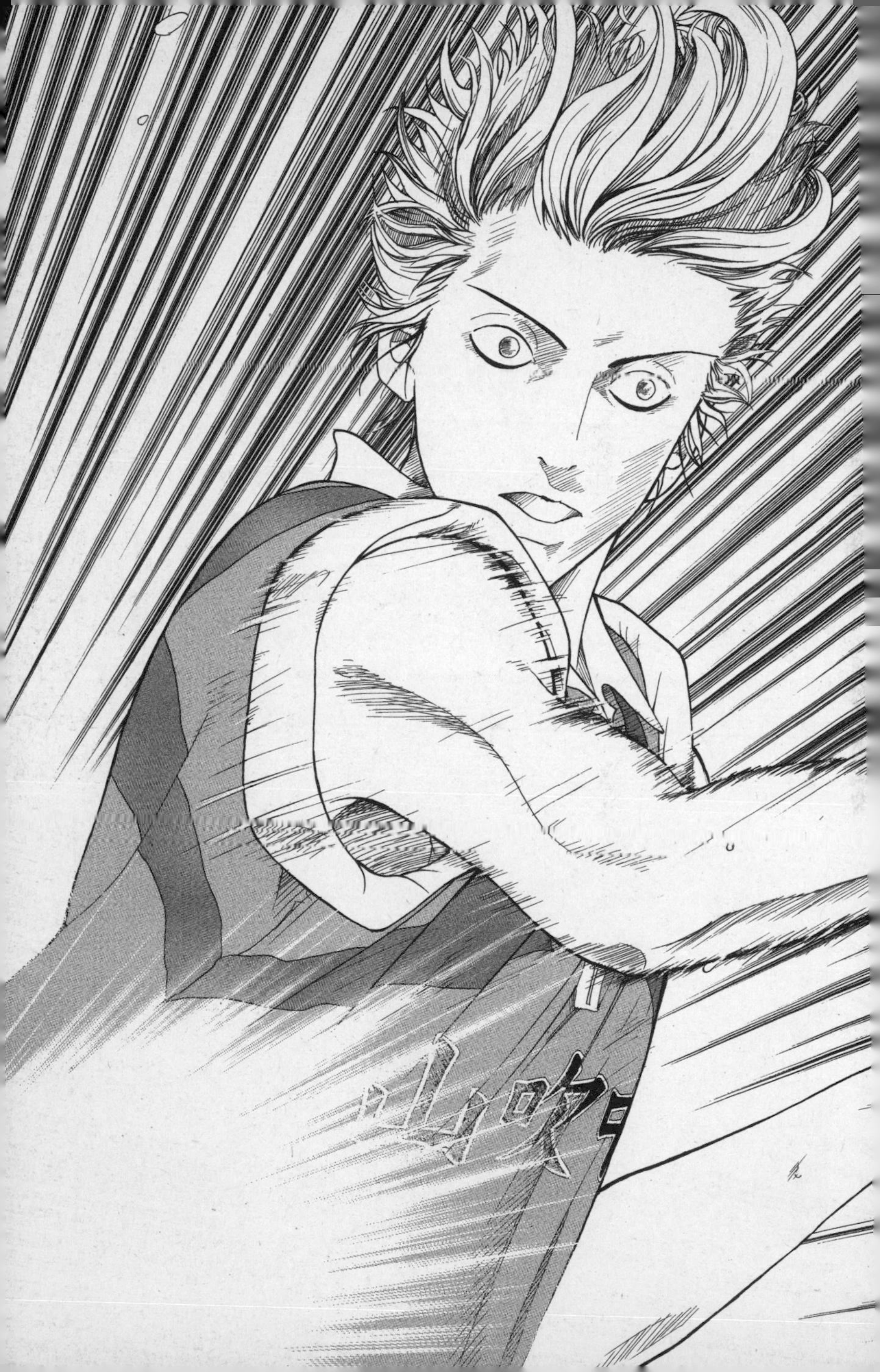

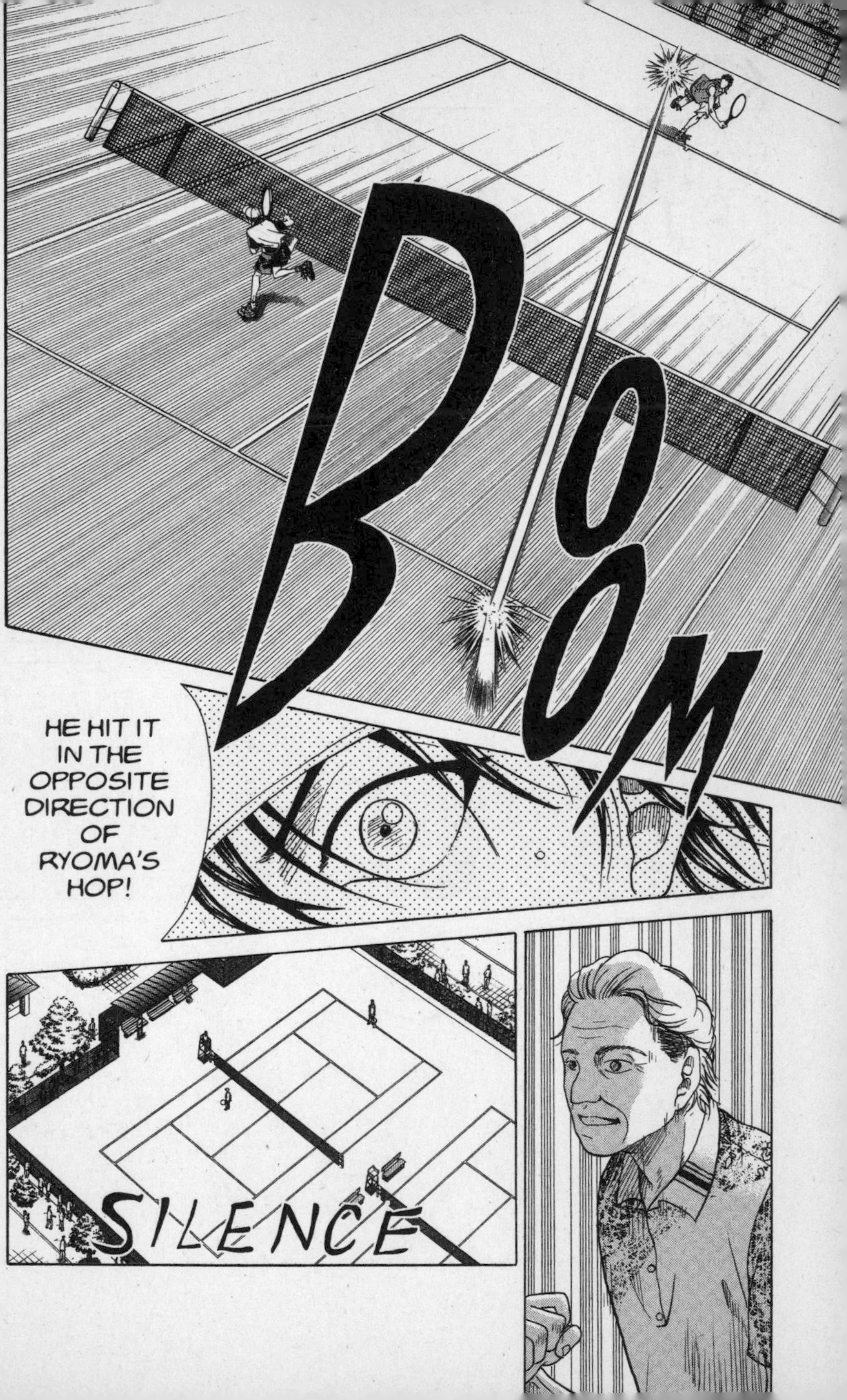
BOOM
HE HIT IT IN THE OPPOSITE DIRECTION OF RYOMA'S HOP!
SILENCE

READ THIS WAY

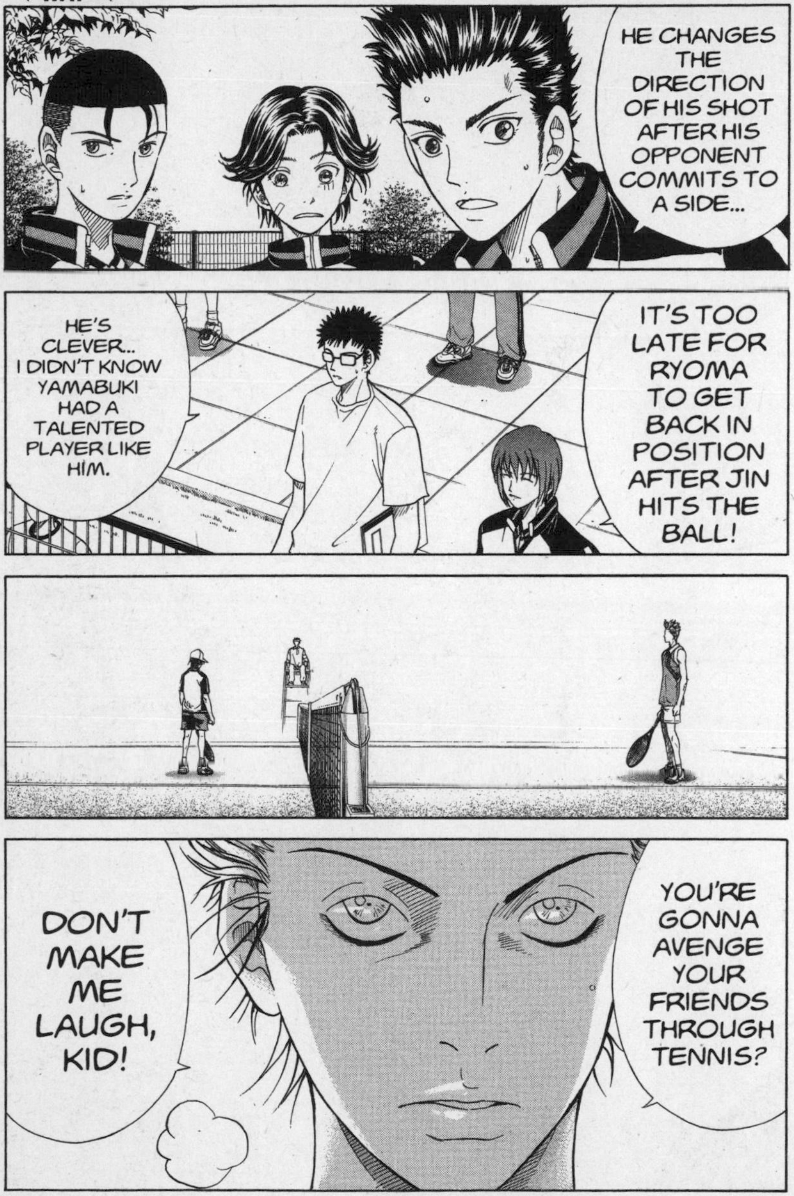
HE CHANGES THE DIRECTION OF HIS SHOT AFTER HIS OPPONENT COMMITS TO A SIDE...
IT'S TOO LATE FOR RYOMA TO GET BACK IN POSITION AFTER JIN HITS THE BALL!
HE'S CLEVER... I DIDN'T KNOW YAMABUKI HAD A TALENTED PLAYER LIKE HIM.
YOU'RE GONNA AVENGE YOUR FRIENDS THROUGH TENNIS?
DON'T MAKE ME LAUGH, KID!

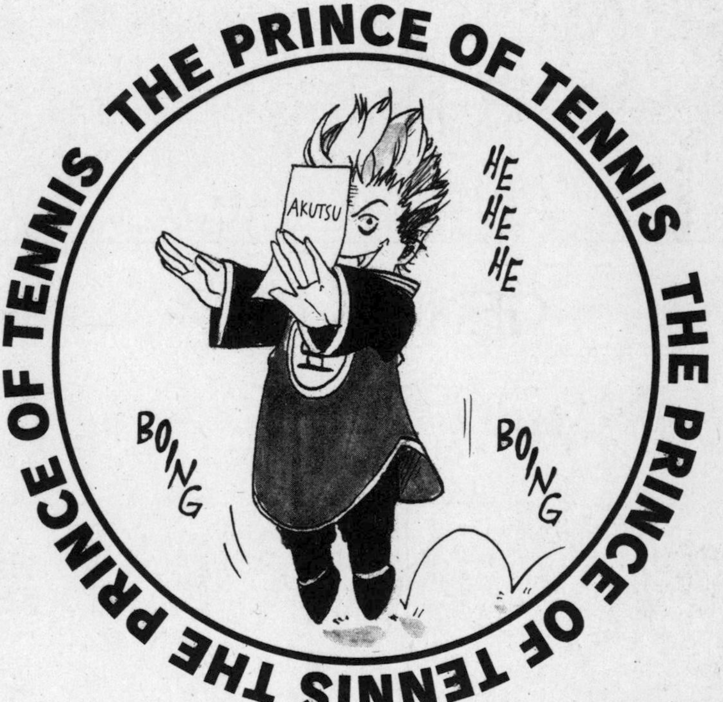
THE PRINCE OF TENNIS THE PRINCE OF TENNIS THE PRINCE OF TENNIS
AKUTSU
HE HE HE HE HE HE
BOING
BOING

5TH MATCH— NO. 1 SINGLES	4TH MATCH— NO. 2 SINGLES	3RD MATCH— NO. 3 SINGLES	2ND MATCH— NO. 1 DOUBLES		1ST MATCH— NO. 2 DOUBLES	
KUNIMITSU TEZUKA (9TH GRADE) BLOOD TYPE: O	RYOMA ECHIZEN (7TH GRADE) BLOOD TYPE: O	TAKESHI MOMOSHIRO (8TH GRADE) BLOOD TYPE: O	SHUICHIRO OISHI (9TH GRADE) BLOOD TYPE: O	EIJI KIKUMARU (9TH GRADE) BLOOD TYPE: A	SHUSUKE FUJI (9TH GRADE) BLOOD TYPE: B	TAKASHI KAWAMURA (9TH GRADE) BLOOD TYPE: A

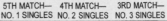

GENIUS 103:

INVINCIBLE MAN

TOJI MUROMACHI (8TH GRADE) BLOOD TYPE: AB	JIN AKUTSU (9TH GRADE) BLOOD TYPE: B	KIYOSUMI SENGOKU (9TH GRADE) BLOOD TYPE: O	MASAMI HIGASHIKATA (9TH GRADE) BLOOD TYPE: A	KENTARO MINAMI (9TH GRADE) BLOOD TYPE: A	ICHIUMA KITA (8TH GRADE) BLOOD TYPE: O	INAKICHI NITO (9TH GRADE) BLOOD TYPE: A

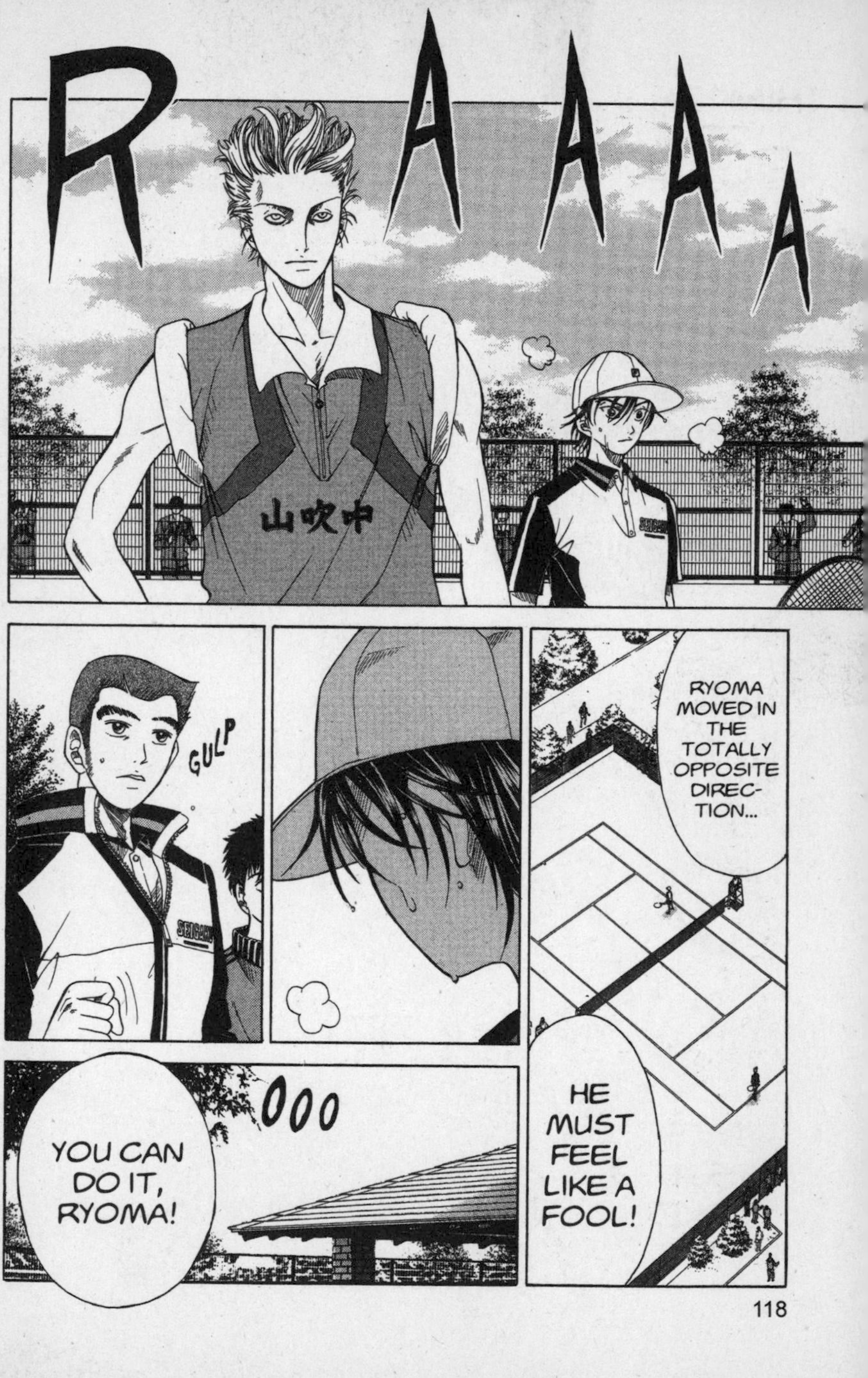
RAAAA
山吹中
RYOMA MOVED IN THE TOTALLY OPPOSITE DIREC-TION...
HE MUST FEEL LIKE A FOOL!
GULP
OOO
YOU CAN DO IT, RYOMA!

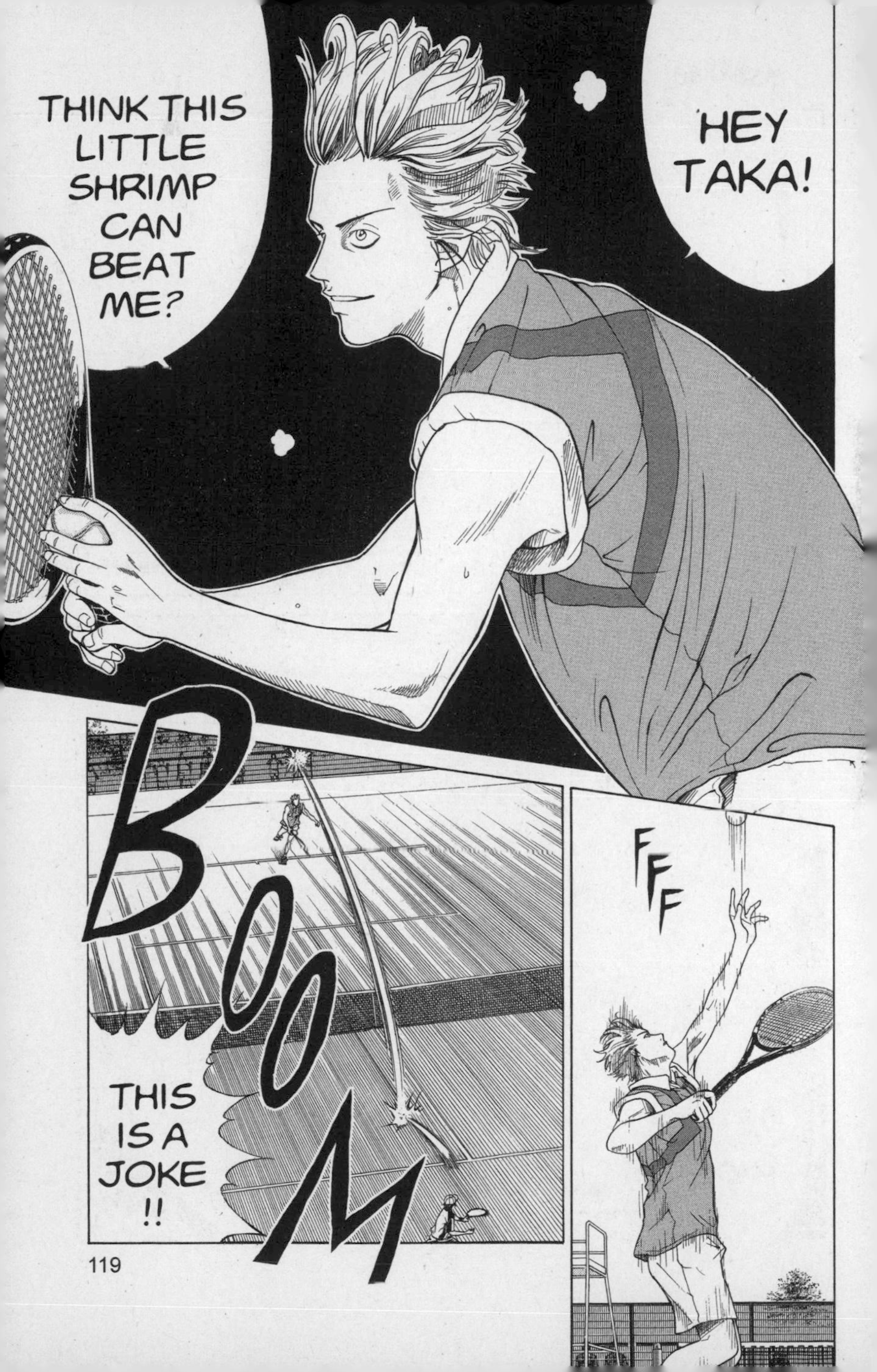
HEY TAKA!
THINK THIS LITTLE SHRIMP CAN BEAT ME?
FFF
BOOM
THIS IS A JOKE !!

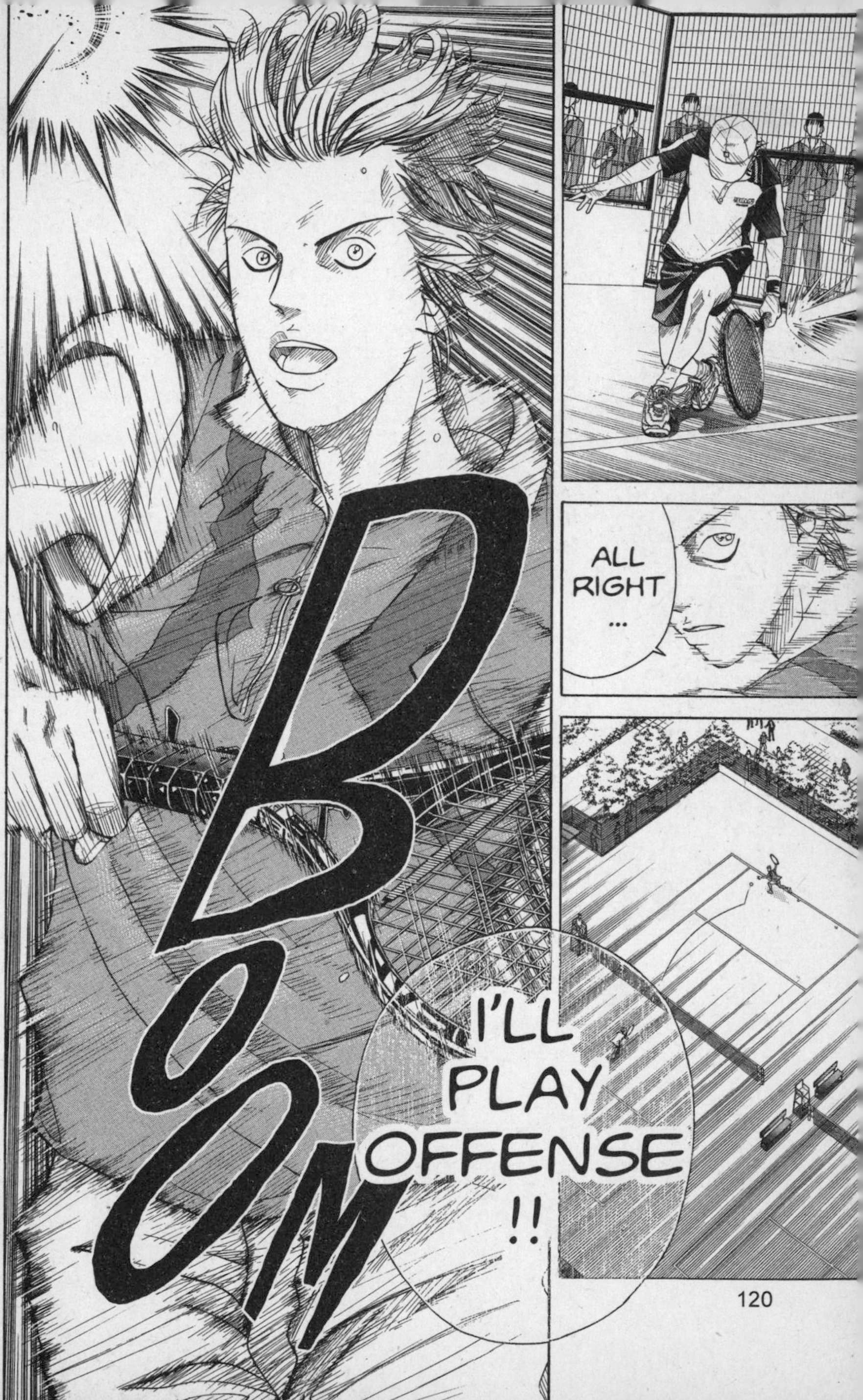
ALL RIGHT ...
I'LL PLAY OFFENSE !!
BOOM

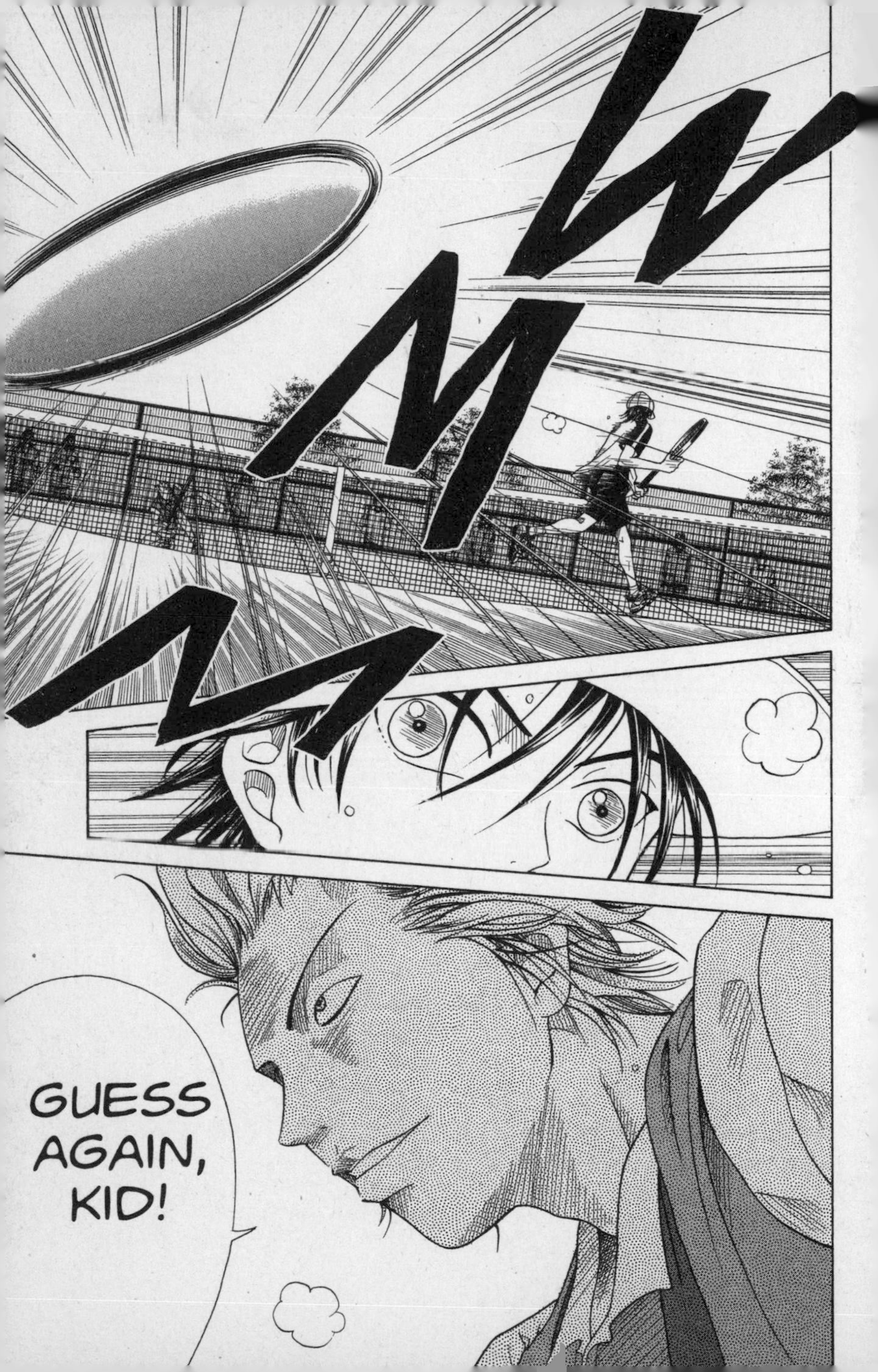
WMM
GUESS AGAIN, KID!

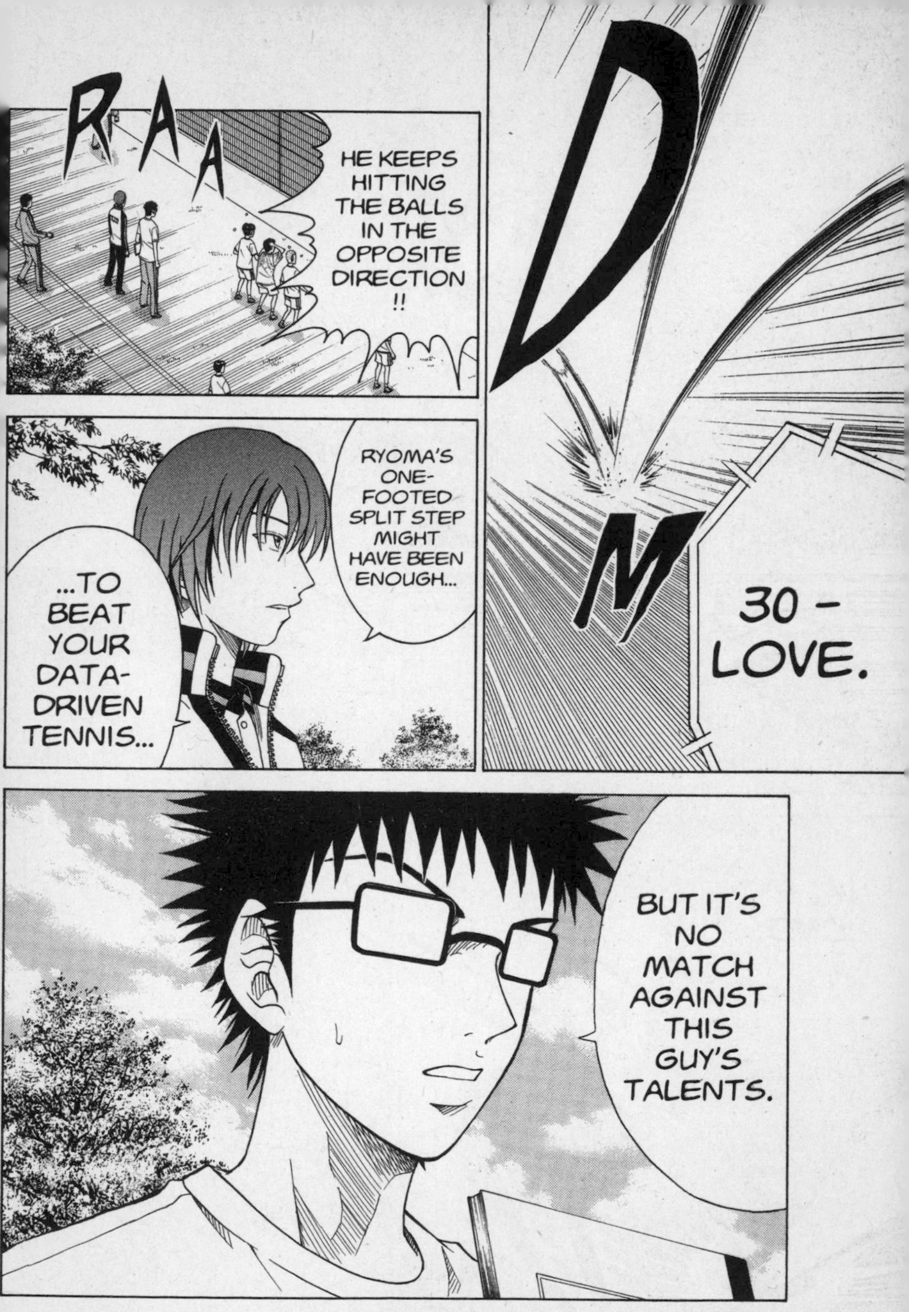
DM
30 - LOVE.
RAA
HE KEEPS HITTING THE BALLS IN THE OPPOSITE DIRECTION !!
RYOMA'S ONE-FOOTED SPLIT STEP MIGHT HAVE BEEN ENOUGH...
...TO BEAT YOUR DATA-DRIVEN TENNIS...
BUT IT'S NO MATCH AGAINST THIS GUY'S TALENTS.

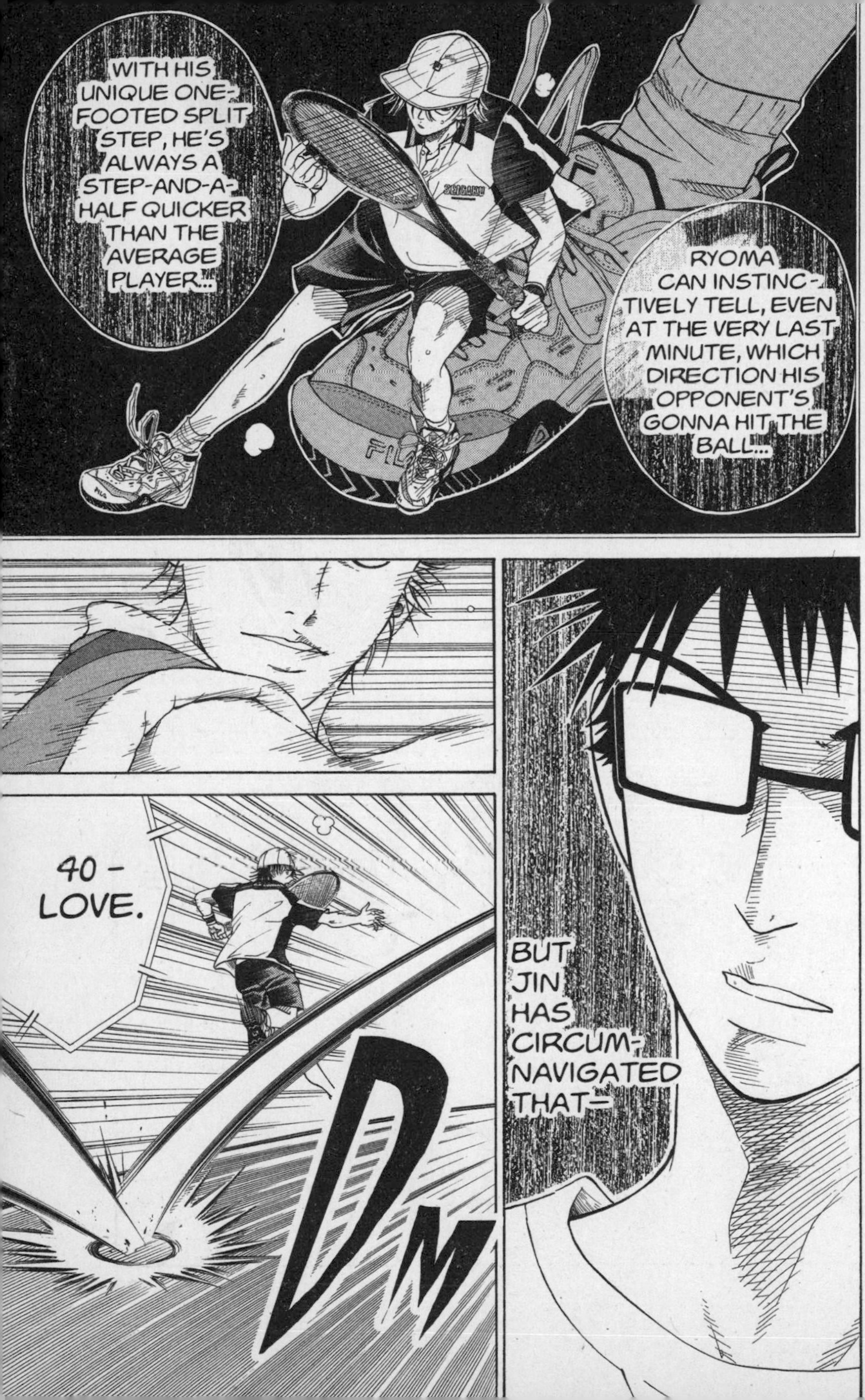
RYOMA CAN INSTINCTIVELY TELL, EVEN AT THE VERY LAST MINUTE, WHICH DIRECTION HIS OPPONENT'S GONNA HIT THE BALL...
WITH HIS UNIQUE ONE-FOOTED SPLIT STEP, HE'S ALWAYS A STEP-AND-A-HALF QUICKER THAN THE AVERAGE PLAYER...
SEIGAKU
FILA
BUT JIN HAS CIRCUMNAVIGATED THAT—
40 - LOVE.
DM

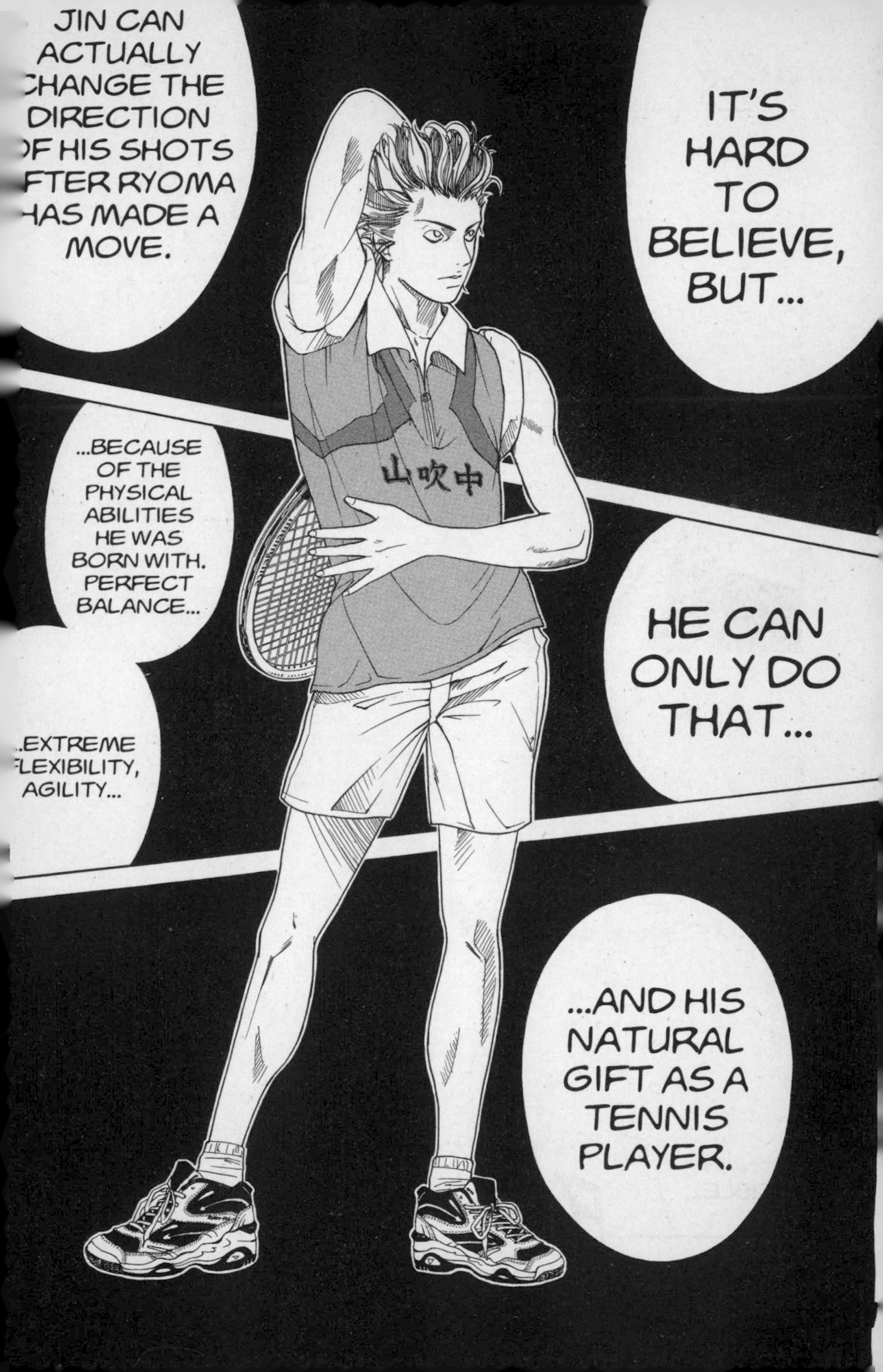
IT'S HARD TO BELIEVE, BUT...
JIN CAN ACTUALLY CHANGE THE DIRECTION OF HIS SHOTS AFTER RYOMA HAS MADE A MOVE.
HE CAN ONLY DO THAT...
...BECAUSE OF THE PHYSICAL ABILITIES HE WAS BORN WITH. PERFECT BALANCE...
山吹中
...EXTREME FLEXIBILITY, AGILITY...
...AND HIS NATURAL GIFT AS A TENNIS PLAYER.

READ THIS WAY

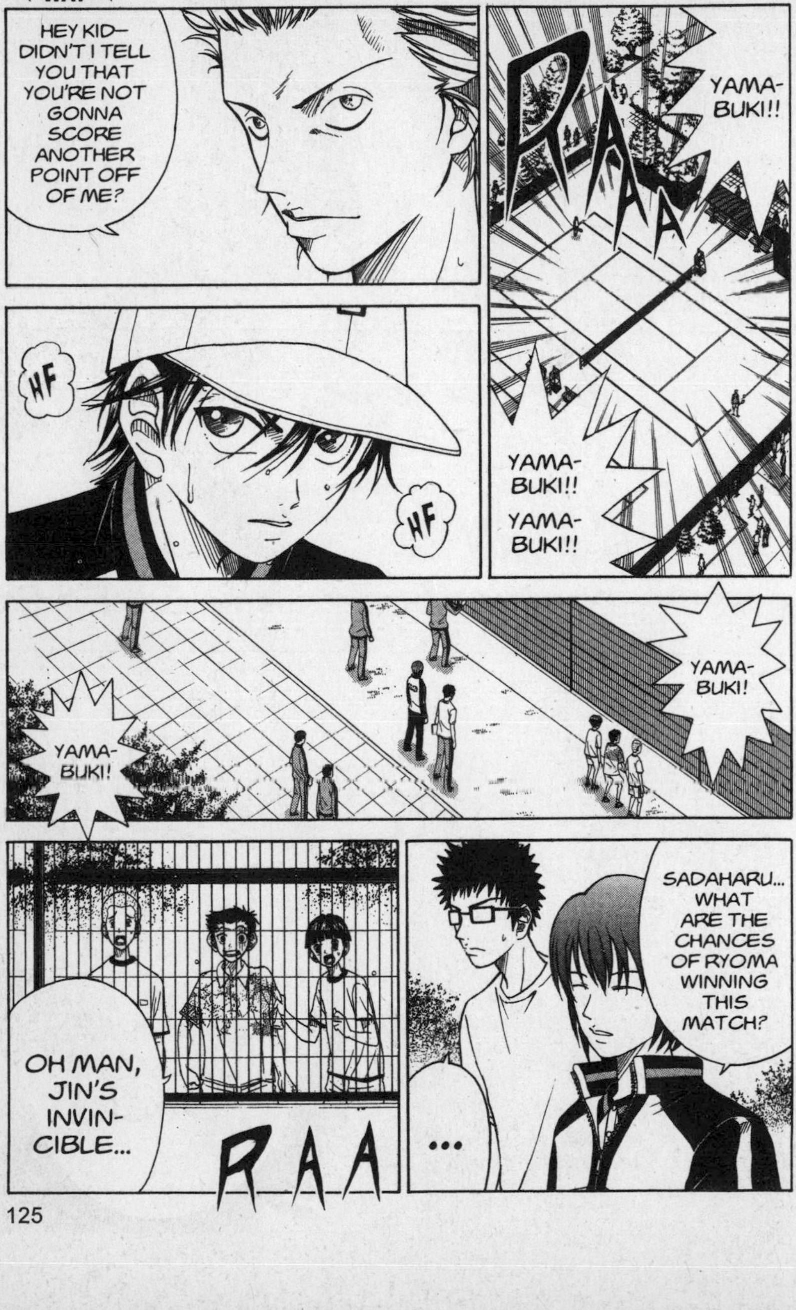

RAA
YAMA-BUKI!!
YAMA-BUKI!!
YAMA-BUKI!!
HEY KID-DIDN'T I TELL YOU THAT YOU'RE NOT GONNA SCORE ANOTHER POINT OFF OF ME?
HF
HF
YAMA-BUKI!
YAMA-BUKI!
SADAHARU... WHAT ARE THE CHANCES OF RYOMA WINNING THIS MATCH?
...
RAA
OH MAN, JIN'S INVINCIBLE...

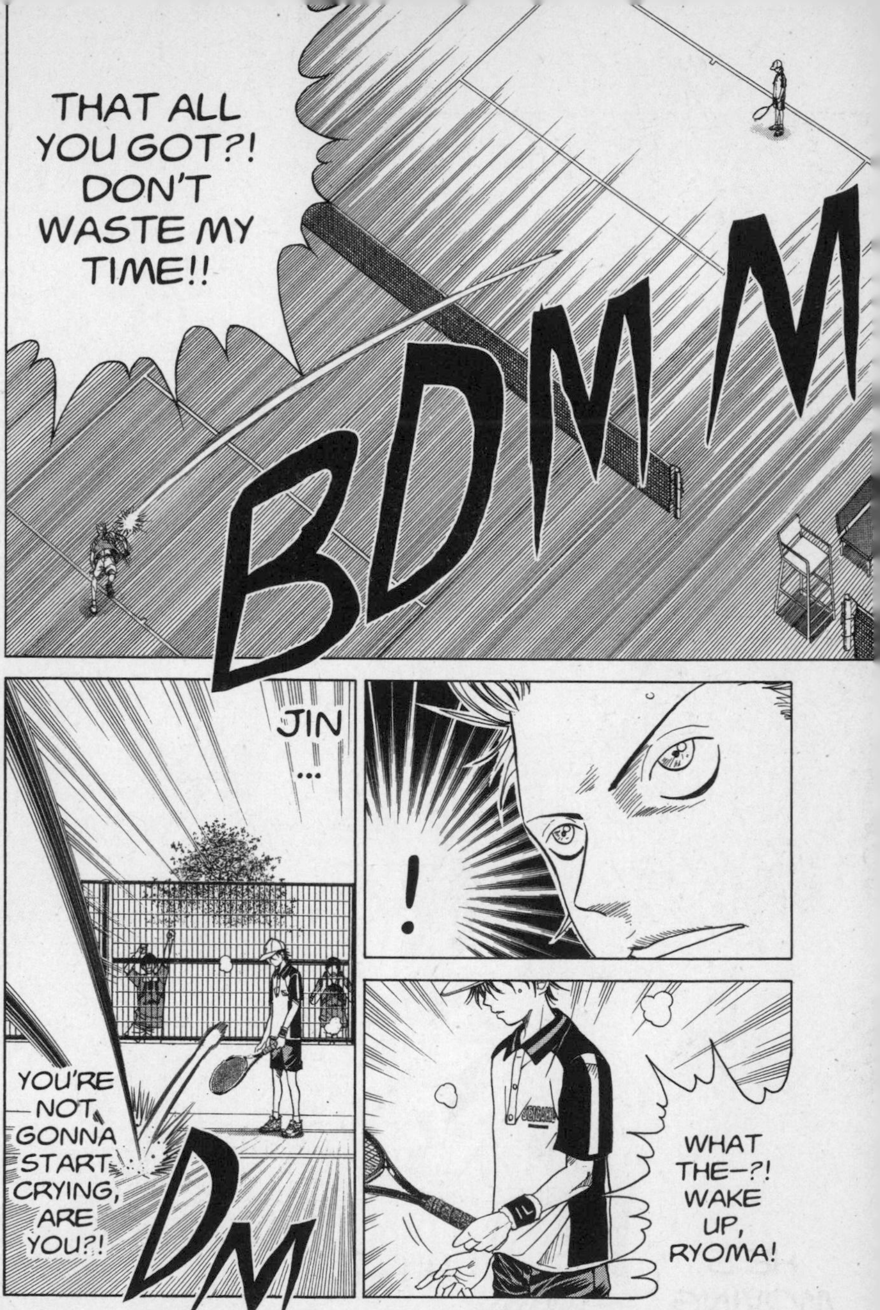
THAT ALL YOU GOT?! DON'T WASTE MY TIME!!
BDMM
!
WHAT THE–?! WAKE UP, RYOMA!
JIN ...
YOU'RE NOT GONNA START CRYING, ARE YOU?!
DM

READ THIS WAY

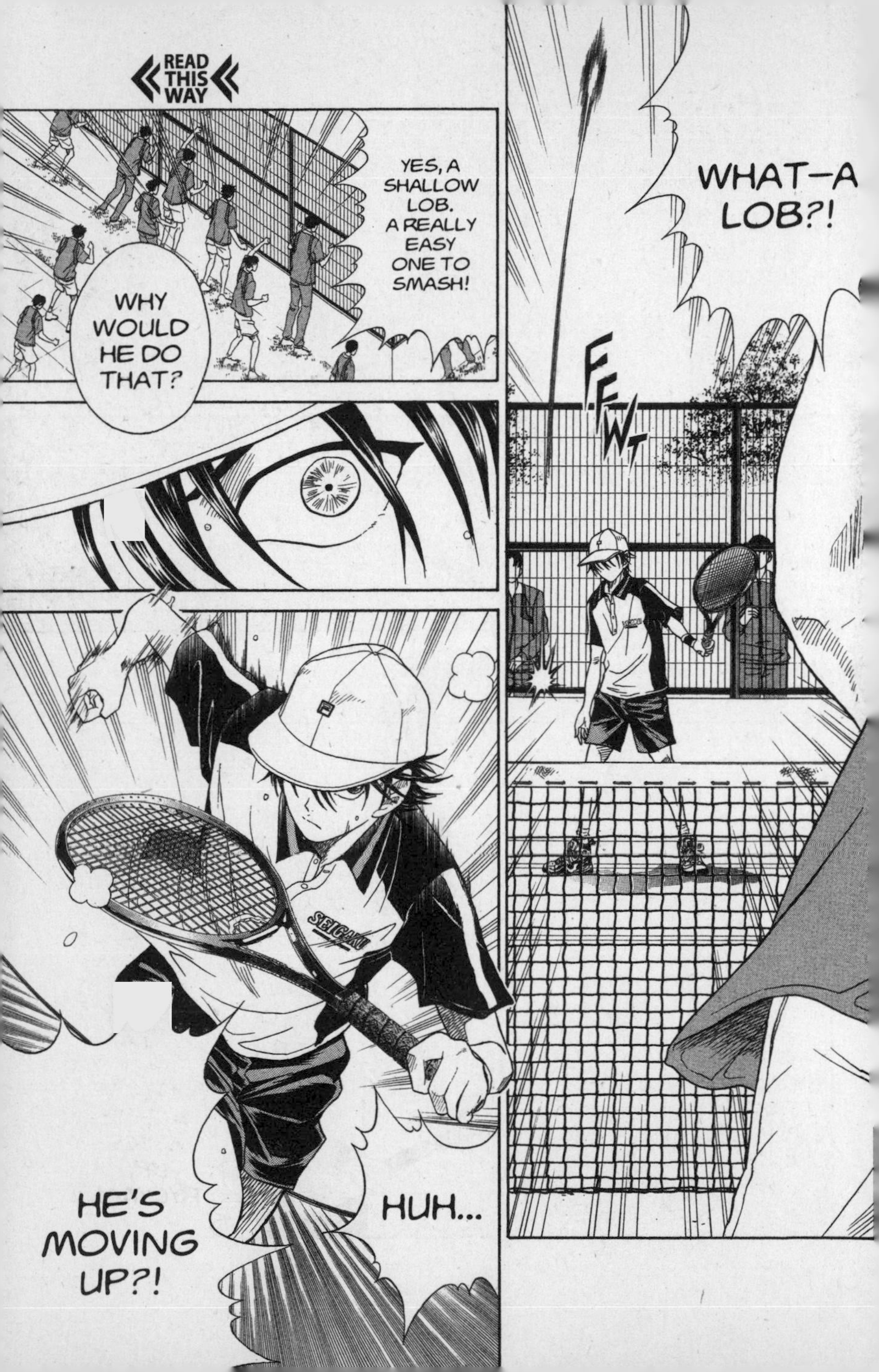
WHAT—A LOB?!
FFWT
YES, A SHALLOW LOB. A REALLY EASY ONE TO SMASH!
WHY WOULD HE DO THAT?
HUH...
HE'S MOVING UP?!

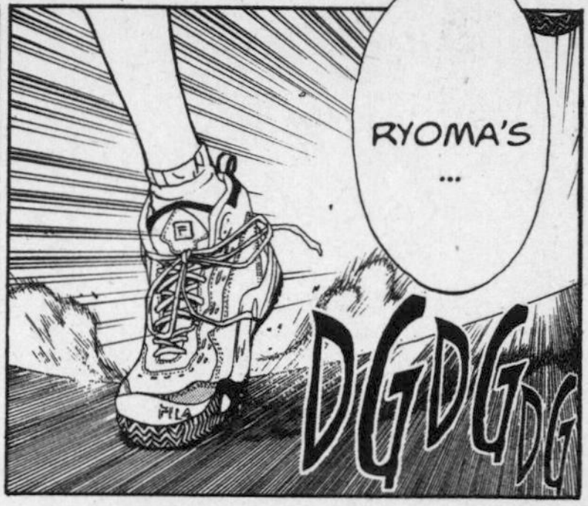
RYOMA'S ...
DGDGDG
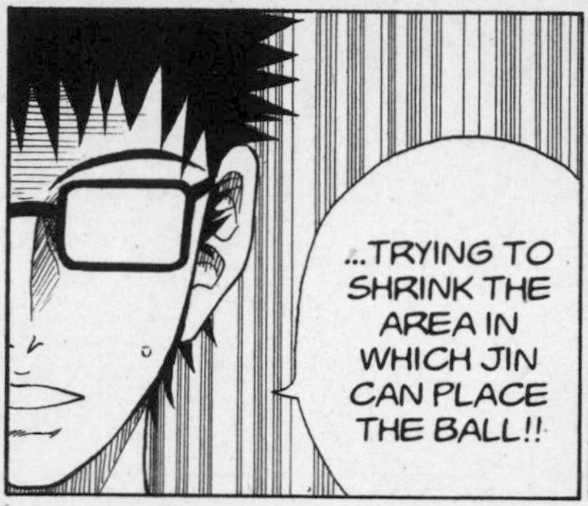
...TRYING TO SHRINK THE AREA IN WHICH JIN CAN PLACE THE BALL!!
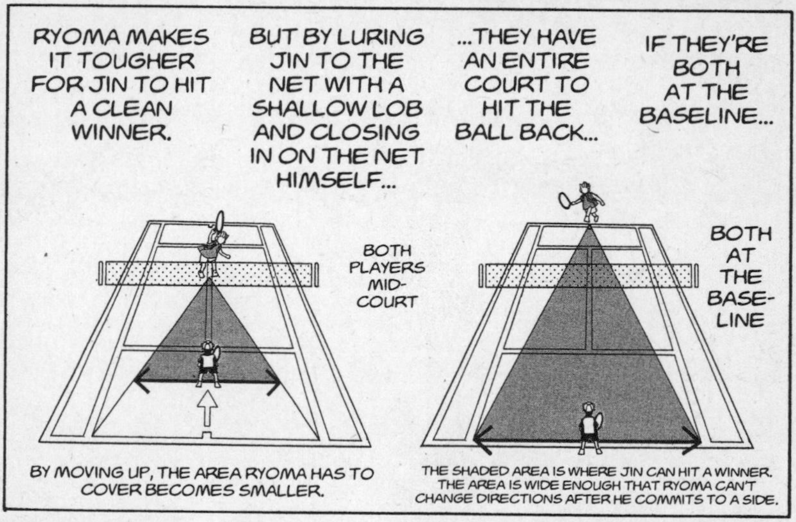
IF THEY'RE BOTH AT THE BASELINE...
...THEY HAVE AN ENTIRE COURT TO HIT THE BALL BACK...
BUT BY LURING JIN TO THE NET WITH A SHALLOW LOB AND CLOSING IN ON THE NET HIMSELF...
RYOMA MAKES IT TOUGHER FOR JIN TO HIT A CLEAN WINNER.
BOTH AT THE BASE-LINE
THE SHADED AREA IS WHERE JIN CAN HIT A WINNER. THE AREA IS WIDE ENOUGH THAT RYOMA CAN'T CHANGE DIRECTIONS AFTER HE COMMITS TO A SIDE.
BOTH PLAYERS MID-COURT
BY MOVING UP, THE AREA RYOMA HAS TO COVER BECOMES SMALLER.
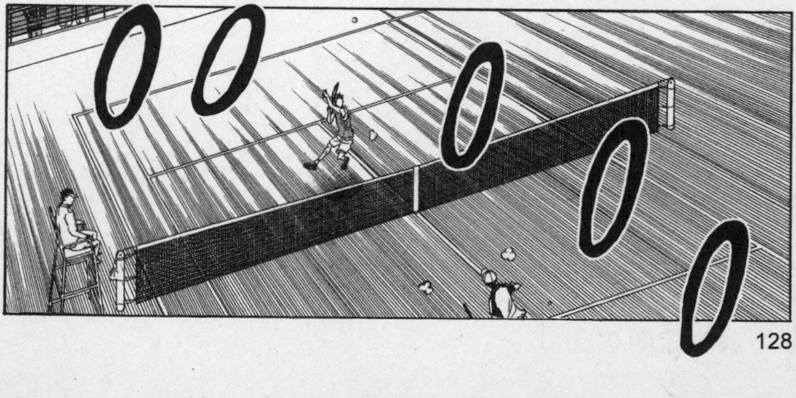

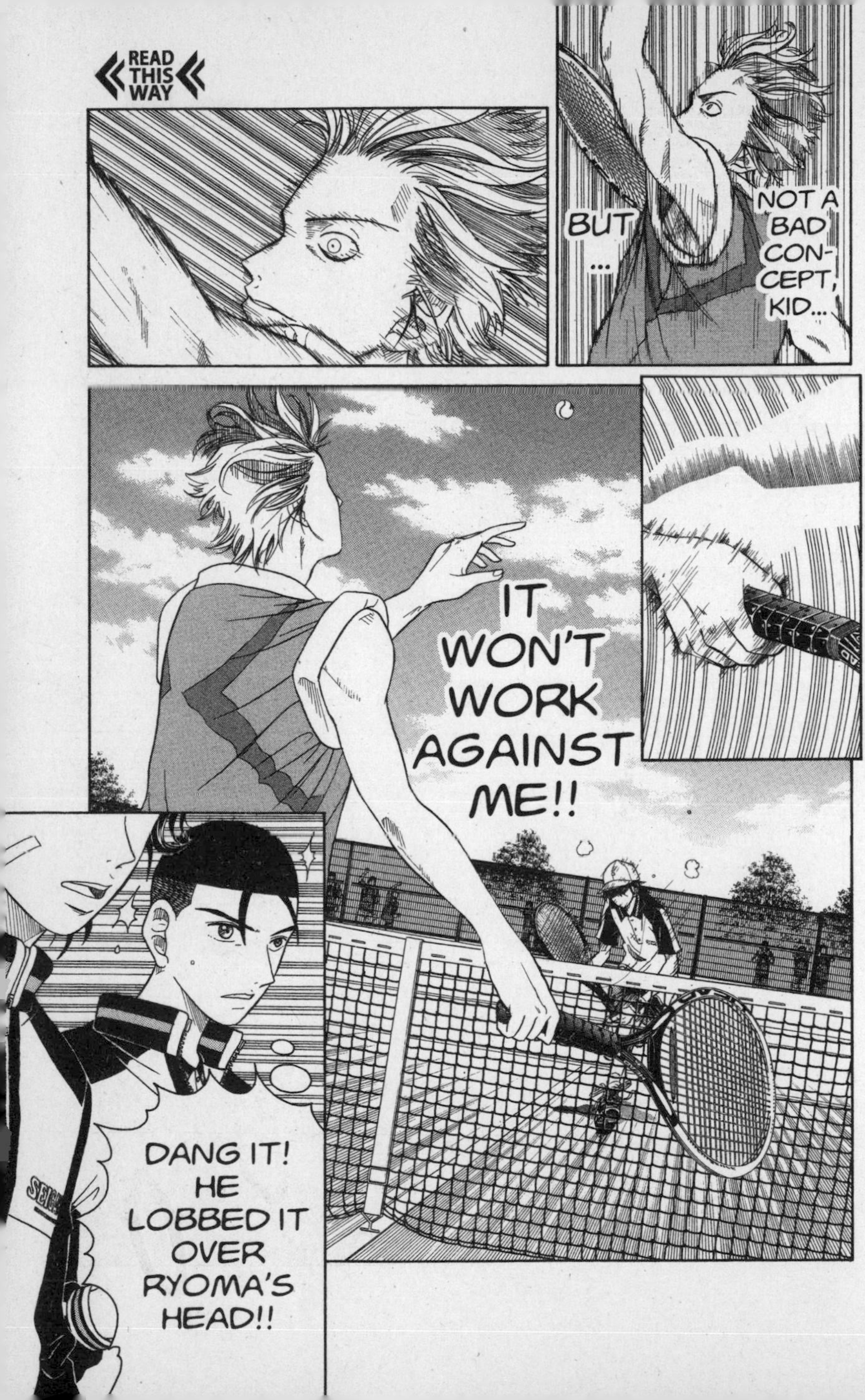
READ THIS WAY
NOT A BAD CON-CEPT, KID...
BUT ...
IT WON'T WORK AGAINST ME!!
DANG IT! HE LOBBED IT OVER RYOMA'S HEAD!!

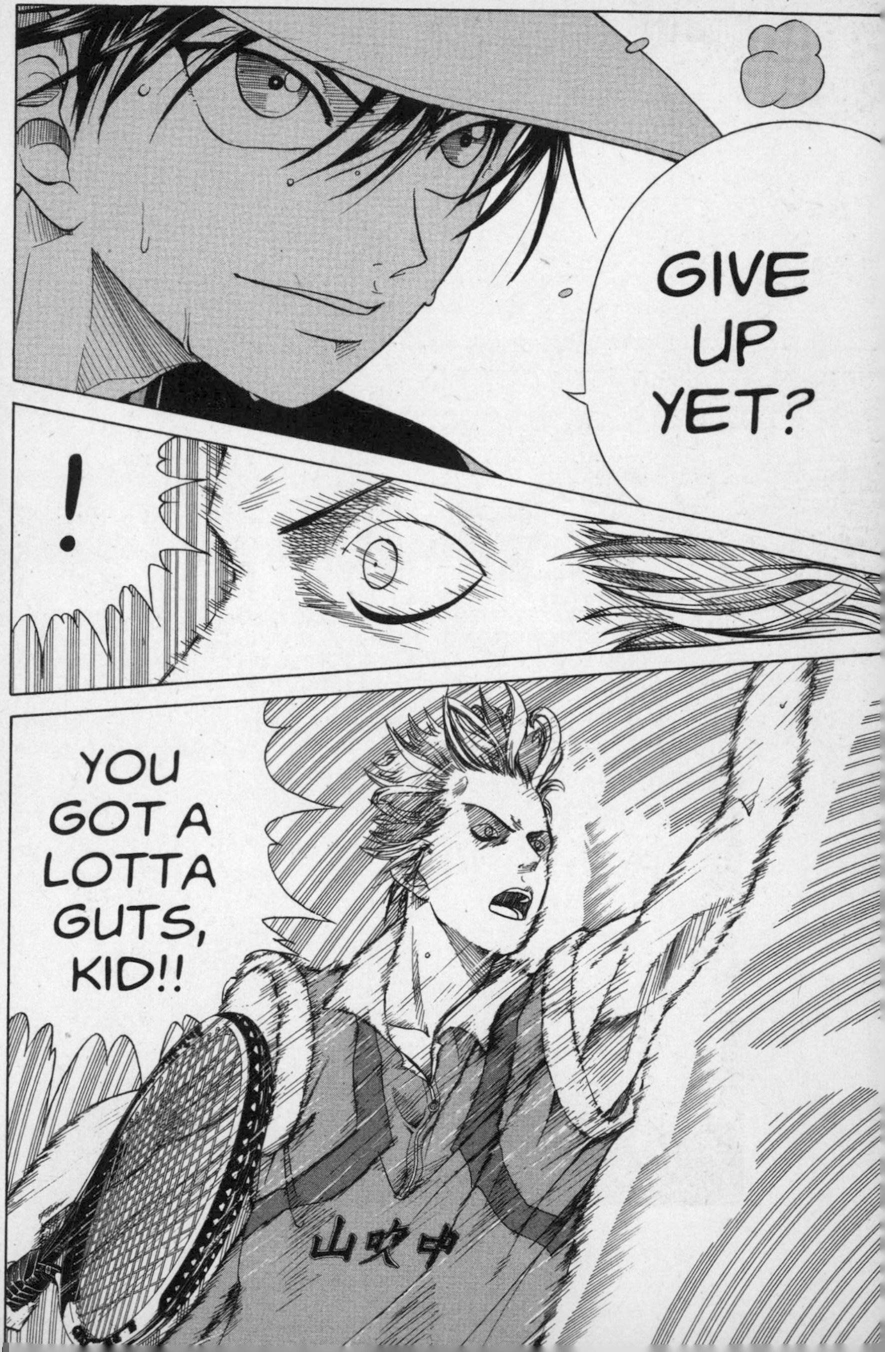
GIVE UP YET?
!
YOU GOT A LOTTA GUTS, KID!!
山吹中

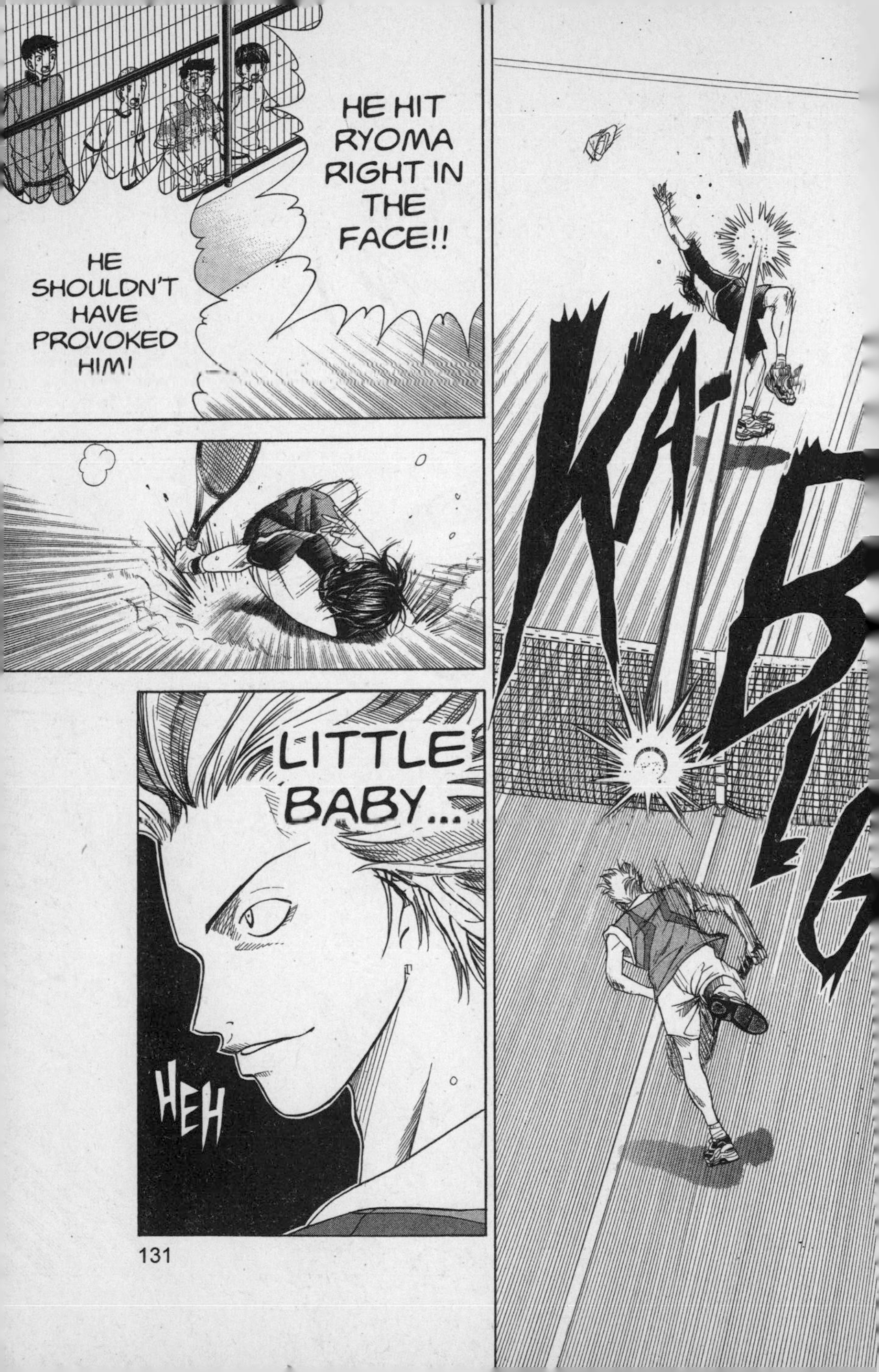
KA-BLG
HE HIT RYOMA RIGHT IN THE FACE!!
HE SHOULDN'T HAVE PROVOKED HIM!
LITTLE BABY...
HEH

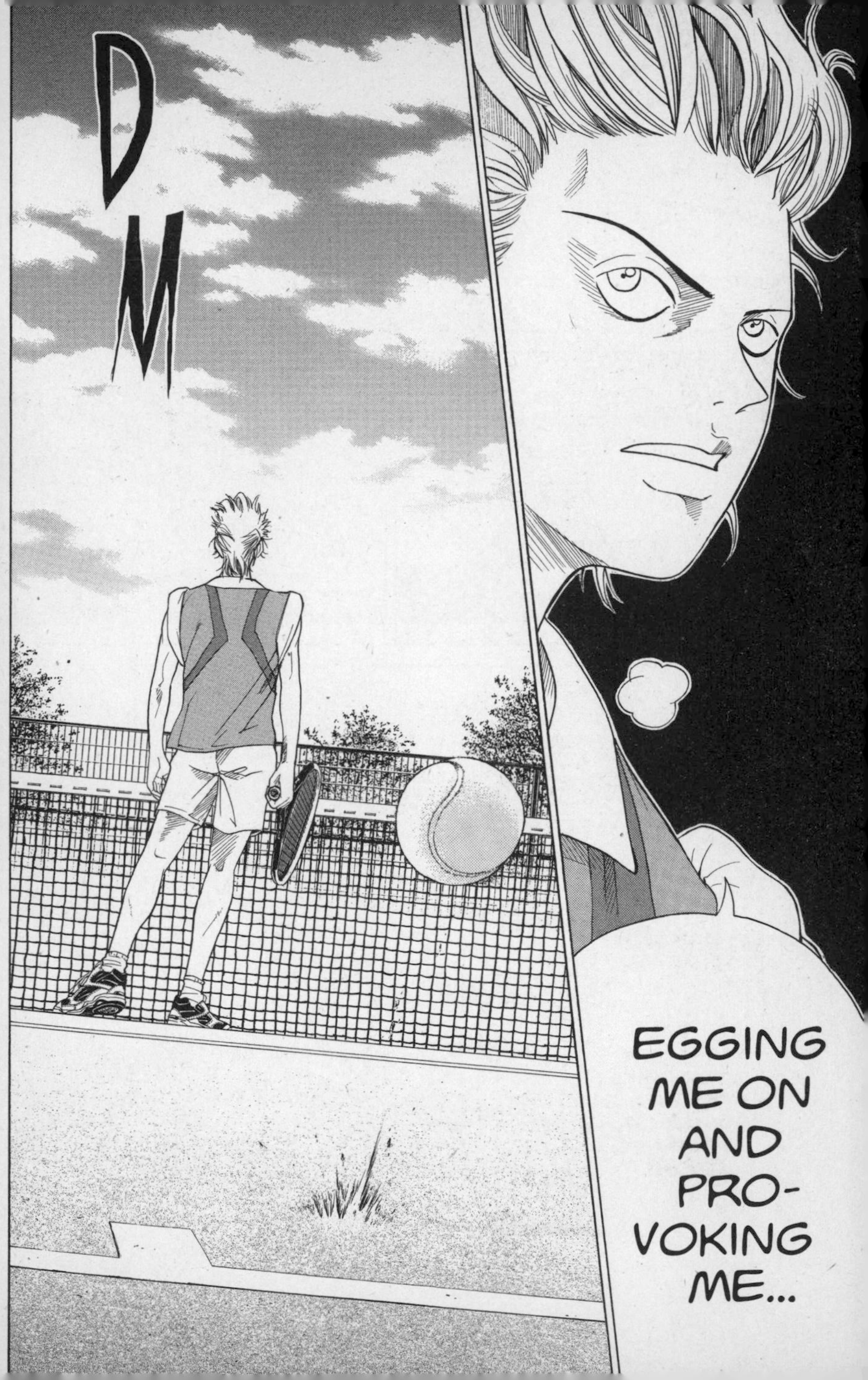
EGGING ME ON AND PRO-VOKING ME...
DM

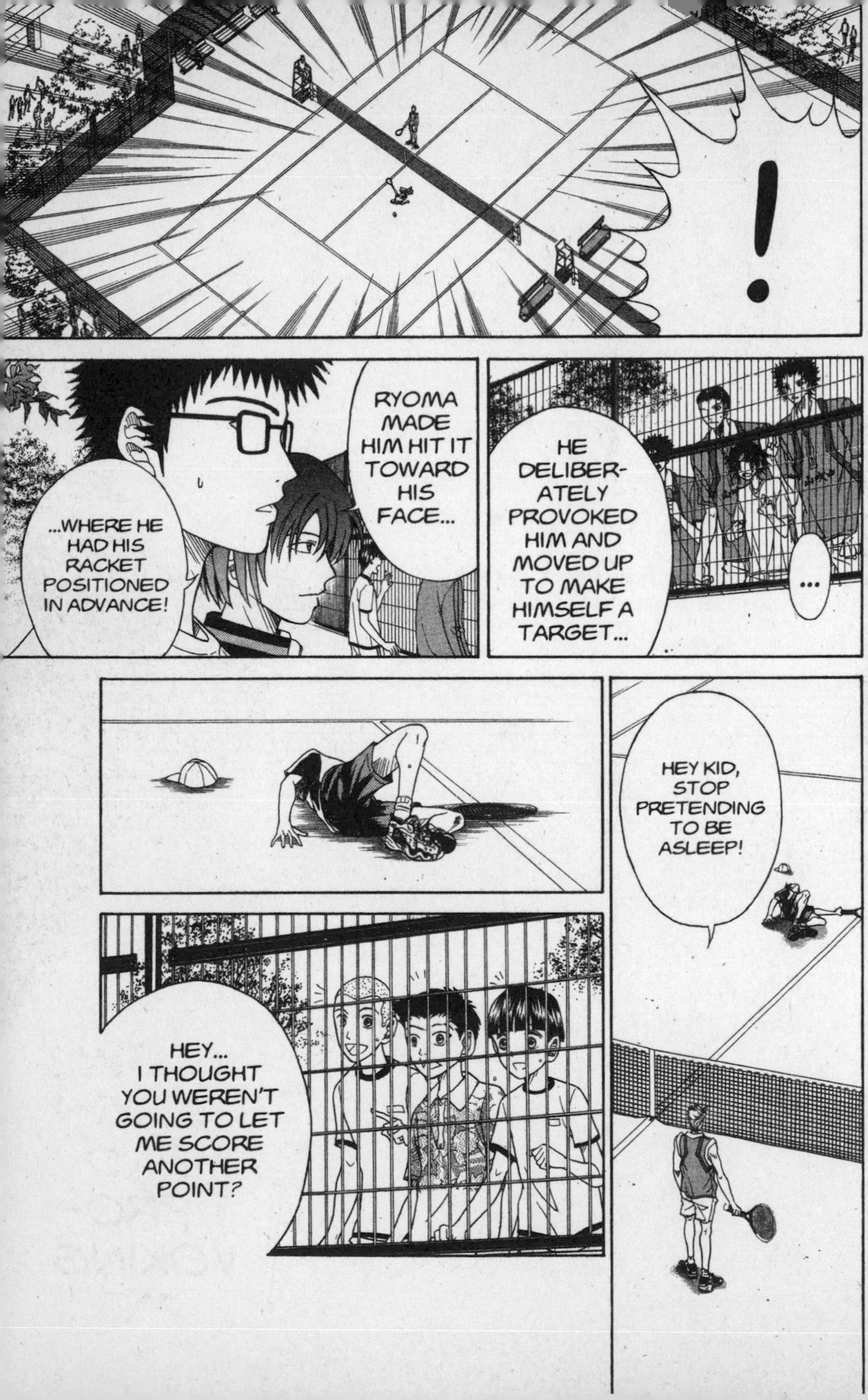
!
HE DELIBER-ATELY PROVOKED HIM AND MOVED UP TO MAKE HIMSELF A TARGET...
...
RYOMA MADE HIM HIT IT TOWARD HIS FACE...
...WHERE HE HAD HIS RACKET POSITIONED IN ADVANCE!
HEY KID, STOP PRETENDING TO BE ASLEEP!
HEY... I THOUGHT YOU WEREN'T GOING TO LET ME SCORE ANOTHER POINT?

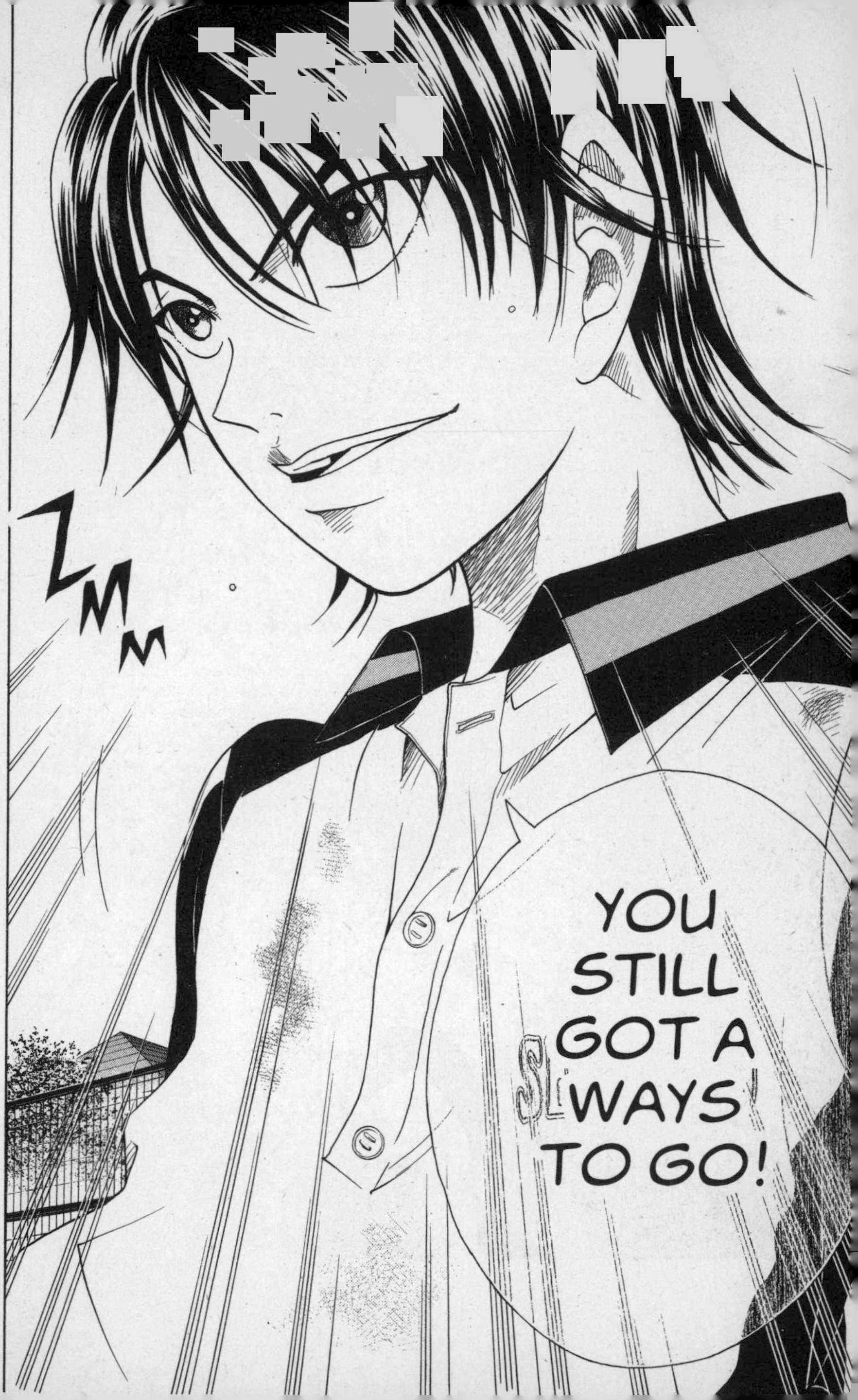
YOU STILL GOT A WAYS TO GO!
ZMm

READ THIS WAY

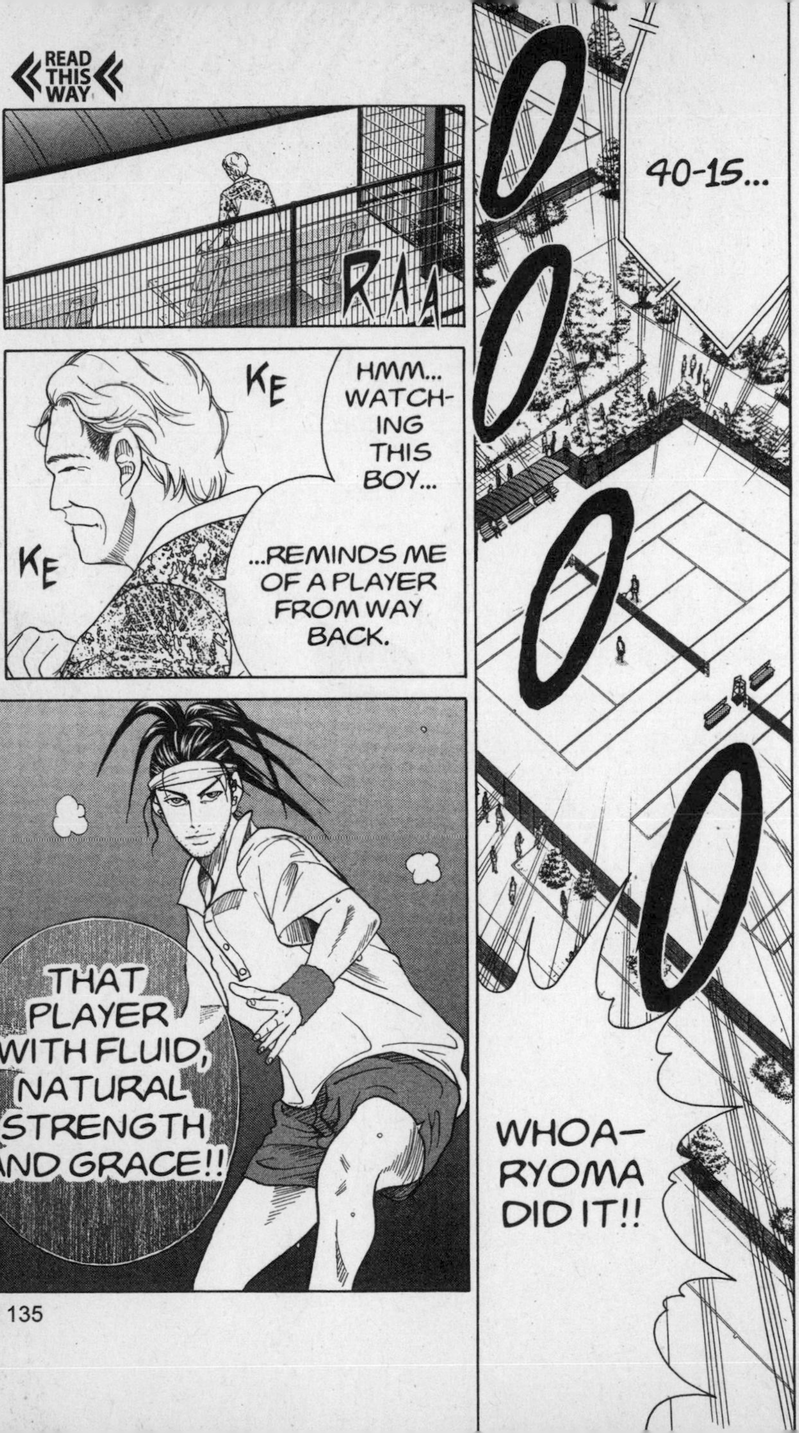
40-15...
OOOO
WHOA—RYOMA DID IT!!
RAA
KE
KE
HMM... WATCHING THIS BOY...
...REMINDS ME OF A PLAYER FROM WAY BACK.
THAT PLAYER WITH FLUID, NATURAL STRENGTH AND GRACE!!

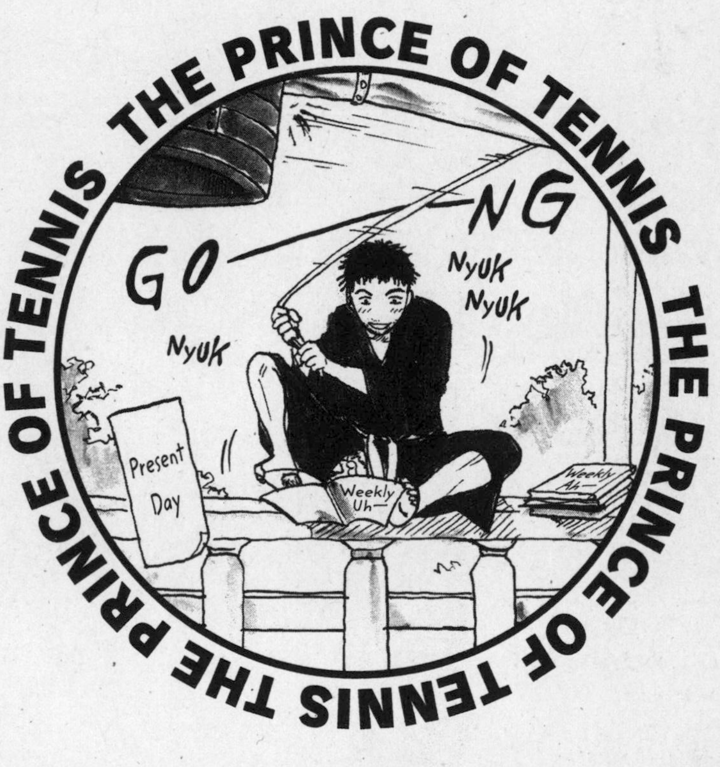
THE PRINCE OF TENNIS THE PRINCE OF TENNIS THE PRINCE OF TENNIS THE PRINCE OF TENNIS
GO—NG
Nyuk Nyuk
Nyuk
Nyuk
Present Day
Weekly Uh—
Weekly Ah—

GENIUS 104: STEPPINGSTONE

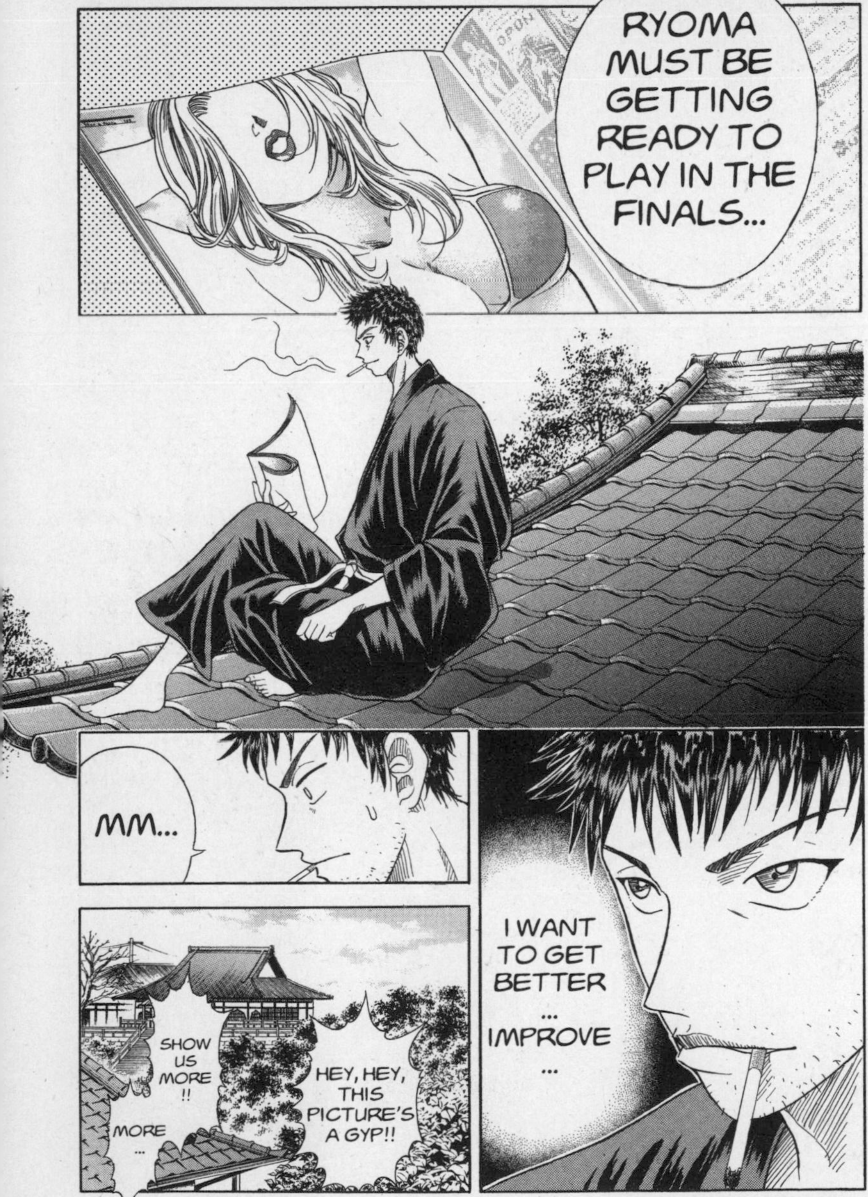
RYOMA MUST BE GETTING READY TO PLAY IN THE FINALS...
MM...
SHOW US MORE!!
MORE ...
HEY, HEY, THIS PICTURE'S A GYP!!
I WANT TO GET BETTER ... IMPROVE ...

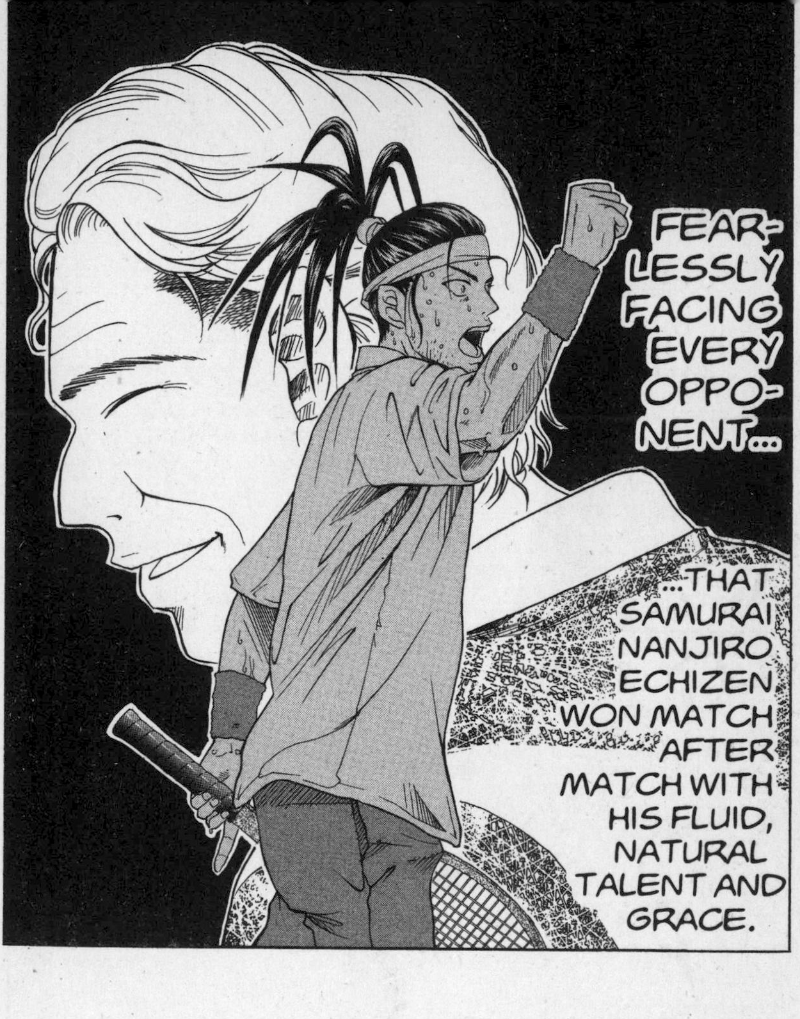
FEAR-
LESSLY
FACING
EVERY
OPPO-
NENT...
...THAT
SAMURAI
NANJIRO
ECHIZEN
WON MATCH
AFTER
MATCH WITH
HIS FLUID,
NATURAL
TALENT AND
GRACE.

GENIUS 104: STEPPINGSTONE

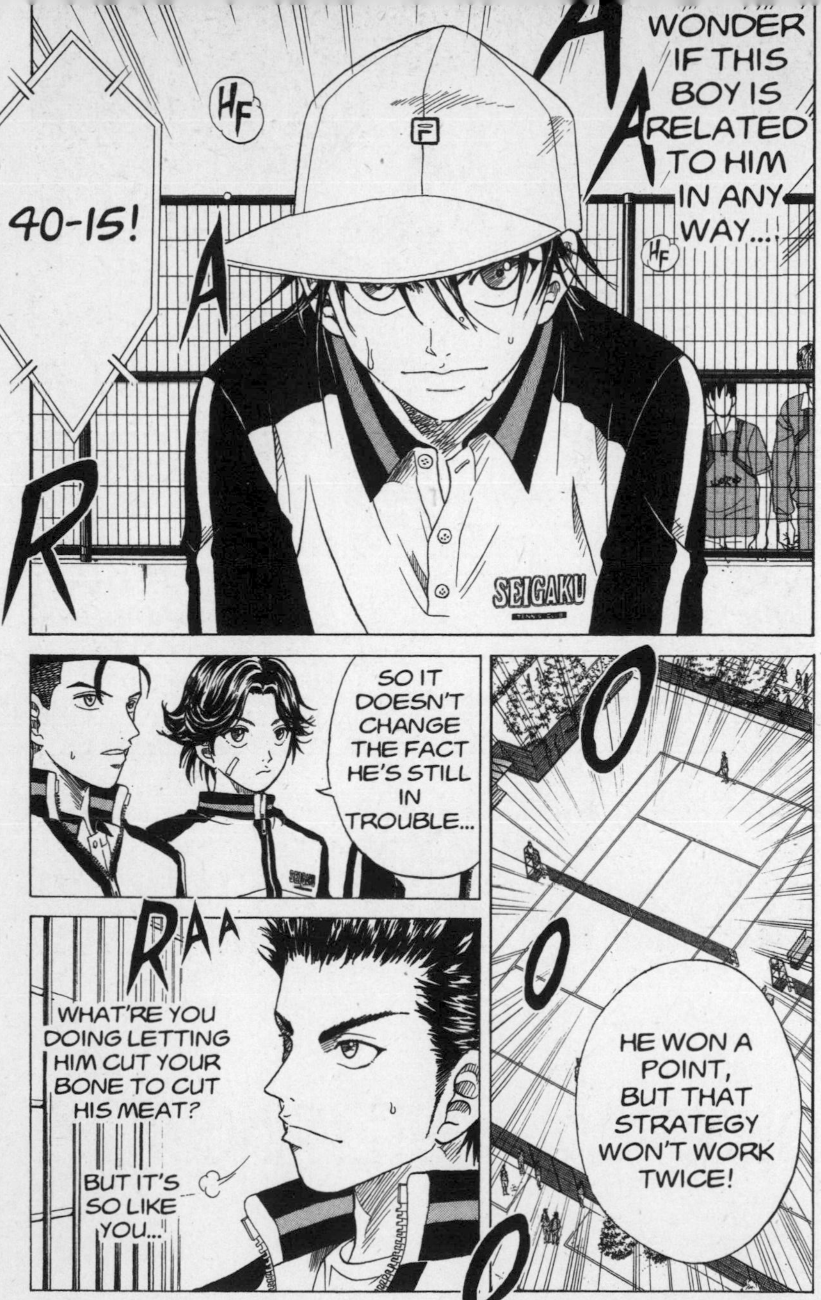
WONDER IF THIS BOY IS RELATED TO HIM IN ANY WAY...
HF
RAAA
40-15!
HF
OOO
HE WON A POINT, BUT THAT STRATEGY WON'T WORK TWICE!
SO IT DOESN'T CHANGE THE FACT HE'S STILL IN TROUBLE...
RAA
WHAT'RE YOU DOING LETTING HIM CUT YOUR BONE TO CUT HIS MEAT?
BUT IT'S SO LIKE YOU...

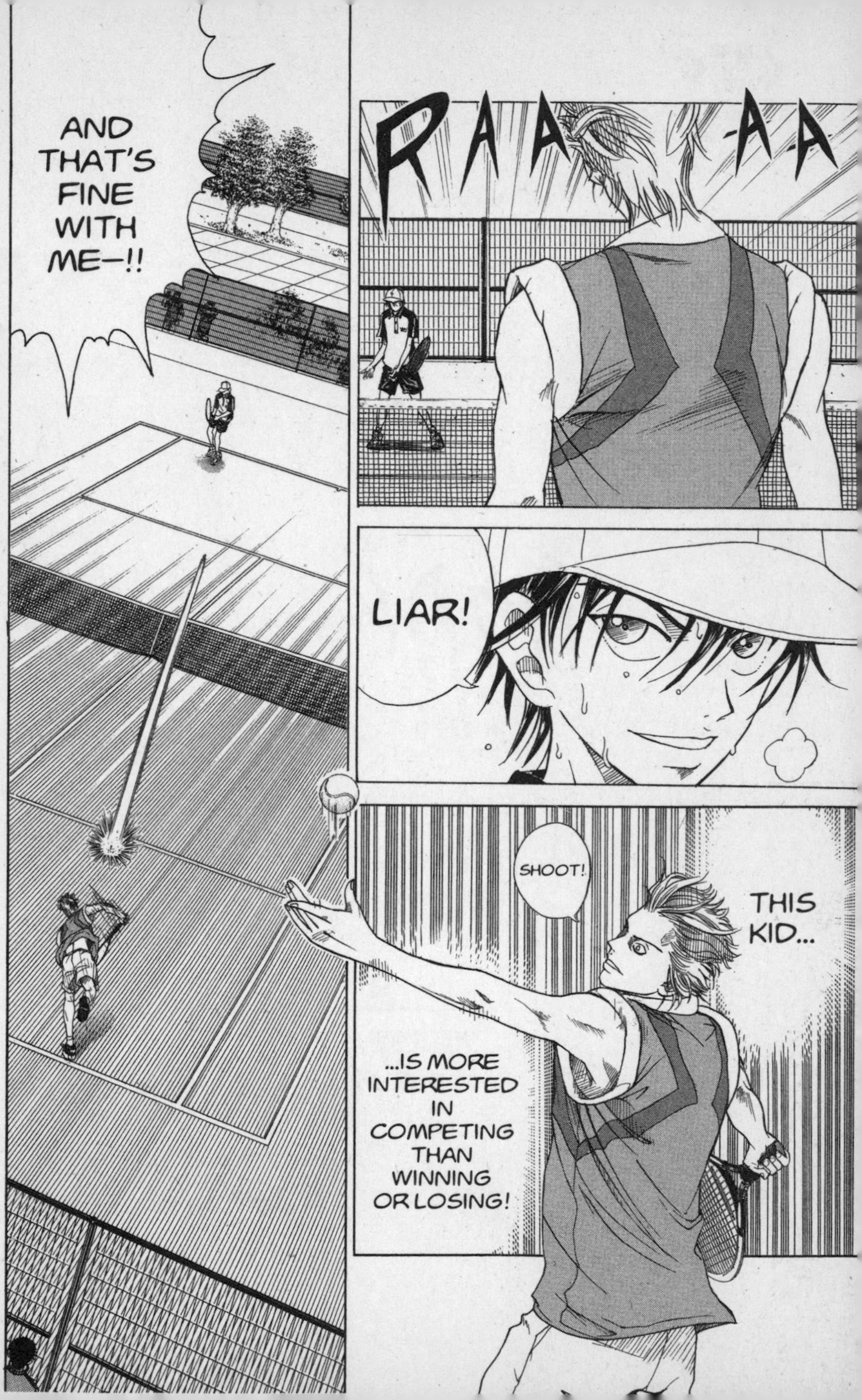
AND THAT'S FINE WITH ME—!!
RAA-AA
LIAR!
SHOOT!
THIS KID...
...IS MORE INTERESTED IN COMPETING THAN WINNING OR LOSING!

READ THIS WAY

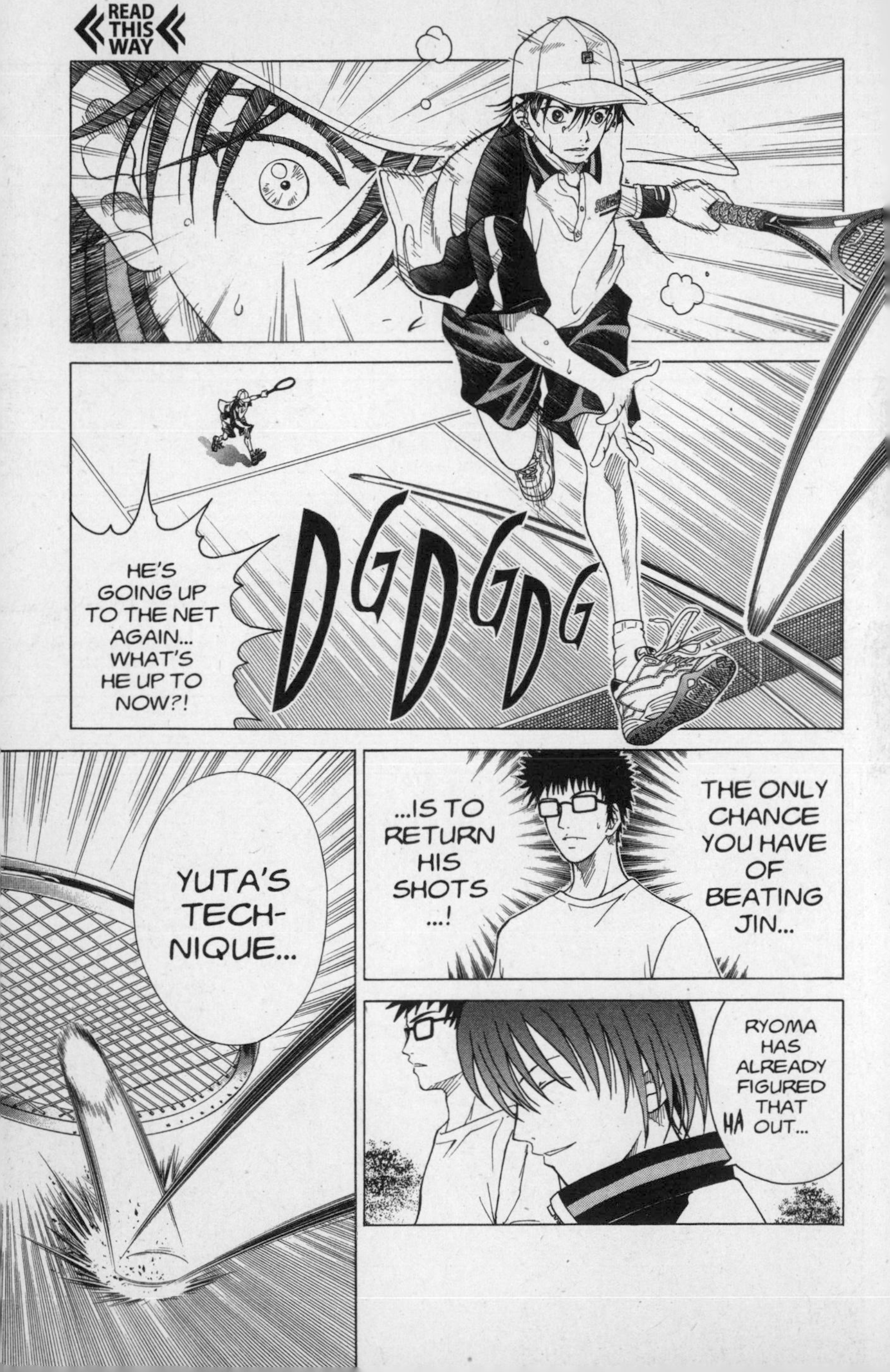
HE'S GOING UP TO THE NET AGAIN... WHAT'S HE UP TO NOW?!
DGDGDG
THE ONLY CHANCE YOU HAVE OF BEATING JIN...
...IS TO RETURN HIS SHOTS ...!
RYOMA HAS ALREADY FIGURED THAT OUT...
HA
YUTA'S TECH-NIQUE...

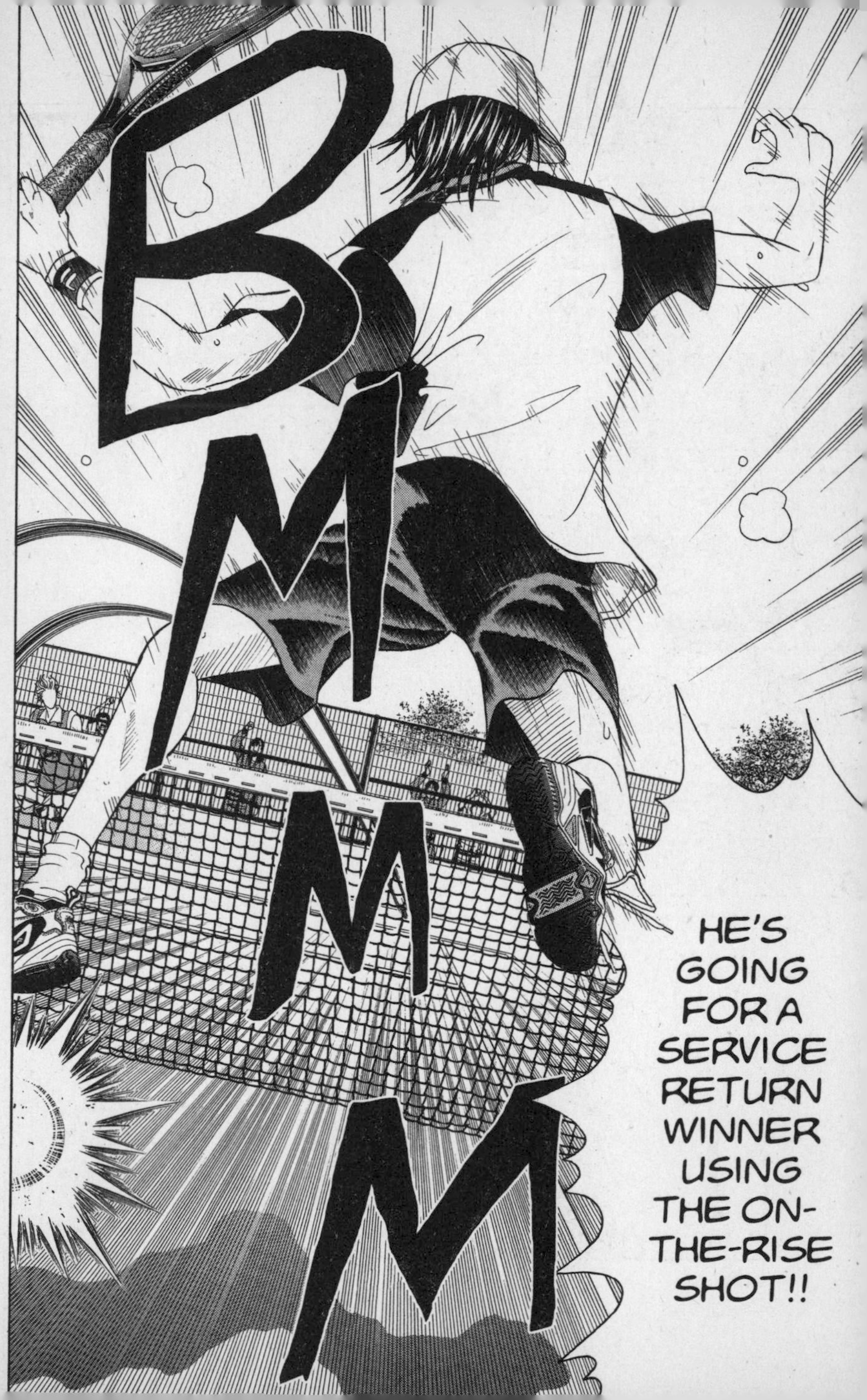
BMMM
HE'S GOING FOR A SERVICE RETURN WINNER USING THE ON-THE-RISE SHOT!!

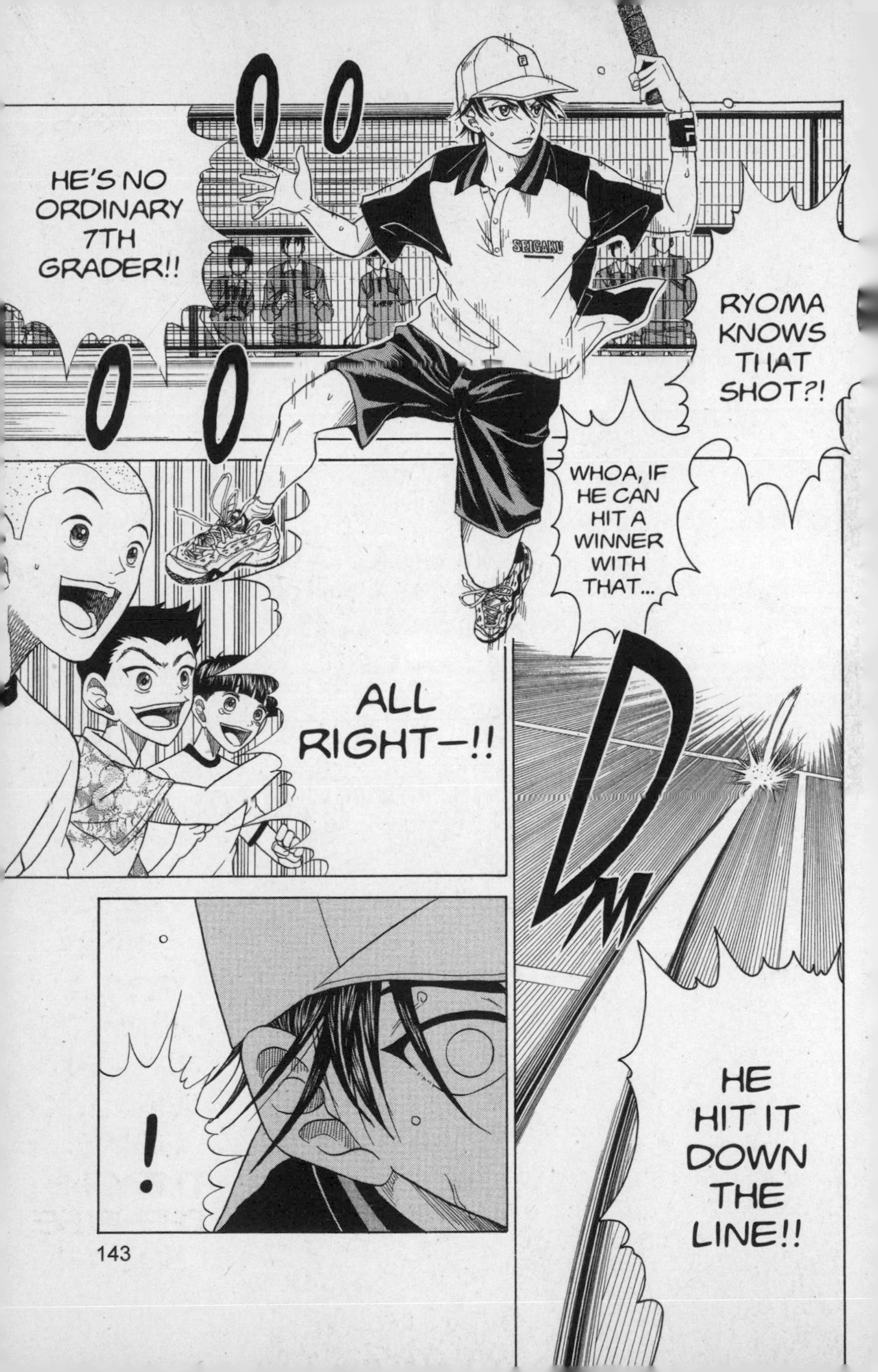
RYOMA KNOWS THAT SHOT?!
HE'S NO ORDINARY 7TH GRADER!!
OO
OO
WHOA, IF HE CAN HIT A WINNER WITH THAT...
HE HIT IT DOWN THE LINE!!
ALL RIGHT—!!
!

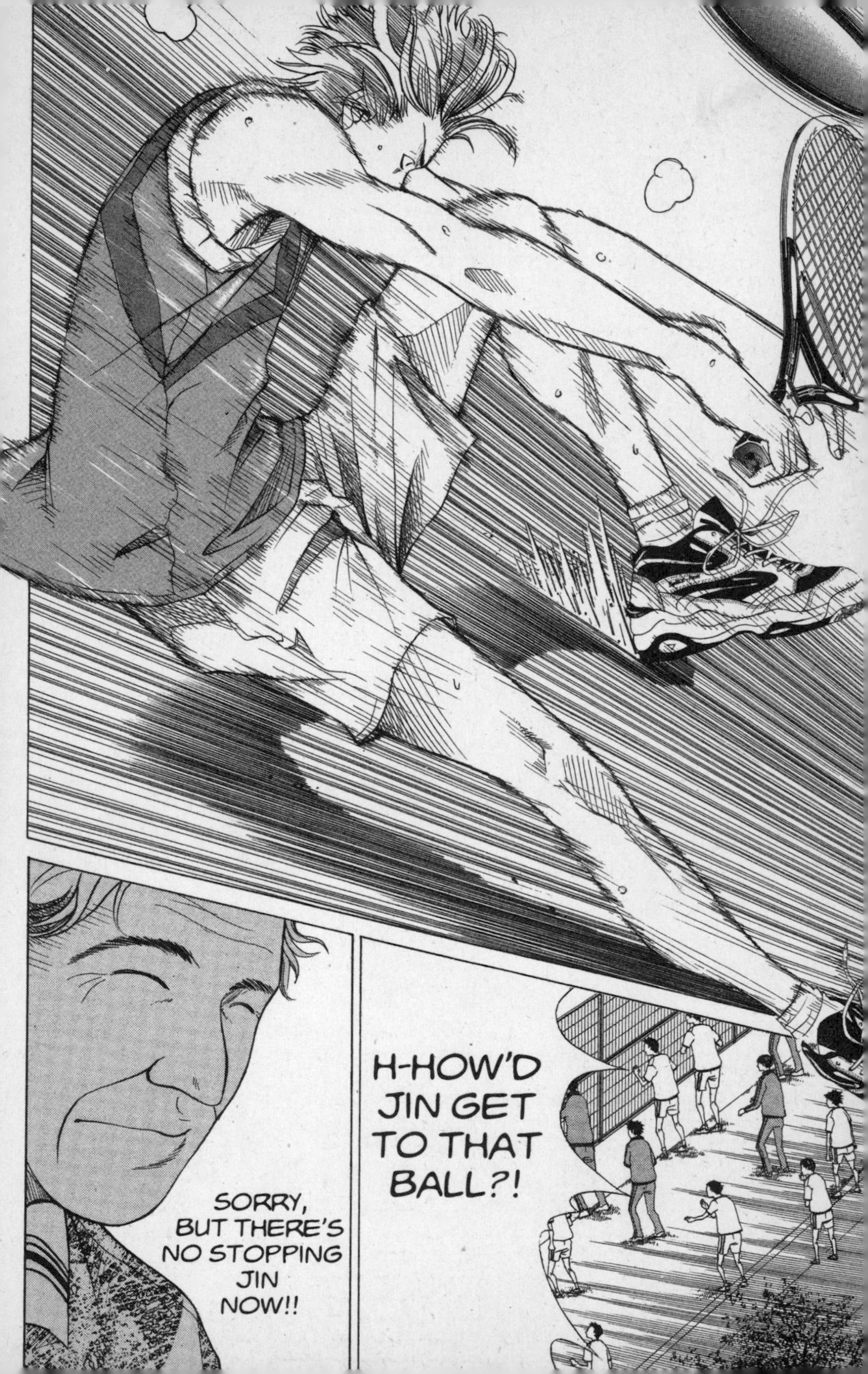
H-HOW'D JIN GET TO THAT BALL?!
SORRY, BUT THERE'S NO STOPPING JIN NOW!!

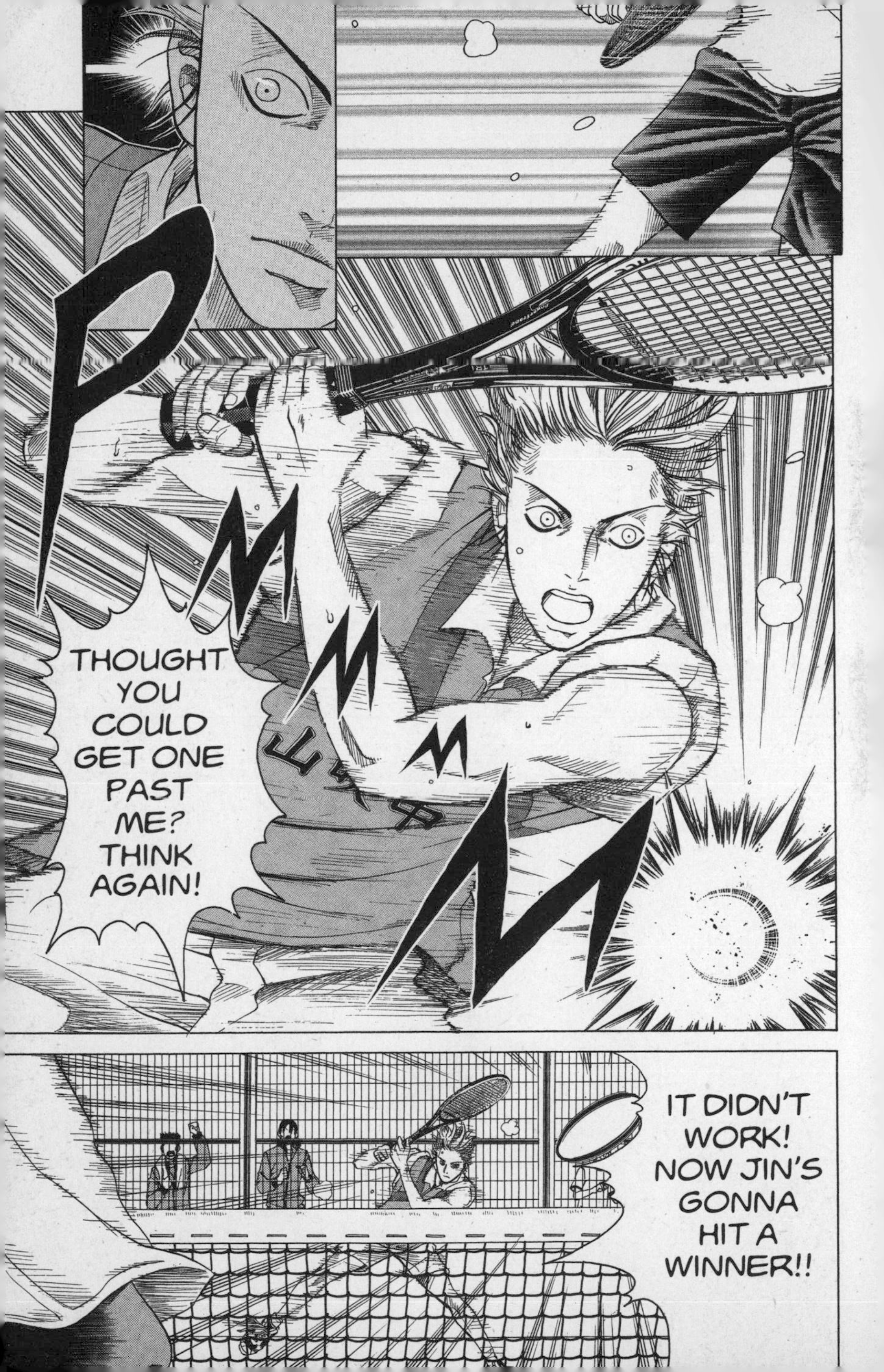
PMMM
THOUGHT YOU COULD GET ONE PAST ME? THINK AGAIN!
IT DIDN'T WORK! NOW JIN'S GONNA HIT A WINNER!!

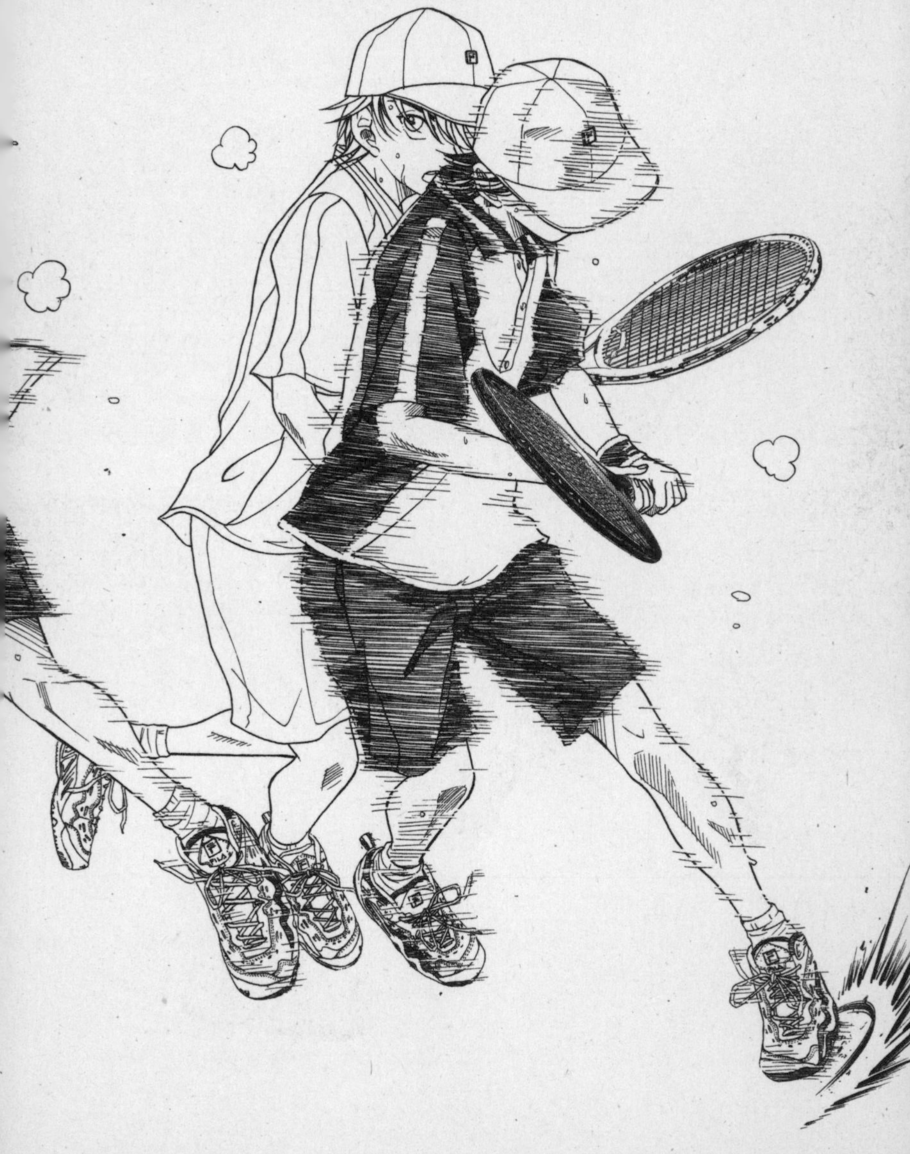

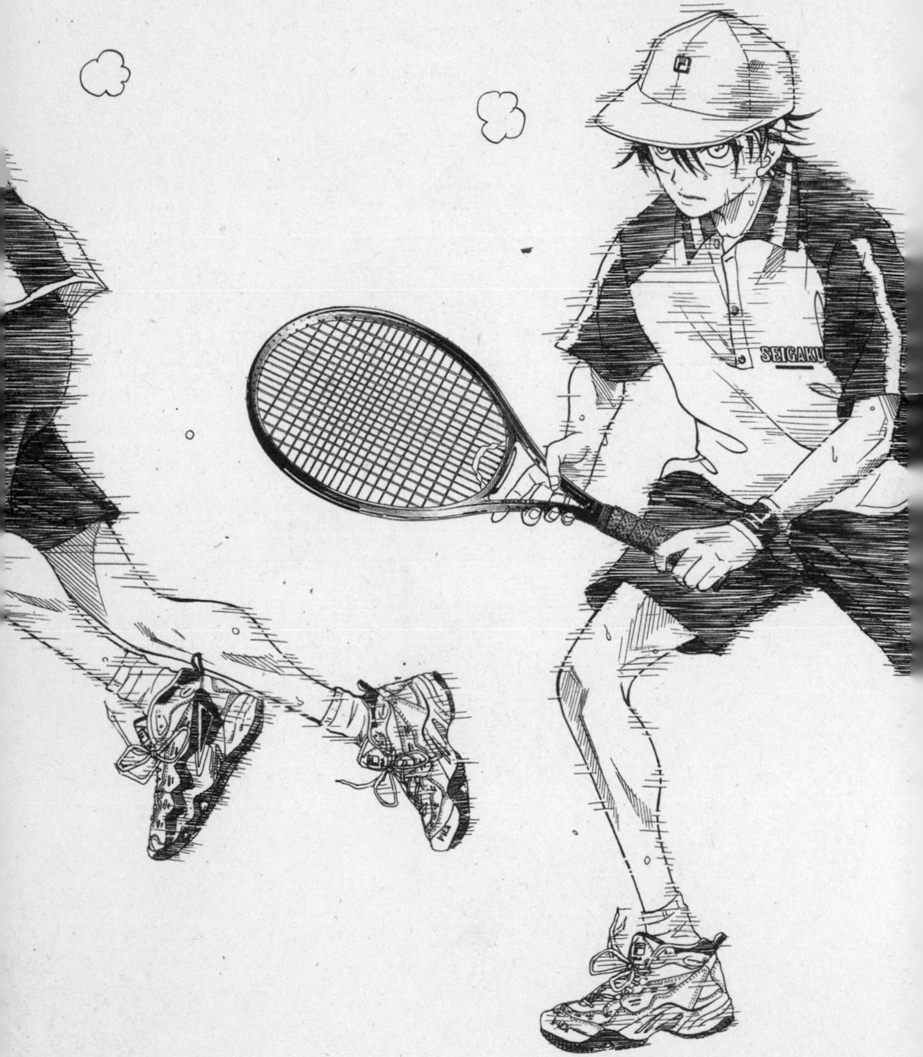
SEIGAKU

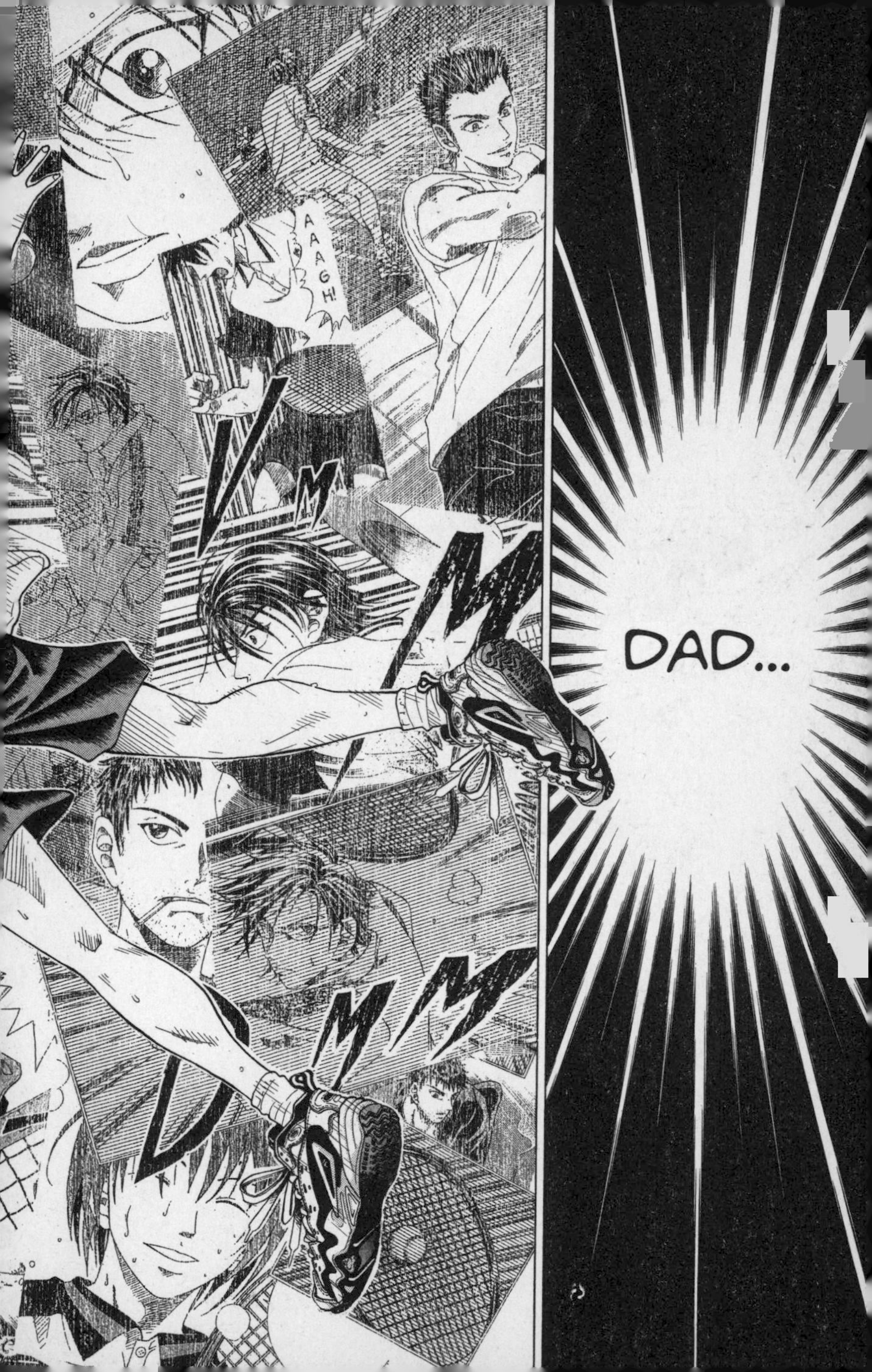
DAD...
AAAGH!

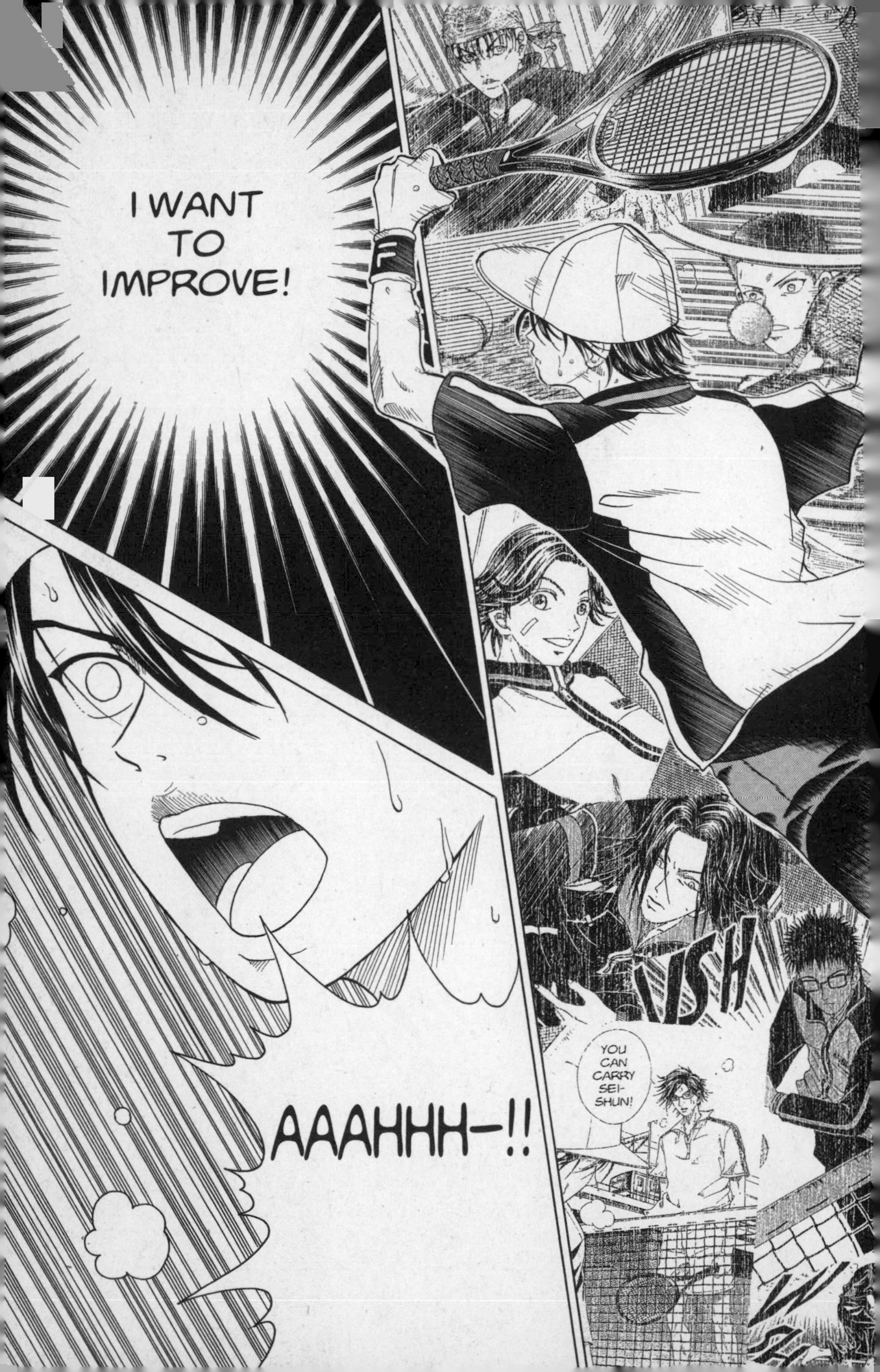
VSH
YOU CAN CARRY SEI-SHUN!
I WANT TO IMPROVE!
AAAHHH—!!

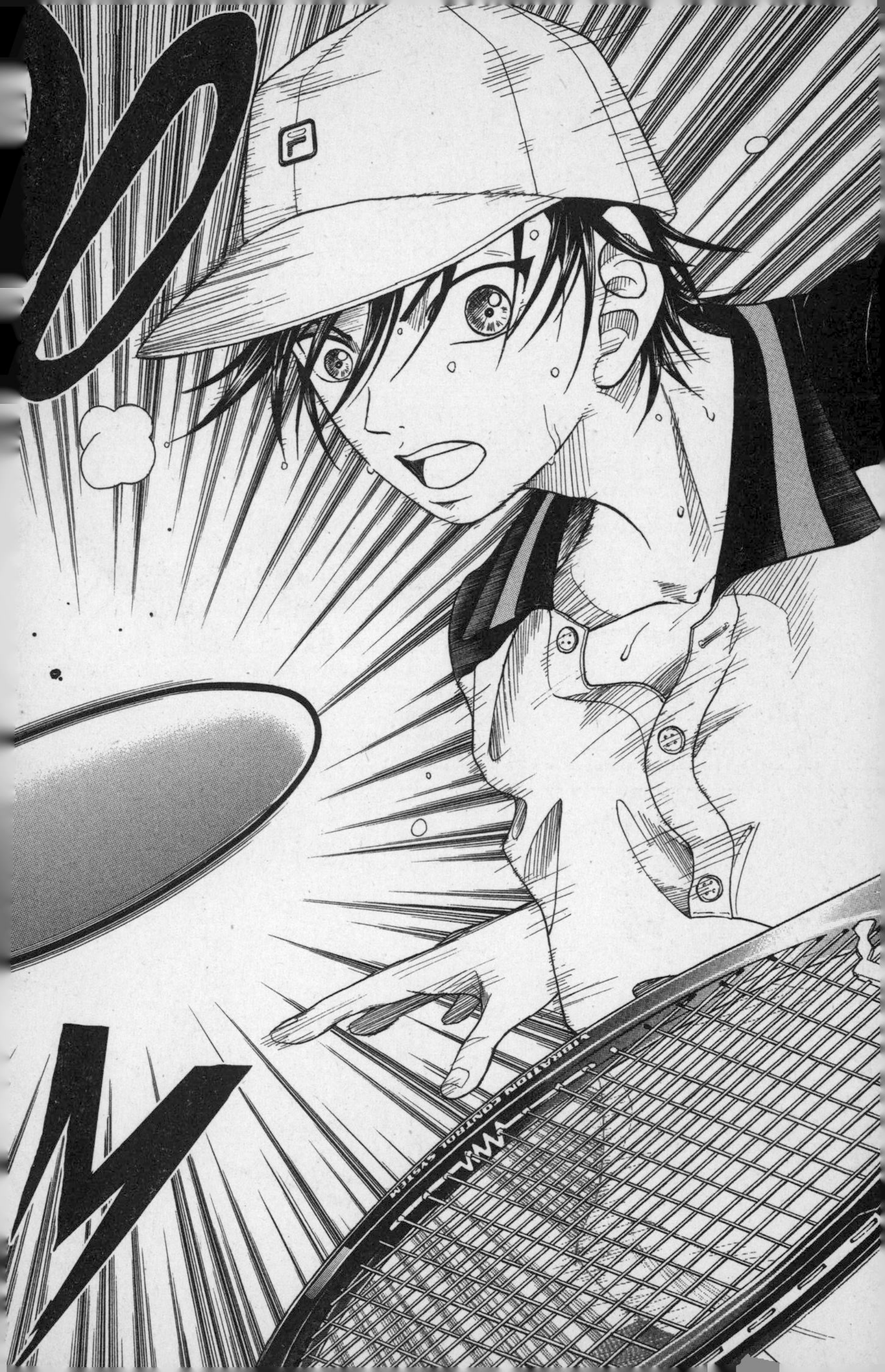
VIBRATION CONTROL SYSTEM

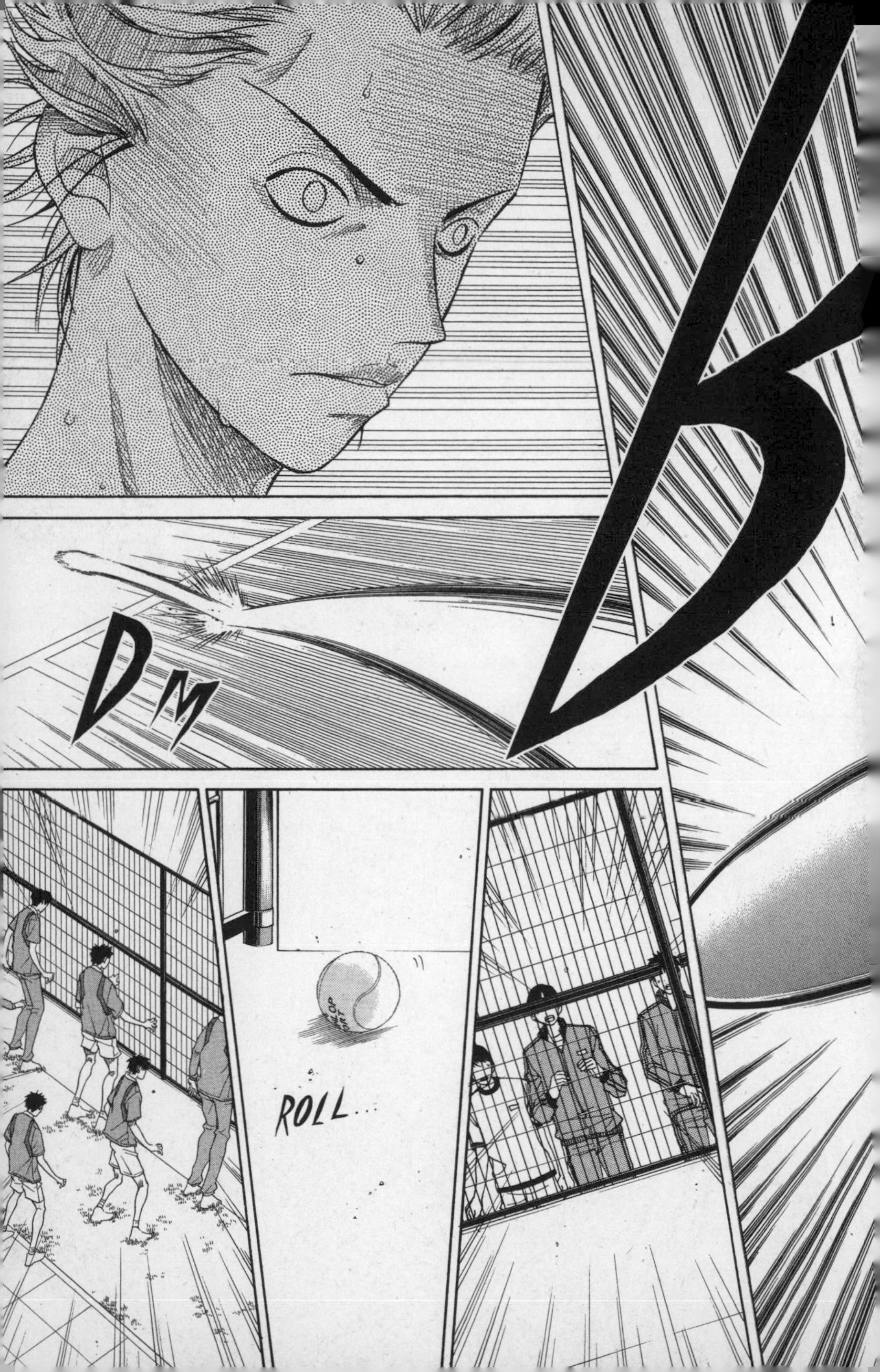
DM
ROLL...

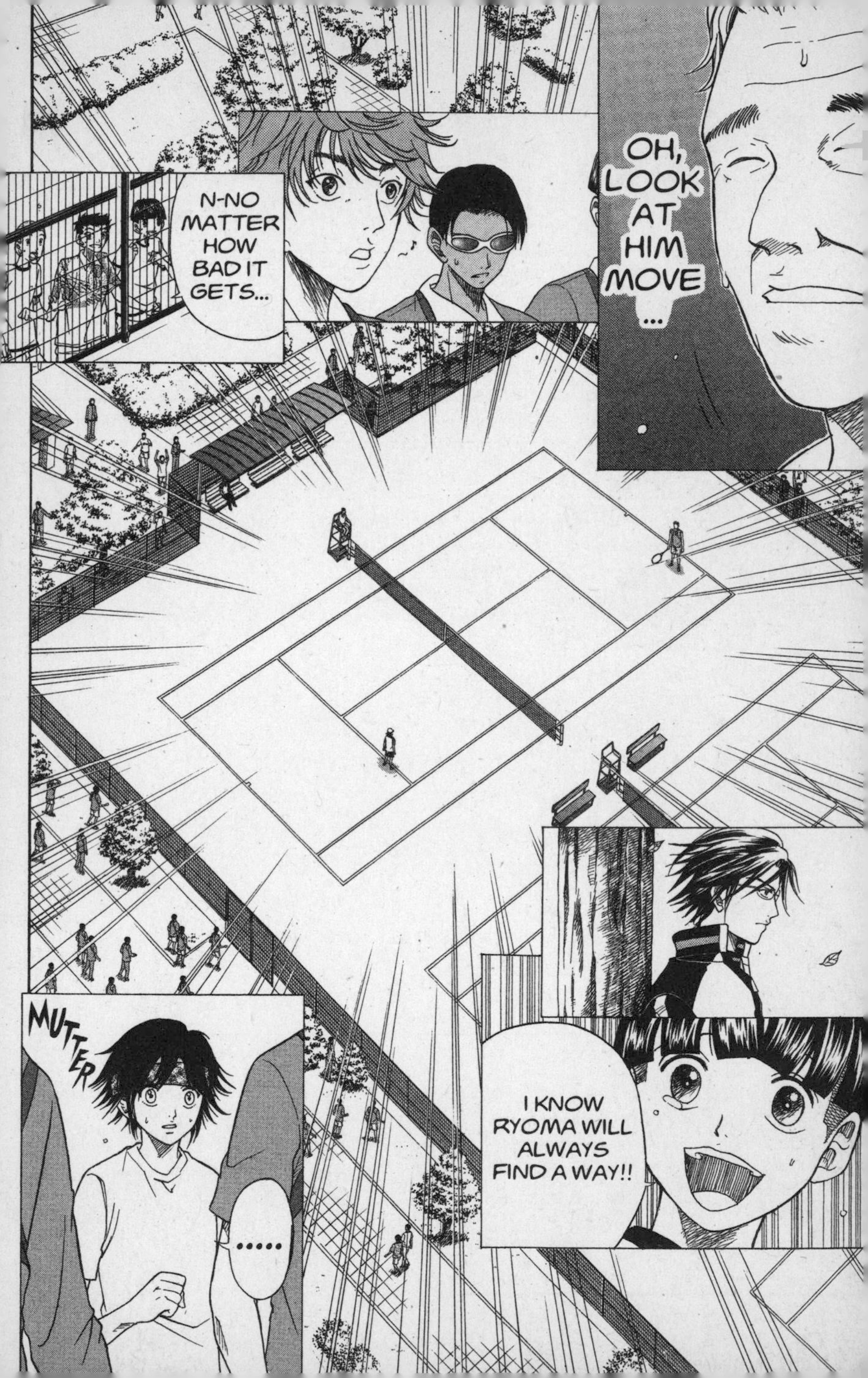
OH, LOOK AT HIM MOVE...
N-NO MATTER HOW BAD IT GETS...
I KNOW RYOMA WILL ALWAYS FIND A WAY!!
MUTTER
.....

READ THIS WAY

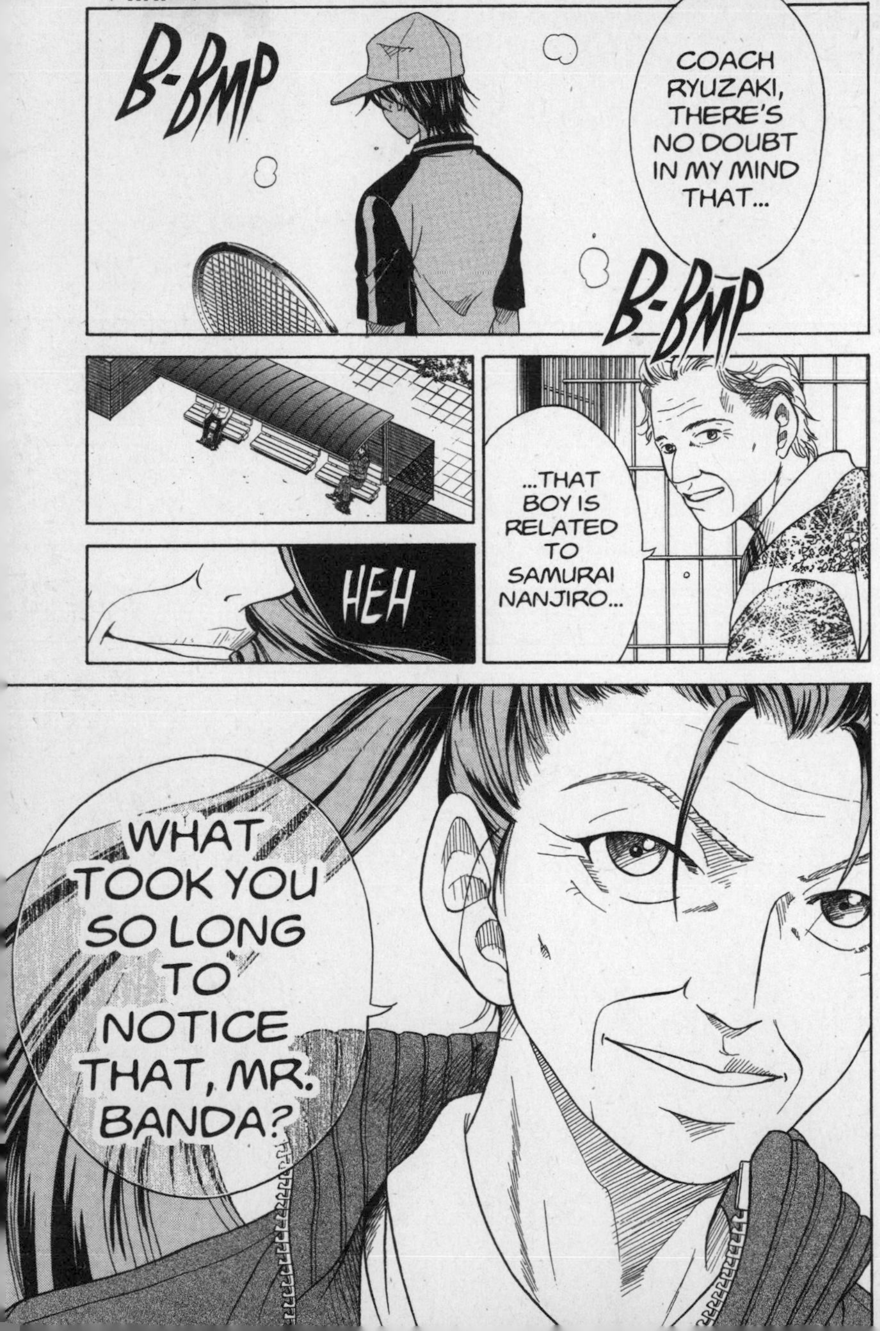
COACH RYUZAKI, THERE'S NO DOUBT IN MY MIND THAT...
B-BMP
B-BMP
...THAT BOY IS RELATED TO SAMURAI NANJIRO...
HEH
WHAT TOOK YOU SO LONG TO NOTICE THAT, MR. BANDA?

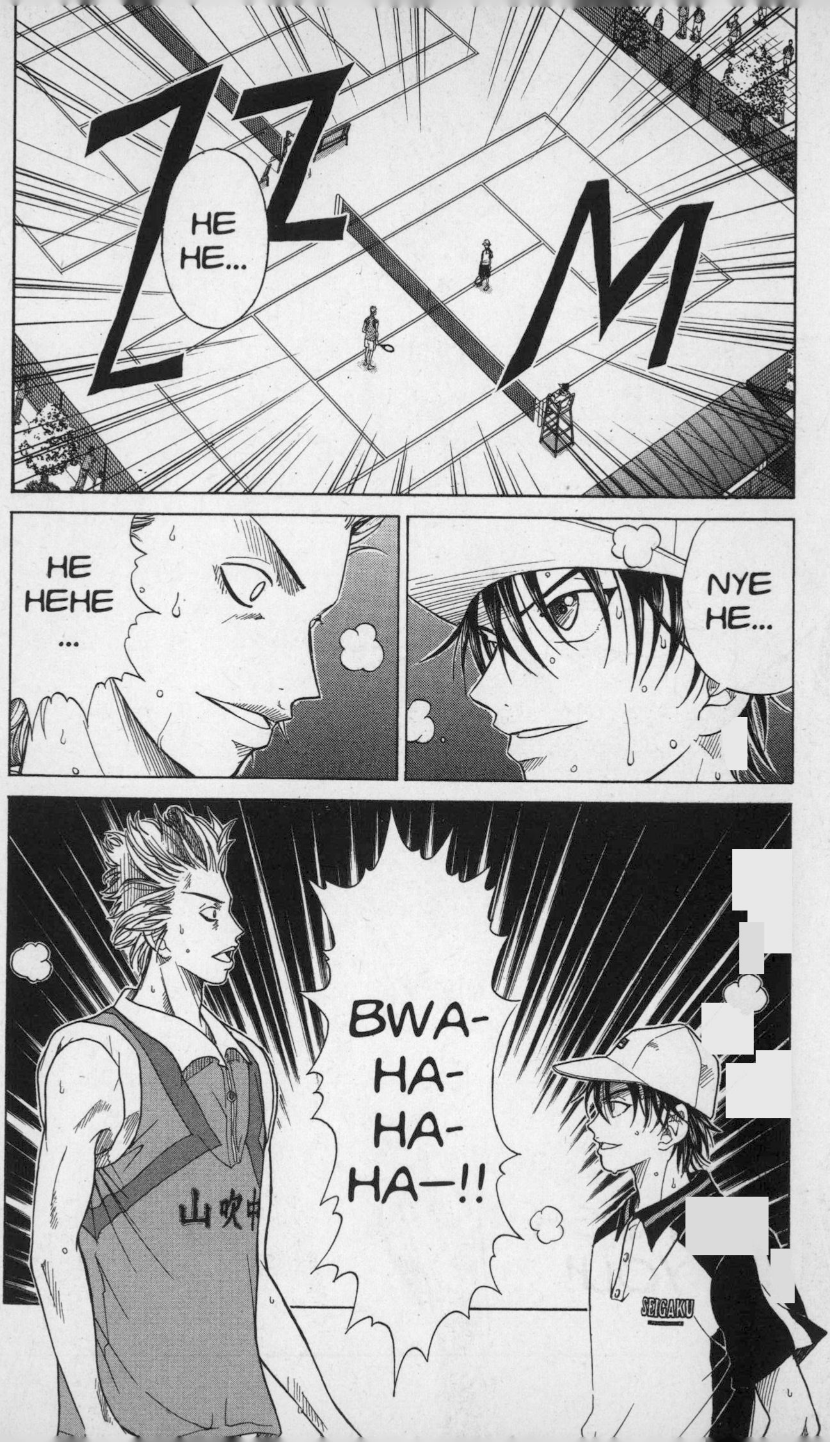
ZZM
HE HE...
NYE HE...
HE HEHE ...
BWA-HA-HA-HA-!!
山吹中
SEIGAKU

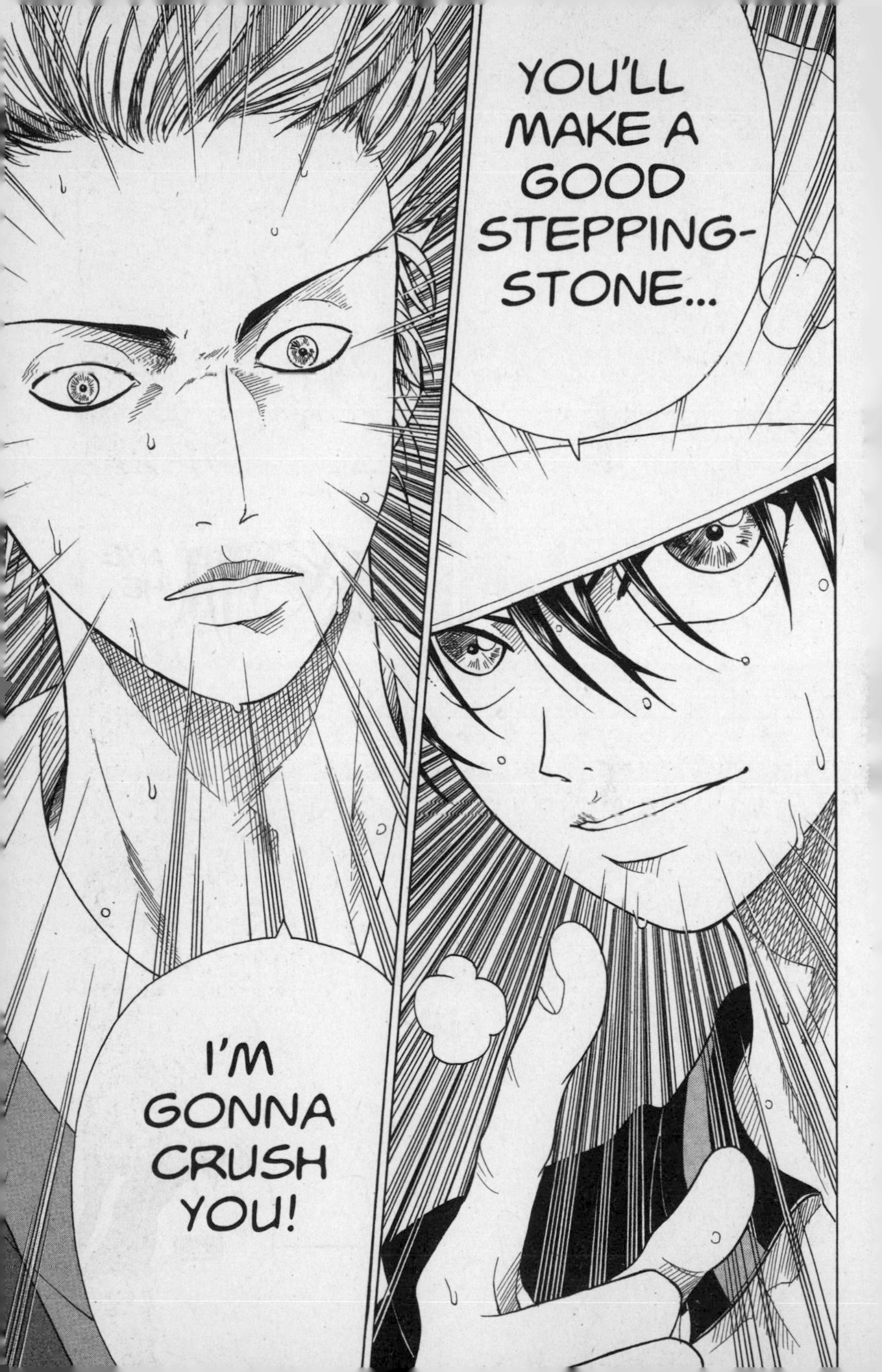
YOU'LL MAKE A GOOD STEPPING-STONE...
I'M GONNA CRUSH YOU!

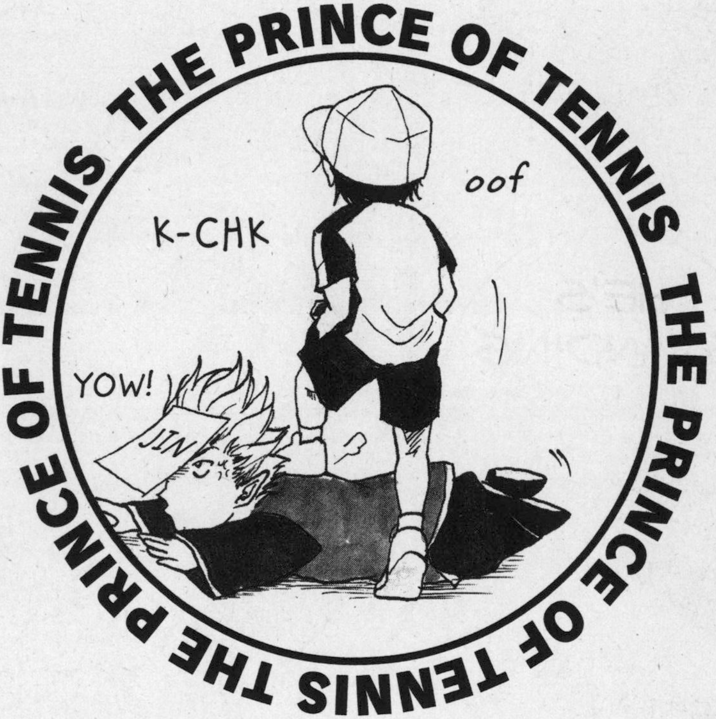
THE PRINCE OF TENNIS THE PRINCE OF TENNIS THE PRINCE OF TENNIS
oof
K-CHK
YOW!
JIN

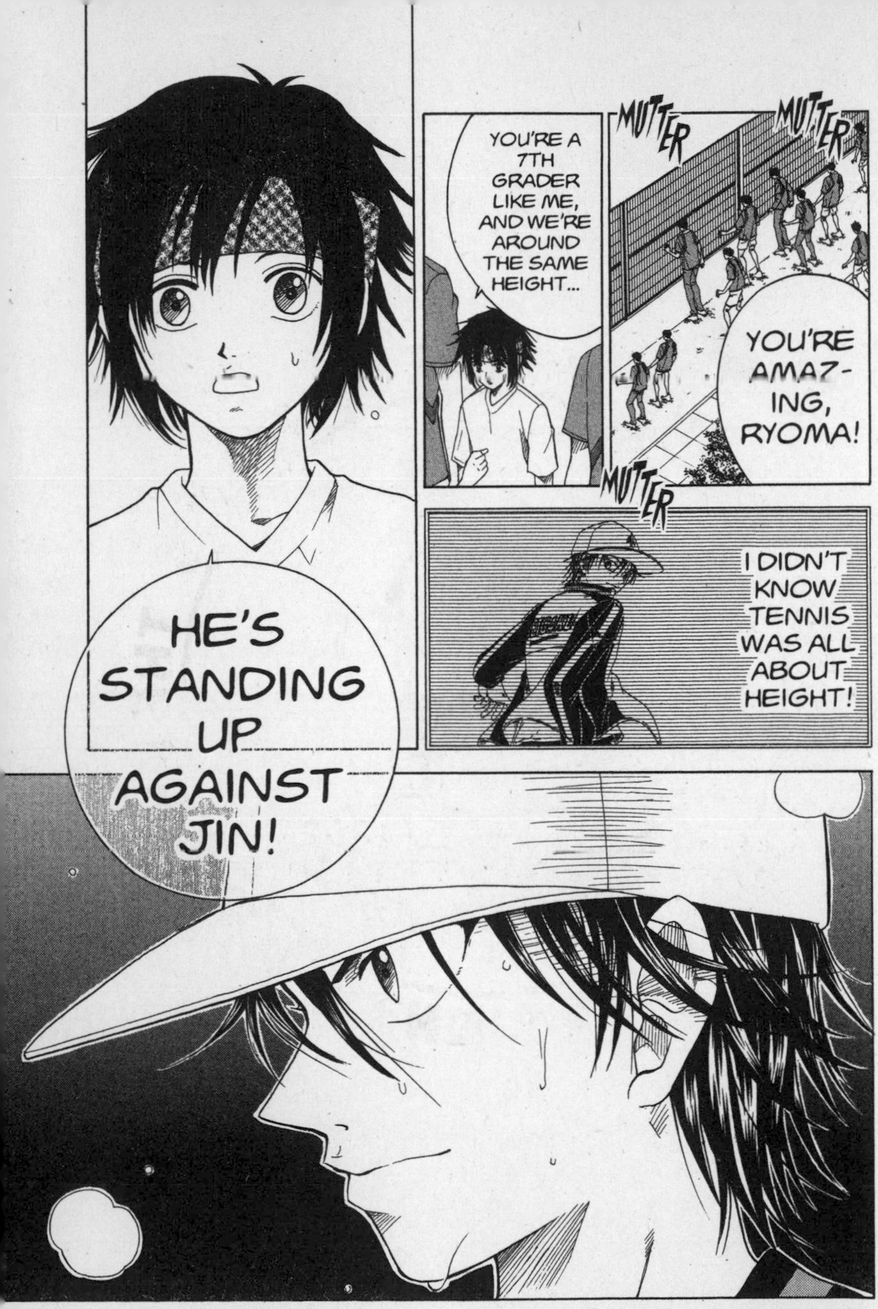
MUTTER
MUTTER
YOU'RE AMAZING, RYOMA!
MUTTER
YOU'RE A 7TH GRADER LIKE ME, AND WE'RE AROUND THE SAME HEIGHT...
I DIDN'T KNOW TENNIS WAS ALL ABOUT HEIGHT!
HE'S STANDING UP AGAINST JIN!

GENIUS 105: NATURAL

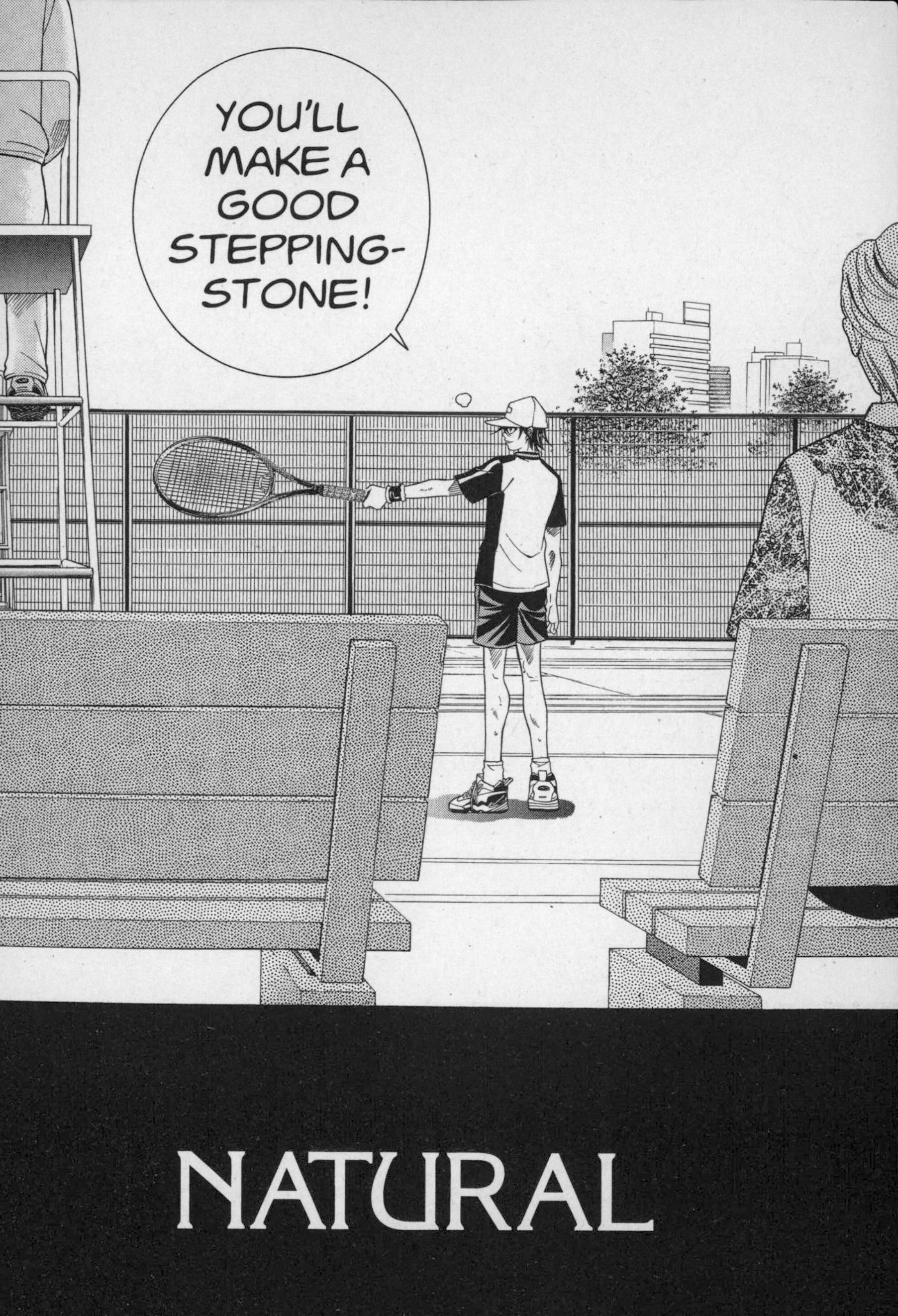
YOU'LL MAKE A GOOD STEPPING-STONE!

NATURAL

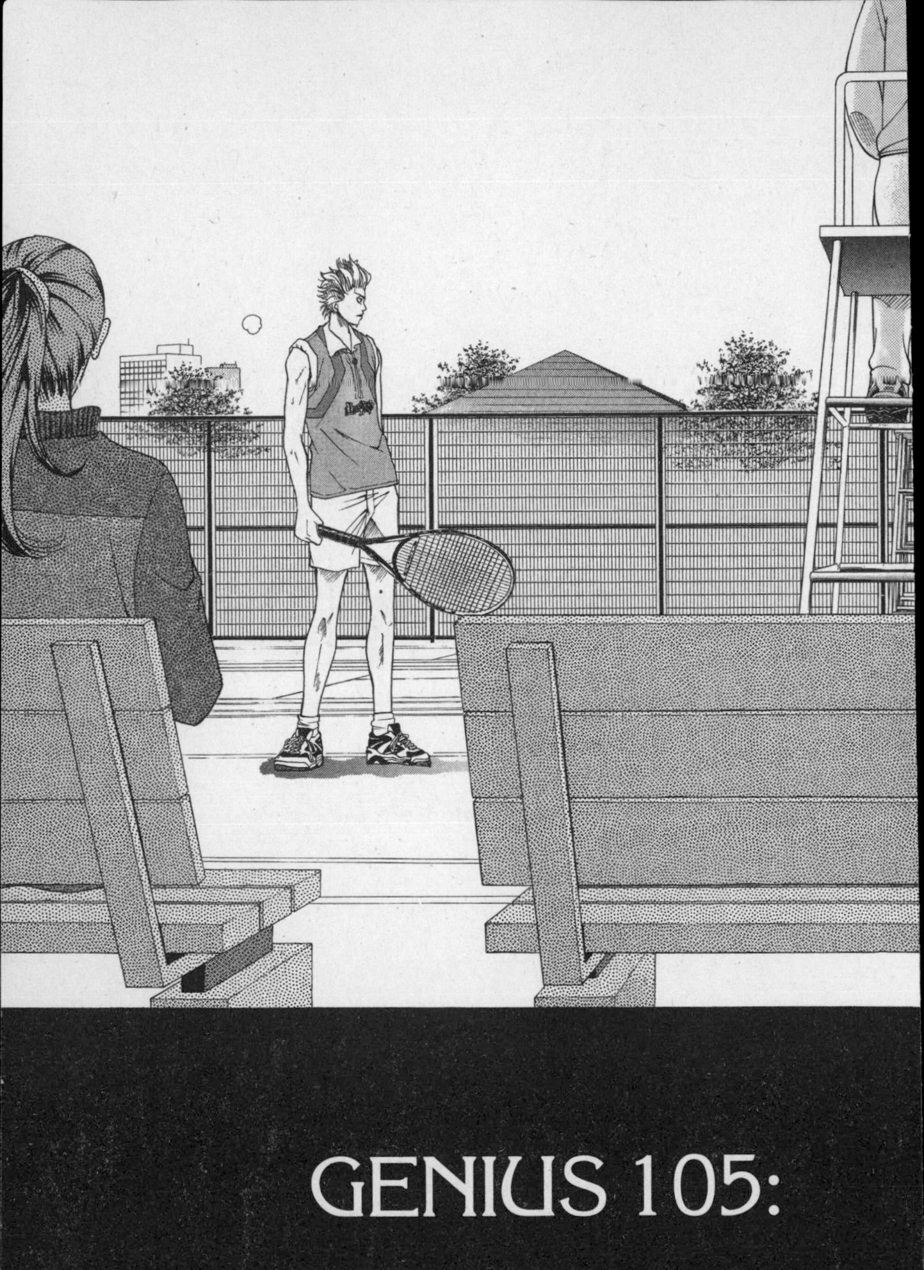

GENIUS 105:

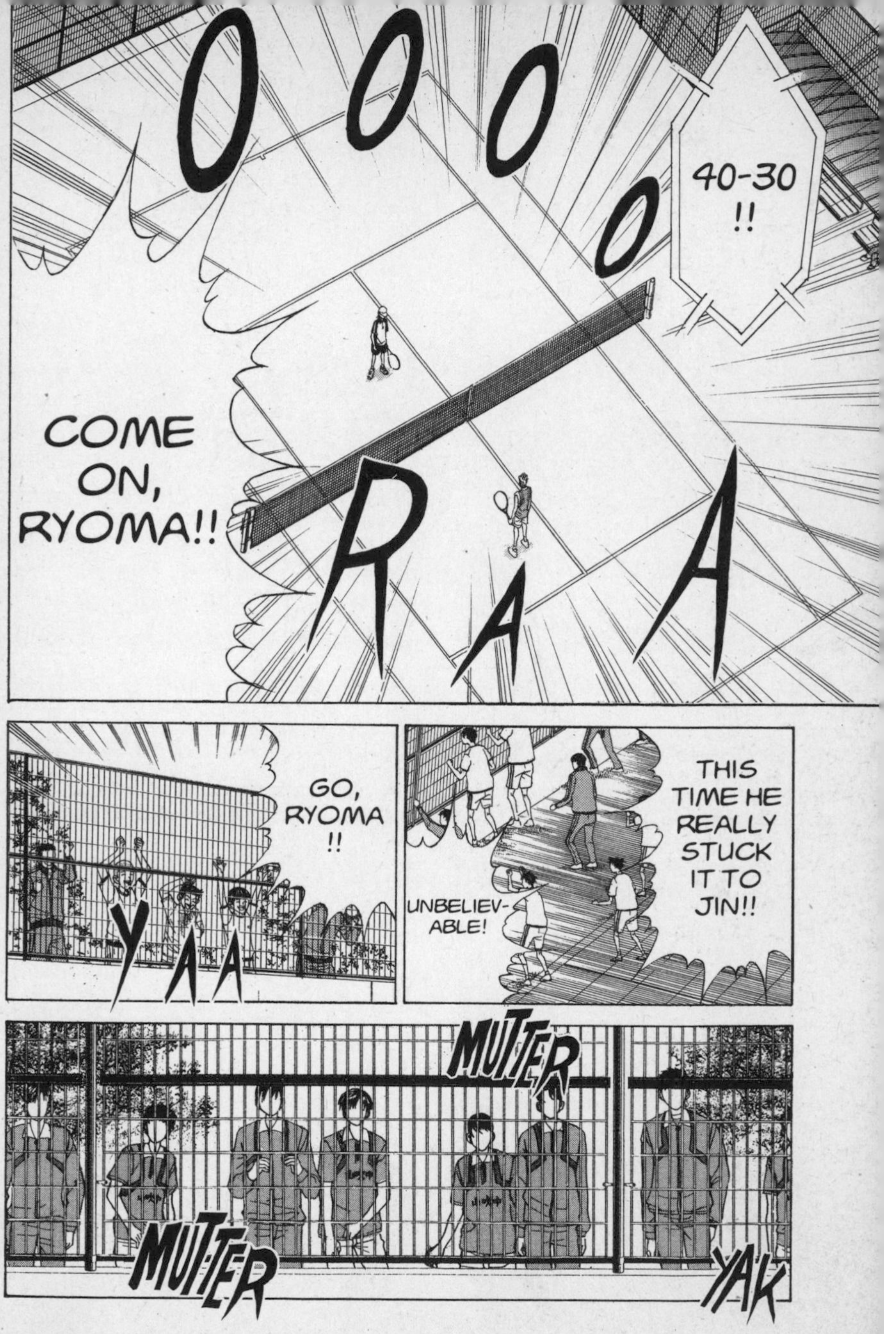
40-30 !!
OOOOO
COME ON, RYOMA!!
RAA
THIS TIME HE REALLY STUCK IT TO JIN!!
UNBELIEV-ABLE!
GO, RYOMA !!
YAA
MUTTER
YAK
MUTTER

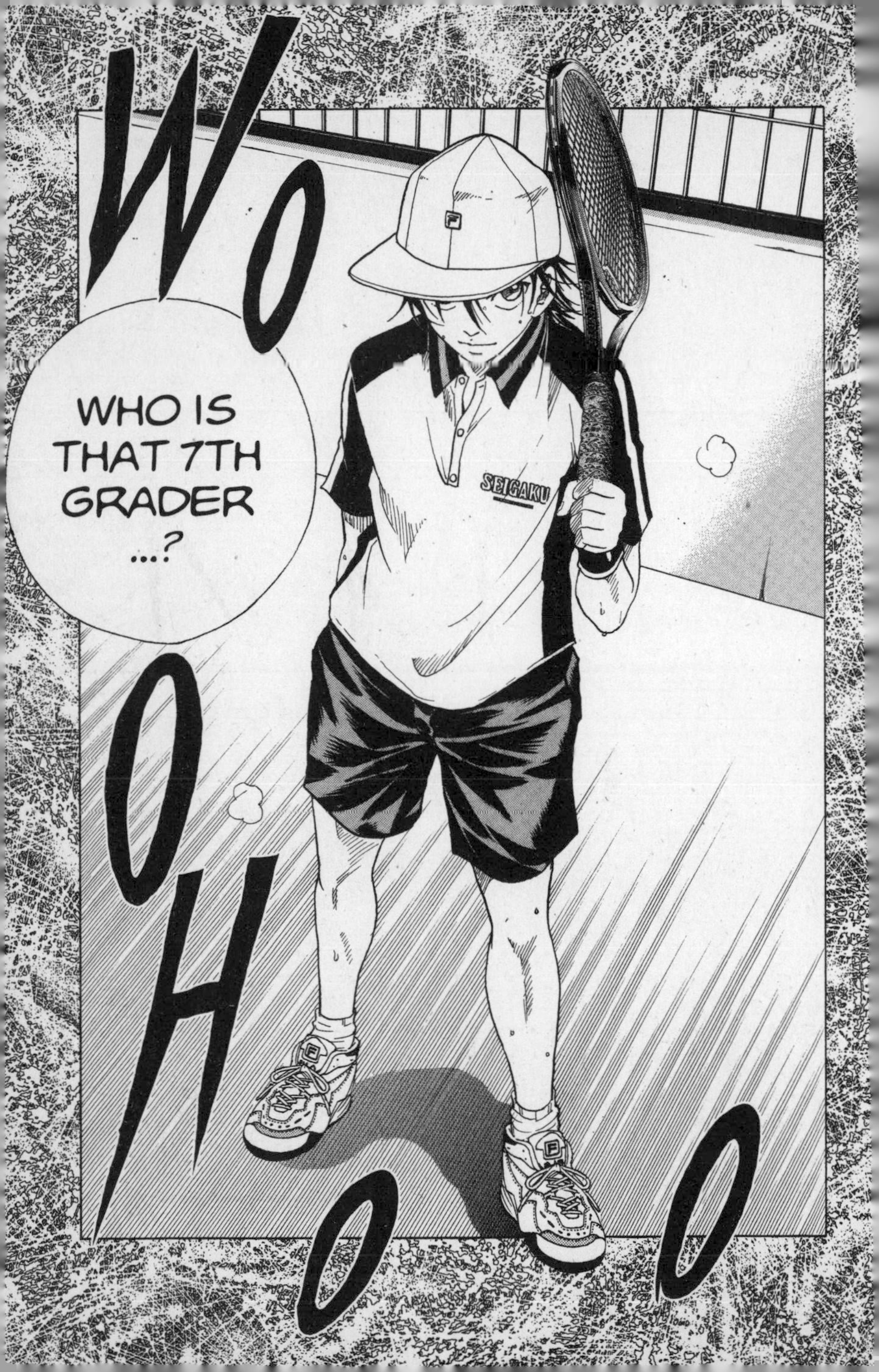
WOOOHOOO
WHO IS THAT 7TH GRADER ...?
SEIGAKU

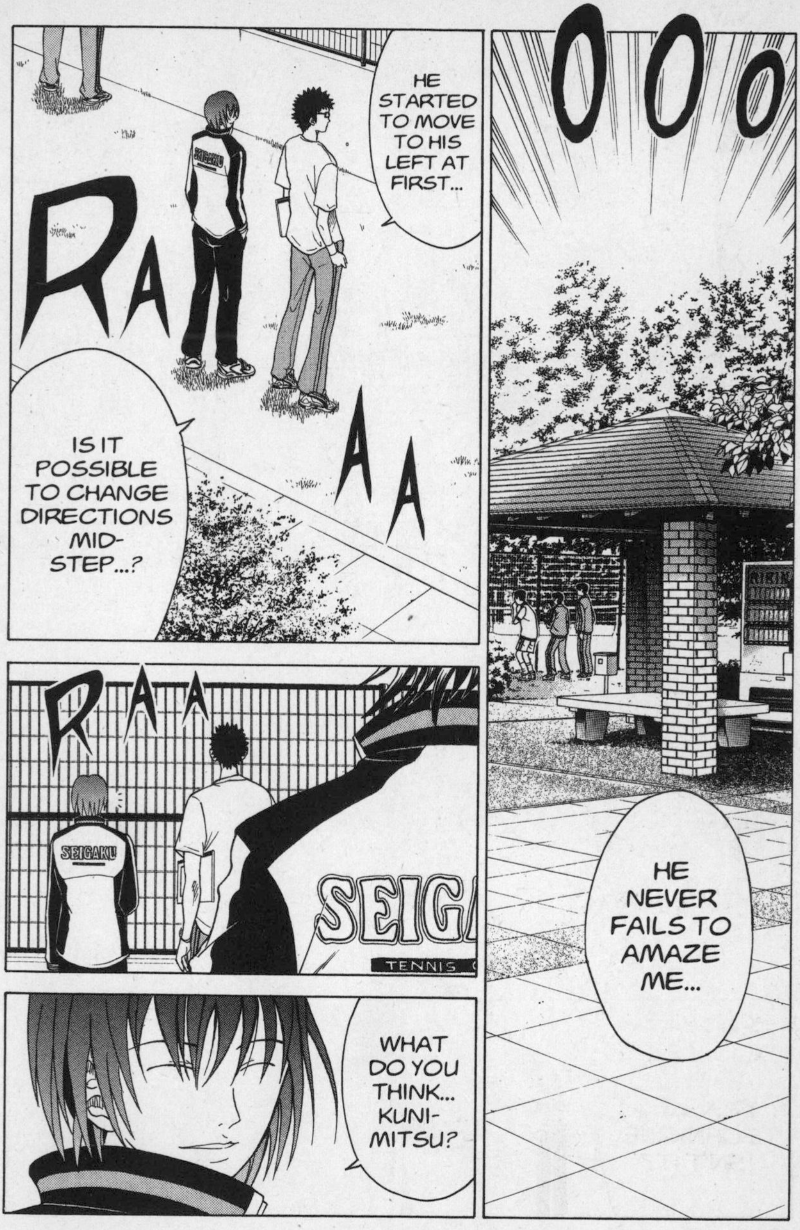
OOO
HE NEVER FAILS TO AMAZE ME...
HE STARTED TO MOVE TO HIS LEFT AT FIRST...
RAAA
IS IT POSSIBLE TO CHANGE DIRECTIONS MID-STEP...?
SEIGAKU
RAA
SEIGAKU
WHAT DO YOU THINK... KUNI-MITSU?

IT WAS POSSIBLE BECAUSE IT WAS A ONE-FOOTED STEP.

BUT USING BOTH LEGS IS THE CLASSIC TECHNIQUE, ISN'T IT?

YOU'RE RIGHT! YOU'D BE A STEP LATE IF YOU USE BOTH LEGS TO MOVE IN ONE DIRECTION. THERE'D BE NO TIME TO SHIFT DIRECTIONS AT THE LAST MINUTE...

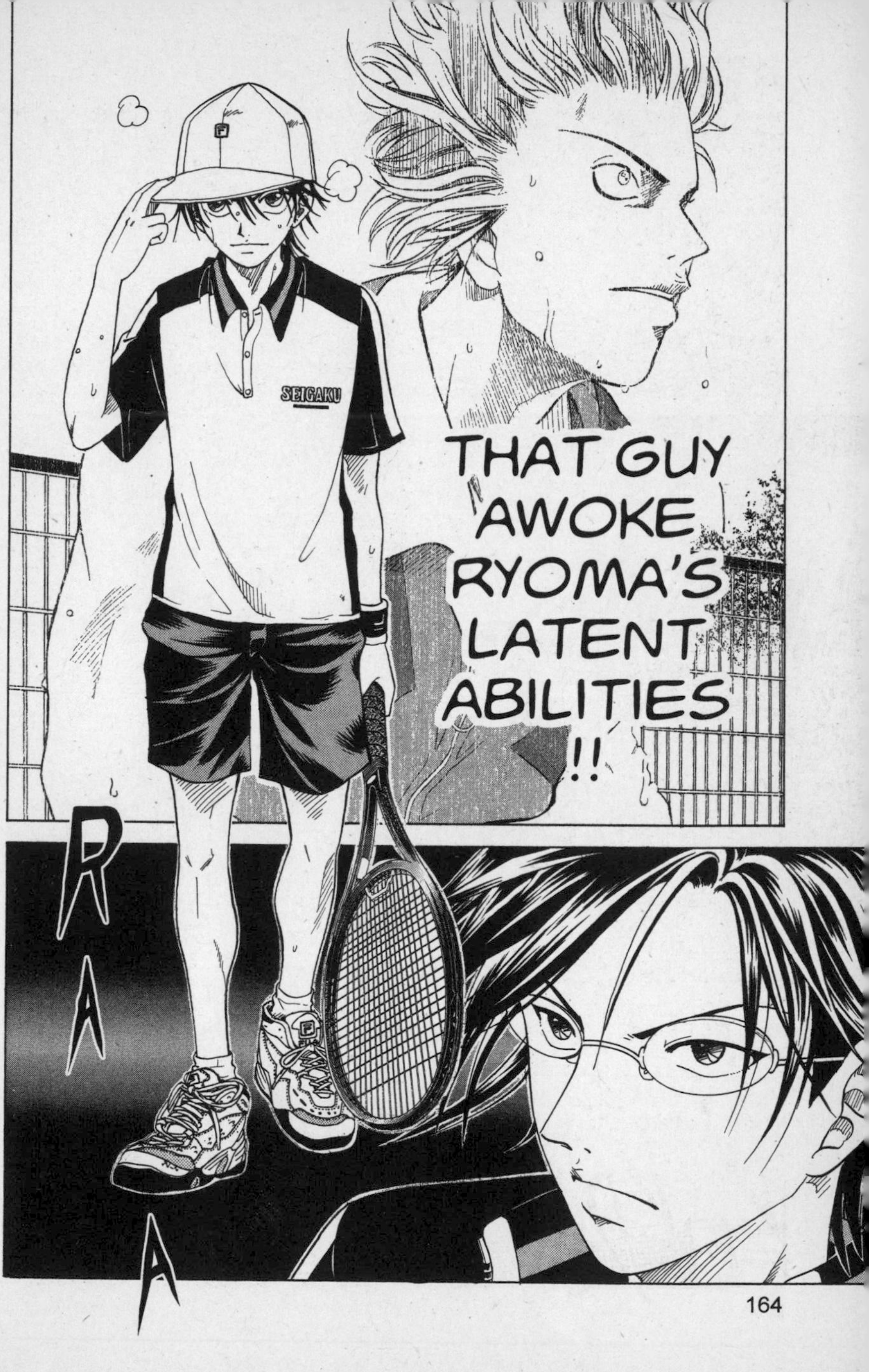
SEIGAKU
THAT GUY AWOKE RYOMA'S LATENT ABILITIES !!
RAA

READ THIS WAY

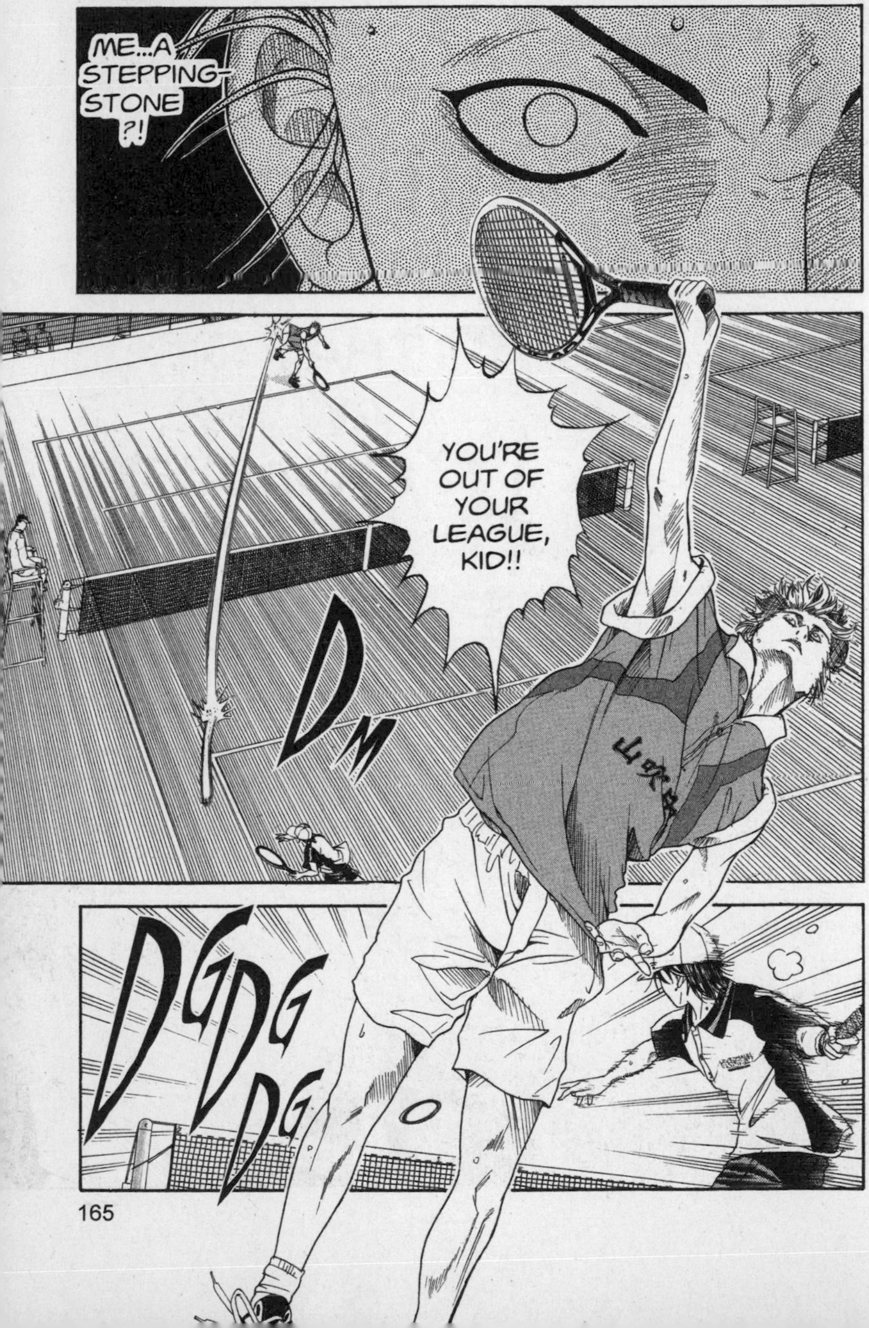
ME...A STEPPING-STONE ?!
YOU'RE OUT OF YOUR LEAGUE, KID!!
DM
DGDG
DGDG

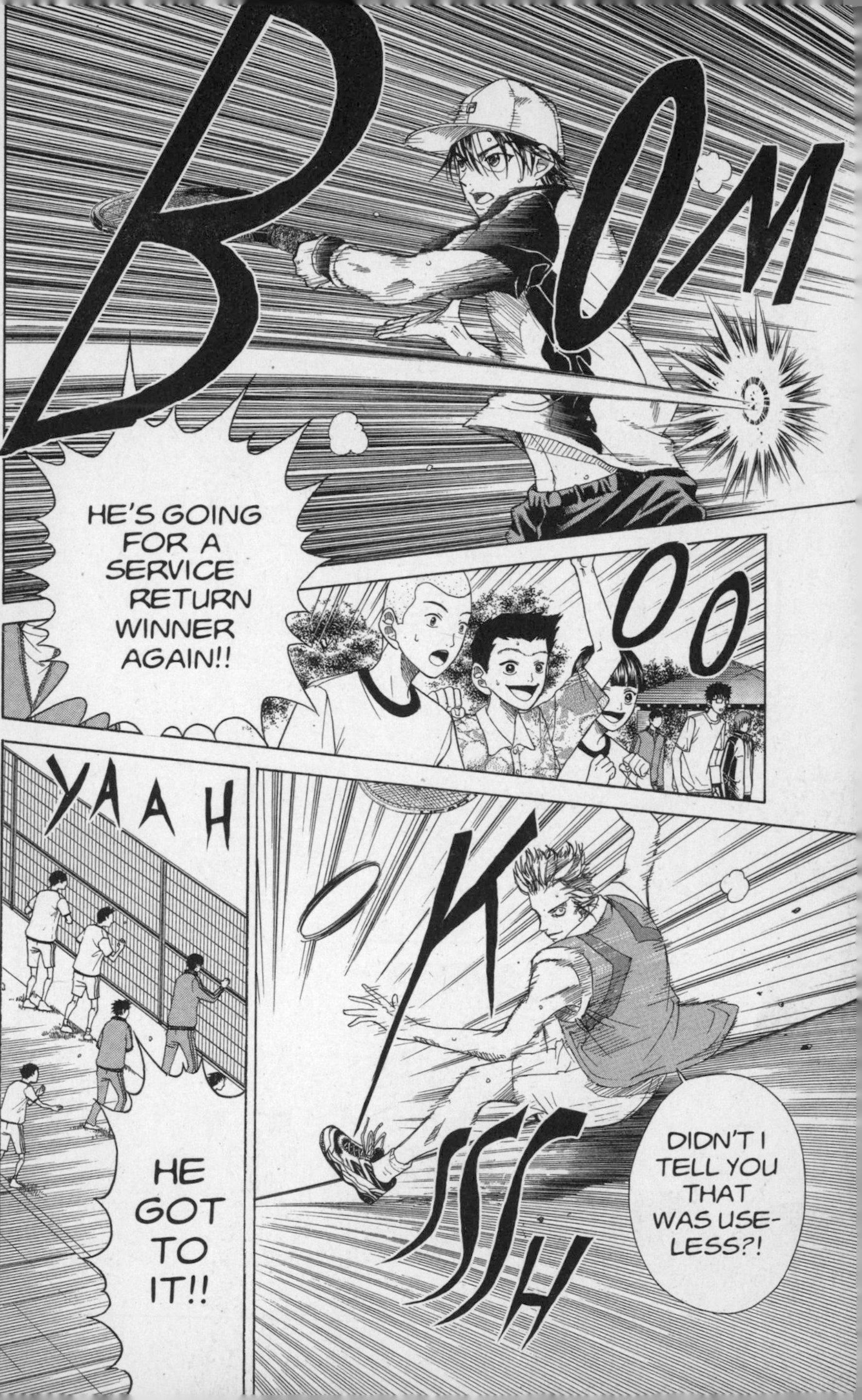
BOOM
HE'S GOING FOR A SERVICE RETURN WINNER AGAIN!!
OOO
K
SSSSH
DIDN'T I TELL YOU THAT WAS USE-LESS?!
YAAH
HE GOT TO IT!!

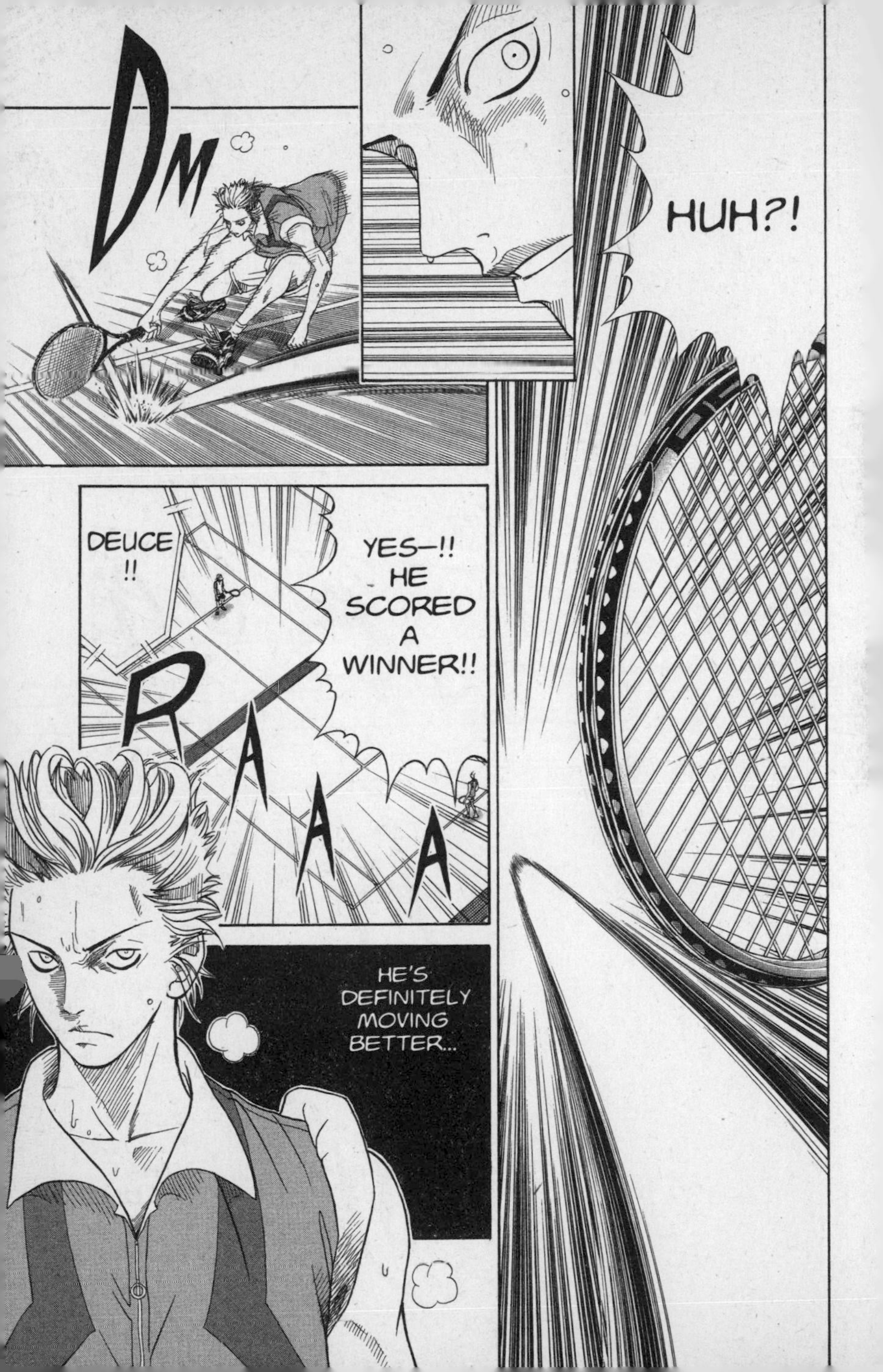
HUH?!
DM
YES—!! HE SCORED A WINNER!!
DEUCE !!
RAAA
HE'S DEFINITELY MOVING BETTER...

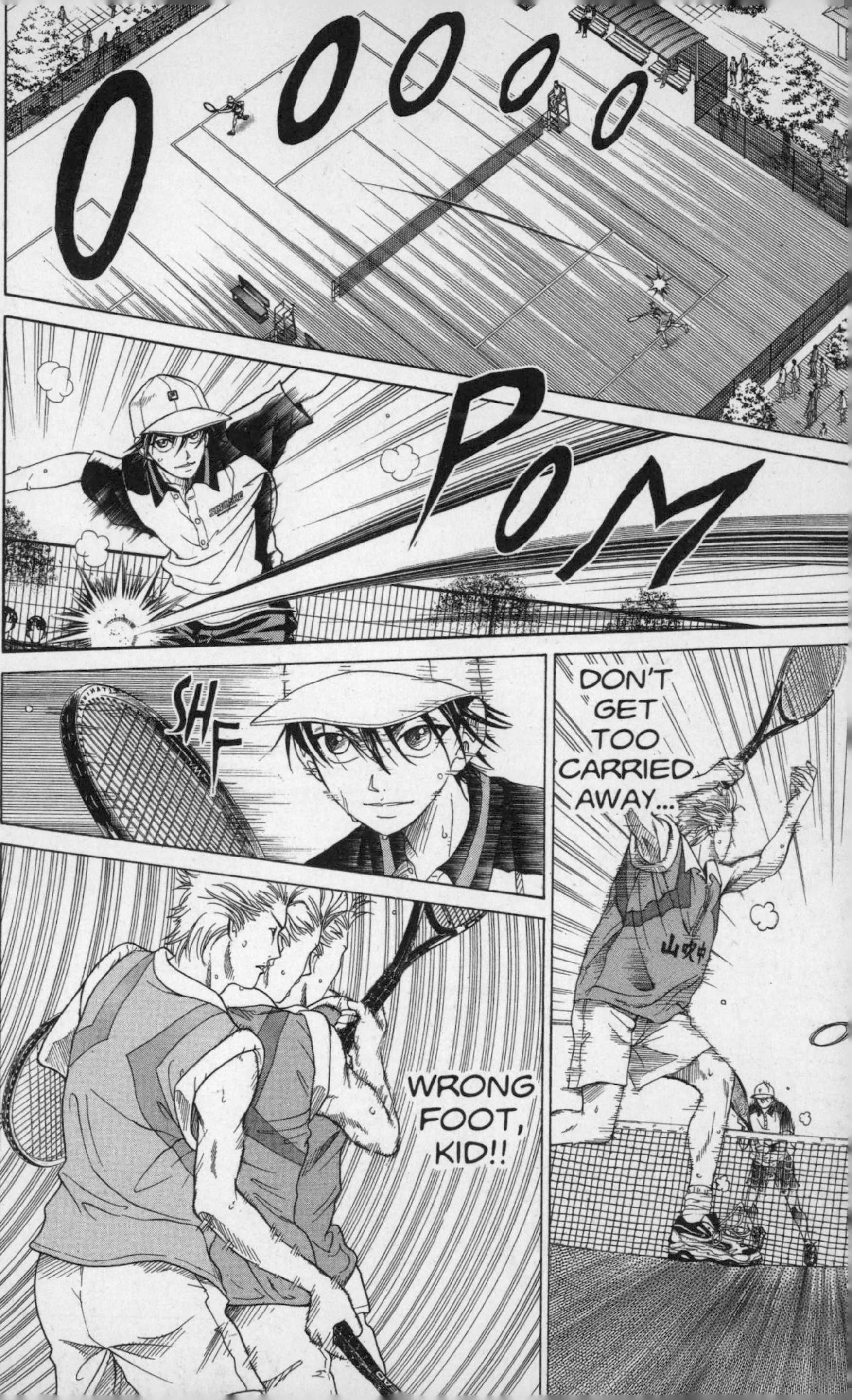
OOOOOO
POM
DON'T GET TOO CARRIED AWAY...
山吹中
SHF
WRONG FOOT, KID!!

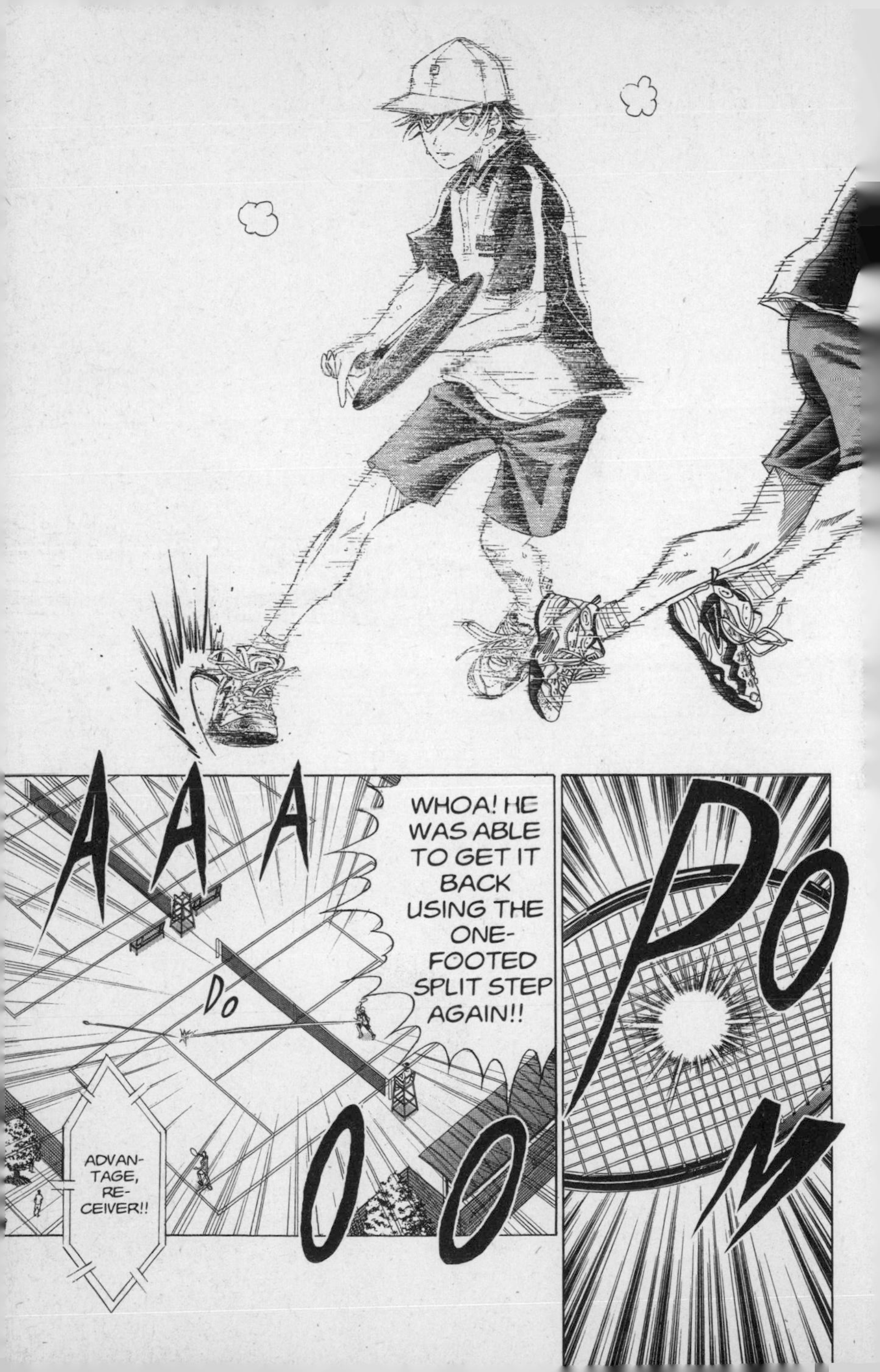
POM
AAA
WHOA! HE WAS ABLE TO GET IT BACK USING THE ONE-FOOTED SPLIT STEP AGAIN!!
Do
OO
ADVAN-TAGE, RE-CEIVER!!

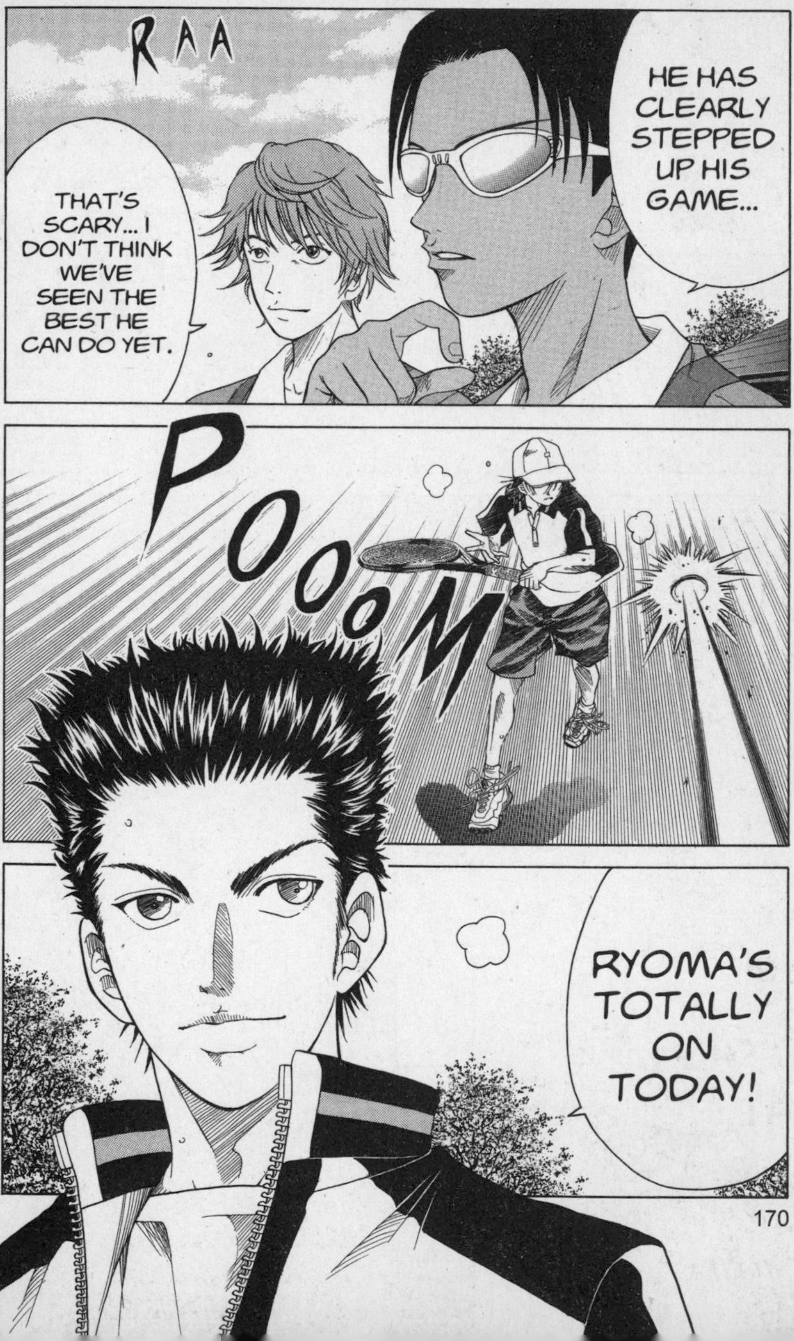
HE HAS CLEARLY STEPPED UP HIS GAME...
RAA
THAT'S SCARY... I DON'T THINK WE'VE SEEN THE BEST HE CAN DO YET.
POOOM
RYOMA'S TOTALLY ON TODAY!

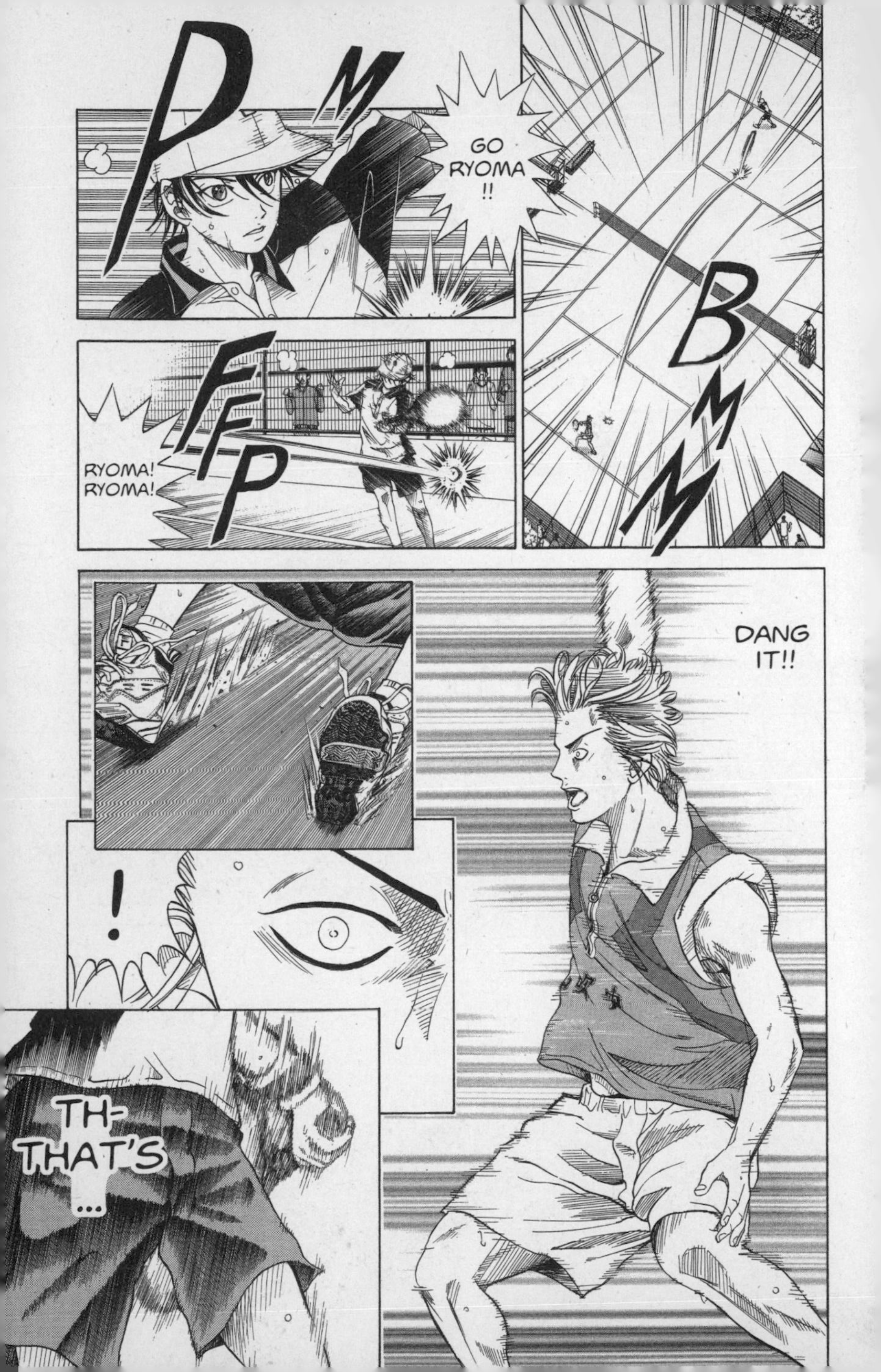
BMMM
PM
GO RYOMA !!
FFP
RYOMA! RYOMA!
DANG IT!!
!
TH-THAT'S ...

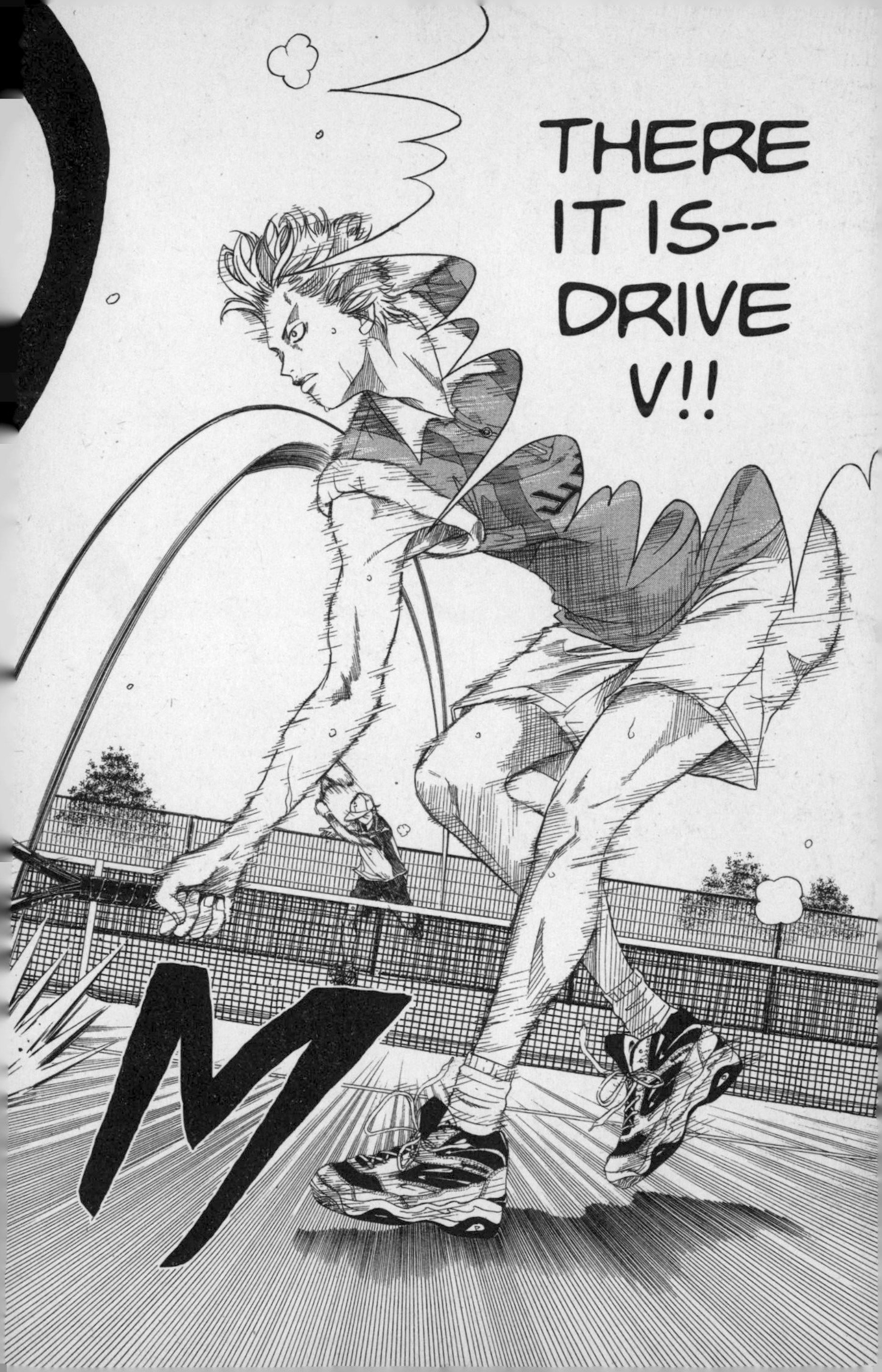
THERE IT IS-- DRIVE V!!

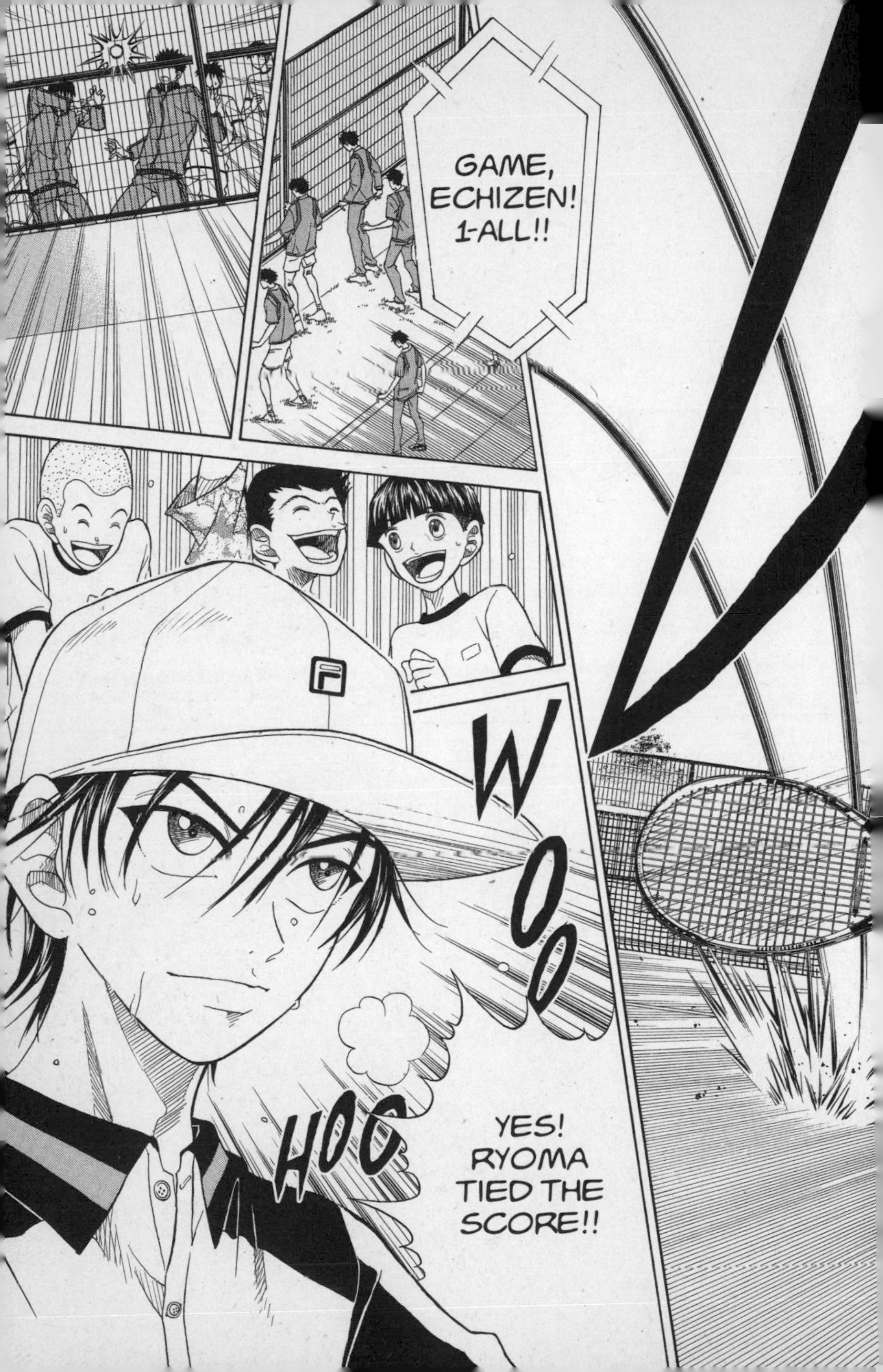
GAME, ECHIZEN! 1-ALL!!
WOOO
HOO
YES! RYOMA TIED THE SCORE!!

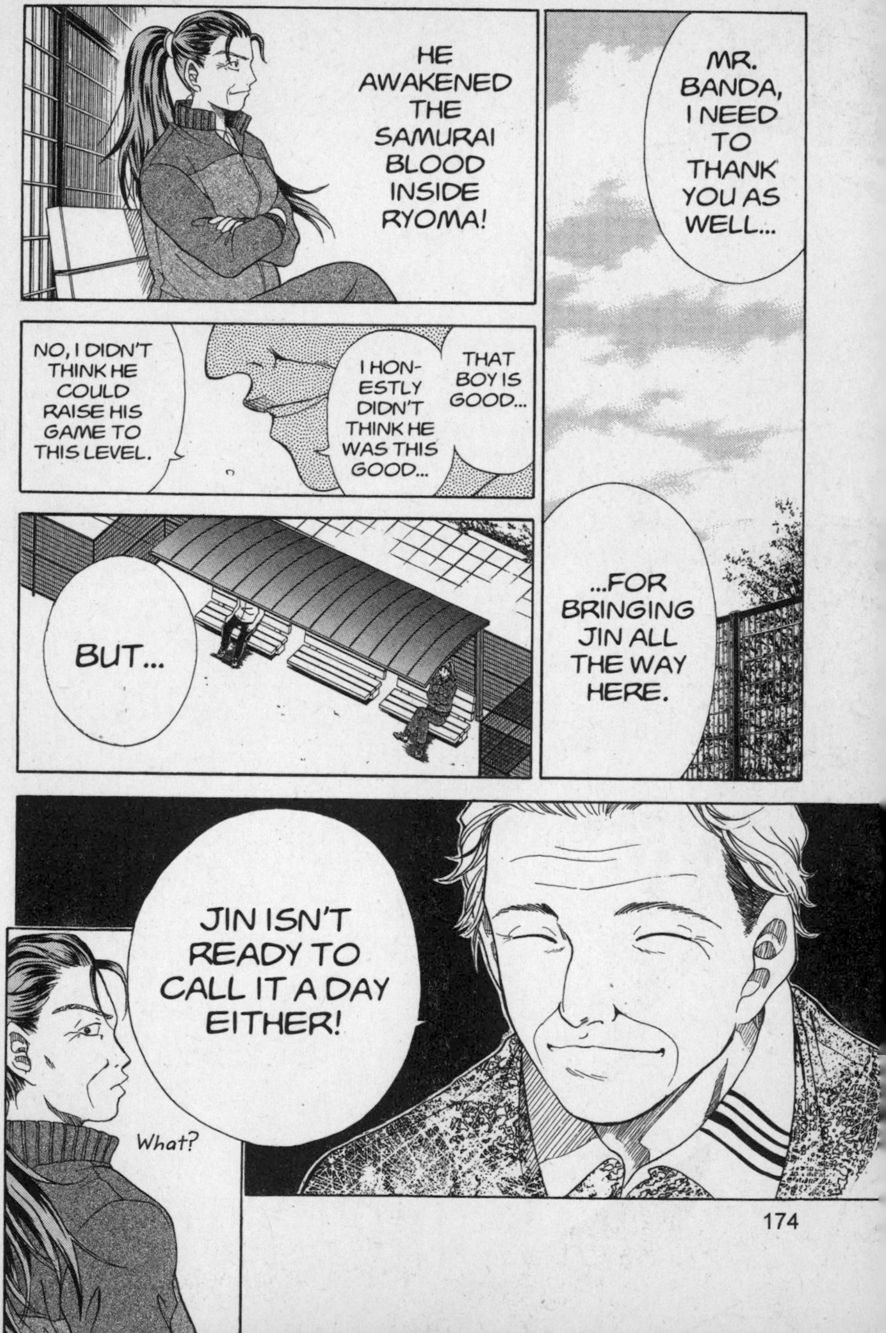
MR. BANDA, I NEED TO THANK YOU AS WELL...
...FOR BRINGING JIN ALL THE WAY HERE.
HE AWAKENED THE SAMURAI BLOOD INSIDE RYOMA!
THAT BOY IS GOOD...
I HON-ESTLY DIDN'T THINK HE WAS THIS GOOD...
NO, I DIDN'T THINK HE COULD RAISE HIS GAME TO THIS LEVEL.
BUT...
JIN ISN'T READY TO CALL IT A DAY EITHER!
What?

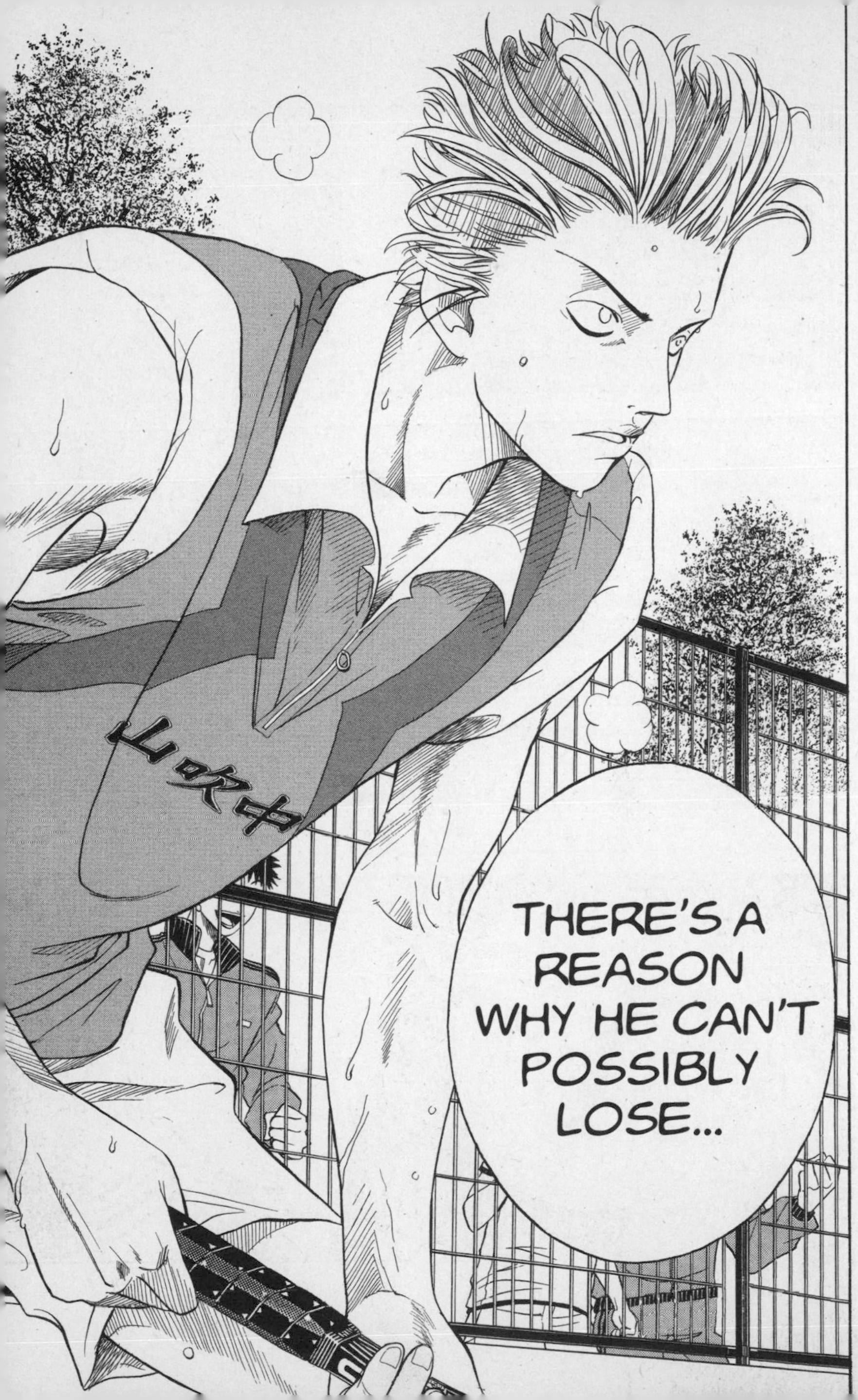
THERE'S A REASON WHY HE CAN'T POSSIBLY LOSE...
山吹中

Finally!!

Seishun Academy's (Suspected) Age-Lying Fighting Machine—
our tennis team Captain!!

Kunimitsu Tezuka! 9th Grade Class 1 Classmate Sign-Up-Contest—!!!

We will be holding another Classmate Sign-Up Contest!! (Those of you who were exhausted from the fan book offensive, are you all right now—?) Deep-rooted popularity! Does not look like a junior high school student!! Seishun's ultimate player, yet he hasn't had a place to shine that much!! He's actually the student council president, truly Seishun's coolest dude!! We are looking for 18 male and 18 female classmates. No age limits. But this time, only postcard submissions will be accepted. (Sorry.)

Please write "Please use my name" where your name would be in a normal fan letter (postcard)! (See volumes 2 and 8 for details). The contest is heating up—Eiji/Shusuke (3-6), Ryoma (1-2), Kaoru (2-7)— so please tell us how much you want to be his classmate!

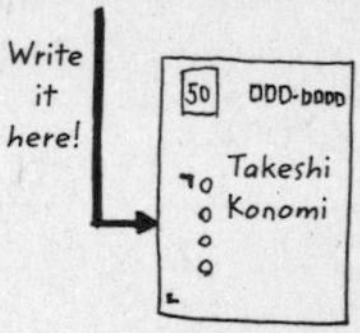
Write it here!
50
DDD-DDDD
Takeshi Konomi

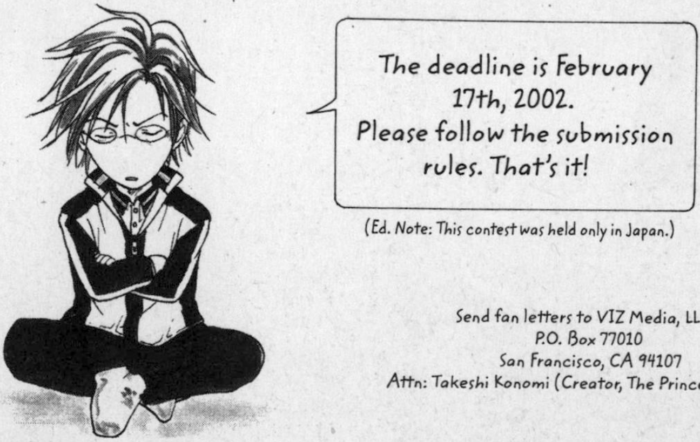
The deadline is February 17th, 2002.
Please follow the submission rules. That's it!

(Ed. Note: This contest was held only in Japan.)

Send fan letters to VIZ Media, LLC
P.O. Box 77010
San Francisco, CA 94107
Attn: Takeshi Konomi (Creator, The Prince of Tennis)

In the Next Volume...

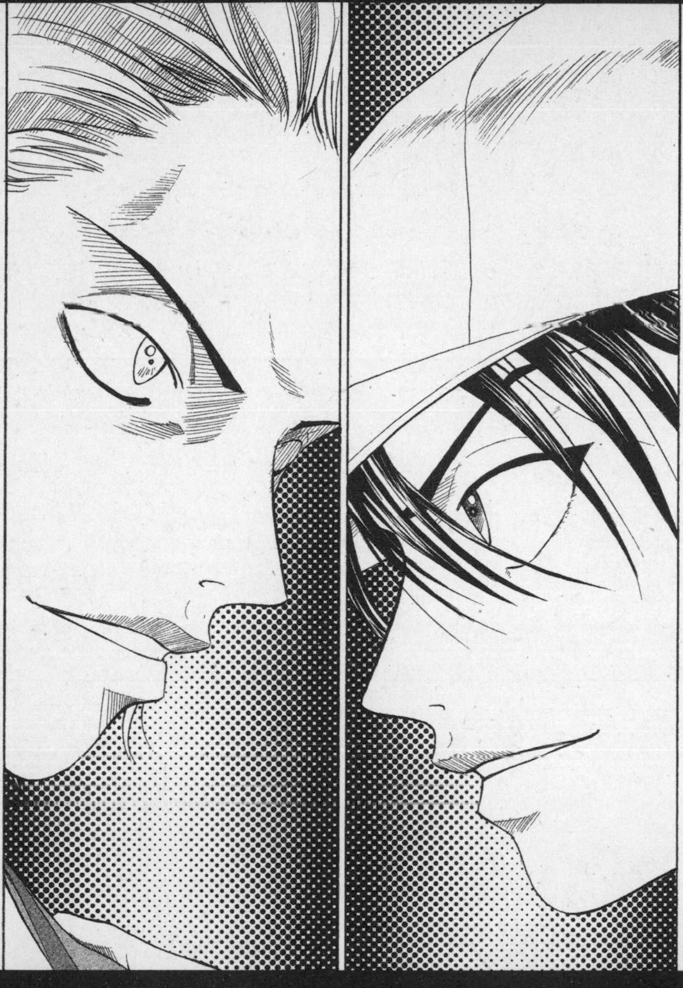

The Prince of Tennis Ryoma Echizen's match against Yamabuki's biggest bully, Jin Akutsu, reaches an unprecedented competitive level, but only one player will walk away with the victory...

Available in May 2006

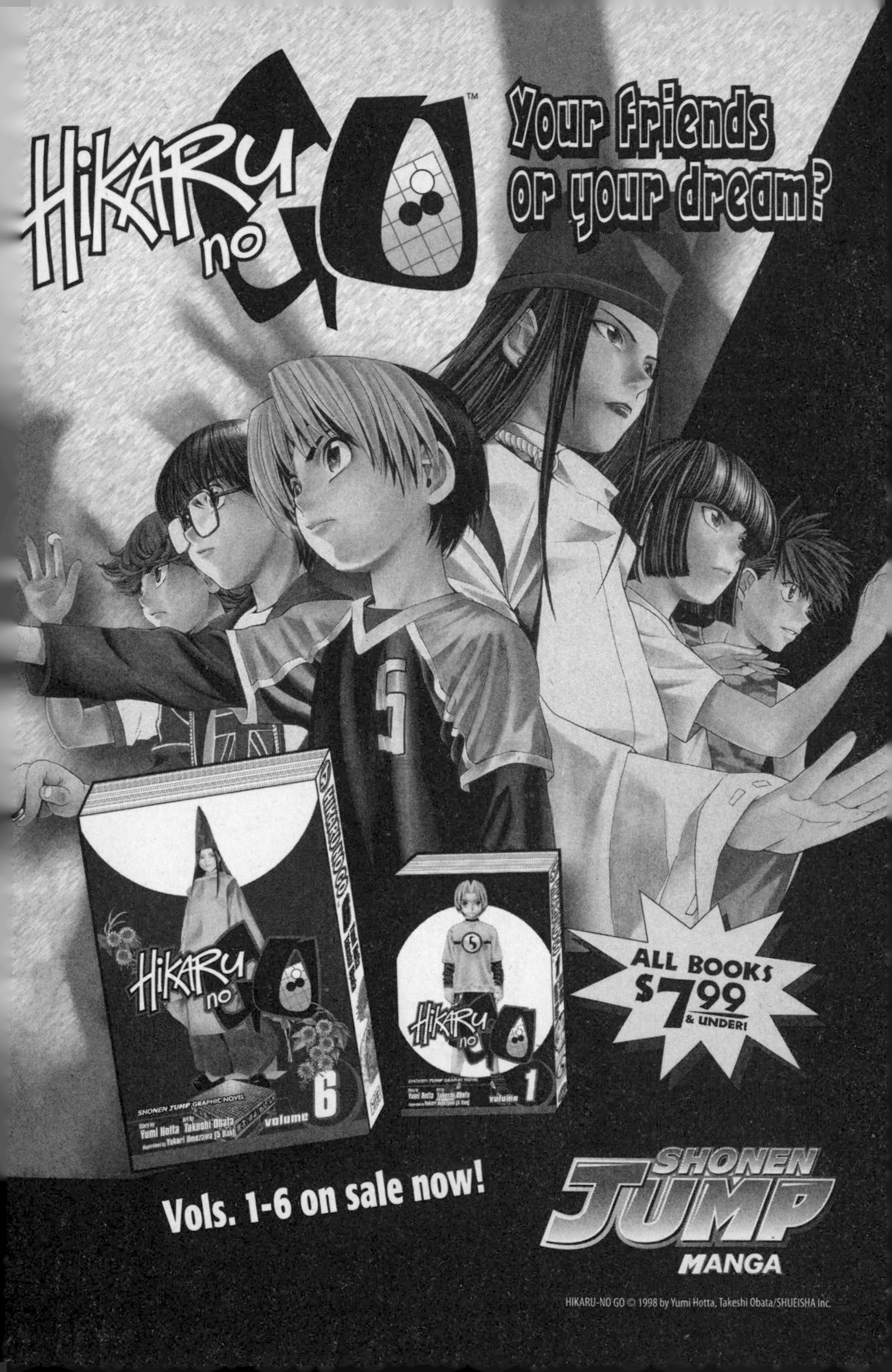
HIKARU no GO™
Your friends or your dream?
ALL BOOKS $7.99 & UNDER!
Vols. 1-6 on sale now!
SHONEN JUMP MANGA
HIKARU-NO GO © 1998 by Yumi Hotta, Takeshi Obata/SHUEISHA Inc.

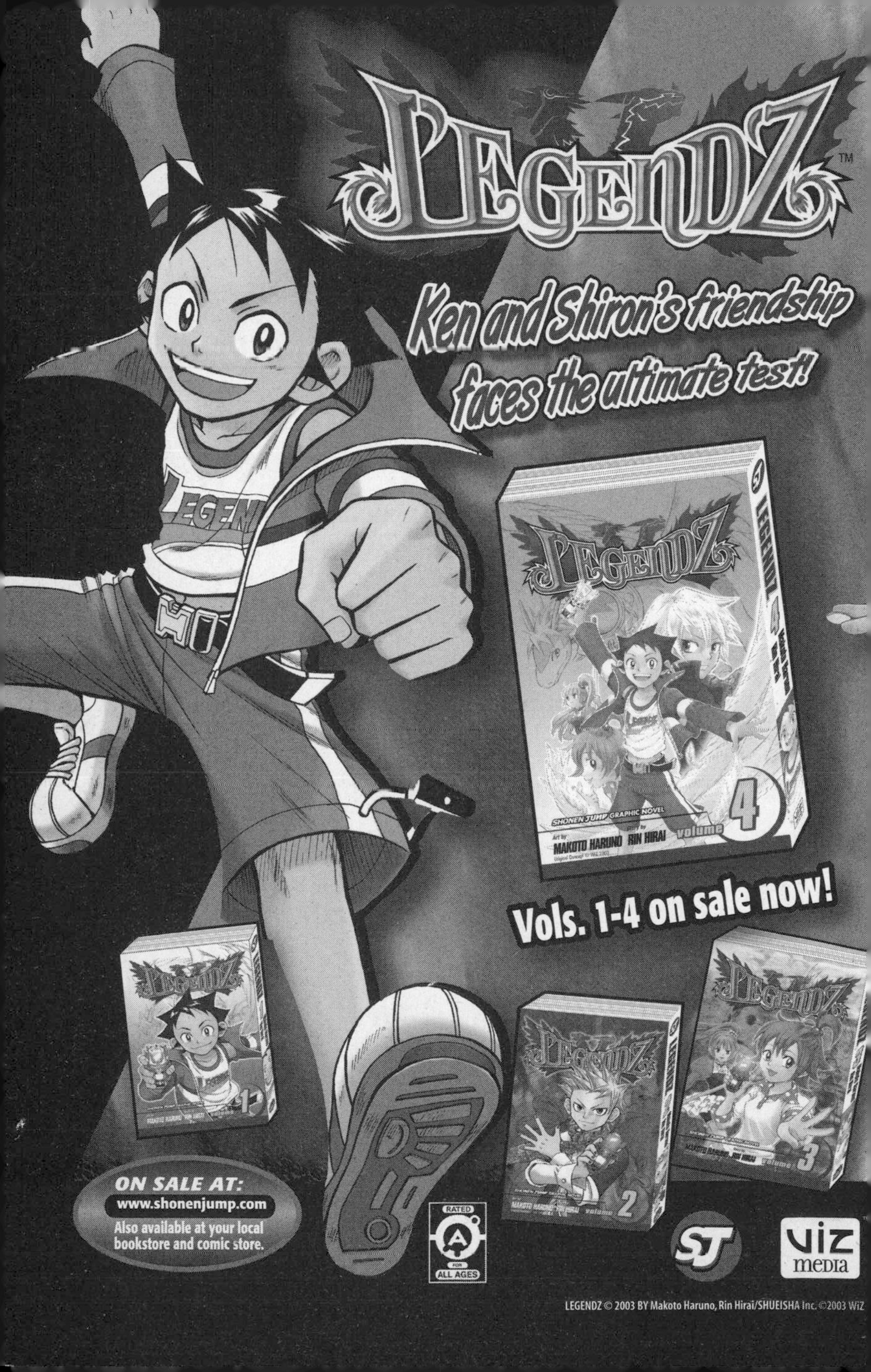

LEGENDZ
Ken and Shiron's friendship faces the ultimate test!
Vols. 1-4 on sale now!
ON SALE AT:
www.shonenjump.com
Also available at your local bookstore and comic store.
RATED A FOR ALL AGES
SJ
VIZ media
LEGENDZ © 2003 BY Makoto Haruno, Rin Hirai/SHUEISHA Inc. ©2003 WIZ

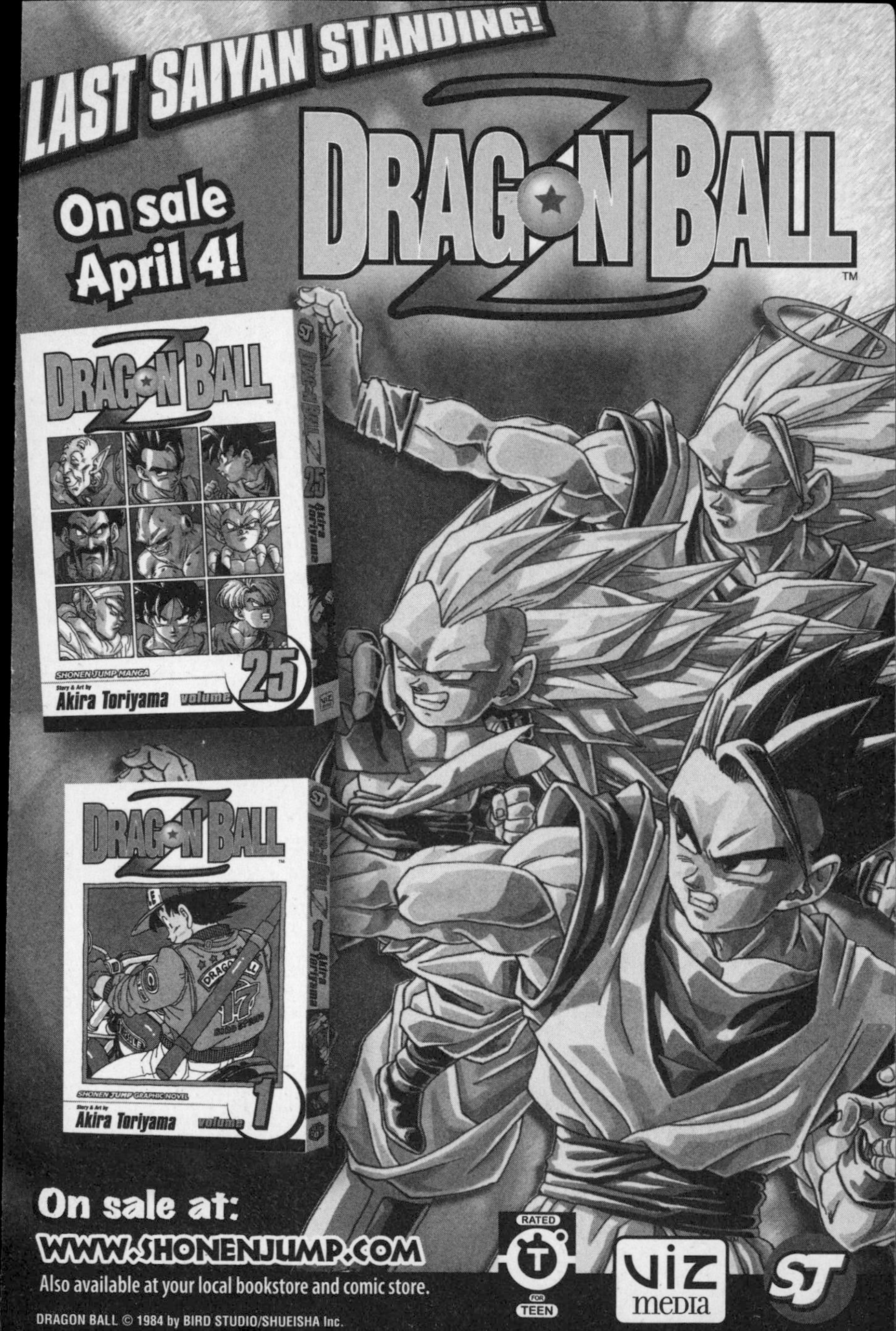
LAST SAIYAN STANDING!
DRAGON BALL Z
On sale April 4!
DRAGON BALL Z
SHONEN JUMP MANGA
Story & Art by Akira Toriyama
volume 25
DRAGON BALL Z
SHONEN JUMP GRAPHIC NOVEL
Story & Art by Akira Toriyama
volume 1
On sale at:
WWW.SHONENJUMP.COM
Also available at your local bookstore and comic store.
RATED T FOR TEEN
viz media
SJ
DRAGON BALL © 1984 by BIRD STUDIO/SHUEISHA Inc.

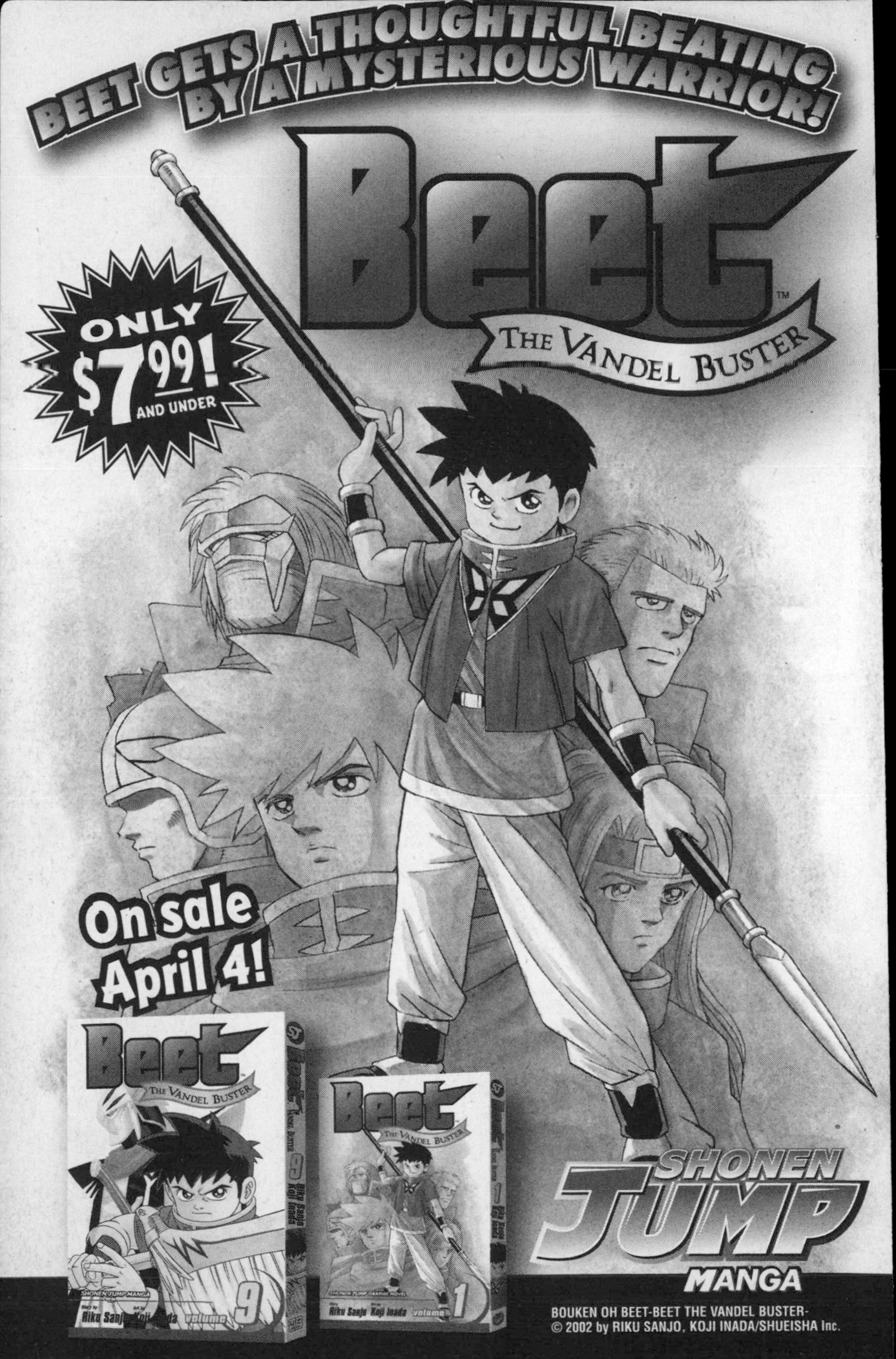
BEET GETS A THOUGHTFUL BEATING BY A MYSTERIOUS WARRIOR!
Beet™ THE VANDEL BUSTER
ONLY $7.99! AND UNDER
On sale April 4!
SHONEN JUMP MANGA
BOUKEN OH BEET-BEET THE VANDEL BUSTER-
© 2002 by RIKU SANJO, KOJI INADA/SHUEISHA Inc.

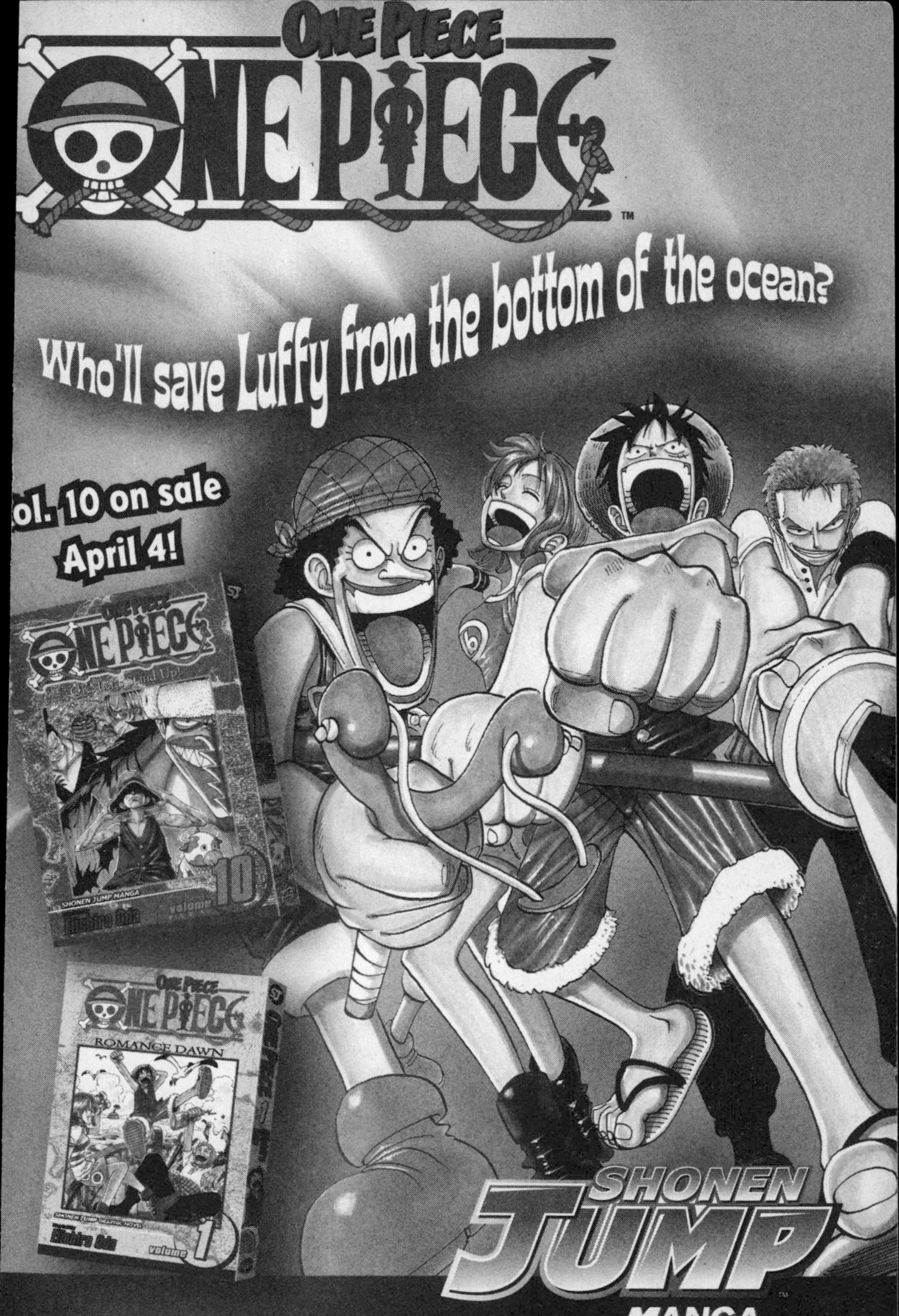

ONE PIECE
ONE PIECE
Who'll save Luffy from the bottom of the ocean?
ol. 10 on sale
April 4!
ONE PIECE
SHONEN JUMP MANGA
10
ONE PIECE
ROMANCE DAWN
Eiichiro Oda
volume 1
SHONEN
JUMP
MANGA

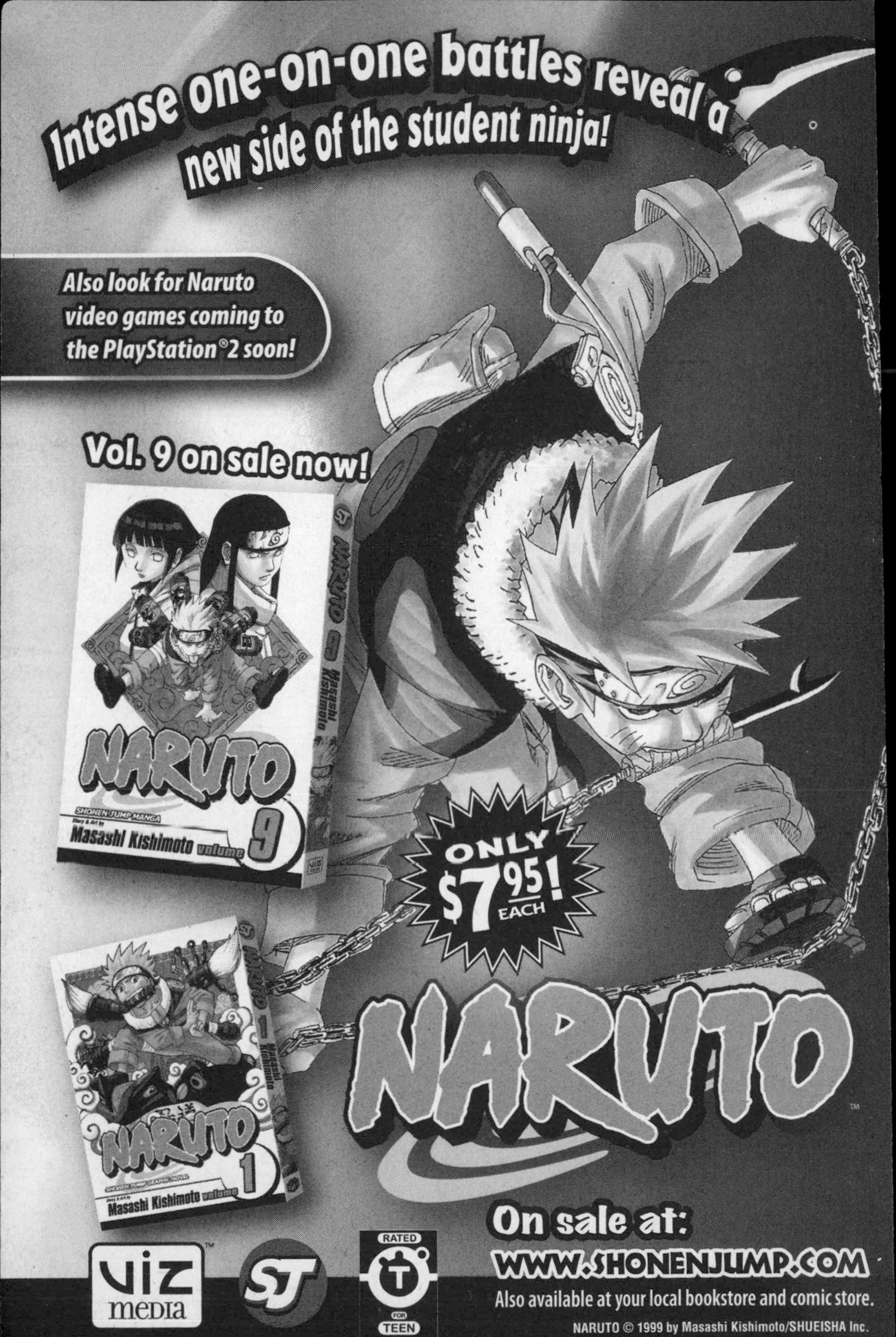
Intense one-on-one battles reveal a new side of the student ninja!
Also look for Naruto video games coming to the PlayStation®2 soon!
Vol. 9 on sale now!
NARUTO
SHONEN JUMP MANGA
Masashi Kishimoto volume 9
ONLY $7.95 EACH!
NARUTO
Masashi Kishimoto volume 1
NARUTO™
On sale at:
WWW.SHONENJUMP.COM
Also available at your local bookstore and comic store.
viz media
SJ
RATED T FOR TEEN
NARUTO © 1999 by Masashi Kishimoto/SHUEISHA Inc.

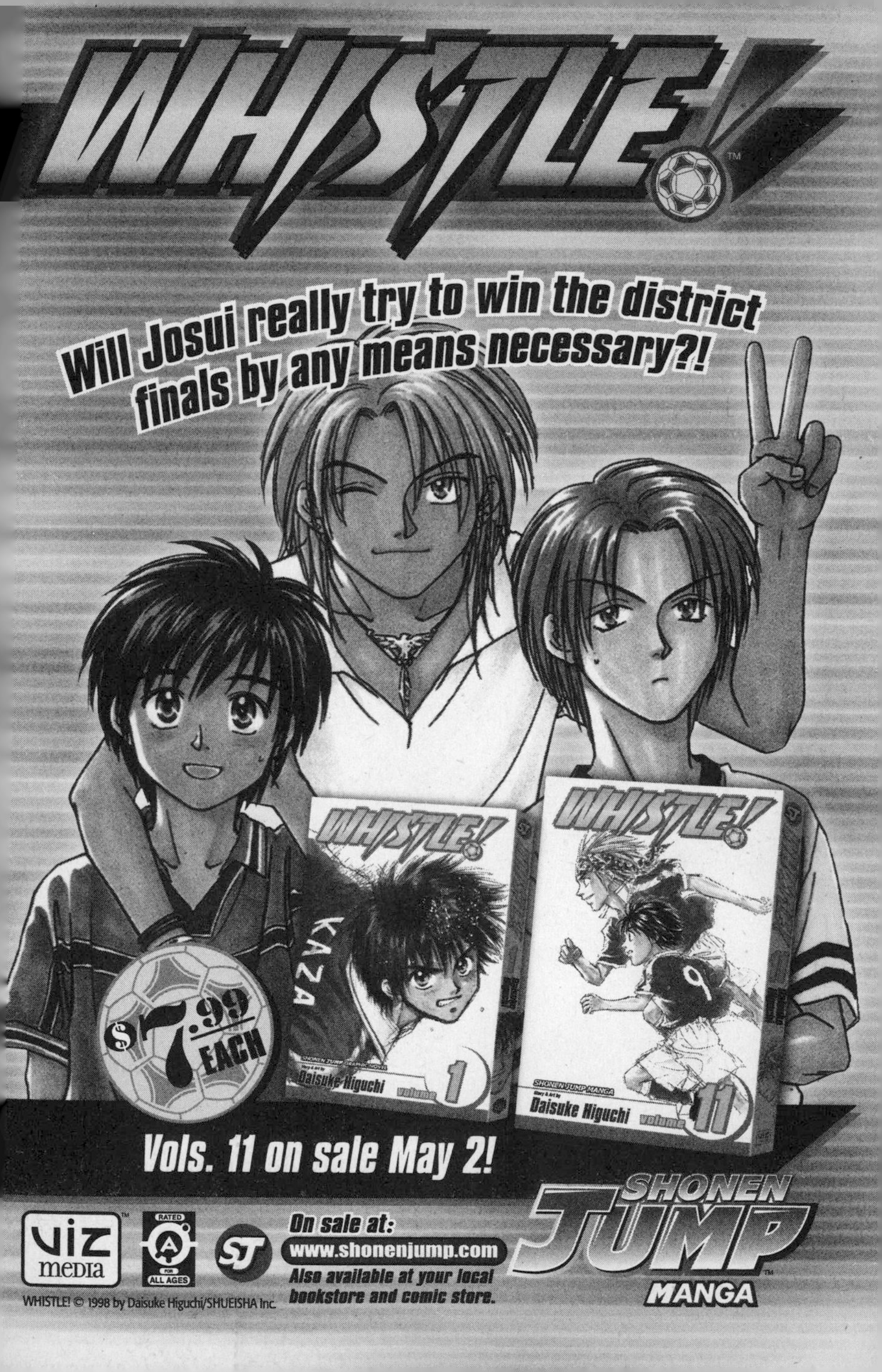
WHISTLE!
Will Josui really try to win the district finals by any means necessary?!
WHISTLE!
Daisuke Higuchi
volume 1
WHISTLE!
SHONEN JUMP MANGA
Story & Art by
Daisuke Higuchi
volume 11
$7.99 EACH
Vols. 11 on sale May 2!
viz media
RATED A FOR ALL AGES
SJ
On sale at:
www.shonenjump.com
Also available at your local bookstore and comic store.
SHONEN JUMP MANGA
WHISTLE! © 1998 by Daisuke Higuchi/SHUEISHA Inc.

Check us out on the web!

www.shonenjump.com